Grounds for Pleasure

DENISE OTIS

Grounds for Pleasure

FOUR CENTURIES

OF THE

AMERICAN GARDEN

HARRY N. ABRAMS, INC., PUBLISHERS

Contents

Page two: The Colonial-Revival garden at the John and Abigail Adams house in Quincy, Massachusetts. Page four: A torrent of naturalized primulas sweeps through woods in Frank Cabot's garden.

INTRODUCTION

Preparing the Ground

"First clear your ground" is as good advice for writing about gardens as it is for making them; an overview of garden design in the United States from the seventeenth century to the present stakes out a lot of ground to be cleared. In the interest of reducing it to more manageable proportions I have concentrated on private gardens created for their owners' pleasure, leaving aside for the most part public parks as well as private gardens primarily devoted to the growing of fruit and vegetables. Pleasure and produce are not mutually exclusive goals in horticulture, but the layout that will promote the maximum production of food may not delight the eye or any of the senses but taste — and that not until after harvest.

The design of the pleasure garden is the object of this investigation, not the plants used to flesh it out, except where they truly determine its visual character. After all, plants from China do not necessarily make a garden Chinese. And from the days of Columbus, American plants have infiltrated European gardens, and European plants, American gardens.

Is there such a thing as an American garden? The often-repeated statement, usually by British observers, that "America is not a nation of gardeners," implies that we have no gardening history and no gardening style worth the investigation. Perhaps not, or not in the way that gardening is imbedded in the cultures of Great Britain or Japan. Yet, having been brought up in a family that always gardened, even under the most adverse conditions — corporate nomadism that left us for the first thirteen years of my life less than two years in any one location — and having heard from childhood of the gardens of my grandparents and great-grandparents, I've always found this judgment both irritating and hard to believe. Were we and our friends odd, atypical, and mildly eccentric, or fairly normal but the victims of a misperception of the nature of American gardens and gardening?

It would not have been difficult to assemble an album of beautiful gardens to demonstrate that this country is well supplied with dedicated and imaginative gardeners and garden designers, and has been for a long time. The du Pont family alone, since it arrived in 1800, has produced six generations with scores of distinguished gardeners. But that would never satisfy the skeptics who subscribe to another standard piece of received wisdom: that all our ideas of garden design are derivative — European fashions fifty years later. True, detecting foreign ideas in American gardens is not a particularly difficult sport for a knowledgeable observer, but it can be practiced in most twentieth-century gardens in the world: a touch of Japanese pruning here, a French espalier there, a very British lawn, or a slightly Spanish patio. In fact the game of what came from where and who borrowed what from whom in what century continues to be the stock-in-trade and favorite source of controversy for garden history scholars.

For all this scholarly activity, the myth of originality, the idea that for any human achievement to be truly creative it must spring clean from the imagination like Athena from the head of Zeus, continues to infest our thinking. And it is a particularly virulent weed in the realm of the arts. Memories, influences, and borrowings are part of the artist's working capital, whether or not he is consciously aware of them. If William Kent "leaped the fence, and saw that all nature was a garden" as Walpole says, it was because he looked with the eyes of a painter trained in the tradition of Claude's Italian landscapes, and his gardens, however revolutionary to eighteenth-century eyes, reflect that training. The observer, critic, or scholar, is on the watch for influences; the creator is trying to solve a problem in the most pleasing way he or she can think of.

The adjustment of existing design ideas to a new set of circumstances can produce an original result; but appealing combinations of plant color and texture, no matter how unexpected, are not quite enough to create a true style of design. "American Garden" does not bring an instant picture to mind, and this is the kernel of truth from which has grown the oversimplified notion that this country has made no contribution to the history of garden design. "English landscape garden," "French formal garden," "Moghul garden" or "Japanese garden" do conjure up distinctive images; but the images are of princely gardens, and princely gardens are something we have never had in the United States. Even the most pretentious of late nineteenth-century robber-baron landscapes were very small by those standards.

Nor have Americans produced a great body of theoretical writing about the design of gardens. Not that this is a prerequisite to style—in most cases theory follows creation at a respectful distance—it simply disseminates style more swiftly and widely. Andrew Jackson Downing, perhaps the single most influential American writer on landscape design, never made any pretence of doing more than adapting English theories to American conditions, bearing out Tocqueville's observation that "The spirit of the Americans is averse to general ideas; it does not seek theoretical discoveries." [1]

The first settlers had little or no time for theoretical speculation; but they soon found blind adherence to custom unproductive. Faced with a new continent and the necessity of adapting to unfamiliar conditions, the American very soon came to, as Tocqueville puts it, "accept tradition only as a means of information, and existing facts only as a lesson to be used in doing otherwise and doing better; to seek the reason of things for oneself, and in oneself alone." [2]

It's not surprising that such an individualistic habit of mind would produce too many different kinds of gardens to sum up in one style or even two. Diversity might be predicted as well from the variety of different climates and terrains in this country. Growing conditions have less influence than one might think, and less than they probably should have. Some planting patterns are widely diffused: The green front lawn is found from coast to coast and north to south; in humid regions where it thrives and in deserts where it doesn't, at least without the expenditure of unconscionable amounts of water.

Where did these patterns come from, and how did they spread? Is there a common thread that links the diversity of garden designs, or, more likely, a set of common threads? And if there are, where did *they* come from and how did they develop? And, most important, has everyone been looking for a style when they should be looking for an attitude?

That there is no comprehensive up-to-date scholarly history of American garden design gave my search for answers the zest of detection and offered enjoyable possibilities for speculation and common-sense deduction. Had the monographs on individual designers and some detailed studies of certain periods by serious garden historians been available when I began my research in 1986, that research would have been much less time-devouring. So far, such studies have served to strengthen my conclusions, but a straightforward history is still needed and I hope it will be written soon. This is not it. Rather, it is a stroll through the history of American garden-making as one might walk through a garden—pausing here and there to make note of an interesting detail or a new idea, retracing steps to reconsider a familiar form, stopping to appreciate a particular effect and figure out how it was achieved, and finally trying to get a sense of the whole.

A lot of evidence of the most useful kind is missing: living gardens. The seventeenth- and eighteenth-century gardens we have are restorations. They have to be if for no other reason than the relatively short life of plants. With the important exception of certain trees, plants do not survive even as long as a century. Add to this the ingrained habit of mobility—noted by Tocqueville in 1831 and confirmed by the latest census figures, which state that Americans move on the average of every seven years. These peregrinations may be chosen, forced by the depletion of the soil—a common problem in the seventeenth, eighteenth, and early nineteenth centuries—or required by employment, but they do confer some validity on foreigners' scepticism about Americans' commitment to gardening. A good garden takes time to create and to mature, and, quite naturally, in a succession of owners some will be committed, others not. A garden left to its own devices will revert to weeds even faster than plowed New England fields revert to forest. Small town, city, suburban, even estate gardens become building sites as population grows and land prices rise. Tastes change and the original design may be so overlaid with revisions as to be unrecognizable. Yet gardens are made and survive, some, indeed a surprising number, still in the families of their creators, others—the most common solution today—as public gardens in the care of not-for-profit institutions.

Garden archaeology, with its increasingly sophisticated techniques offers the most valid information about our earliest gardens, and the best guidance for their restoration. Archaeologists can tell us where paths and fences, garden structures and trees were placed, often when the garden was made, or if not, when it was abandoned. Analysis of seeds and pollen found in the soil will identify the plants that grew in it. But not every site that one would like to see examined can be. How many arguments would be settled if we could know what a seventeenth-century Manhattan *bouwerie* looked like, or the Boston garden into which Governor John Winthrop invited three visiting French officials for a private walk while he attended an interminable Puritan Sunday service in 1646.[3]

Written accounts—diaries, letters, wills, travel books—continue to tell us most of what we know about gardens of the past, but the pictures they conjure up can be misleading. So much depends on familiarity with what the writer meant by the words he used: When Dr. Alexander Hamilton visited Captain Malbone's "magnificent dwelling" outside of Newport in 1744[4] and praised the canals in its "pretty gardens," his contemporaries would visualize long, narrow ornamental pools; we would be unlikely to. And even those acquainted with the vocabulary of a period are unavoidably influenced by what appeals to the eyes of their own era, as those who work in garden—and house—restoration know only too well. With each generation come revisions.

Gardening friends from abroad have been quick to point out what they have seen as typically American gardens, but alas they haven't been very articulate about what made these gardens so "American." Yet foreign observers always notice just the things that custom makes invisible to natives. And they notice what is different from what they themselves habitually see. As I have tried to piece together a character for the American garden and find out where it came from, interested and observant European travelers from the seventeenth century to the present have offered some of the most illuminating insights, even if almost none of these ladies and gentlemen were as precise and detailed reporters as I would have liked.

Still, making the acquaintance of so many observant and opinionated gardeners, travelers, and horticultural writers, past and present, has been an unforseen bonus of pleasure in researching and writing this book.

PART ONE

Building
a Design
Vocabulary
Over Time

Europeans Colonize a New World

WHAT THEY FOUND OR THOUGHT THEY FOUND AND WHAT THEY BROUGHT WITH THEM

Typical of seventeenth-century plans, the Plimoth Plantation garden of John and Priscilla Alden combines sturdy fences, raised planting beds framed with rocks or planks, and work spaces.

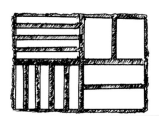

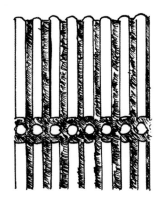

These now-vanished ridged fields, however decorative, were built to an agricultural scale according to measurements published by Bela Hubbard in *The American Antiquarian*, 1878. In the detail from a 150-acre checkerboard near Kalamazoo (top) the narrow beds were six feet wide and eighteen inches high, with paths four feet wide and twelve to forty feet long. The other two were of similar size.

The first gardens that we think of as American were necessarily European in design. Whether or not we are a nation of gardeners, we are a nation of immigrants. And each immigrant brings with him the memory of the plants and gardens he grew up with. In addition, the first immigrants who came to the part of North America that would become the United States did not find a gardening tradition already in place to modify the models they carried in their minds — or, at least, not one that they recognized.

All the early accounts found by this author show that the Indians that the Europeans encountered did not cultivate what we call pleasure gardens, although many tribes had agricultural systems well worked out for their needs and numbers. But Indians did not lack aesthetic sensibility. Explorers commented on the decorative brilliance of their clothing, body painting, pottery, or basketwork, depending on the tribe. Whether or not the natives turned their talents to ornamenting the land around their dwellings we may never know. A paragraph in the description of sunflower planting given in the late nineteenth century by the then-elderly Hidatsa Maxi'diwiac, or Buffalo Bird Woman, suggests that they might have:

> Usually we planted sunflowers only around the edges of a field. The hills were placed eight or nine paces apart; for we never sowed sunflowers thickly. We thought a field surrounded thus by a sparse-sown row of sunflowers, had a handsome appearance. [1]

The much earlier and more complex civilizations that left behind the Serpent Mound in Ohio and such tantalizing ruins as Cahokia and Casa Grande may well have been garden-makers as accomplished as the Aztecs. William Bartram, a late eighteenth-century plant collector and careful observer, encountered many abandoned mounds and terraces in his travels through Georgia, the Carolinas, and Florida. At Port Royal, on the St. Johns River, in Florida, he sketched and described the ruins of what sounds like a splendid piece of probably ceremonial landscape design:

> At about fifty yards distance from the landing place, stands a magnificent Indian mount.... [T]here was a very considerable extent of old fields round about the mount; there was also a large orange grove, together with palms and live oaks, extending from near the mount, along the banks, downwards... But what greatly contributed towards completing the magnificence of the scene, was a noble Indian highway, which led from the great mount, on a straight line, three quarters of a mile, first through a point or wing of the orange grove, and continuing thence through an awful forest of live oaks, it was terminated by palms and laurel magnolias, on the verge of an oblong artificial lake, which was on the edge of an extensive green level savanna. This grand highway was about fifty yards wide, sunk a little below the common level, and the earth thrown up on each side, making a bank of about two feet high... The glittering water pond played on the sight, through the dark

grove, like a brilliant diamond, on the bosom of the illumined savanna, bordered with various flowery shrubs and plants. [2]

When Bartram returned fifteen years later, highway, bank, and pond were gone, and all but the mount plowed under by settlers. He offers no speculation as to the site's creators.

And what was the purpose of the elaborate, geometric "Garden Beds" covering sometimes as much as three hundred acres in Michigan and reported by the French explorer La Verendrye in 1748? The clearly defined beds, raised about eighteen inches above the surrounding prairie and arranged in both wheel-shaped and rectangular designs with paths between them, were investigated and documented by Henry Rowe Schoolcraft in the 1840s. He reported that an oak growing on top of one bed was found when cut down in 1827, to date from 1502. [3] Similar but simpler ridged fields have been discovered in Wisconsin and the Mississippi Valley, all of which resemble those recreated in the Andes as an experiment in reviving ancient farming techniques: The Michigan examples show a greater variety of patterns than straightforward agriculture would require. The Algonquins, who occupied this area when the French came, did not know who had made them nor, for sure, does anyone else, although they are now thought to date from the Woodland Period (500 B.C.– 1000 A.D.).

Could the Indian American have shared what would turn out to be the European American tendency to create gardens that gave pleasure from their design and their produce alike? The question has been little explored, perhaps because conventional wisdom has always assumed that there were no pleasure gardens in the United States before the eighteenth century anyway. Most authors writing about seventeenth-century North America still accept the myth that the English found impenetrable forests on the Virginia and New England shores. They did not. What they found was something similar to the forest in an English royal park. As disinterested observers of the period and modern historians like William Cronon have established, the Indians burned forests periodically to keep down the undergrowth and provide forage attractive to game. [4] It was their equivalent, and a rather sophisticated one, to stock-raising.

The opinions of seventeenth-century Puritans can be quite misleading. "Wilderness," as these writers used the word, is often a metaphor, with biblical overtones, for the unknown, unpopulated, or unchristian, rather than an accurate delineation of the natural world. The English settlers would indeed find impenetrable forests, but only later, as they moved north or west from the territories of the agricultural Indians living along the East Coast to those of hunter-gatherers.

Maps, prints, and drawings offer some graphic evidence that gardens existed early in the North American colonies, but these documents are usually tantalizing in their lack of detail and therefore subject to a variety of interpretations. What is known as the Castello plan of New Amsterdam, a map of New York City drawn in 1660, shows a multitude of garden plots, some obviously orchards, but others with formal beds and parterres. Most garden historians have dismissed these as decorative figments of the map-maker's imagination on the grounds that colonists had to work too hard for survival to have time for pleasure gardening. Both assumptions are questionable. In many years of working with artists and draftsmen, this author has almost invariably found that their seeming flights of fancy turn out to be grounded in visual fact. And the Dutch were passionate gardeners: Where but in a garden-loving country would there have occurred a speculative bubble like the tulipomania that swept Holland in the 1630s? According to a census of the same date that identifies all lot-holders, the most elaborate layouts belonged respectively to the governor and to the West India Company. By 1660 the Dutch had been in the New World for more than thirty years, time enough to go beyond subsistence agriculture; and many colonists were merchants and ship-owners, engaged in occupations that are exacting but not physically demanding and furthermore build capital to hire work done. Also, by then there were African slaves in the city. In fact, a retaliatory massacre of 200 settlers by local Indians in 1655 was set off when a Manhattan garden-owner shot an Indian woman who was stealing his peaches![5]

Written records of the period confirm the existence of gardens, but do not describe them. Adrian Van der Donck, who came to New Amsterdam in 1642, gives a long list of the flowers grown, both native and imported, including fine tulips.[6] New York peaches recur in the narrative of Jasper Danckaerts who came with Peter Sluyter in 1679, after the British had taken over:

> As we walked along we saw in different gardens trees full of apples of various kinds, and so laden with peaches and other fruit that one might doubt whether there were more leaves or fruit on them. I have never seen in Europe, in the best seasons, such an overflowing abundance.[7]

Danckaerts, an austere man in search of good farmland on which to settle the members of his church sect, Protestants known as Labadists, makes no mention of flowers, but he does note in traveling through New Jersey an island that "formerly, belonged to the Dutch governor, who had made it a pleasure ground or garden." Several accounts of New Jersey and Pennsylvania in the 1680s mention flower gardens, and in 1698 Gabriel Thomas waxed truly enthusiastic over the garden of the wealthy merchant Edward Shippen, although he didn't get the name quite right.

> There are very fine and delightful Gardens and Orchards, in most parts of this Countrey; but Edward Shippey (who lives near the Capital City) has an Orchard and Gardens adjoyning to his Great House that equalizes (if not exceeds) any I have ever seen, having a very famous and pleasant Summer-House erected in the middle of his extraordinary fine and large Garden abounding with Tulips, Pinks, Carnations, Roses, (of several sorts) Lilies, not to mention those that grow wild in the Fields.[8]

The idea that colonists had no time, energy, or desire to create attractive surroundings for themselves until well into the eighteenth century is proving to be questionable indeed. True, there were enough unfamiliar and devastating insects, predatory wild beasts, and untrustworthy Indians to make the household garden in the New World, as J. B. Jackson maintains, "play the role of frontier outpost, a defense against a hostile world." In helping the colonists tame an unknown landscape, the earliest gardens served the same purposes as the primitive gardens of prehistoric Europe: "the protection of the group, the providing of food and materials, and the transition between the community and its surrounding environment."[9]

But the settlers were accustomed to more than primitive surroundings. Coming from an environment that had been cultivated for a couple of thousand years, they could remember gardens that were places of refreshment and delight, even works of art. And if you remember you can reproduce, although you may have to simplify or adjust. Nor does the very real brutality and violence of life on what was, after all, a frontier of conquest necessarily exclude the desire for and appreciation of aesthetic pleasure. One has only to think of the gardens built by the moghul conquerors of India. There are enough references, even if they are sketchy, in seventeenth-century American letters and diaries to suggest that from Massachusetts to the Carolinas, gardens were a source of pleasure as well as produce to at least a few of the first and second generation colonists. This is not to suggest that the American seaboard was a model of high cultivation in the seventeenth century any more than it is today. Undoubtedly, then, as now, the householders who demonstrated total indifference to the appearance of their surroundings or who kept them up only to the minimum necessary for social acceptance out-numbered those who tried to beautify those surroundings. But as long-lost or buried documents continue to surface, we may find that the latter were more numerous than we suspect. After all, Danckaerts's diary was not discovered and translated until the end of the nineteenth century. It was only in the 1940s that a scholar deciphered William Byrd II's early eighteenth-century shorthand and brought his Secret Diaries to light. And in 1985 archaeologists produced the most exciting and material evidence regarding the dating of early ornamental gardening with the discovery of a large 1680 garden at Bacon's Castle in Virginia.

Gardens existed by both choice and necessity in the north, and by law as well in Virginia—an ordinance of the 1624 Jamestown General Assembly. But what did they look like, how were they used, and what grew in them? That there was a distinction between orchard and garden is clear from early wills and travelers' accounts that mention them separately. It is usually assumed that all the gardens are what we would call kitchen gardens rather than pleasure gardens. In truth, it is quite possible that some considered the orchard rather than the garden the pleasure ground. Fruit trees in flowery meadows have attracted pleasure seekers—and artists—since at least the Middle Ages: What else are the Unicorn Tapestries? How could a gardener resist that seventeenth-century champion of the orchard, William Lawson?

What can your eye desire to see, your eares to heare, your mouth to taste, or your nose to smell, that is not to be had in an Orchard? with abundance and variety? What more delightsome than an infinite varietie of sweet smelling flowers? decking with sundry coloures the greene mantle of the Earth, the universall Mother of us all.[10]

The idea that the Puritans could take pleasure in an orchard or a garden or anything at all for that matter, is something most people can't seem to accept. Yet estate inventories show that better-off Puritans had turkey carpets on their tables, pictures on their walls, velvet cushions to sit on, and down mattresses to sleep on. Nor did they dress in sober black, eat plain food, and drink plain water. Somehow people of the twentieth century find it extremely difficult to comprehend that a human being can be ardently religious and deeply sensual at the same time, an idea that people in the seventeenth century didn't think to question. Indeed, if any pleasurable activity were acceptable in the Puritan "City on a Hill," it would be gardening. Milton, after all, had Adam and Eve pruning trees in Paradise before the Fall.

Seventeenth-century writers do tend to emphasize the practical when they list the plants grown in New England, naming herbs, vegetables, and fruit trees individually, but with the exception of roses, lumping together in a single phrase the "fine flowers many." Since most of these accounts were written for the benefit of future colonists, it made sense to be specific about the plants and seeds one would have to bring for survival.

Herbs and vegetables make up the bulk of a bill from Robert Hill in London dated July 26, 1631 and endorsed by John Winthrop, Jr.; but tucked in among the cabbages and radishes, basil and marjoram are hollyhocks, violets, columbines, and stock gillyflowers.[11] And Governor William Bradford speaks of "The fair white lily and sweet fragrant rose"[12] growing in the gardens of Plymouth some dozen years after the first famine-plagued winters. Although his adjectives are appreciative and not practical, both these flowers and most others, as well, were prized for their medicinal value, as Ann Leighton quite correctly points out in *Early American Gardens "For Meate or Medecine."* Take the rose: the flower essence distilled in rosewater was an antiseptic; the hips were a scurvy preventative, that is, a source of Vitamin C. Indeed, a late seventeenth-century New England physician's compilation listed 163 medicinal uses for the rose.[13] Thus it is no accident that the doctor's garden in the carefully researched recreation of the Plymouth settlement called Plimoth Plantation is heavily planted with roses. But the stock gillyflower on the Winthrop list, which we know as stock, was grown then as all those flowers are now, for scent and color: contemporary herbalists couldn't seem to find any medicinal virtues in it.

Common sense, as well, suggests that the first American pleasure gardens were a blend of the useful and the enjoyable. You could enjoy the roses you were going to turn into conserves or rose water. The tree you sat under to shell peas or sip canary wine might very sensibly have borne pears or apples; pinks and poppies might grow in beds with lettuce and parsley; and the vines shading the arbor might produce grapes. Any herb or vegetable that needed protection from predators animal and human could share space with what we now think of as the raison d'être of a pleasure garden, flowers, in the walled or fenced enclosure near the house that seventeenth-century people thought of as a garden. Also, order in itself provides a fair amount of pleasure to the spirit, even if the plants ordered are all there for practical purposes. Although land was cheap, labor was dear then, and through much of American history, except to some degree in the areas where slavery flourished. The separation of vegetable and flower gardens was not as practical a solution as it seemed to the writers of English garden books at the time. What was fenced in was what the proprietor — usually the housewife — with minimum help could take care of.

In the absence of pictures or detailed descriptions, English garden books do offer useful clues to the layout of early American gardens. John Parkinson's 1629 *Paradisi in sole, Paradisus Terrestris* was widely distributed in New England according to Ann Leighton. Parkinson, like Lawson, feels that "The foure square forme is the most usually accepted with all, and doth best agree to any mans dwelling," and recommends laying it out with

convenient roome for allies and walkes; for the fairer and larger your allies and walkes be, the more grace your Garden shall have, the lesse harme the herbes and flowers shall receive, by passing by them that grow next unto the allies sides, and the better shall your Weeders cleanse both the beds and the allies.[14]

Parkinson goes on to diagram elaborate ways to form these four-square beds into fashionable "knots," as parterre designs were then called. One may seriously question that the first settlers went in for knots, which by Parkinson's own admission take considerable work to keep in order.

Even without Lawson, Parkinson, and their fellow writers we might presume a design of rectangular beds, usually raised, with walks between them as a matter of what one might call folk memory. The earliest illustrations of medieval gardens show just such an organization, which is not so very different from the ancient Persian ones quartered by streams of water. That the Spanish in Florida, the French in Canada, the Dutch in New York, and the English in New England and Virginia all laid out their plant beds to this design is indicated on every map of the period that shows gardens. The same layout went west with the pioneers, and still appeals to many present-day gardeners. It is a part of our heritage that we never let go out of fashion very long.

Plank fences, slightly lighter than the riven oak palisade around Plimoth Plantation village, protect the terraced garden built up with stone retaining walls beside the Stephen Hopkins house. Asparagus forms a feathery hedge on the top level in late September, but many of the vegetables have already been harvested.

The Colonists
Settle In

GROWING AFFLUENCE
STIMULATES THE DESIRE TO
TRY NEW GARDEN IDEAS
FROM EUROPE

The summerhouse and chinoiserie bridge shown in Charles Willson Peale's 1772 portrait of William Paca were rebuilt in his restored garden. His fish-shaped pond suggests a sense of humor.

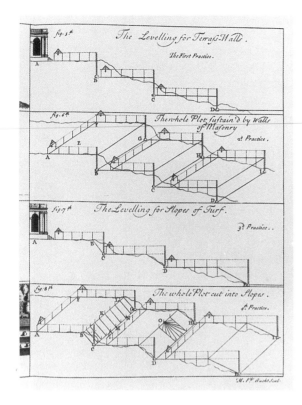

Diagrams from *The Theory and Practice of Gardening* illustrate eighteenth-century proportioning of retaining wall terraces, and sloping or falling ones. Dimensions were related to the height and width of the house as well as the terrain. Overall size was decided first, then divided.

While the colonists in North America were raising fences to make gardens in the wilderness, landscape designers in France — André Le Nôtre and his contemporaries — were revolutionizing garden design by sweeping away walls. Before the innovations of Le Nôtre and his contemporaries walled, enclosed compartments had represented gardens in France for even the greatest palaces, which had simply featured more and larger such compartments than private houses. In the new French gardens vista replaced enclosure as the dominating principle of the design. In Le Nôtre's gardens at Vaux-le-Vicomte and Versailles, green architecture of precisely cut hedges and regimented lines of trees now drew the eye outward, and provided a theater for the activities of king and courtiers. These landscapes seem bounded only by the horizon, and all of their divisions are composed into a single, albeit complex, integrated plan. To achieve his effects, Le Nôtre not only manipulated optical illusions with great sensitivity, he also remodeled the land on a scale impressive even to our bulldozer-obsessed culture.

Vaux-le-Vicomte, finished in 1661, and Versailles, on which Le Nôtre was still working at the end of the century, were immediately recognized as masterpieces and imitated by the kings and great noblemen who could afford them. Charles II even tried, unsuccessfully, to lure Le Nôtre to England, and it was not long before books appeared adapting his principles for those with more modest — but still abundant — resources.

For North American settlers, the new French style did not have immediate appeal; protection was paramount, labor was scarce and expensive, and one could enjoy striking views without having to create them in the garden. Not that Americans were unaware of the new fashion: They read the books and visited gardens on their trips back to England. Among the English gardens mentioned in the diaries of Samuel Sewall at the end of the seventeenth century and William Byrd II a bit later were newly made ones influenced by French practice, either directly or filtered through Dutch adaptations. It would take a good fifty years before Americans began assimilating these new ideas of garden design to their own circumstances, and here, perhaps, is the origin of the myth that American garden-makers have always tagged along fifty years after European ones. The most elaborate American example of Baroque garden design — adapted, as such designs frequently were, to the layout of a city — is the L'Enfant plan for Washington. Although the plan was commissioned at the very end of the eighteenth century, the same principles in much simpler form had been expressed at the end of the seventeenth in the plans proposed for Annapolis and Williamsburg by Sir Francis Nicholson, successively the English governor of Maryland and Virginia.

By the second decade of the eighteenth century Governor Spotswood at the palace in Williamsburg and gardeners among the Tidewater planters were cutting "falls," or terraces, down to the rivers like those illustrated in John James's 1712 *The Theory and Practice of Gardening*. James's book was a translation of an influential treatise by the French theorist Dezallier d'Argenville. At the same time, New England merchant magnates were seeking sites offering distant prospects and raising up their residences on grassy plinths.

One spectacular and imaginative adaptation of the formal vista garden to the American landscape still exists: Middleton Place in South Carolina, begun in 1741. Descriptions of vanished gardens like Thomas Hancock's on Beacon Hill, Captain Malbone's in Rhode Island, and William Penn's Pennsbury, as well as the overgrown but still discernible terraces on many Virginia and Carolina plantations, make clear that by the middle of the eighteenth century wealthy landowners up and down the coast were experimenting with the geometrically organized vista garden. Even those who continued to make fenced and inward-looking gardens began to replace simple rectangular raised beds with new-style parterre patterns from the new English garden books.

These experiments with the architectural style landscape did not mean that Americans had abandoned their practical bent: they simply carried out designs with productive trees or plants. Travelers repeatedly note that the formal allées leading to country houses in the East were composed of cherry trees. If the trees that made up the allées of the Southeast from the Carolinas to Texas were shade trees, well, shade was a real need in those climates.

The working parts of an estate were not banished from proximity to the pleasure grounds nor, in most cases, even concealed, as they would invariably have been in Europe. True, the ornamented farm had had its English advocates at the beginning of the eighteenth century and would have another in John Claudius Loudon at the beginning of the nineteenth, but Humphry Repton, who had no use for it, was more typical. He preached what most of his predecessors had practiced:

> Since the beauty of pleasure-ground and the profit of a farm are incompatible, it is the business of taste and prudence so to disguise the latter and to limit the former that park scenery may be obtained without much waste or extravagance; but I disclaim all idea of making that which is most beautiful also most profitable: a ploughed field and a field of grass are as distinct objects as a flower-garden and a potato-ground.[1]

The American attitude was the exact opposite: Thomas Hancock would not "Spare any Cost or pains in making my Gardens Beautifull or Profitable . . ."[2] Judging from the plants he ordered, he intended to make his profit from fruit growing. At Middleton Place, the cash crop was rice, and the rice fields are clearly visible, integrated successfully beside the principal vista. Whether there was also an attempt made to solve the more difficult problem of fitting into the overall design the buildings and yards devoted to all the crafts needed on such a plantation, which had to be self-sufficient, is not known. Quite possibly, there was. Eighteenth-century southern landowners often tried to integrate the plantation street or plantation village into their ornamental landscapes. The neat white buildings on the plantation street at Tuckahoe, near Richmond, were probably neither as neat nor as decorative as they are today when they were really functioning, but their placement and their architectural style indicate a serious effort to compose a harmonious and symmetrically balanced plan for the grounds. Less evidence has survived from the great estates in the northern colonies, but some owners may also have attempted to give their barns and barnyards an ornamental role. The 1792 engraving of the seat of the Hon. Moses Gill, Esquire, in Princeton, Massachusetts, shows a cupola-topped barn and neat barnyard balancing the formal gardens on the other side of the front lawn. It may seem to overlook a simple hayfield, but according to a contemporary "The prospect of this seat is extensive, and grand, taking in an horizon to the east, of seventy miles at least."[3]

The Gill estate is a frontier version of the architectural vista garden—not very large, drastically simplified, but carefully and symmetrically balanced. That the flower garden appears to be laid out in the old raised-bed pattern rather than in one of the newer parterre designs is characteristic of the way that Americans assimilate changes in garden style. In general, new theories, new ideas do not sweep out the old, but are simply added to the repertory. Elements of the architectural style—symmetry, topiary, terraces, long straight allées of trees, bowling greens, parterre patterns, boxwood borders—sometimes singly, sometimes in combination, moved west across the country in the gardens of the pioneers. But they were almost never pulled together into the kind of elaborate and integrated ornamental design found in

European garden books. When first made, they had to share space with the herbs, fruit, and vegetables needed to support the household. Later when buying produce became easier and cheaper than growing it at home, they had to compete with still newer design ideas.

As formal vista gardens began to be made in America, they began to come under attack in England. In 1712, the very year that saw the publication of James's *Theory and Practice of Gardening*, Joseph Addison in *The Spectator*, called for a more natural approach to garden design:

> I would rather look upon a Tree in all its Luxuriancy and Diffusion of Boughs and Branches than when it is thus cut and trimm'd into a Mathematical Figure; and cannot but fancy that an Orchard in Flower looks infinitely more delightful, than all the little Labyrinths of the most finish'd Parterre.[4]

In the next year came Alexander Pope's proclamation—along with a satirical attack on topiary work—in *The Guardian* that "all Art consists in the Imitation and Study of Nature."[5] These were early salvos in a revolution of taste that, in the name of Nature, would transform the spatial organization of the vista garden from architectural to painterly, symmetrical to asymmetrical, regular to irregular, and create what we know as the English Landscape Garden.

The new English attitude presented a way of looking at garden design much more sympathetic to American circumstances. An American landowner could see realistic possibilities in Addison's program:

> But why may not a whole Estate be thrown into a kind of Garden by frequent Plantations, that may turn as much to the Profit, as the Pleasure of the Owner? A

As restored by Colonial Williamsburg one of the "falls" or terraces descending to the James River at Carter's Grove is laid out as a kitchen garden defended by a ten-foot-tall palisade, a height suggested by the size of the post holes uncovered by archaeologists.

Command center for a 3000-acre estate, Moses Gill's house in western Massachusetts also commanded a view, on good days, to Boston Harbor. His garden and farmyard show care for design, but if having a vista was a matter of pride for the judge he was not concerned that its foreground was a hayfield.

Marsh overgrown with Willows or a Mountain shaded with Oaks, are not only more beautiful, but more beneficial, than when they lie bare and unadorned. Fields of Corn make a pleasant Prospect, and if the Walks were a little taken care of that lie between them, if the natural Embroidery of the Meadows were helpt and improved by some small Additions of Art, and the several Rows of Hedges set off by Trees and Flowers, that the Soil was capable of receiving, a Man might make a pretty Landskip of his own Possessions.[6]

In the New World, at least most of the time, you didn't have to plant trees: all you had to do was thin them out judiciously to create natural-seeming vistas. That these new ideas immediately struck a responsive chord we have to infer from literary sources. We have no clear physical evidence from the beginning of the century of American gardens in the Landscape Garden style, and that is likely to remain true unless some unknown drawings turn up; without the guidance of plans or detailed descriptions it is difficult for the archaeologist to distinguish between real and contrived nature.

William Byrd II was one Virginia gardener who had seen first-hand what was happening in England, and had assimilated the fashionable way of viewing the landscape as a series of paintings, to judge from his descriptions of vistas in *The History of the dividing Line Run in the Year 1728*, of which this is a particularly telling example:

The tent was pitched up on an Eminence, which overlookt a wide Piece of low Grounds, cover'd with Reeds and watered by a Crystal Stream gliding thro' the Middle of it. On the Other Side of this delightful Valley, which was about half a Mile wide, rose a Hill that terminated the view, and in the figure of a Semicircle closed in upon the opposite Side of the Valley. This had a most agreeable Effect upon the Eye, and wanted nothing but Cattle grazing in the Meadow, and Sheep and Goats feeding on the Hill, to make it a Compleat Rural LANDSCAPE.[7]

Byrd admired ex-governor Spotswood's terraces on his estate at *Germanna* on the upper Rappahannock, and his diaries testify to both his pleasure in his own garden at Westover and his efforts to improve it and "put it into a better fashion." Unfortunately, the diaries offer no descriptions, and the garden at Westover has been made over many times in the past two hundred and fifty years. What is there today, walled and laid out in squares, might be the garden Byrd inherited from his father in 1705. Undoubtedly a walled garden was incorporated into his new landscaping: most landscape gardens in the New World, quite understandably, included walled or hedged areas well into the nineteenth century. Whether Byrd's landscaping was in the geometric or the natural style or a blend of the two is matter for speculation. The last is more likely. To our eyes, most early gardens of the English landscape school, even in England, look very much as if Art and Order still had Nature in firm control. Literary references and architectural allusions to Classical Rome or Medieval England abounded, and the serpentine paths owed as much to the compass and T-square as had the avenues and goose feet of the earlier period. The style developed freedom slowly. The seemingly undesigned pastoral gardens of Capability Brown, Humphry Repton, and their followers that epitomize it to us were not created until the second half of the eighteenth century.

Although there was more traveling back and forth to England in the eighteenth century than we tend to realize, most garden-makers on this side of the Atlantic had to depend on magazines — *The Spectator* was widely read — and books from Europe to learn about the new fashions in gardening. And not just in gardening. Paper was scarce and type was scarcer, which, as Daniel Boorstin points out, discouraged colonial Americans from expressing their ideas and sharing their experiences in book form.[8] When they tried to visualize the working out of the ideas they read about in English garden books, they were doing it in terms of very different land forms and agricultural practice. To further complicate matters, popular early eighteenth-century books preached the new gardening ideas in their texts; but Stephen Switzer's *Ichnographia Rustica: or, The Nobleman, Gentleman, and Gardener's Recreation* (1718), Philip Miller's *Gardener's Dictionary* (1731) and *Gardener's Kalendar* (1731), and Batty Langley's *New Principles of Gardening* (1727) faithfully reproduced in their illustrations, diagrams, and plans the geometric layouts and symmetrical vistas characteristic of what Switzer called the French "Grand Manier." No wonder it was hard to break away from the habit of symmetry.

But break away they did, at least some of them did in some part of their gardens; painterly garden vistas need as much acreage as architectural ones. Eliza Lucas's description, written in the early 1740s, of Crowfield, one of the Middleton family plantations in South Carolina, might be of an English garden in the style of the early part of the century, except for the birds and trees named. The outlines that can still be traced in this century bear a strong resemblance to Batty Langley's garden plans: formal layouts to be loosely planted. Incidentally, Langley's book was published only two years before one of the anglophile Middletons acquired the property.

> From the back door is a spacious walk a thousand feet long, each side of which nearest the house is a grass plat ornamented in a Serpentine manner with flowers; next to that on the right hand is what immediately struck my rural taste, a thicket of young, tall live oaks where a variety of airey choristers pour forth their melody, and my darling the mocking bird joyn'd in the artless Concert and inchanted me with his harmony. Opposite on the left is a large square bowling green, sunk a little below the level of the rest of the garden, with a walk quite

around composed of a double row of fine, large flowering Laurel and Catalpas which afford both shade and beauty.

> My letter will be of unreasonable length if I don't pass over the Mounts, Wilderness, etc., and come to the bottom of this charming spot where is a large fish pond with a mount rising out of the middle the top of which is level with the dwelling house and upon it a Roman temple; on each side of this are other large fish ponds properly disposed which form a fine prospect of water from the house. Beyond this are the smiling fields dressed in vivid green.[9]

Later, married to Charles Pinckney, the garden-loving Eliza spent six years in England and saw at first hand the new style developing. On her return she found her own garden reverted to forest, but as she wrote an English friend in 1762 "indeed it was laid out in the old taste, so that I have been modernizing it which has afforded me much imployment."

Another American garden-maker, William Paca, had just returned from a year's study at the Inner Temple in London when he began to build his house and garden in Annapolis, Maryland. That his walled town garden included a Wilderness on its lowest level (see p. 19) indicates that he was quite aware of up-to-date English fashion, and well able to blend it successfully with the ordered falling terraces more usual in this country. Barbara Paca, a landscape historian as well as a direct descendent of William, has established the precision of the garden's mathematical structure, underlying even the more informally arranged wilderness.[10]

The marquis de Chastellux, traveling in North America in the early 1780s, noted landscape gardens in the English style in New Jersey— "if this lawn were better taken care of, one would think oneself in the neighborhood of London rather than that of New York" — and in Virginia, "which yields not in beauty to those English models which we are now imitating with much success."[11] Both would have to have been made before the beginning of the American Revolution, probably around mid-century.

Fifteen years later, the duc de la Rochefoucauld-Liancourt, who admired the English landscape style to the point of fanaticism and, like his fellow countryman, deplored the low quality of American maintenance, thought Middleton Place badly taken care of and overrated on his trip to South Carolina. He was more impressed with the well-established— it is mentioned in the *Gentleman's Magazine* in 1753 — garden at neighboring Drayton Hall:

> We came at last to dine with Dr. Drayton at Drayton Hall, an old house, comfortable and fairly well built, and a garden better laid out, better maintained, planted with better trees than any I have yet seen in this country. To have an agreeable garden here it is only necessary to bring to it the rich gifts of the surrounding forest, isolate them so they show to better advantage, place shrubs artfully in front of the trees, and the trees according to the height their species will reach at maturity. This is just

The terraced falls between house and wilderness in Paca's garden, built between 1763 and 1765, are unusual only in that the center walkway is not centered on the house, but the off-set axis is precisely placed within a geometric grid favored in the period.

how Dr. Drayton's father, also a physician, began the garden, and his son, who seems to find his only pleasure in country life has, with great taste, continued it.[12]

However enthusiastically Americans embraced the theories of the landscape garden, their application in this country produced results rather different from those in England, which European observers did not always appreciate. Unretouched Nature didn't offer the kind of "*piquant*" vistas La Rochefoucauld-Liancourt felt were the proper culmination of a garden. What he found appealing was a highly cultivated countryside like that between Portsmouth, New Hampshire, and Boston, which he described as "a continuous garden," and which was as rare in eighteenth-century America as wild nature was abundant. Even more important, as J. B. Jackson points out, in England "the invasion of the park and garden by lawn represented the triumph of the pastoral landscape, the triumph of sheep over horticulture."[13] The lawn eventually triumphed in America, but sheep never did. In *The Shaping of America*, D. W. Meinig uses sheep-raising as an example of the way in which colonists were forced to change their patterns of subsistence in the New World:

. . . despite repeated and extensive efforts, especially by British colonists, sheep never became important in any of these colonial regions, whereas in some hogs thrived beyond all expectation. Sheep suffered from harsh winters, dense forest, poor fodder, natural predators and a shortage of shepherds, while swine, omnivorous, prolific, and fiercely protective of themselves, ran wild to become a staple and a nuisance. . . . That twentieth-century Americans consume nearly twenty times as much pork as lamb and mutton is a direct legacy of this seventeenth-century pattern.[14]

These very American, adaptable pigs would delay the spread of the unenclosed garden in many areas until they were legally restrained in the nineteenth century. However, American landowners did not cease to experiment with the form, simply because they were engaged in a different pattern of agriculture.

Fortunately two very different but equally splendid eighteenth century adaptations of English-landscape design theories to the American landscape still remain: George

Washington's Mount Vernon, and Thomas Jefferson's Monticello. Both gardens are restorations, but restorations based on an unusually large amount of documentation. Interestingly, both men attempted to raise and breed sheep for both wool and meat but seem to have produced only enough of both for household consumption. Whether their flocks were pastured at the mansion-house plantations to play their old-world role as lawn mowers seems quite probable but is undocumented.

As with the architectural style, one of the major American modifications of the natural style was the incorporation of practical necessities like vegetable gardens, smoke-houses, "necessaries" (privies), laundries, and all the workshops of the plantation street in the landscape design. Jefferson reached an imaginative but partial solution by moving the kitchen, the dairy, the ice house, the stables, some storage and some slave quarters underground—really under terraces flanking the house. Based on Palladian examples and made possible by his hilltop site, this innovation was rather too special to be widely imitated. Nor did it take care of the messiest and noisiest of the workshops, the nailery and the joinery. One has a feeling from the documents that Jefferson's visitors were bothered much more by the intrusion of all this necessary but unpicturesque activity into the designed landscape than Jefferson himself was. He could afford to sacrifice that particular vista. After all, he had plenty of views from his "little mountain" as he wrote to William Hamilton:

> Of prospect I have a rich profusion and offering itself at every point of the compass. . . . To prevent a satiety of this is the principal difficulty.[15]

In the same letter Jefferson brings up for modification another aspect of the English models he so admired:

> Their canvas is of open ground, variegated with clumps of trees distributed with taste. They need no more of wood than will serve to embrace a lawn or a glade. But under the beaming, constant and almost vertical sun of Virginia, shade is our Elysium . . . The only substitute I have been able to imagine is this. Let your ground be covered with trees of the loftiest stature. Trim up their bodies as high as the constitution & form of the tree will bear, but so as that their tops shall still unite & yeild dense shade. . . . Then, when in the open ground you would plant a clump of trees, place a thicket of shrubs presenting a hemisphere the crown of which shall distinctly show itself under the branches of the trees.

By the last decades of the eighteenth century, even in England, voices were raised to point out that the broad sheep-sheared lawns of the pastoral landscape park were not suitable to all climates or terrains. Proponents of "the picturesque" found the wild, romantic landscapes of Salvatore Rosa more appealing as models than the equally seventeenth-century but peaceful Claudian views that had inspired earlier designers. The war of words that ensued, fought on the battleground of aesthetic principle, did not much interest Americans: they were fighting a real war.

Monticello's hilltop site enabled Jefferson to screen some plantation workspaces and vegetable gardens from the pleasure grounds and protect his distant vistas. Mulberry Row, on the right in the photograph, was in his day the site of the nailery, joinery, stables, and some of the slave quarters.

A New Nation
Experiments

AND FINDS IT MUST ADAPT OLD
WORLD GARDEN IDEAS TO NEW
WORLD CONDITIONS

A mid-nineteenth-century American innovation, the affluent suburb with open tree-shaded lawns and curving streets, perfected in Olmsted and Vaux's design for Riverside, Illinois

When the country had pulled itself together after the Revolution and new gardens began to be made, the naturalistic or painterly style in both its pastoral and picturesque forms came into its own. William Birch, in his 1809 *Country Seats of North America*, shows two picturesque gardens, one of them his own; and a variety of pastoral landscapes. True, geometrical landscapes continued to be created from the 1780s through the first twenty years of the 1800s; but Americans had gained a good deal of confidence in adjusting their layouts to their topography. On hilly land in Medford, Massachusetts, in 1809, Thomas Kidder composed such elements of order as terraces, linear planting, allées, and fences with freedom and sensitivity to produce for his estate, The Lilacs, a fresh and original design. It is highly likely that many equally individual interpretations enlivened gardens of the early republic: the documents have not been found.

Nurserymen were the leaders in popularizing the natural or "modern" style of garden design. In 1806, the same year as the letter from Jefferson to William Hamilton quoted above, Bernard McMahon, an Irishman transplanted to Philadelphia and one of Jefferson's suppliers, published *The American Gardener's Calendar*, the first widely disseminated attempt to adapt European horticultural information to "the peculiarities of our climates, soils, and situations."

Although McMahon was a recent immigrant, he displayed the true American reluctance to relinquish any design possibility. In his chapter on "The Pleasure, or Flower Garden," he explains in simplified form the canons of the natural style, or as he calls it, "modern taste" in garden design, but he cannot bring himself to rule out entirely "straight ranges of the most stately trees . . . which, though prohibited in many modern designs, always exhibit an air of grandeur." And he even has some good words for topiary as providing "an agreeable variety by diversifying the scene in contrast with the rural works."

Early nineteenth-century American seedsmen and nurserymen, recent immigrants and native-born alike, didn't just sell trees and plants. They explained growing techniques and offered hints on design in their catalogues. They wrote books and magazine articles, and some started their own magazines. They were often leaders in forming the agricultural and horticultural societies dedicated to the improvement of farming and gardening that proliferated in the new republic. All century long, in fact, they continued to make major contributions to what became a flood of gardening books and periodicals eagerly consumed by a population that was always on the move. A letter from Peoria in the August, 1847, issue of *The Horticulturist*, during Andrew Jackson Downing's editorship, indicates how much these publications were valued by those who lived on the frontier.

> I have been looking over the first eight numbers of your journal, lately received from Albany in one package; and be assured, this is one of the *best treats* enjoyed during a residence of eleven years upon the prairies. While perusing the pages of this beautiful work, I no longer feel myself an isolated being, far out upon the borders of the cultivated portions of our land, but in the

midst of highly gifted and refined minds, sensibly alive to the best interests of our common country.

Downing, born in 1815, was by far the most influential of those nurserymen who turned to writing, magazine editing, and landscape design. His books, in particular the first, *A Treatise on the Theory and Practice of Landscape Gardening* of 1841, went through many editions in his century and are still being reprinted in ours; the ideas and designs in them were copied all across the country, with and without acknowledgment. The Swedish novelist and social critic, Fredrika Bremer, was told by the popular novelist Catharine Sedgwick in 1850 that "nobody, whether he be rich or poor, builds a house or lays out a garden without consulting Downing's works. Every young couple who sets up housekeeping buys them."[1] Downing's tragic death at the age of thirty-seven in a Hudson River steamboat accident was mourned by the press and his contemporaries as a loss to the nation.

Downing did not claim originality. He saw himself as an adapter to American circumstances of European landscape gardening theories, especially those set forth by Humphry Repton and John Claudius Loudon. He corresponded with the latter and, although he didn't much admire Loudon's designs, he did admire his thinking and eulogized him as "one who has done more than any person that ever lived, to popularize, and render universal, a taste for Gardening and Domestic Architecture."

As far as the United States is concerned, Downing's words could serve as his own epitaph. He was a brilliant popularizer and his timing was perfect. When he started writing for the horticultural press in the 1830s, the economy had recovered from the war of 1812 and taken off, those two great American wealth-builders, mass-production and overseas commerce, in the lead. At the same time, a wave of European immigration, Irish for the most part, poured into the Northeast, providing the not-so-cheap labor that made a certain amount of large-scale gardening feasible and increasing the city congestion that gave suburban life its appeal. More and more businessmen were acquiring the money to create country estates, and even the modestly successful might aspire to the suburban cottages that increasingly efficient mass transportation made available. Here was the audience for Downing's clearly and engagingly presented blend of good sense, scientific understanding, sound practical advice, and aesthetic guidance.

His contemporaries also considered him a gifted designer, and the demand for his professional services was such that he felt obliged to publish a schedule of his fees in horticultural magazines. So little evidence of his landscapes is left that it is hard for us to evaluate them. We have descriptions and a few engraved views of his own house and grounds; his plan for a public park on what is now the Mall in Washington, D.C.; and the recently uncovered grounds of the Headley House in Newburgh. The house itself appears in *Cottage Residences*, but the engraving shows little of the landscaping, and without more documentation it is difficult to tell just how much remains of his work. For the fairly large but ruinous remnant of Springside, the estate he planned for

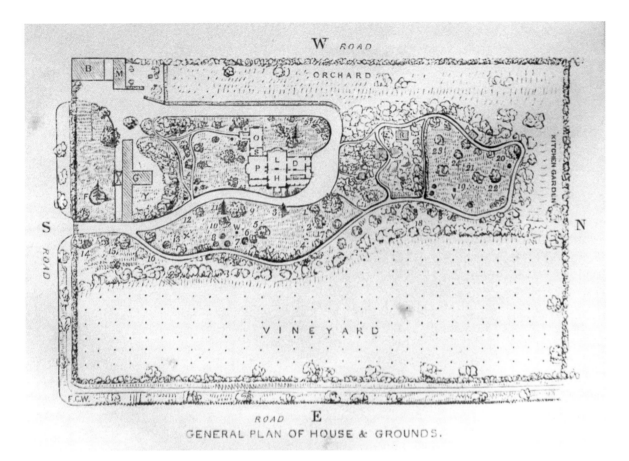

GENERAL PLAN OF HOUSE & GROUNDS.

Matthew Vassar, sufficient documentation does exist so that it could be restored and re-created. But, illuminating as it would be to walk through a picturesque landscape of the mid-nineteenth century rather than trying to visualize it from plans and period engravings, Downing's importance in his own day depended on his writings and not his commissions, and it still does in ours. He contributed articles to several horticultural magazines, served as editor and editorial writer of *The Horticulturist* from 1846 until his death, edited a couple of English books for American publication, and wrote three books in addition to the *Treatise on Landscape Gardening. The Fruits and Fruit Trees of America* (1845) became a standard reference work. His two architectural pattern books, *Cottage Residences* (1842) and *The Architecture of Country Houses* (1850), were reissued throughout the century, and both contained information on the planning and planting of home grounds, updated in later editions by his brother Charles and Henry Winthrop Sargent.

Downing was an acute observer of his countrymen and the changing society of his time. He had something to say about almost every strand in the web of American attitudes to the garden and the larger landscape. He noted new wealth's love of display and pointed out the difficulty of sustaining it with expensive but unskilled labor. He warned of the pitfalls of "borrowed taste," but felt that everyone possessed the capacity for refinement. He shared the belief of contemporary social critics in the positive moral and social influence of an attractive domestic environment and in the importance of contact with nature for physical and mental health. He put forward the idea that the individual house with a modest surrounding garden, what he called suburban country living, would best meet these requirements for the

largest number of people. Downing saw the beginning of suburban real-estate development in the Hudson valley, and made suggestions for improving the design of suburbs very similar to those advocated by town planners of our own day. He advocated the planting of street trees and the creation of city parks to make contact with nature available to those for whom the suburban or agrarian ways of life were unachievable. Quite aware of his countrymen's utilitarian mind-set, he realized that they had to be sold on the value of anything that was not an actual or potential money-maker, and were best persuaded by a combination of example and appeal to national pride. The enlightened citizen was to provide both the example and the leadership in organizing the community groups needed to bring about civic improvements in a democracy.

James Vick was too much a nurseryman to disparage bedding out; but he did grant that it looked stiff. Although succulents made up this pyramid from the February 1878 issue of his magazine, "in our dry climate," he wrote, "we cannot but feel that plants so situated must be uncomfortable."

Downing shared the view of many thoughtful commentators, both native and foreign, that, in a country without laws or customs to promote the intact inheritance of large estates over generations, the future of landscape design as high art lay in public commissions. Only parks, cemeteries, or town plans would allow the gifted designer enough money and enough land to work with. His hope was that everyone could learn the principles of taste, and in learning them would realize that moderation in both size and embellishment best suited the abilities of those homeowners, the great majority, who would be landscaping their property without professional help. He gave his middle-class readers simple and usable versions of garden-design theories current and historic, plant lists, and construction and maintenance tips. As his experience broadened—especially after an 1850 trip to England—he became more and more convinced that Americans should favor their native vegetation rather than trendy exotics in planting their properties. Still, he was careful to keep his audience up to date on the latest European gardening fashions that he thought adaptable to this country.

Two of these, bedding out—the practice of massing flowers or foliage of a single color in shaped beds—and what Loudon called the gardenesque—specimen trees and shrubs displayed individually on greensward—were instantly added to the American design repertory. In many ways, both were responses to the steady stream of new and exciting flowers, trees, and shrubs brought to Western Europe and Eastern America by the proliferation of plant hunters roaming the globe in the early nineteenth century. By the 1880s, circles or stars packed with precise rows of brightly colored blossoms or foliage—coleus and alternanthera were great favorites—decorated the front yards of farmhouses and city bungalows and erupted from the lawns of private estates and public parks. Who could blame passionate gardeners for polka-dotting their lawns with Douglas firs or Japanese cherry trees, or filling their carpet beds with the new petunias from South America, zinnias from Mexico, phlox from Texas, or tuberous begonias from Africa and the Andes? In fact, some critics did, arguing that enthusiasm for individual plants tended to trivialize the garden's design; that many exotics demanded continual intensive care and even then didn't really look healthy; that these vulgar displays of color had more to do with dressmaking than gardening. Such criticism has been given plenty of justification, but bedding out and specimen planting, used with imagination, can be valuable additions to the designer's kit. Both have played a large role for good and ill alike in public parks and gardens. And they still do.

Bedding out is highly labor-intensive. Bulbs of the same size carefully planted to the same depth can be counted on for one-color blocks or bands in the spring. But to keep blocks and bands—carpet or ribbon beds—in continuous bloom, bulbs must be removed when the blossoms fade and replaced with flowers or foliage of even height and matching color. Beloved of seedsmen and nurserymen who provided the plants and the propaganda, and of professional gardeners

because it showed off their skills, bedding out demanded from most American homeowners a degree of dedication they didn't always possess, or the help of trained gardeners they couldn't always find. Nor did Americans rush to take up Loudon's suggestion that "A Green-house, Orangery or Conservatory ought if possible to be attached to every suburban residence"[2] despite all the technological advances that made such structures cheaper to build and more effective.

Americans did do a lot of rushing in the mid-nineteenth century, but not of a kind conducive to elaborate gardening. Above all, they rushed to multiply. According to D. W. Meinig, the population grew from 5,306,000 in 1800 to 23,192,000 in 1850, with less than a quarter of the increase provided by immigrants.[3] Still the stream of immigrants continued to swell to the end of the century, interrupted only briefly by the Civil War. To observers at the time the whole country seemed in motion. Native-born citizens and immigrants alike moved west or north or south in search of more fertile land, richer mines, or better opportunities; then moved back east again to display their success if they were successful and lick their wounds if they were not. The trained gardeners among the immigrants—there weren't many—soon found that commerce offered them the best rewards. The untrained were little help to equally untrained homeowners in the finicky aspects of garden-making.

Westward moving Americans were less likely to put into practice the latest fashions in garden design than to re-create, for reasons of practicality and nostalgia, the old-fashioned vernacular mixture of fruit and flowers, vegetables, and herbs. Making the carefully packed and nursed seeds and cuttings they carried with them thrive in unfamiliar, often inhospitable soil gave pioneer women enough challenges.

Immigrants from a variety of European countries continued to infuse new life and variety to the mixed garden with their own traditional plans, plants, and horticultural techniques. A few were knowledgeable botanists and horticulturists like Eleuthère Irénée du Pont de Nemours. In the first years of the nineteenth century, du Pont's Delaware orchard and garden had demonstrated the horticultural and decorative value of espaliers, a long-practiced French technique for fruit production.[4] Other immigrants were intellectuals fleeing political turmoil, like the Germans Olmsted encountered in Texas, or simple farmers seeking better land and better opportunities.

Few pioneer groups included as many trained horticulturists or were given as much encouragement in garden-making by their leaders as were the Mormons. Their success in truly making a desert bloom offered comfort and encouragement to later migrants passing through Utah on the way to California and Oregon. Yet from all accounts, the Mormons' earliest gardens followed the traditional pattern of mixed plantings in rectangular beds. Local historians have also noted that the settlers, Americans as well as those who came directly from Europe, would plant in their gardens favorites from their native lands. You could usually tell where a householder came from by looking at what grew in his garden.[5]

Back East, the old-fashioned garden had its champions even at the height of the fashion for bedding out. A star of well-pinched coleus on the front lawn did not preclude an old-fashioned garden in the backyard or by the kitchen door, and photographs of carpet-bedding schemes show that their box-edged paisley-form beds were often planted with a mixture of annuals, perennials, and flowering shrubs. From magazine descriptions, most of the city gardens that won prizes in competitions sponsored by companies like National Cash Register or civic improvement groups were similar mixtures. Such competitions proliferated at the turn of the the twentieth century, since gardening was considered an easily learned craft conducive to domesticity by reformers bent on keeping workmen out of taverns. In fairness, it should be registered that these reformers were almost always zealous gardeners themselves.

The old-fashioned garden, as Anna Warner demonstrated in her popular 1872 *Gardening by Myself* was supremely adaptable. Its straightforward orthogonal beds could develop curves, and its unconstrained mix of plants welcome exotic newcomers to the company of long-loved favorites. As the nineteenth century moved on, fruit and vegetables contributed less and less to that mix. More and more Americans moved to the cities and went to work in factories, leaving little time and space for household self-sufficiency. Railroads and refrigeration brought reasonably priced and sometimes superior produce to local shops and markets. Horticultural books and journals started suggesting that homegrown fruits and vegetables were luxuries that even a suburban homeowner could well forgo unless he or she were truly interested in the process of raising them. By the time that distinctively American branch of the Arts and Crafts Movement, the Colonial Revival, took up the old-fashioned garden in the last quarter of the nineteenth century and endowed its beds with boxwood edging they rarely had—except in the South—in the seventeenth and eighteenth centuries, its promoters could unblushingly refer to it as the "flower garden of our grandmothers."

Bedding out and the vernacular garden weren't the only contenders for command of American garden design. The principles of the landscape style in either of its forms, which Downing called The Picturesque and The Beautiful—read pastoral—guided the layout of many large public and private gardens and were even miniaturized for the small house lot with varying degrees of success. As time went on, these principles were more and more often adjusted to enhance the distinctive character and variety of American landscapes. Early in the nineteenth century designers stuck close to the models provided by the parklands of great English estates and their adaptations by the French, the so-called *jardins Anglo-Chinois*. Nature's landscapes were still considered to need taming and civilizing, although for decades there had been some who deplored the wholesale and wasteful razing of the forests. At mid-century attitudes began to change. Many thoughtful Americans came to believe that both mindless exploitation and imitation of foreign examples were destroying the very thing that made their country unique: its

great natural beauty. And as travelers and settlers fanned out across the continent they saw that this country contained even more varied and remarkable scenery than they had imagined. When Frederick Law Olmsted and his brother John, already well-acquainted with England and the continent, visited Texas in 1853, they were enchanted by the Western Prairies:

> The live-oaks, standing alone or in picturesque groups near and far upon the clean sward, which rolled in long waves that took, on their various slopes, bright light or half shadows from the afternoon sun, contributed mainly to an effect which was very new and striking, though still natural, like a happy new melody.[6]

Soon came the discoveries of still more extraordinary landscapes like Yosemite, Yellowstone, and the Grand Canyon.

"Shouldn't an effort be made to save some of this spectacular beauty?" asked writers and painters. For the man who would provide the philosophical basis for wilderness preservation, it was a matter beyond beauty; it was a matter of spiritual survival. In 1851 Henry David Thoreau declared to a Concord audience "in Wildness is the preservation of the World," and in an 1858 issue of *Atlantic Monthly* he called for the creation of "national preserves," which would include not just mountains and forests, but also Indians and wild animals and allow them to continue their way of life. Momentum built. Even the Civil War did not stop it, but the Indians and the animals were left to fend for themselves, when not actively hunted. On July 1, 1864, President Lincoln signed a bill presenting the Yosemite Valley and the Mariposa Big Tree Grove to the state of California for public use for resort and recreation for all time. In 1870 Yellowstone became the first national park—Yosemite would become one in 1890. By reserving areas of great scenic or scientific interest for public enjoyment, the United States opened up a new and distinctively American chapter in the art of landscape design. Designers were challenged to make those areas

Specimen tree planting in the gardenesque style as interpreted by Frank J. Scott in 1870. This collection of trees and shrubs from *The Art of Beautifying Suburban Home Grounds* forms a quite harmonious composition, but a lot of cutting or transplanting will be needed as the specimens grow up and out.

accessible to that public without destroying the very thing it came to enjoy, a challenge continually renewed as more and more people with more and more leisure time find it easier and easier to visit the national parks.

Many supporters of wilderness preservation, writers such as William Cullen Bryant and Washington Irving, were also instigators of another mid-century phenomenon: the city park movement. City parks, by exposing the public at large to pastoral and picturesque landscapes, did a lot to popularize the styles. The catalyst was New York's Central Park, designed by the team of Frederick Law Olmsted and Calvert Vaux, the young English architect brought to this country as a business partner by Downing, who had led the campaign for the park's creation. Olmsted and Vaux's prize-winning Greensward Plan of 1858 was a resounding success, and set off a surge of park-building across the country, interrupted by the Civil War, but not for long.

Olmsted, who would dominate landscape design for the rest of the century, truly learned his art by practicing it. It took him a while to find his calling. In succession a clerk for a dry-goods merchant, a China-trade seaman, a farmer, a magazine editor, and a book publisher, he was well-known as a journalist and social critic when he became Superintendent of Central Park, but he came from a family of nature-lovers and scenery connoisseurs. If as a boy he spent more time roaming the New England countryside than sitting in the schoolroom, he had studied civil engineering for a short time and taken a course in scientific farming at Yale. An omnivorous reader, he knew the major British landscape gardening texts, and he had seen a variety of British and continental parks and gardens during a seven-month European walking tour in 1850.

Very little escaped Olmsted's attentive observation, and he turned out to be a brilliant and far-sighted designer. This gift he was slow to recognize; he tended to think of himself as an organizer and administrator. Self-expression meant far less to him than social responsibility. Even after the success of Central Park, he took leave during the Civil War to serve as Executive Secretary of the Sanitary Commission, from which the American Red Cross would develop. Then came a brief but very illuminating period managing a California gold mine—we are at last beginning to heed his warnings that imitation Eastern landscapes of lawn and trees can only be maintained at great environmental cost in California. At the age of forty-three he returned to New York and to the profession, landscape architecture, that he and Vaux would name.

Olmsted is best known for his large public projects. He devoted considerable thought and energy to wilderness preservation and the creation of state and natural parks, and is considered the father of city planning in this country. To mention only a few highlights, he and his firm designed parks and parkway systems from Brooklyn, Boston, and Buffalo to Louisville and Detroit; the Stanford University campus; and the site plan for the 1893 Chicago World's Fair. Much of his private work was on a similar scale. Indeed, the acreage of the Biltmore Estate in North Carolina was far larger than

Soon after he settled in Delaware in 1802, Eleuthère Irénée du Pont de Nemours planted an orchard and a garden patterned after those in his native France, a horticulturally sophisticated vernacular garden with espaliered, pleached, and cordoned fruit trees. The simplified reconstruction designed by William H. Frederick, Jr. derives from both archaeological exploration and a plan sketched by du Pont's granddaughter Victorine in 1925 from childhood memories.

that of most city commissions. And Biltmore, with its introduction of managed forestry, reflected his overriding concern with the welfare of society as a whole. To him, high art and social responsibility were not, or need not be, conflicting goals for landscape architects. His point of view, whether honored or not in practice, has persisted as an ideal for the profession in this country.

Olmsted sincerely valued the stimulation of city life as much as he valued health-giving contact with nature. Given his experience with the economic and political realities of the city, he came to feel, as Downing had, that well-planned, easy-to-reach suburbs would offer the most balanced life for the middle class. Suburbs as such weren't new. We tend to think of the rush to the suburbs as a nineteenth- and twentieth-century phenomenon, a child of the Industrial Revolution, and in particular of the streetcar, the train, and the automobile. In certain ways it is, but historians with a longer view point out that suburbs have sprouted around cities right from the start, whether those cities began in Mesopotamia, China, India, Egypt, Europe, or pre-Columbian Meso-America. The cities of French and British North America, "parachuted" into the wild, were no exception. They followed, without realizing it, the great and mysterious metropolis of Cahokia, which flourished between 1050 and 1250 A.D. on the banks of the Mississippi across from present-day St. Louis. Estimates by archaeologists have given Cahokia a core population of 15,000, with double that number in its suburbs and satellite villages.

In the first chapter of *Crabgrass Frontier*, his astute analysis of the suburbanization of the United States, Kenneth T. Jackson quotes from a letter written on a clay tablet in 539 B.C. that could have been written today, or, as he acknowledges, two thousand years before.

> Our property seems to me the most beautiful in the world. It is so close to Babylon that we enjoy all the advantages of the city, and yet when we come home we are away from all the noise and dust.[7]

Some historians like to point out that many suburbs were home to trades too disreputable, too noisy, too smelly, or too land-hungry to be welcome in the heart of town. We still have these, but usually we reserve the term "suburb" for the residential kind, and call territory occupied by used-car lots, auto repair shops, motels, fast-food chains, shopping centers and lumberyards "strip" or "slurb." Where there is attractive land residential suburbs tend to grow up, but in this country, as Downing pointed out, they don't always make the most attractive use of that land.

Enter the planned garden suburb, designed to do just that. The first was Llewellyn Park in New Jersey, organized by Llewellyn Haskell, a New York businessman, in 1853. He and a group of his friends bought land on the side of the Orange Mountains in New Jersey facing New York City across the Hudson. Alexander Jackson Davis, an architect who had often worked with Downing, laid out the landscape and was one of the property owners. Roads followed, where possible, the contours of the land, as did the lot lines—no grid here—

and a fifty-acre strip, much of it left wild, was reserved for community use. Llewellyn Park was a community from the start. Individual owners joined together and placed their properties under a covenant that barred any industrial activity, stipulated that houses could not be built on less than an acre of land, and bound them to contribute to the upkeep of roads and common lands. Such covenants became typical of planned suburbs and many were highly restrictive both socially and aesthetically. Although Llewellyn Park put no restrictions on the style of house or garden that an owner could build, most owners there tended to follow in their own gardens the lead of the suburb's picturesque landscape layout.

Chestnut Hill, just inside Philadelphia, and Lake Forest, north of Chicago, soon followed, but probably the most influential of these new developments was Riverside, designed by Olmsted and Vaux in 1868 for a tract of land along the Des Plaines River west of Chicago. Olmsted offered a carefully thought-out program to create a harmonious setting for family life. It combined a sensitive layout based on the character of the site with a soundly constructed infrastructure to create a design so pleasing that it became the prototype for the tree-shaded, lawn-bordered curving streets of the affluent American suburb.[8] Not only did Olmsted and his sons design several hundred suburbs and subdivisions, but the style was, and still is, imitated by developers and designers all over the country, often on the cheap and without Olmsted's serious study of the land, the climate, and the needs of future inhabitants.

For Olmsted there was a real distinction between landscape architecture and gardening. The difference was a matter of intent not of scale: He created a successful miniature landscape on his own one-and-three-quarter acre property in Brookline. And he devised for *Garden & Forest* "A Plan for a Small Homestead" to accommodate on a steep half-acre lot the requirements of a suburban household—fruit and vegetable garden, stable for horse and cow, with carriage room and lodgings for a man; a place to sit outdoors; and a flower garden—and still provide a landscape experience.

> The only valuable landscape resource of the property lies in the distant view eastward…it can evidently be improved by placing in its foreground a body of vigorous dark foliage in contrast with which the light gray and yellowish greens of the woods of the river bottom will appear of a more delicate and tender quality, and the grassy hills beyond more mysteriously indistinct, far away, unsubstantial, and dreamy.[9]

The foreground foliage was to be composed of intimately mingled forms and colors to produce "such intricate play of light and shade that…the eye is not drawn to dwell upon…details." Olmsted had been profoundly impressed by such effects in the Panamanian rainforests he had seen on his way to California, and would be influenced by them in his planting plans for the rest of his career. The aim of landscape architecture, he believed, was to create a work of art that would stir the emotions, as music did "back of thought." Trees, foliage textures, stone, water, sun, shade, views, and

perspective were so many elements that the artist used to outline "a picture upon which nature shall be employed for generations before the work he has prepared for her hand shall realize his intentions." [10] Gardening, in his eyes, was about growing plants. In what he thought of as a garden individual plants counted for much more, and its design might well be determined by the kind of plants to be grown. He would make gardens for clients who wanted them, but he separated and screened them from the landscape, and it was the design of the landscape that really engaged his interest.

Few people in Olmsted's time or since have understood this distinction, or, even if they have, have been able to hold to it in practice, verbally or visually. It's not just that the subject could use a larger vocabulary, although that does cause part of the confusion. In his popular 1870 book, *The Art of Beautifying Suburban Home Grounds*, Frank J. Scott offered a solution by substituting the term "home grounds" for both garden and landscape. Full-scale landscape gardening—a term that he was not alone in preferring to landscape architecture—Scott claimed, "is only to be accomplished in public parks and cemeteries," at least in this country. The city businessman seeking a suburban home should "take country life as a famishing man should take food—in very small quantities. *From a half acre to four or five acres will afford ground enough to give all the finer pleasures of rural life.*" Fair enough, but when the discussion turns to decorative planting—not an adjective Olmsted would have

approved—a difficulty arises. Scott lists a variety of motivations for improving one's surroundings, ending with what he calls the highest of all, the desire to create *"lovely examples, in miniature, of what we call landscapes."* But as is clear from subsequent chapters in his book and even more from the plans he proposed, Scott was not willing to give up flower beds, collections of trees and shrubs, and vegetable gardens, not to mention the occasional allée of trees and a few touches of topiary. Alas, no discipline, no work of art. At least not in a suburban lot. And it was the owner of a suburban lot that the tastemakers addressed.

Llewellyn Park, this country's first planned suburb begun in 1853 was probably also its first gated community. Laid out in the picturesque landscape style by Alexander Jackson Davis on a steep slope in Orange, New Jersey, it still retains much of its nineteenth-century character.

PART ONE CHAPTER FOUR

The American Tycoon Appears

NEW TECHNOLOGIES BUILD VAST WEALTH AND OPEN THE WORLD FOR DESIGN INSPIRATION

Preceding Page:
A sense of theater played a considerable role in the design of Italian Renaissance gardens, which inspired many American estates. A "room" might even be laid out as an actual theater with clipped cypresses for wings and a grassy stage like that painted by Maxfield Parrish at La Palazzina in Siena for Edith Wharton's *Italian Villas and Their Gardens*.

Right:
Even more theatrical, Versailles was as much a set for plays, mock battles, fountains, fireworks, and the display of courtiers' beautiful clothes as it was a complex architectural landscape. At Nemours, the Beaux-Arts architects Carrère and Hastings translated it to this country for Alfred I. du Pont.

The desire to have a little of everything operated particularly powerfully on the turn-of-the century American tycoons, who could buy up several hundred acres for a country estate. How could you choose among the new and different garden styles beckoning? How could you sort out those with which you were already familiar? Especially when money was no barrier. Like large fortunes, enticing possibilities multiplied so fast in the years after the Civil War that trying to introduce their arrival in strict chronological order would create a dizzy-making crazy quilt of dates. It is better to consider them one by one with the understanding that they all entered the garden-maker's field of view during the same period of time, roughly 1870 to 1910.

Foreign travel picked up speed in the mid-nineteenth century, first with fast American packetships and clippers and then, British steamships. And once the transatlantic cable was in place in 1865, businessmen could comfortably spend several months examining European cultural icons and absorbing the latest fashions, yet still keep a firm hand on profit-making by telegraph. On their grand tours these eager-to-learn plutocrats and their families saw first-hand how aristocrats lived, and determined to do as well, if not better. They collected garden styles and garden furnishings on their travels just as they collected paintings and sculpture, carpets and tapestries, and even whole rooms and whole castles. Italy was a favorite destination, not surprising for people whose education usually included at least a smattering of Latin and some exposure to the work of artists like Michelangelo and Raphael. Italian gardens and their artifacts — urns, balustrades, sculptures — became prime souvenirs.

Italian gardens of the Renaissance proved a fertile source of inspiration for tycoons' country house gardens. As they were built up from a series of compartments or "outdoor rooms" that could be arranged either symmetrically or asymmetrically, they were well adapted to the irregular terrain that characterized much of the American countryside. Clearly defined compartments within the same garden could be planted in very different ways but maintain some kind of coherence, unlike "gardenesque" arrangements of carpet or ribbon beds and specimen plants, which all too often became fussy, gaudy, and confused. That time, nature, and neglect had given Renaissance gardens a patina that charmed both classicists and romantics is clear from two influential American books on the subject: Charles Platt's *Italian Gardens*, published in 1894 and Edith Wharton's *Italian Villas and Their Gardens*, 1904. In the gardens designed by Platt, the richness and exuberance of the planting softened the geometry and created an equivalent to the charm of patina.

Platt, who had started as a painter, gradually turned his talents to landscape architecture, then architecture. He was extremely successful at both. His own landscape designs were carefully adjusted to their sites and he had clearly absorbed what he felt was the most important lesson of the Italian Renaissance garden:

> The problem being to take a piece of land and make it habitable, the architect proceeded with the idea that not only was the house to be lived in, but that one still wished to be at home while out-of-doors; so the garden was designed as another apartment, the terraces and groves still others, where one might walk about and find a place suitable to the hour of the day and feeling of the moment.[1]

Frequent trips to study European gardens became an important source of education for landscape designers, since professional training at university level was not available in this country until 1900. Such trips were particularly important for women, who entered the field of garden design as

Horatio Hollis Hunnewell laid out much of his estate in the naturalistic style favored in 1851, but included an Italian and a French garden between the house and Lake Waban. For his terraces of topiaries he tried shearing balsams, arborvitaes, English maples, beeches, and Scotch firs. He was particularly successful with native white pines, a real first.

professionals around the turn of the century. Many brought a great deal of practical knowledge gained as hands-on gardeners; but they were often barred from university programs and rarely encouraged to learn by apprenticing themselves to an established practitioner. Women of the first generation absorbed the principles behind the design of the Italian garden as thoroughly as Platt had and used them with even more freedom and imagination. Fortunately we still have left a few examples of the memorable country-house gardens created by such designers as Beatrix Farrand, Ellen Shipman, Marian Coffin, and Florence Yoch.

American respect for European culture certainly played a role in the renewed popularity of the so-called formal garden. So did the fact that many American architects of the period were trained at the Ecole des Beaux-Arts in Paris: Architectonic garden layouts made better settings for their European-inspired buildings. When they designed gardens theirs tended to be francophile, and the adjective Beaux-Arts applied to garden design usually calls up images based on French royal gardens. But Beaux-Arts designers never hesitated to mix motifs drawn from several different countries or architectural styles or periods. Geometrically structured gardens, whether French or Italian or an eclectic blend, were seen as well suited to the cultivation of flowers — an important point, since many of these architects, and their clients as well, believed as one of them, Guy Lowell, put it, "that the sole purpose of a garden is to grow flowers."[2] That statement would have astonished the creators of the European gardens he so admired.

Beyond these motivations, as anyone who watches the ebb and flow of architectural styles can testify, was simply the human desire to try something different. Even the British, the inventors of the landscape style, had begun to build Italianate gardens in the middle of the nineteenth century. What Henry Winthrop Sargent, in his 1859 supplement to

the sixth edition of Downing's *Landscape Architecture*, called the first successful Italian garden in this country was inspired, according to its creator, by a British garden in the Italian style. If Horatio Hollis Hunnewell drew ideas from Elvaston Castle's topiary, and in another part of the estate, its pinetum, his Italian garden is far more truly Italian in spirit than the fantasyland that illustrations show Elvaston to have been. Clearly he had also seen in England some of the more authentic gardens and terraces designed by Sir Charles Barry and William Nesfield before he began in 1851 to transform about forty acres of "flat, sandy, arid plain" on Lake Waban in Wellesley, Massachusetts.

The renewed interest in the architectural garden led, in England, to a vituperative verbal battle in books and magazine articles between Reginald Blomfield, author of *The Formal Garden in England*, and William Robinson, author of *The Wild Garden*, and their supporters. From an American point of view this seemed absurd, as a respected American art and architecture critic, Mariana Griswold Van Rensselaer, indicated in 1893:

> In truth, if we use our own minds and eyes, we find no reason to think that formal gardening and naturalistic gardening are deadly rivals, each of which must put the knife to the other's throat if it wishes itself to survive.
>
> No garden can be absolutely artificial, and none can be absolutely natural; and this is enough to show that the elements theoretically proper to the one style may sometimes be very freely introduced in a general scheme which we class as belonging to the other style.[3]

American tolerance of variety and lack of interest in theoretical correctness made American landscape design particularly susceptible to the collecting instincts of turn-of-the-century Americans and to Beaux-Arts eclecticism. The

Right:
At Sonnenberg in Canandaigua, New York an early twentieth-century anthology garden survives into the twenty-first, given an exemplary and well-maintained restoration. Typically for the period the Italian Garden mixes Italianate pergolas and exedrae with French-derived parterres bedded out in a fleur-de-lys pattern.

Opposite:
The Pansy Garden, one of a series of intimate garden rooms near the house designed by John Handrahan. Named for and planted with Mrs. Thompson's favorite flowers, it included a fountain and birdbath.

country estate became an anthology of gardens, which might include a French flower parterre, an old-fashioned American garden, an Italianate pergola and terraces, a Japanese tea garden, an arboretum, a rock garden, and a fernery, plus herb, cutting and vegetable gardens, all set into a landscaped park. Often added to these were plant-lovers' displays of all the newest plants as they were introduced. Such anthology gardens also appeared in England and on the Continent; it was both an eclectic and a museum-making period in Western Civilization. But the pattern was more widespread and longer-lived here since the American country estate was most often a summer place, without traditions to uphold, or the practical constraints of a full-time agricultural enterprise to consider.

Even when operated as public gardens, most such estates have undergone drastic simplification. Sonnenberg, a fifty-acre estate in Canandaigua, New York, offers a rare chance to see an anthology garden in its full Victorian glory. In 1863 the New York City banker Frederick Ferris Thompson and his wife, Mary Clark Thompson, bought a farmhouse with twenty acres on the highest point in the town where Mrs. Thompson had grown up. Over the next thirty-six years they added farmland, orchards, and greenhouses, and replaced the farmhouse with a forty-room mansion. After Thompson's death in 1899, his wife focused her formidable energies on redesigning the whole estate, adding more property, traveling to Europe for inspiration, and hiring a Boston landscape architect, Ernest Bowditch, to help her. In 1907 she replaced Bowditch with his construction supervisor, John Handrahan, an engineer who worked with her until her death in 1923. In its prime, Sonnenberg offered every fashionable amenity—nine different gardens, a deer park, an aviary, a nine-hole golf course, a tennis court, a swimming pool, a bowling alley—

and extensive practical ones, including a large greenhouse complex, a six-acre utility garden and a cannery. Mrs. Thompson was generous in sharing her achievements, not just with her guests, but also with the public. On one of her summer open days, she might have 5,000 visitors.

As was usually the case with anthology gardens, most of the pleasure grounds were laid out in pastoral style with sweeping lawns and specimen trees. The Italian Garden, the Rose Garden, the Old Fashioned Garden, the Sub Rosa Garden, the intimate Blue and White, Pansy, and Moonlight Gardens, all of them rather architectural in character, were clustered around the house in the northeast corner of the estate. Somewhat away from this complex to the north was the Japanese Garden designed by K. Wadamori, and to the east, the natural-seeming Rock Garden created by Handrahan.

Unable to keep the estate up during the Depression, Mrs. Thompson's nephew, who had inherited the property, sold it to the U.S. Government. After some vicissitudes, in 1970 local volunteers were able to form a non-profit educational corporation, obtain a charter from New York State, and reclaim Sonnenberg. Hundreds of volunteers and a small professional staff have made a great success of its ongoing restoration and maintenance, no easy task since they are operating without an endowment.

An anthology landscape can seem fragmentary and disjointed in spite of the excellence of one or another individual part. It takes a truly gifted designer to weave disparate elements into a coherent work of art, and often proprietors, untrained but emboldened by the American do-it-yourself tradition, acted as their own designers or hired a different designer for each different section.

More elements were still to be added to the mix. Hunnewell's friend Henry Winthrop Sargent, whose estate

Built by Japanese craftsmen to replicate one in Kyoto, the Tea House perches on the rocks above a stream in the 1906 Japanese garden. Naturalistic in style like the Rock Garden, it was also located at some distance from the mansion, a characteristic arrangement in the period.

was also an anthology and even more horticulturally directed, justified the approach because

> ... in this country where we have no rural sports as in England, nothing in fact for the amusement of our friends and visitors, except what is beautiful or interesting on our grounds or in our gardens, we have always thought it highly desirable ... to set aside in different and distant portions of the place all our objects of interest; a flower garden in one spot, the vegetable garden in another, an arboretum or pinetum in a third and so make and multiply as it were, various interests in different parts ... which shall furnish to our guests excuses for a walk, and give to a small place the appearance of a large one ...[4]

Within a decade of Sargent's writing, "rural sports" would become one of the most popular of those "various interests," as we have seen at Sonnenberg. Plans in Scott's *Suburban Home Grounds* make room for croquet and archery lawns—not a difficult design problem, even on a fairly small houselot. In the 1880s tennis courts would demand their share of space, which was more of a challenge. The usual, and successful if carefully sited, solution was to treat them as outdoor rooms, walling them in with hedges or vine-covered fencing. Right on their heels came swimming pools. Despite their special requirements, these can be easily integrated into either architectural or naturalistic gardens given the will to do so. Too often, even today, they are simply plopped down with no attempt to suit shape or color to their surroundings. The golf course, which became a specialized branch of landscape architecture in itself, adapts more easily to a layout in the pastoral style. Although a dozen or so tycoons gave themselves the pleasure of a private golf course, designers didn't face this challenge very often. Not many estates were large enough to justify one. Golfers played at suburban country clubs, an institution that Henry James called "a clear American felicity; a *complete* product of the social soil and air which alone have made it possible."[5] By the 1920s most affluent suburbs could boast one or more of these. Still, sports, rural or otherwise, had entered the garden to stay. And along with them came the idea that a garden should be a setting for active recreation in which plants and their care play a minor and supporting role. With more and more hours of leisure time available to more and more people in the twentieth century, the provision of the right kind of space for the householder's favorite outdoor activities has become a consideration in the design of a garden, whether the garden occupies a few hundred square feet or several dozen acres.

The truly exotic gardening world of the Orient, particularly Japan, began to attract Americans in the last half of the nineteenth century. When Japan yielded to Commodore Perry's forceful persuasion in 1853 and opened its ports to the Western world, it was not immediately overrun by American or European tourists—fortunately, for they would not have been welcome. West and East had to adjust to each other's customs, and that took time. The first wave of visitors—

sailors, diplomats, and traders—stimulated curiosity about the island empire with their reports and the artifacts they brought back. Some also brought back plants, and these were immediately and enthusiastically embraced both by knowing amateurs and nurserymen. The Japanese flora was a rich one, and well adapted to temperate North America. Too well adapted in some cases. Among the eagerly received plants brought to the Parsons nursery in 1861 by George Rogers Hall, a medical doctor turned trader, was the beautiful, fragrant, vining honeysuckle, *Lonicera japonica*, which has run wild and become a real pest in parts of this country. But that was in the future, and the honeysuckle was the only one of Hall's popular introductions to misbehave.

Knowledge and appreciation of the distinctive Japanese approach to garden design took longer to build. The artists and intellectuals who formed the second wave of travelers to Japan were entranced by its gardens. But most Americans were introduced to those gardens in the exhibits sent by the Japanese government to American and European World's Fairs, like the simple tea house and garden at the 1876 Philadelphia Centennial Exposition. Even more influential were the larger and more completely developed gardens at the 1893 Columbian Exposition in Chicago, and the 1894 California Midwinter Exposition in San Francisco's Golden Gate Park.

That all of the country-house owners who tucked a Japanese garden into their grounds understood its symbolism or truly wished to create the peaceful retreat for quiet contemplation that such a garden represented for the Japanese is questionable. They undoubtedly appreciated its charm, but it seems likely that in many cases they were motivated by the desire to display their sophistication and to surprise and entertain their friends. Nor did everyone who wanted a Japanese garden truly study its principles of composition. Some settled for a simple arrangement of appealing artifacts—a stone lantern and basin, a bridge or torii gate—with a maple or a weeping cherry. Others, determined to get it right, brought in a Japanese landscape designer. Still others learned from magazines. The pioneer *Garden and Forest*, conducted, as he put it, by Charles Sprague Sargent, founder of the Arnold Arboretum in Boston, ceased publication in 1898. But it was followed almost immediately by somewhat less intellectual magazines devoted to the house and its surroundings such as *House & Garden, The Garden, Country Life in America, House Beautiful,* and *The Craftsman.* In the first fifteen years of the twentieth century, the Japanese garden seems to have been a favorite topic for all of them. *Country Life in America* proposed studying its principles to create a "condensed landscape" for a small yard; *House & Garden* suggested "Artistic Japanese Features for Garden and Country Estates." Most published photographs of American adaptations at least once a year. Exotic curiosity, source of techniques, stimulus to the imagination, the Japanese garden, once encountered, has never lost its fascination for us.

In the eyes of mid-nineteenth-century intellectuals and tastemakers, the industrialization that created the fortunes that created the estates did not exercise a particularly beneficent influence on art and design. Just as the New England Transcendentalists had rejected the materialism of industrial capitalism on moral and spiritual grounds beginning in the 1830s, so beginning in the 1840s the British critics and designers we group together as the Arts and Crafts Movement rejected it on social and aesthetic grounds. On both sides of the Atlantic moralists and social critics exalted home life as an antidote to what they considered the dehumanizing influence of commerce and industry. Too much of what that industry chose to produce or reproduce for the home seemed to all of them — and often does to us — designed to show off the dexterity of its machinery with more regard for showiness than for use or beauty. Products proudly displayed at World's Fairs like London's 1851 Crystal Palace or Philadelphia's 1876 Centennial Exhibition competed to be the biggest, the most colorful, the most elaborately ornamented. Or, at the other end of the scale, machine-made ornament was used to disguise poor construction. Unworthy goals, unsuitable furnishings for middle class dwellings, produced under unhealthy conditions judged Englishmen like John Ruskin, William Morris, and Charles Eastlake.

Focusing their attention on architecture and domestic furnishings, Arts-and-Crafts artisan-designers and theoreticians believed in the superior beauty of objects made by hand of good materials soundly put together, and in the importance of handwork to the intellectual and emotional health of the worker. They sought design inspiration in their country's Medieval and Elizabethan past, in its vernacular culture, and in the natural world around them. The movement was far from monolithic. Some of its partisans rejoiced in ornament, others rejected it; some experimented with flowing, vegetative forms, others preferred geometric simplicity, still others followed the form-follows-function principle well before it was proclaimed; but all shared one goal, the integration of all the arts. And all rejected the notion of copying past forms: These were to be just guides to the proper procedures for satisfying modern needs and tastes. The sources of inspiration are not too hard to spot, such protestations notwithstanding.

The ideas and artifacts of English Arts and Crafts lost little time in crossing the Atlantic, even though many design historians seem to date the beginning of the American Arts and Crafts Movement to the proselytizing of Gustav Stickley at the end of the century. Charles Eliot Norton, who founded the Fine Arts Department at Harvard in 1873, had made friends with Ruskin in Europe and promoted his ideas. Clarence Cook's *The House Beautiful*, an 1877 compilation of articles previously published in *Scribner's Weekly*, is full of praise for the designs of William Morris and the color palette of the closely associated pre-Raphaelite painters. Cook, much more influenced by Japanese design than the British, exhibits an important difference in the way Americans approached Arts and Crafts. While the enemy for both was gaudy, slipshod, meretricious industrial production, Americans did not reject the machine. Cook, like Stickley — the publisher of *The Craftsman*, premier promoter of hand-made furniture, and inventor of the Mission Style — admitted that only machine production could produce fur-

nishings in sufficient quantity at affordable prices. Indeed, machines were used for some processes in Stickley's furniture production. Craftsmen would have to depend on the upper middle class to buy their work but could demonstrate to the public the value of better design and better construction and ideally guide manufacturers in that direction. Also, there was a big do-it-yourself component in American Arts-and-Crafts thinking, not unexpected in a country with so recent a pioneer past. Stickley encouraged everyone, middle or working class, to learn the skills and share in the construction of their houses and furnishings, and the making of their gardens, all of which should "embody the Craftsman principles of utility, economy of effort and beauty."[6]

The English Arts and Crafts Movement is often credited with introducing the idea of treating the garden as a series of outdoor rooms, but, as we have seen, this was already present in the contemporary revival of the Italian garden. And after all, the compartmented Elizabethan garden they often took as a model — and romanticized — had itself been heavily influenced by Renaissance Italy. The two really pervasive effects on the design of gardens were renewed devotion to hardy herbaceous plants — William Robinson's wild garden was not closed to all but British natives; any exotic that could survive on its own was welcome — and a veneration of the vernacular. The latter was expressed in an attempt to suit design and materials to regional customs, the use of local stone and stoneworking techniques in constructing a garden framework, and the appreciation and adaptation of the contained but informal luxuriance of that mid-eighteenth-century artifact, the cottage garden. Two legacies of English Arts and Crafts to American garden design were the herbaceous border and Gertrude Jekyll, an artist turned garden-maker and writer. She herself never came to the United States, but her books and her ideas did, and, as we shall see, were immensely influential.

By the 1880s the ground in this country was well prepared to accept both these gifts. As we have noted, the exuberantly planted old-fashioned garden had never completely gone out of fashion. Very often a border of flowering shrubs or tall perennials lined its fences. It took no great stretch to imagine much wider borders separated by a strip of lawn or a wide path, and backed by a hedge or planted at the base of a retaining wall. In his additions to the 1873 edition of Downing's *Cottage Residences*, Henry Winthrop Sargent, who had hemmed a drive with ribbon bedding at his Hudson River estate, noted that "the tide has commenced to turn and is slowly rolling back to the good old herbaceous borders of the past." He quoted at length a rapturous description of its possibilities from Robinson's magazine, and offered a plant list for beginners. To Alice Morse Earle thirty years later, "that very trying expression of which we weary so of late — herbaceous border" seemed to have been invented by architects, as a way to distinguish mixed plantings from bedding-out schemes. A very anti-poetic term it was, in her eyes. It must have been the name, not the design, that bothered her, since the photographs that illustrate her 1901 book, *Old Time Gardens*, show, anachronistically, a number of what we would call herbaceous borders. Both name and design have stuck, and

Today's garden at the house in Quincy, Massachusetts that John and Abigail Adams bought in 1787 is a simplified version of the Colonial Revival style, which probably had less lawn and more flowers when it was first created by Mrs. Charles Francis Adams at the turn of the century.

Plantation Revival is a better word for early twentieth-century parallels to Colonial Revival gardens in the deep South. The house at Shadows-on-the-Teche was begun in 1830 at the heart of a 200-acre plantation, and the gardens were embellished over the years by four generations of a garden-loving family. As painted by Adrien Persac in 1861, the landscape on the bayou side of the house consists of a lawn with ornamental trees, among them two live oaks and a white crepe myrtle near the house. An unusual feature is the V-shaped flower garden.

Persac also painted the street entrance to the house from what is thought to be the estate's kitchen garden on the other side of the road. The rectangular beds do seem to be bordered with flowers and an agave can be identified, an arrangement typical of the period. Today the house is no longer white. It has been returned to the original 1830s unpainted brick.

indeed enjoyed an enthusiastic burst of popularity in the last twenty years: one more addition to the garden-designer's repertoire, one that has proved adaptable to both large estate and small suburban gardens. As for the contributions of Gertrude Jekyll to the planting of the flower garden, it is a rare gardener who is not receptive to some new ways to think about color in the garden, and she had plenty to offer.

By the last years of the nineteenth century, serious gardeners, designers, writers, and magazine editors in this country, England and the Continent had woven from their shared interest networks in which ideas passed rapidly back and forth across the Atlantic. They visited each other's gardens, they corresponded, they quoted each other's books. Colonial Revival and Arts-and-Crafts devotees often linked up. Sarah Orne Jewett, a popular novelist and preserver of old New England houses and gardens, put a William Morris carpet on the stairs and Arts-and-Crafts wallpapers on the walls of her eighteenth-century Maine house. Although members of the Beaux-Arts web might appear to have little in common with those in the Arts-and-Crafts web, even they crossed over from time to time. For more than thirty years after the publication of her first book, *Wood and Garden*, Gertrude Jekyll was a major figure. Beatrix Farrand, Edith Wharton's niece, whose design education was to a large degree shaped by her aunt's enthusiasm for Renaissance Italian gardens, was at the same time a great admirer of Jekyll. She visited Jekyll's garden

at Munstead Wood, and was responsible for saving her papers and finding a home for them in this country.

A painter and craftswoman, who turned to garden design after deteriorating vision forced her to give up her original vocations, Gertrude Jekyll was a master colorist. With the eyes of a painter, like her Impressionist and Post-Impressionist contemporaries, she studied the ways in which light affected color, colors affected each other, and after-images affected our perceptions of color. The combinations of color and texture, and the planting plans that Jekyll drew from her studies were so appealing that they have influenced the composition of flower gardens to this day. But unlike the painter, the garden designer must share with nature control over the materials in his or her palette. Jekyll's compositions often could not be duplicated in this country with the same varieties and cultivars that she used. Savvy American gardeners, like Louisa Yeomans King, for whose much reprinted *The Well-Considered Garden* Jekyll wrote the preface, understood. They used the plantings she described as inspiration not as recipes, and worked out their own schemes on the ground with flowers that would thrive for them.

Gertrude Jekyll, in the true Arts-and-Crafts manner, was a dedicated student of rural traditions. These antiquarian interests were a bond with Alice Morse Earle, who sometimes endorsed Jekyll's ideas about color and sometimes disagreed with them. Earle understood that the past to which Americans looked for inspiration was their own pre-Revolutionary one, and tried to document it with varying degrees of historical accuracy. She pointed out correctly that tiger lilies and bleeding heart were nineteenth-century introductions but unfortunately fell into the boxwood-in-Colonial-New-England trap.

An early contribution to, if not the origin of, rising public interest in the architecture, artifacts, and gardens of the thirteen colonies and the early republic was the national campaign that resulted in the purchase in 1858 of Washington's Mount Vernon, to be restored and managed as a national monument. With this agenda, the Mount Vernon Ladies Association also kicked off the historic preservation movement, which for many years was entwined with the Colonial Revival. The two have increasing diverged over the years. Historic preservation has not just expanded the past it wants to preserve. It has become more and more concerned with historical accuracy and has developed better and better techniques for finding out what the past might really have looked like. The Colonial Revival was looking for a past more beautiful than the present, a refuge from the all-too-frequent ugliness that industrialism stamped on the landscape. It consciously or unconsciously eliminated the compost piles, dung heaps, and all other unpicturesque if practical elements from the gardens it created or "restored." It also gave them a polish that, if travelers' accounts are to be believed, they rarely had: "High keeping" was not considered an American trait. Nevertheless, there were exceptions; there always are. Barbara Wells Sarudy's reading of the garden diary that an Annapolis craftsman, William Faris, kept between 1792 and 1804 reveals that he was meticulous about maintenance and furthermore, that his garden had box-edged beds, lots of flowers, with tulips an especial favorite, and even a statue,

With no heirs, William Weeks Hall, the last owner, always intended Shadows-on-the-Teche to open to the public eventually. This influenced the way he planned the reconstruction of his family's garden. "The principle of design was to keep open centers and vistas; and to confine planting to the borders," he wrote. Hall gave the property to the National Trust for Historic Preservation on his death in 1958, and the trust has been working on the landscape restoration since 1990. Here, aspidistra and boxwood with fern accents line the path around the house to the bayou side of the garden.

along with vegetables, cow shed, and bee skep. Her reconstruction of Faris's garden plan with its rather complex layout indicates that there might very well have been some eighteenth-century precedents for Arthur Shurcliff's Colonial Williamsburg "restorations" of the 1920s and 30s, which have been much criticized as too decorative.[7]

Given a big push by the 1876 Centennial celebrations and again by Colonial Williamsburg in the 1920s, the Colonial Revival soon developed regional variations: The historic Charleston Garden, the New England Dooryard, and, in the Deep South, the Plantation Garden, to name a few. Today, many consider the Colonial Revival a twentieth-century style related to historic Colonial gardens in much the same way that late eighteenth- and nineteenth-century Neo-Classical architecture related to that of historic Greece and Rome. Of all the nostalgic styles, it was the easiest to adapt for a small suburban garden.

The Arts-and-Crafts search for grounding in the American past did not always follow the Colonial Revival path. Arts-and-Crafts designers actually amplified this country's appreciation of its diverse past by adding the Southwest's Spanish heritage, ably abetted by the propaganda of transcontinental railroads seeking passengers for their trains and tourists for their hotels. Pueblo Revival still has its devotees in New Mexico and Arizona, and California provided the source for Stickley's much-imitated Mission Style. In fact, the Mission Revival was probably more responsible for the Spanish Colonial patios of turn-of-the-century Florida resorts than anything from that state's genuine Spanish past. Just like Colonial Revival gardens in the East, the patios re-created at the missions and ranch houses around the turn of the twentieth century were flower-filled romantic fantasies highly unlikely to have had many precedents in the frontier California of the late eighteenth and early nineteenth century. The more important and less superficially apparent contribution of California and its patios to the design of the suburban garden began quietly at that time with books like Keeler's *The Simple Home* and occasional articles in *The Craftsman*. The real impact of the patio came later, as we shall see.

Arts-and-Crafts thinking also helped to nurture an emerging appreciation for regional differences in topography, climate, and vegetation, and to encourage designers to seek their materials and their design vocabularies in regional characteristics. Often gardeners tend to crave exotic plants and turn up their noses at the beautiful wildlings growing all around them. And often it takes an immigrant, as we shall see many times, to open their eyes. One such was Theodore Payne, an Englishman and a trained horticulturist who came to California in 1893 at the age of twenty-one. Ten years later, after working as an estate gardener and nursery manager, he opened his own nursery and began to promote the native flora of California, which he had fallen in love with. He collected seeds, learned how to propagate them—no easy task—and in 1906 issued his first wildflower catalogue. At first he had more response from Europeans and Easterners, but after he planted demonstration gardens in Hollywood

and Pasadena, local interest picked up. According to Victoria Padilla, "Payne introduced into cultivation in California between 400 and 500 species of wildflowers and native plants and made them available for general use."[8] Ironically many of these had been introduced in Europe many years before.

Payne did more than just grow and sell wildflowers. He launched a campaign, in articles and lectures, to save the wildflowers and native landscapes, which he realized were fast disappearing. He also designed landscapes for many estate owners, among them Cima del Mundo, for Lora Knight. Payne filled the rolling meadows of the spectacular landscape around Knight's house with wildflowers, but mixed natives and exotics in the courtyard garden. He had learned, as have many lovers of wildflowers, that only certain kinds will do well in a small garden. Many resent disturbance, as David Streatfield has pointed out in his immensely valuable history of California gardens,[9] or succeed only where they have room to roam.

In 1915 Wilhelm Miller, professor of horticulture and editor of *Country Life in America*, dated what he called variously "The Prairie Style in Landscape Gardening" or the "Middle Western Movement in Landscape Gardening" to 1878 when Ossian Cole Simonds began work on Chicago's Graceland Cemetery. In addition to Simonds, Miller also named as leading proponents Walter Burley Griffin and Jens Jensen, who would become the best known and most influential of the Prairie Style group. Miller was quite clear that "There is nothing new about the principles used in the prairie style: only their applications are new." The style was "based on the practical needs of the Middle-Western peo-

ple," he argued, and its principal features were "preservation of typical western scenery," "restoration of local vegetation," and "repetition of the horizontal line of land or sky which is the strongest feature of prairie scenery."[10] What we think of as landscapes of the Prairie School are idealizations of natural Middle-Western scenery, its landforms, and patterns of vegetation, but Miller felt that it was quite possible to interpret that scenery in an architectonic manner. This does not seem to have happened very often, perhaps because most designers who embraced Beaux-Arts eclecticism, the Prairie School's major competitors for estate commissions, had little interest in plants, plant communities, or the new science of ecology. They tended to stick with a limited palette of plants that could be manipulated easily; their clients tended to want the most colorful flowers, or, if horticulturally inclined, the newest introductions. It would seem that anyone hoping to interpret a particular landscape, whether in architectonic or in painterly form, had better understand and appreciate its native vegetation.

PART ONE CHAPTER FIVE

Confidence Breeds Innovation

TRADITIONAL INFLUENCES, NEW ART AND SCIENCE ARE ASSIMILATED, MODIFIED, AND RECOMBINED

Preceding page:
Dan Kiley's landscape
design for the J. Irwin
Millers' ten-acre property in
Columbus, Indiana, brought
a breakthrough demonstra-
tion that the elements of the
classical geometric style
could be used to create
thoroughly modern spaces.
Kiley had been excited by
the allées, bosques, quin-
cunxes, and *tapis verts* he
had seen in Europe, and
with this 1950s commission
"the pieces were all in place:
the architect, the client, the
site and my vision." From
the ridge containing the
house designed by Eero
Saarinen, a serene expanse
of lawn slopes gently westward down to the wooded
banks of a creek, left in their
natural state.

The palm tree that has
strayed into one of its prim
boxwood-edged beds tells
you that this Colonial
Revival garden is not in
New England. In fact it is
one of several gardens in
different styles on the estate
of Mrs. J. E. Jardine in
Pasadena, California.

During the first half of the twentieth century, the most talented landscape architects of the eclectic persuasion—whether
trained at the Ecole des Beaux-Arts, an American university,
or self-educated—were trying to integrate a rich variety of historical influences and motifs into coherent designs rather than
continuing the disjunctive anthologies characteristic of the
preceding decades. Despite the strictures of modernist critics,
ideas from other times and other cultures were and are a perfectly legitimate resource for the garden maker seeking the
best possible solution to the demands of a specific site and
client.

Unfortunately, eclecticism could and often did slide gradually into a creativity-stifling insistence on inflexible axial layouts and the exact reproduction of historic details, particularly
in the academic world. In short, imitation not assimilation.

By the late nineteen-thirties, students, more interested in
the experimental modernism of European art and architecture, castigated the schools for this by-the-book historicism,
and for treating garden history as a grab bag of mix-or-match
garden features. If modern painters, sculptors, and architects
could look at the world with fresh eyes, why could not landscape designers? These critics had plenty of justification for
feeling that design solutions, pastoral or architectonic, intended for powerful aristocracies did not address the needs, realities, or ideals of a twentieth-century democracy. But a certain
share of the blame for the grab-bag approach must fall to the
many clients who felt more comfortable with derivative work.
Familiar design ideas were easy for them and for their friends
to understand, and they were fashionable, an important consideration for those who were not really that interested in plants
and gardens but wanted a setting appropriate to their money
and their aspirations. Familiarity can often breed comfort.

The magazines concerned with landscape and garden
design were not a great deal of help, principally because they
very rarely gave any critical analysis or appraisal to the projects they showed. They did report the new work being done
in France and Germany, and when the landscape architect
Fletcher Steele wrote about modern gardens in 1930 for both
Landscape Architecture and *Country Life in America*,
he offered some analysis of gardens by French designers like
Legrain and Guevrenkian. Earlier in the same year *House
& Garden* had proposed a model modern house, and in
explaining its garden, which reflected in simplified form
some of those French ideas, the editors proposed a set of
principles for the modern garden: simplicity of plan, clear
articulation of functions, unity of design, and minimum of
upkeep. This was in essence the program of the modernists.
All that needed to be added was the notion that the designer
should look to the site and the needs of the client and not
some past style for inspiration. However, if the magazine editors intended to imply this, they did not state it clearly. For
the most part thereafter, the national magazines simply presented the work of pioneering modernists as representative
of one style among many—and most of the "many" were
eclectic. In the East, Colonial Revival details—picket
fences, summerhouses, arches, not to mention the inevitable
boxwood-edged beds—were often combined with Italianate
pergolas, marble benches, and little temples. The Midwest
seemed more inclined to fieldstone walls, terraces, and steps
with broad Arts-and-Crafts borders in the English manner, or
to crisply delineated stone balusters, belvederes, and pools
clearly French or Italian in inspiration. On the West Coast,
too, Italian spatial organization and architectural details were
much copied, and often combined with equally popular
Hispano-mauresque patios, tiles, and fountains. But you
never knew; Spanish Colonial patios might turn up in New
Jersey, or Colonial Revival rose arbors in California. The
strongest unifying element of these schemes was exuberant
planting. Flowers and shrubs billowed over paths; roses and
vines cascaded over fences and arbors. That, by the way,
meant a maximum of upkeep. Text and illustration alike generally treated the planting plan of a garden in more detail
than the overall organization of the space. Such coverage is
often adequate for a small garden. To comprehend a large
estate from a collection of details is not so easy.

Contrary to the conventional wisdom, the 1929 stock
market crash did not completely put an end to the creation
of country estates; the outbreak of World War II did. True, not
as many large estates were built during the thirties, but most
established designers had enough clients and commissions
to keep going. Still, few could expand their offices and many
had to reduce staff. Professional landscape designers had
very, very rarely concerned themselves with small gardens,
except as part of the land planning for large suburban developments, and not very many of these were going forward.
Small, private gardens continued to be created, as they
always had been, by their owners, who gleaned ideas from
books and magazines and advice, often less than artistic,
from nurserymen. But during the Depression, the small garden began to attract the attention of landscape architects and

took on a new role as a laboratory for change.

At first, younger and newly graduated landscape architects found government programs such as the Civilian Conservation Corps, the Tennessee Valley Authority, the Works Progress Administration, and the National Park Service their best and often only source of work. The demand for their services in these programs was enormous. It was said that during the Depression ninety percent of the landscaping profession was employed by governments national and local.[1] From a design point of view, government administrators tended to be deeply conservative, and welcomed if they did not encourage the adaptation of Beaux-Arts monumentality to municipal rose gardens, and the Rustic Picturesque to the furnishing of roads and structures for state and national parks.

Dissent was stirring. Young landscape designers who did not enter government service found that there were clients who wanted professional expertise applied to their modest properties. Many were also receptive to a different approach, one that responded directly to their interests. Although garden books and magazines had been promoting the garden as an outdoor living room since the turn of the century, the plans they proposed offered little more than a level and shaded place for a table and chairs, and a suggestion that children could play on the lawn. In a 1932 book devoted to small backyard gardens called (what else?) *The Outdoor Living Room*, photographs typically show either miniaturized naturalistic or simplified Italianate layouts with lawn areas cut up by ornamental pools or flower beds, leaving not much place to play. More truly suited to outdoor living were the historicizing patios, partly or wholly encircled by rooms, shown in California magazines of the twenties and thirties.

Not surprisingly, it was a Californian who put forward the earliest program for a garden to live in that was at once realistic, imaginative, and contemporary. In 1933, a young Berkeley and Harvard trained landscape architect, Thomas Church, began a series of articles in *California Arts & Architecture* by proposing a New Deal for the Small Lot.[2] He wrote:

> ... many of our existing gardens are over-planted and under-kept. With the return of the arts to a new-found simplicity, we find the design of gardens being governed by such principles as these: Function, beauty, adaptability, convenience and economy of upkeep.

Neatness was clearly important to Church and the examples he showed were clean-lined and simple, although rather classical in plan. In later articles in the series his designs would seem more modern. They would also show more clearly their debt to California's patio tradition: the concept of a garden as an enclosed space for human activity, its plants, often in containers, suited to a hot, dry climate. Provision was made for practicalities like garbage cans and clotheslines, but most of the activity was intended to be pleasurable. Carrying the lines and materials of the house into the garden, Church felt, was important in unifying house and garden. "Horticultural excellence in the garden can never compen-

The outdoor living room as conceived in the first two decades of the twentieth century was usually an open lawn screened from neighbors by a perimeter planting of shrubs, either informally grouped as in this plan or clipped into hedges supplemented by trees for shade and accent.

sate for fundamentally bad layout," he declared.[3] He continued to design small gardens throughout his career. Even clients who owned large ranches or vineyards often did not feel they needed or wanted to care for gardens of more than an acre, and Church was known for his sensitivity to their needs and wishes. Some of his gardens appear quite traditional, although under scrutiny they display considerable ingenuity in accommodating complex sets of demands to the conditions of their sites.

Church felt comfortable using an idea from the past if it seemed the best solution to a particular problem, but younger landscape architects, or at least some of them, seemed to reject all traditions. Describing one of his own student projects for developing a city block in the September 1937 issue of the architectural journal *Pencil Points*, Garrett Eckbo posed a question:

> This is the United States of America 1937 A.D.—automobiles, airplanes, streamlined trains, mass production, the machine, new materials, new thoughts, new social concepts, a more abundant life. Why not express that, instead of English Tudor, or Italian Renaissance, or French modernistic, or Spanish-Moorish?[4]

In the October 1938 issue of *Pencil Points*, James Rose fired a salvo straight at the landscape design schools. His article "Freedom in the Garden" blasted their commitment to exclusive study of the past. He condemned the axial layouts and rigid geometry of the so-called formal style as inappropriate to contemporary life and dismissed the informal or natural style as a failure, because "its roots were in literature and sentiment rather than form and arrangement."

> When man arranges nature or nature arrives at an arrangement perceptible to man, the thing acquires form and meaning. . . . Informality does not exist for us except as an effect coming from the looseness and free-

Right:
Backyard garden plans by modernist landscape architects in the 1940s and 50s look very different and are intended for very different kinds of use. Dan Kiley's 1954 plan for Howard H. Wallace, Jr. in Hollin Hills near Washington, D.C. provides parking space for three guest cars in front with direction to the front door, reserving driveway, carport, and terrace entrance, for family. Separated from street traffic by shrubs, the "front lawn" becomes a safe play area.

Upper far right:
Irregular, angular terraces reflect the original contours of a San Francisco hillside and provide living and gardening space for plant-collecting clients. Slices of redwood logs compose the paving in Garrett Eckbo's 1939 design, and redwood makes up the rest of the garden's constructed elements.

Right:
James Rose's system of modular units could be assembled in different configurations with appropriate planting. Worked out in 1946 for *Ladies Home Journal*, these consisted of an angular trellis, a basket-weave fence, plus interchangeable three-foot-square precast concrete pavers and metal pool pans. Planting beds could be varied by lifting and replacing pavers.

Lower far right:
Thomas Church planned this garden to accommodate the activities of energetic children—he had carefully observed how children really like to play—with a design that could easily be adjusted to the changing wishes of teenagers and then adults.

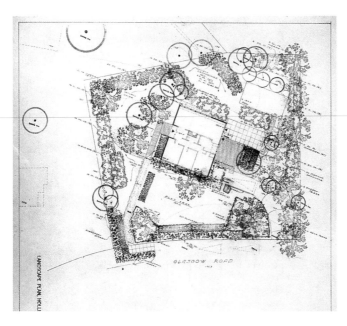

dom in the use of form; the "leave nature alone" attitude is complete childish romanticism, and, more important, an impossibility.[5]

In subsequent articles Rose went on to reproach the Beaux-Arts landscape architects for their lack of interest in and knowledge of plants, and their consequent limited plant palette and inability to use vegetation except in static masses. With some knowledge they might have been able to create form and articulate space with individual trees and shrubs. It should be noted, parenthetically, that modern architects of the so-called International School knew no more and were no better. Rose also suggested that science offered the landscape designer all kinds of unexplored possibilities. He was

joined by Eckbo and Dan Kiley—all three rebels among the students in the Harvard Graduate School of Design—in a series of articles for *Architectural Record* outlining the challenges they felt landscape architects *should* be exploring: "Landscape Design in the Urban Environment," "Landscape Design in the Rural Environment," and "Landscape Design in the Primeval Environment." These pieces for the most part concentrated on recreational landscape design, a particularly 1930's concern. Interestingly, they all but ignored suburban development, which, fueled by government policy, would become explosive after World War II. Perhaps, having absorbed rather uncritically the Europe-based social agendas of the Bauhaus architects they admired,

Rose, Eckbo, and Kiley failed to recognize the enormous importance of suburban life as an American aspiration. This is ironic because, at least in the beginning, the suburban garden would be the vehicle for the dissemination of their design ideas. And it is also sad, because in their indifference—at times hostility—to suburbia they missed the chance to influence for the better its development.

All three became distinguished landscape architects, each with a distinctive design personality. Kiley, based in Vermont, has built most of his career on public projects around the country, but he has always had a number of pri-

vate clients. Rose, who lived in New Jersey, devoted his design talents to private gardens commissioned by homeowners or corporations; his writing talents to magazine articles and books addressed to laymen as well as professionals; his reforming zeal to teaching. Eckbo, a Californian, returned to his home state and over time came to concentrate on large public projects, although he never stopped writing and teaching.

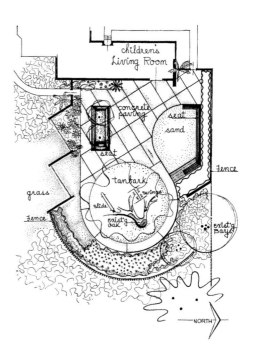

"Most of the forms we were using came from intensive looking at modern art," Eckbo told an interviewer in 1981.[6] Marc Treib's juxtaposition of a Suprematist composition by Kasimir Malevich with a drawing of Eckbo's ALCOA garden in *Garrett Eckbo: Modern Landscapes for Living* makes the point clearly. Eckbo also acknowledged the impact on his imagination of Pierre-Émile Legrain's Tachard garden in Paris, and Dorothée Imbert's research has shown that French designs of the 1920s by LeGrain, Guevrenkian, and Mallet-Stevens that reflect an Art-Deco sensibility were widely studied in this country.[7] But it was modern painters, under whatever label — Cubism, Constructivism, De Stijl — with their rejection of traditional perspective, who really empowered landscape designers to reexamine the organization of the garden. They discovered the energy that could be achieved by bending or breaking an axis and changing the balance of forms as a visitor moved through a space. Natural land and vegetation forms often turned out to be just the complements or contrasts needed by constructed geometric ones. Straight lines and curves could co-exist. In sum, there weren't any rules; designers simply had to train and trust their eyes.

It was the Californians who had the most pervasive influence on the design of American gardens, particularly small ones, in the decades after World War II. Servicemen who had been stationed in or passed through the West Coast were enchanted by its outdoor way of life, and wanted to take home with them the backyard swimming pools, barbecues, decks, and terraces they saw there, whether or not these were practical where they lived. In response, popular magazines promoted as examples the designs of Church, Eckbo, and younger men like Lawrence Halprin and Douglas Baylis. The work of these Californians was sensitive to the landforms and vegetation of their region. Unfortunately, most of the suburban developments that burgeoned in the forties and fifties were not. Land was bulldozed flat; trees, vegetation, in many cases even topsoil, removed. This provided a perfect canvas for the working out of an oversimplified version of what was perceived to be Californian thinking: plants take too much work. If you want a garden that is easy to care for, pave it over. In fact, Thomas Church's own garden exhibited a great love for plants, which he used with almost a nurseryman's knowledge. However, "pave it over" is what a reader might have gathered from his 1955 book, *Gardens Are for People*:

> Most of us, however, need a garden area which is always neat and ordered with a minimum of work. Sacrificed are the heady delights of dividing perennials in the fall, mulching the hibiscus for winter, and the thousand and one fascinating chores that need doing through the year.

Minimizing maintenance was a powerful goal in the 1950s, so any ambiguity in this statement was missed. Gardens were paved or decked. Or where grass remained more practical than paving, as in the Northeast, with its freeze and thaw cycles, backyard lawns hosted play equip-

Left:
A broad paved terrace for entertaining was essential to the live-in landscape. So was shade. In Thomas Church's California garden for Dr. Leisure a tree casts dappled shadows over the dining table and its built-in benches, a woven reed roof over part of the pergola gives more substantial shade next to the house designed by Douglas Honnold.

ment and above-ground swimming pools, their boundaries, with luck, traced with hedges not bare chain link fences. It was not until the 1970s that large numbers of Americans again began to find that growing and caring for plants could be a really pleasurable thing to do.

Still more important, what had not been understood by the simplifiers of the gardens-as-outdoor-rooms message was that the above-mentioned designers and others like them created true outdoor rooms with walls and passages, floors and ceilings. Usually the ceiling was the sky, but it was the sky made visible through tree branches. Partial ceilings of trellis,

canvas, or, experimentally, plastic, might offer shelter. In their gardens plants, trees, and manufactured materials were composed to create spaces one could move through and experience. Too often, alas, suburban backyards became assemblages of artifacts for specific activities with a few flowers patched in for decoration.

Yes, good gardens were created between the mid-forties and the seventies. Henry Francis du Pont and Marian Coffin were revising, refining and adding to the gardens at Winterthur. The Californians mentioned and Florence Yoch were all working, as were James Rose and Dan Kiley. A. E.

Above:
When du Pont needed architecturally structured spaces he called on his long-time friend, landscape architect Marian Coffin. She designed the Italianate staircase that descends from a wing added in 1928 to what was then the swimming pool, now a reflecting pool. Recently the boxwood has been restrained, restoring the steps to their original width.

Far left:
Starting in 1902 Henry Francis du Pont laid paths and planted banks of hybrid azaleas in open woodlands at Winterthur. A consummate plantsman and colorist, du Pont went on creating new garden experiences, and refining the succession of bloom until his death in 1969.

Left:
Like William Robinson and Gertrude Jekyll, both of whom he had visited, du Pont's idea of a wild garden made no distinction between native and imported species if they would naturalize. He swept grand drifts of native may apples and Virginia bluebells and Spanish bluebells through the Azalea Woods.

Bye, who manipulated natural forms in surprising new ways, had embarked on major works by the mid-sixties. Fletcher Steele was still active. In fact, two of the great icons of modern garden design were created during the period: Thomas Church's El Novillero for the Dewey Donnells in 1948, and Dan Kiley's garden for the J. Irwin Millers in 1955. They represent the two basic approaches to landscape design as filtered through sensibilities that had assimilated the lessons of modern art. The Dewey Donnell garden is composed of natural forms, highly stylized but sympathetic to the landscape of its Sonoma Valley location. In contrast, although some

Precisely ordered outdoor rooms and groves rotate around the podium on which the house rests, among them the hedge-enclosed swimming pool, two orchards, and a grove of redbuds. An allée of moraine honey locusts, protecting the house from sun and wind, runs the length of the podium on the west and is anchored by a Henry Moore sculpture at the northern end, a fountain at the southern. Mature horse chestnuts shade the entry drive, and staggered hedges consisting of twenty-foot segments of clipped arborvitae behind lines of red maple trees screen the house from the streets without seeming a solid barrier.

native landscape remains at its western end, the Miller garden is made up for the most part of geometric forms, its architectonic allées and clipped hedges in a dynamic arrangement with no central axis.

Even before these two landscapes came into existence, John and Jane Platt were well into the making of their marvelous, continually evolving Oregon garden, a reminder that not all good gardens are made by professionals. The race of plant-lovers, who tend to create gardens without a designer, had not been wiped out by any means, although for a while it seemed not to be adding new generations.

Many explanations have been offered for the still-rising swell of interest in plants, gardens, and garden design that began in the nineteen-seventies, and probably all of them played a part. Interest seemed to start in the late sixties with a rage for houseplants—perhaps, at last, Americans were starved for green, growing things. In addition, prosperity and a strong dollar had made foreign travel available to most people of the middle class and they rushed to enjoy it. As always, with travel came exposure to new experiences and new tastes. But if these new travelers wanted to reproduce the wonderful salad they had eaten at a charming two-star auberge, they had to grow their own tarragon and chervil, and their own lettuces. All the grocery store had to sell was iceberg. As interest in fine food and cooking grew, more people saw value in tending a garden. Americans began to plant ever more elaborate herb gardens and vegetable plots. As a plus, those who worried about what went on or into the food they were eating had control over that when they grew their own vegetables and fruits. Moreover, practical gardens could be good to look at. With their amazing variety of foliage tints and textures, herbs, in particular, turned out to have great ornamental as well as savory potential.

It wasn't long before flowers charmed their way back into the gardening mainstream. Even if they did not seek them,

travelers were also exposed to enticing ornamental gardens, and they were inspired by them. We still feel the influence, not always benign, of the English passion for horticultural superiority and the kind of garden design it tends to produce. Still, the rediscovery of Gertrude Jekyll's books, to take just one example, has been a positive force in creating a demand for a wider range of plants in a wider range of colors than were available commercially in America during the forties and fifties.

Probably the most powerful legacy of the late sixties and early seventies was a new perception of the relationships among humanity, nature, art, and science. Its spokesmen emerged from a variety of disciplines, but they produced a constellation of interrelated and mutually reinforcing ideas. As is the case with most new insights, when first expressed they were attacked and ridiculed, but in the long run they would profoundly affect the design, first of large-scale landscape projects, then by the end of the century of domestic gardens.

Concern for the health of the natural environment on the part of scientists began to penetrate public consciousness. Aldo Leopold's *Sand Country Almanac* had been published in 1949; but the real wake-up call was Rachel Carson's 1967 *Silent Spring*, which documented the frightening cost of all those chemicals we had believed made our lives easier. In the same year, Michael Heizer sank an open cube into the ground in the Sierra Nevada, but the earth sculpture that really caused a furor was his 1970 *Double Negative*, a 1500 by 50 by 30 foot slash cut across a Nevada mesa. His work was soon accompanied by that of friends and fellow sculptors, Walter De Maria—*Mile Long Drawing*, two chalk lines in the Mojave Desert (1968)—and Robert Smithson, whose 1970 *Spiral Jetty* curled into the Great Salt Lake. They worked on a gigantic scale and none of their creations could be separated from its environment. Nor could their sculptures be experienced from any one viewpoint. They had

Instantly recognized as a landmark, the swimming pool complex created by Thomas Church and his associates Lawrence Halprin and George Rockrise for Dewey and Jean Donnell was published even before it was completely finished. The Donnells had selected an oak-mantled ridge on their ranch north of San Francisco with a view across salt marshes to the ocean. Church extended a wooden deck over the south slope, bringing a small grove of live oaks into the design, and placed a sculpture by Adaline Kent in the iconic free-form pool.

to be entered, walked through, and pulled together in the imagination. They could not be displayed in a living room or sold in a gallery, freeing them from what these artists believed was commercial pressure that turned art into merchandise, and a focus on formalism that alienated it from the real world. What really happened was that their work was mostly experienced by the public in drawings and photographs—in galleries. Thus, it is no accident that Robert Smithson's highly photogenic *Spiral Jetty* became the best known example of Land Art, as the movement came to be called. Although Land Art did not address the practical and social requirements that landscape architecture has to fulfill, its potential for influencing that discipline is obvious.

Ecological considerations, which had been ignored in the years of Beaux-Arts ascendancy, resurfaced among landscape architects at the same time. In that seminal year, 1967, Lawrence Halprin produced comprehensive studies of the ecology of the site to guide his and architect Charles W. Moore's design of the Sea Ranch, a second-house development north of San Francisco. His groundbreaking analyses documented the effect over time of both human interventions and natural processes—geologic, oceanic, climatic, zoologic, and vegetative—and acknowledged that neither interventions nor processes would ever end. Two years later came Ian McHarg's highly influential *Design with Nature,* a forceful proclamation of the idea that landscape design should be rooted in scientific knowledge, one that would have a far-reaching effect on the teaching of landscape architecture.

Gradually newspapers and popular magazines made at least some of the public aware of the long-term consequences of habitual horticultural practices. Concern about the effect of all the fertilizers, pesticides, and herbicides that they had been told were needed to produce an acceptable lawn, for example, led many gardeners to look for substitutes. Wildflower meadows became a popular choice. In fact,

lawns do not require massive chemical fixes in all parts of this country, wildflower meadows are far from being maintenance-free, and they don't work as a substitute for turf in all situations. However, their new popularity served as a harbinger of the importance that sustainability and ecological responsibility are coming to have in the design of gardens and landscapes. Garden-makers still have much to learn about how their decisions affect the health both of the garden and of its surroundings, but more and more are accepting this as a challenge that can be met by many different kinds of designs. They are finding that attention to ecology has brought into their field of vision many splendid but long overlooked native plants, and that it has stimulated new approaches to the planting and shaping of space.

If art is limitation, as G. K. Chesterton claimed, sensitivity to ecological process may well be the limitation that garden-making needs today. Nostalgia is losing some of its power. Function is not enough for us anymore. We also want meaning, stimulation, refreshment, beauty: the gifts of art.

The beginning of the twenty-first century is an exciting time for American garden design. We have drawn on the whole world, as well as on our own experience over the centuries to assemble a repertory of ideas and techniques. We have a vast range of materials, natural and manufactured, to compose with. We have assimilated the lessons of modern art, and, it seems, freed our thinking from such irrelevant either/ors as geometrical forms vs. natural forms, and architectural organization vs. painterly organization. Landscape architects, at least for the time being, have plenty of clients with the money to carry projects to speedy fruition. That gives them a lot of freedom, which is producing some fascinating gardens and innovative garden-makers. At the same time, professionals and amateurs both, even the most forward-looking, are still creating variations on the oldest and most basic garden plan, the plan that came here with the first European settlers.

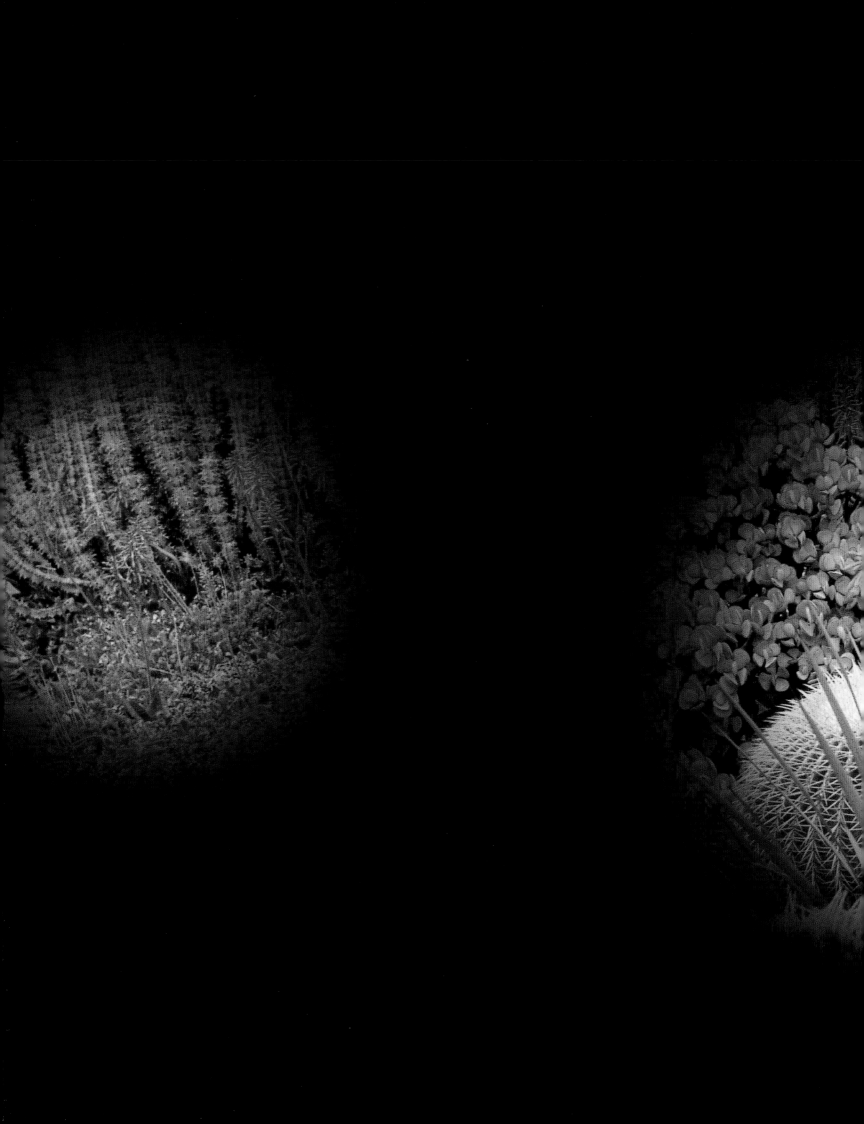

The Forms
American
Gardens
Have
Taken and Some

Digressions

on the Customs or

Conditions That

Influenced Them

The Enclosed Garden

Preceding page:
Archaeological evidence
and informed guesswork
both contributed to the
reconstructed 1680 garden
at Bacon's Castle in
Virginia. Beds in front of the
brick wall, sun-trap and
wind-shelter, were used at
the time to start plants.
Benches set in hedge stand
in for exedrae thought to
have terminated crosswalks.

Right:
The painting "How the
Indians Garden and Plant"
in the sixteenth-century
*Histoire Naturelle des
Indes* shows a raised
seedbed within a woven
enclosure. An ethnobotanist
has identified typical tropical Amerindian plants
including papaya, manioc,
gourds, maize, and beans.

We always think of the enclosed garden and the raised bed as European horticultural patterns laid on American soil but they may have been indigenous to this continent as well, although not as far as we know to New England. Depradation of unfenced Indian cornfields by Puritan cows and pigs was a major instigator of hostility. However, a drawing in the remarkable *Histoire Naturelle des Indes*, usually known as the "Drake Manuscript," c. 1590, in the Morgan Library titled "La manière et façon de jardinier et planter des yndiens . . ." shows, behind a wattle fence, an Indian holding a planting stick and sowing seed in a raised rectangular bed which appears to be neatly framed in dressed timber. The Indian's manner and style of gardening was probably not much influenced by contact with the Spanish who were there to mine gold and silver not raise crops. And this means that such a garden plan, which appears in Egyptian tomb paintings, Pompeiian frescoes, Medieval manuscripts, Renaissance altarpieces, and Persian and Indian miniatures, was archetypical beyond the cultures of the Middle East and Europe. It would not surprise the thoughtful gardener: It is a supremely practical plan.

There are three elements to the layout, which might be called the basic European garden: monks, princes, and peas-

ants all hewed to such a layout or elaborated on it from the Middle Ages on through the sixteenth and seventeenth centuries when colonists brought it to the New World. Each of these elements can have a separate life in garden design but judging from European illustrations, they were almost always joined.

Enclosure was the essential. Invariably the plot of land set aside for a garden, whether for pleasure or produce was defined by brick or stone walls, paled or woven fences, hedges or trellises. In fact, the very word garden, like its siblings yard and garth, comes from an Indo-European root that implies enclosure. The enclosures shown in illustrations are most often rectangular, although from time to time you see a circular plot fenced with woven wattle. The latter shape was not recommended by garden writers when they came on the scene at the end of the Middle Ages. Believing that the garden should adjoin the house if at all possible, they felt that it was too difficult to reconcile a circular garden with a four-square house. However the enclosure was shaped, invariably the ground within was divided geometrically into paths and planting beds. Most often the beds were rectangular, but more ambitious gardeners sometimes incorporated circles or triangles in their designs.

The planting surface of the beds was in the great majority of cases raised above the level of the paths. While the raised bed did not have quite the universality of enclosure and geometric subdivision, it was often advocated, particularly to improve drainage. In 1594 Didymus Mountain gave the fifth-century Neapolitan, Pallidius Rutilius, as his authority for suggesting

> In a moiste and waterie Garden-plotte...that the beddes in the same ground be reared two foote high, for the better prospering of the seedes . . . But in a drie grounde, the edges of the beddes raysed a foote high, shall well suffice.[1]

His illustrations show beds with quite elaborate wooden edgings and finial-topped posts at the corners. Raised beds are so much more often illustrated than discussed in garden texts that one must conclude that they were the norm. Indeed, John Parkinson assumes that the beds will be raised through most of his analysis of materials for the laying out and bordering of knots—what we would call parterre patterns—in the pleasure garden. Only at the end does he allude to and make suggestions for "levelled" knots.[2]

Knots were embellishments for the pleasure garden, but the basic plan was also applied to the growing of herbs and vegetables. With this one remembered model the first settlers could satisfy all their design requirements, no matter how large or small the plot. And so they did, according to the maps that bother to record garden plots. The earliest garden laid out to this design in North America for which we have actual physical evidence is a very large and rather sophisticated one. The recently excavated 1680 garden at Bacon's Castle in Virginia—three hundred sixty feet long and one hundred ninety-five feet wide—was divided by white sand paths into six raised rectangular beds and ringed by a border of narrow beds outside the outer path. It appears to have been furnished with brick pavilions or exedrae or both, garden amenities that Sir Francis Bacon advocates in his much quoted essay.[3] There was a brick wall across the north end—now restored as a forcing wall—but so far fence lines have been found on the other three sides only for later centuries. On the basis that hedges often provided the enclosure in English gardens of the time, landscape architect Rudy Favretti has planted hedges of mock orange along two sides of the current reconstruction. The disposition of the furrows in the large central beds suggests that they were used for the production of vegetables, but only two of the six are so planted. The other four have been grassed over for reasons of maintenance. The border beds display the mixture of herbs, flowers, fruit, and vegetables so often mentioned in contemporary written descriptions.[4] In fact gardens in this style, both grand and humble, were often planted with such a mixture well into the nineteenth century. The garden at Nomini Hall in Virginia as recorded by Philip Vickers Fithian in 1774 is typical:

> After school, I had the honour of taking a walk with Mrs. Carter through the Garden—It is beautiful, & I think uncommon to see at this Season peas all up two & three

Inches—We gathered two or three Cowslips in full-Bloom; & as many violets—The English Honey-Suckle is all out in green & tender Leaves—Mr. Gregory is grafting some figs—Mrs. Carter shewed me her Apricot-Grafts; Asparagus Beds & c."[5]

Given the American bent to practicality, it is not difficult to understand why the enclosed garden of raised beds continued to be made in this country long after it was considered totally outdated in Europe. The advantages of enclosure are abundant. Of supreme importance to the first settlers—and to the pioneers as they went west—fences or walls or hedges protect the garden's contents against two-footed and four-footed predators. In addition, they can provide shelter from the wind, trap the sun's heat, and create micro-climates that permit the cultivation of plants otherwise unsuited to the location. They provide privacy for the designer's self expression and the owner's enjoyment. Whether built primarily for horticultural or social reasons, they can serve as an architectural extension of the house into the landscape, a comfortable way to manage the transition between house and natural environment. The desire to integrate gardens into their surroundings without or with minimum visible enclosure is a rather recent development and one less than universally shared.

The straightforward division of the garden plot into rectangles with paths between them is also very easy for the amateur to manage. It only requires a rule, a line, some stakes, a spade and the understanding that the beds should be narrow enough to weed without stepping into them. The raised beds can be arranged in many ways. A good sense of proportion improves the aesthetic effect, but is not strictly needed to produce acceptable results.

Raised beds fall out of fashion from time to time and then someone rediscovers their advantages and they become popular again. They did not appeal to nineteenth-century lovers of the "natural garden," but by the beginning of the twentieth century garden writers were starting to suggest them again for flat lands in need of improved drainage. Landscape architect Thomas Church, whose work in the 1940s, 50s, and 60s influenced the style of so many American gardens, employed them in geometrically and in informally organized designs, both for practical reasons:

> The rose garden and vegetable beds are raised, not only for neatness and convenience, but because they are built on a rock base. It proved to be a much more economical way to get sufficient topsoil than to excavate and drain the garden planting space."[6]

And for aesthetic ones:

> A garden can be easier to look at, as well as to maintain, if certain planting areas are raised above the main grade. If you have a high retaining wall or fence and want to reduce its visual impact, a raised bed at the base will do miracles. Your eye will subtract the lower level from the over-all vertical height and negate the problem.[7]

Knots, interlacings of herbs and evergreens with brick dust or colored gravel between them, were promoted by sixteenth and seventeenth century garden writers like John Marriott from whose 1618 book these came. Too time-consuming for colonists, knots had to wait for present-day herb enthusiasts.

A Curious fine Knot.

A flourishing Knot.

Above:
With only a narrow rocky ridge to hold house and garden Thomas Church gave over much of the space to raised beds, which limited the amount of topsoil that had to be brought in and formed neat and pleasing patterns.

Right:
Despite a few historical inaccuracies, the Whipple House garden shows how attractive early vernacular gardens could be, even if they lacked today's brightly colored annuals. As it was originally a town house the garden would have been by the kitchen door rather than in front as at present.

Church also recognized that raising planting beds can eliminate a lot of bending and stooping and aching backs for gardeners.

Given the basic form a surprising number of different effects can be achieved, depending on the plants chosen and the way in which they are arranged and tended. The following gardens, one modern, the others reconstructed in this century according to older models, suggest the ways it can serve the imagination.

WHIPPLE GARDEN

The Whipple House in Ipswich, Massachusetts was built about 1640 by the Puritan younger son of a wool merchant, added to later in that century by his increasingly prosperous descendants, and from then on maintained without major alteration by the family and subsequent owners until its purchase by the Ipswich Historical Society in 1898. In 1927 it was moved to its present site, but oriented as it had been originally. In the 1940s, Arthur A. Shurcliff, a landscape historian and the landscape architect for the garden restoration at the Governor's Palace in Colonial Williamsburg, whose summer home was in Ipswich, designed a dooryard garden for the Whipple House. Appropriately, it is divided into six raised beds about ten feet square with chamfered corners where the clamshell paths between them cross. A low split-paling fence surrounds the plot and there is a narrow raised border across one end. The planting of the beds was entrusted to a committee of the Ipswich Garden Club chaired by Mrs. A. W. Smith, better known by her pen name, Ann Leighton. She decided that she would "make the work worthwhile by using only plant material for which I could find contemporary documentary evidence, starting as near the site as possible, and that I would write a book about it as I went along." That book, the delightful and ground-breaking *Early American Gardens "For Meate or Medecine,"* led to two others, one on eighteenth and one on nineteenth-century gardens, all of which are essential reading for anyone interested in the history of American gardening.

She wasn't able to make the garden quite as authentic as she had hoped: "Harison's Yellow" roses had been planted in some of the beds before she took over and she kept them "for sentiment" although that rose was introduced some two hundred years after the Whipple House was built. And neither she nor anyone else to my knowledge has been able to document the first appearance of the lilac in the New England dooryard. While we're on the subject of authenticity, the present fence would not stop a determined pig, let alone a deer or a rabbit, and all three were major menaces of the time. But these are very minor lapses, and, in particular, the true-to-period tall fence with palings set close together would not be nearly as attractive.

Ann Leighton was able to document the seventeenth-century neighborhood presence of all the other plants she put in the garden, about eighty-four different kinds, and she made a strong point of using only those valued for their culinary, medicinal, cosmetic, or household uses. In the latter category, for example, the seed head of the teasel is used in weaving, and the leaves of *Saponaria officinalis* or bouncing bet are still recommended for the washing of fine fabrics.

The garden at the Whipple House is essentially an herb garden, a tapestry of foliage in greens and grays flecked with flower color off and on through the growing season. Each of the beds is centered with a rose bush—other tall plants like hollyhocks and sunflowers are kept in the border—with a variety of herbs radiating out in concentric circles to the mixed edgings of ground-hugging species. On paper the design seems quite rigid, but on the ground it softens and almost disappears: plants are not clipped and there are so many different kinds with so many leaf textures and habits of growth.

The garden could have been made more colorful without sacrificing authenticity. Not all the flowers that could have been included were; one must remember that a display of flower color throughout the growing season only became possible in the nineteenth century after the massive introductions of plants, particularly annuals, from Africa, South America, and the Orient. In gardens of earlier centuries, fragrance was as cherished a garden pleasure as color. It is a pleasure that we have not explored as much as we might in this country, or at least in this century, and one that an herb garden is well equipped to provide. In addition, herbs are mostly hardy creatures that do not need rich soil in order to thrive. The roses in the Whipple house garden would have to be fed, the rosemary and perhaps the lavender brought in for the winter; but on balance, history provided Ann Leighton with a plant list and a garden plan that do not require a lot of skilled gardeners. But put in the same beds a selection of the same plants, set them out according to one of the diagrams in Parkinson or Marriott, keep them meticulously clipped and pinched, and you have a knot garden. Informality or formality is in the style of maintenance.

AN ISLAND GARDEN

Celia Thaxter's garden on Appledore, one of the Isles of Shoals off Portsmouth, New Hampshire is also a reconstruction: it had been destroyed when her cottage burned in 1914. In 1976 John M. Kingsbury, the first director of the Shoals Marine Laboratory, which had been established on the island under the auspices of Cornell University and the University of New Hampshire, undertook the restoration of Celia's garden. In this case the restorers knew just what it looked like and what grew in it. It had been painted many times by the American Impressionist Childe Hassam, and it had been photographed. Most important, in *An Island Garden* written in 1893, the year before she died, its creator left a plan, a detailed inventory of plants, and a description of her planting methods. Research was still necessary, but of a different kind: Most of the flower varieties she grew—fifty are listed in the book—are no longer common and many may have disappeared.

Dr. Kingsbury notes that the rebuilders had wondered why the garden was surrounded with such a heavy board fence. Once they started planting they knew: it kept the strong and constant island winds from flattening the flowers. The garden is fifty feet long by fifteen feet wide, sloping to the south, and in Celia's day sheltered from the north winds by the vine-hung piazza—what we would call a veranda—that overlooked it and by the cottage itself. Virginia Chisholm, who with members of the Rye Driftwood Garden Club still plants and maintains the garden, would very much like to have the cottage restored. The foundations are clearly visible; the structure well documented; and the garden needs the shelter. Then, perhaps Mrs. Chisholm and her colleagues could get the vines over the entrance arch to flourish again.

The garden is divided into nine free-standing raised beds, with a raised border all around inside the fence. The beds are simple rectangles boxed in wood. When Celia was cultivating the garden, judging from the illustrations in *An Island Garden*, beds and borders literally overflowed with flowers, perennials as well as the annuals that so extended the possibilities for garden color in the nineteenth century. Celia grew far more different kinds than she names in her book. Mrs. Chisholm continues to find letters that lengthen the list; but she has also found that many modern versions of these varieties don't grow as tall. They have been bred for compactness. Still, if the restored garden is somewhat less luxuriant, it displays its layout more clearly than does the original in Hassam's paintings.

Celia was an unashamed flower-lover "born to happiness in this vale of tears, to a certain amount of the purest joy that earth can give her children" in spite of a life that was anything but easy. Her enthusiasm might cloy were it not for the venomous determination with which she pursues the slug and the cutworm, and the wealth of useful information that she has learned from experience, and shares. She expresses the wish that seedsmen would print such information on their seed packets:

> For instance, why not say of Mignonette, It flourishes best in a poor and sandy soil; so treated it is much more

When Celia Thaxter's cottage on Appledore burned down in 1914 along with her family's hotel, it deprived her garden of both a background and part of its shelter from fierce north winds, so vines planted to grow up the arch are winter-killed most years.

Garden plants have been bred for compactness since 1893 when Celia Thaxter wrote *An Island Garden* adding to the challenge faced by today's gardeners as they try to recreate the impressionistic thickets of flower color that Childe Hassam's paintings made famous.

Hollyhocks have escaped modernization so they still stand tall among the cosmos, California poppies, bachelor's buttons, zinnias, and nasturtiums in the raised beds, which Thaxter, a large woman, is said to have weeded while lying down between them.

Another change since Thaxter's day: the pests. Instead of the slugs and sparrows she battled, gardeners now have to deal with muskrats, gulls, and poison ivy, newcomers to the Isles of Shoals.

fragrant than in rich earth, which causes it to run to leaves and makes its flowers fewer and less sweet. Or of Poppies, Plant them in a rich sandy loam, all except the Californias (*Eschscholtzia*), which do best in a poor soil. Or of Pansies, Give them the richest earth you can find, no end of water, and partial shade. Or, Don't worry over drought for your Nasturtiums; they will live and thrive with less water than almost anything else that grows. . . . Or, Give your Zinnias a heavy soil; they like clay. Or, Keep Sweet Peas as wet as you can and make the ground for them as rich as possible. Or, Keep barn manure away from your Lilies for your life! they will not brook contact with it. . . . But transport to your garden a portion of the very barnyard itself in which to set Roses, Sunflowers and Hollyhocks, Honeysuckles and Dahlias.[8]

Along with some of the flowers that grew in Celia's consciously "old-fashioned" garden, this passage suggests still another great practical advantage to the garden of raised beds: they make it much easier in a limited space to give a wide variety of plants the kinds of growing conditions they like. And it was Celia Thaxter's attention to and skill in giving her flowers what they liked that turned her tiny garden into a jungle of bloom so generous that she could cut continually for the house without affecting the view from the veranda. This was a very labor-intensive garden, albeit a labor of love, and as such something a good many Americans love to look

at but don't feel they have the time to create and maintain.

We probably have at least some more effective weapons against blights and bugs than she had, but otherwise her book would still be a very good guide for making a small flower garden. In order to plan precise color schemes or grow annuals of unusual color or particularly fine fragrance you still have to buy the seeds and raise them yourself as she did, unless you are lucky enough to find a local grower who will do it for you. The flats sold in garden centers don't offer enough choice for subtle or unusual effects. But one would not need to attempt as many different kinds of flowers as Celia did. What really gave the garden its visual richness in her day was the massing of each kind of flower, the explosions of poppies, the armloads of coreopsis and cornflowers, the groves of hollyhocks.

A MODERN WALLED GARDEN

Babs Simpson's Long Island walled garden is anything but old-fashioned even if the beds are raised and we have seen some of the same herbs and flowers at the Whipple House or Celia Thaxter's. Both plants and plan are developed in a very modern manner, in harmony with the house designed by Paul Lester Weiner and built in 1959. The garden's design, an important reminder that raised beds don't have to be arranged chequerboard fashion, was created by Rachel Lambert Mellon and executed by Judith Heller. "Because the house was modern, Bunny's thought was Mondrian for the garden; but it was Judy" Mrs. Simpson continues, "who suggested varying the ground level and the heights of the beds."[9]

The garden, twenty-two by forty-four feet, is sunken below the level of meadow and terrace and surrounded by a white-painted concrete wall twenty-two inches high on the outside, high enough to keep out the wind and the rabbits. The gate and the redwood timbers that frame the beds, like the house trim, are stained with a black protective stain. Chips of bluestone or white marble cover the walking and sitting spaces, completing a composition in black, white, and blue-gray that makes a sympathetic background for almost any choice of plants.

Although there are some constants—the center bed always holds herbs for scent and flavor—the combinations of plants change almost yearly. Mrs. Simpson finds that the plantings have become more architectural over the years.

I added two espaliered pear trees to the long bed, and two additional ones flanking the one against the wall of the house. Originally the highest beds, at either end,

each held a hardy orange tree (*Poncirus trifoliata*). They weren't hardy enough. I had to replace them with dwarf apple trees.

Except for the espaliers the plants are allowed to grow naturally and not sheared, but because she feels that it is important to see the structure of the garden she has "to be so careful about scale." Plants that grow too tall or too big and bushy are banished and other kinds brought in. The garden as photographed is composed in silver, mauve, and shades of blue and white, with a "dash of the scarlet geum 'Mrs. Bradshaw' for pep." But she is already planning to change the scheme.

The walled garden is only one element in the larger landscape of Mrs. Simpson's house. About six acres of wildflower meadow surround the precisely delineated house-terrace-garden complex.

When I first built the house I decided I didn't want a lawn—it seemed to me that my parents spent all sum-

In high season thriving plants mask the Mondrian-esque composition of raised beds on different levels in Babs Simpson's walled garden. Hardscape elements—concrete walls, board-boxed beds, and gravel paths—are white, black, gray, and no competition for any planting scheme.

She plants the central bed with salad greens and culinary herbs, and fills the beds around the birdbath with lavender. Otherwise, plantings change almost yearly. Here, the silvery foliage of artemisia and santolina are seasoned with dashes of scarlet geum.

mer fretting about their lawn. And I had never forgotten a charming little cottage on Nantucket set in a field of wildflowers.

Now indigenous wildflowers—black-eyed susan, oenothera, coreopsis, butterfly weed—and garden escapees naturalized since the seventeenth century—daisies, Queen Anne's lace, bouncing bet—dapple native grasses all summer. She had wanted to have poppies as European meadows do, but they refused to reproduce.

Unless you can afford to plow up a meadow and reseed every few years, you cannot grow wildflowers from other parts of the country or the world; the natives will crowd them right out.

Her meadow is mowed once a year in the autumn after the flowers have gone to seed to keep down brambles and seedling trees. Otherwise the bordering woods would soon repossess the land.

Actually the meadow is not totally encircled by trees: along one side it is separated from a neighboring field by a rose and hawthorn hedge. Out in the field in front of the hedge another garden has developed, the Rose and Lily garden.

Remember the Sargent painting *Carnation, Lily, Lily Rose*. It's that idea. First white Madonna then rubrum 'Uchida Pink' lilies growing up through the roses. It wasn't intended as a garden but as cutting beds—it also has monbretia, nasturtiums, peonies and raspberries plus four bird baths—but it has turned out

to be delightful. And from the house the wire fence is covered by the meadow grass.

The popularity of the wildflower meadow as a model for landscaping home grounds is a very recent phenomenon, whose labor-saving aspects have been rather overstated by press and seed companies. But the incorporation of an enclosed garden, usually near the house, into more naturalistically treated surroundings has a long history in this country. Practical considerations certainly have some influence: protection, of course, but also limitation of the amount of space that needs careful cultivating to the amount of time and energy available. Not that wildflower meadows — or pastoral landscapes for that matter — don't need maintenance. They do indeed, as Mrs. Simpson emphasizes. But not the daily

weeding and deadheading of a flower bed, nor the weekly mowing and raking and watering of a lawn. But one comes to suspect that many, many times the practical argument is a very American way of justifying a design that reminds us of a field of flowers we once saw from the road or the trimly fenced grandmothers' gardens we loved: a design whose looks we like.

Mrs. Simpson's house and garden are set into a wild-flower meadow, mowed once a year to prevent the encroachment of encircling trees. A dwarf apple tree anchors each end of the garden. Along the long wall espaliered pears are echoed by a trio, less tightly pruned, against the end wall of the house.

Walls and Fences, Piazzas and Porches

The enclosed garden may never have lacked some American admirers, but what strikes foreign observers most forcibly when they visit residential neighborhoods in the United States is the openness, the lack of enclosure, the absence of walls or fences or hedges, particularly on the street side of the houses. The reactions of two contemporary British observers are typical. Joan Dutton Parry, who visited gardens all over the country in the 1950s, writes "If I were asked if there was one single feature of American gardens as a whole which had caught my attention, I would unhesitatingly say the lack of hedges."[1] She also makes clear that to her hedges stand for all forms of enclosure. Christopher Tunnard, in *The City of Man*, linked this openness to the pioneer's clearing in the forest:

> [T]he tradition of the clearing lingers in the open lot of the suburban villa, the house placed in a "clearing," the ornamental trees scattered on the shady lawn. How different this placing of the house is from anything in Europe, where one does not see the continuous lawn in front of several houses or sense the feeling of the "clearing," which in spite of recent trends to enclosure still remains![2]

In fact, enclosure came first; but travelers have noted, almost from the beginning and usually with surprise, the amount of land around the houses in American towns and cities. As one visitor, Samuel Maverick described Newbury, Massachusetts in 1660:

> [T]he Houses stand at a good distance each from the other, a feild and Garden between each house and so on both sides the street for four miles or thereabouts.[3]

So the Swedish botanist Peter Kalm described Trenton, among other towns in New Jersey, Pennsylvania and Delaware, in 1747:

> The houses stand at a moderate distance from one another. They are commonly built so that the street passes along on one side of the houses, while gardens of different dimensions bound the other side. . . . [4]

And a hundred years later, a Swedish visitor, Fredrika Bremer sounded the same note:

> The streets in the lesser cities of America are a succession of small detached villas, with their grass plots, elegant iron palisading, and fine trees in front of the houses. It is only in those portions of the towns in which shops are to be found that the houses are built close together, and rather with an eye to the advantage of business than for beauty.[5]

It is tempting to see this pattern of land use originating in the memory of the clearing in the forest, but under examination the idea holds up better as descriptive analogy than as

actual derivation. Except in the very first years, as several historians have pointed out, it was not the man who cleared the land who settled it—farmed it and built a permanent dwelling—but the man to whom he sold it before moving on west to clear more land. In any case this scenario really applies to farmsteads; most towns were settled by groups. Plots of land were apportioned by the group and assigned to its members. Or, when the town was founded by a speculator it was the speculator who subdivided the tract. There was plenty of land, so the portions could be generous. They had to be: Garden space was a necessity on the frontier. And, as was rarely the case in Europe, it was land that the settler could own, freehold land. One can make a good case for the American single family house in the center of its lawn—the shrunken head of the English manor—as a symbol of the right to own land, whether it was land you cleared yourself, bought from the man who cleared it, or, as became more and more the case, bought from a land company or a speculator.

In the beginning and for at least two centuries, that land was either partly or fully enclosed. According to the unknown author of the 1635 "Essay on the Ordering of Towns" in the *Winthrop Papers* it is not necessary to require fencing for

> he that knoweth the benefit of incloseing, will omit noe dilligence to brenge him selfe into an inclusive condicion, well understanding that one acre inclosed, is much more beneficiall than 5 falling to his share in Common.[6]

What constituted the enclosure has varied with time and region. The wooden fence probably came first wherever wood was plentiful, since it could be put up faster than any other barrier. It is unlikely, however, that the fastest and easiest of all wood fences, the worm fence, which is made from logs or rails laid horizontally in a zig-zag, was often used to enclose gardens. It occupies a strip of land about ten feet wide, which makes it more suitable for farmland. Most scholarly investigation of American fences has concentrated on those types that played a role in agriculture or stock-raising. Some of these, like the post-and-rail and the board fence were also used around gardens; but what was probably the most common garden fence, the picket fence, would have been too expensive to build around cornfields and pastures.

Although seventeenth-century writers don't bother to describe fences, they often use the word "paled" or "empaled" as equivalent to "fenced" in referring to gardens, implying fences of stakes, or pales, driven into the ground and stabilized by cross-pieces between heavier posts. Sharpen the points of the pales and the paling fence becomes the picket fence. Paint it white and it becomes an American icon. But unfinished paling and white picket fences alike are depicted in late seventeenth century paintings of English country houses, the former always for defensive purposes, the latter sometimes simply as a decorative territorial marking. This was a role that the American picket

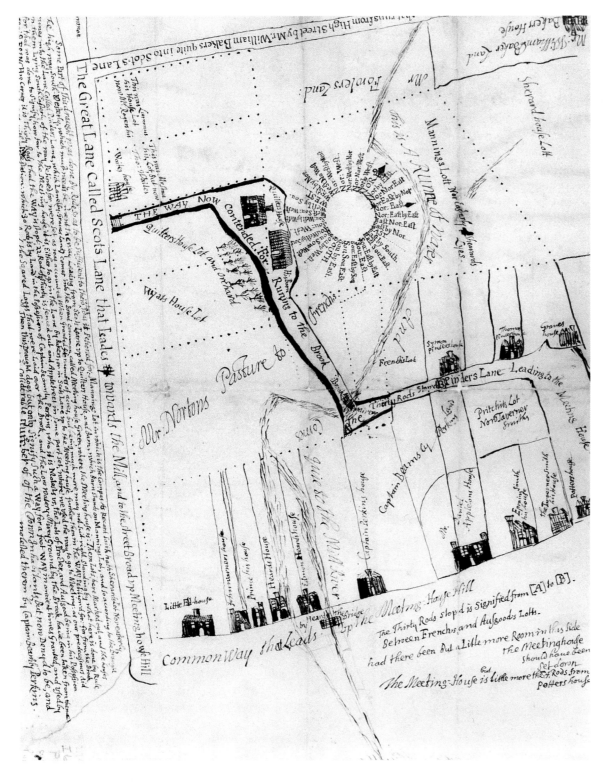

A 1717 map of Ipswich drawn for a court case concerning the closing of a customary right-of-way shows the wide spaces between houses in Massachusetts towns, already noted by Samuel Maverick more than a half-century earlier.

fence was not able to relax into until late in the nineteenth century when the Colonial Revival refurbished its popularity. Archaeological findings have confirmed that the citizens of Williamsburg did choose to build picket fences to comply with the 1705 fence law: The Colonial Revival got it right in this case.

Defensive fencing—as much against free-ranging domestic animals as against wild ones—was so necessary for garden plots that a Virginia planter in 1735 laying out his axial "falls" to the river would enclose his with a ten-foot paling even on the principal axis, as the excavations at Carter's Grove, and estate on the James River, have shown.[7] Jefferson too, seventy years later and farther west, was specific about the need to protect his vegetables and young fruit trees:

His first work is to pale in the garden, with a paling 10. feet high. the posts are to be of locust, sufficiently stout, barked but not hewed, 12 f. long, of which 2-1/2 f. are to go in the ground . . . The pales are to be of chestnut, riven, & strong . . . & should be so near as not to let even a young hare in.[8]

Mixed fences were the rule in rural America from the beginning, with variations depending on materials at hand. In stony Massachusetts a farmer has enclosed his front yard with an almost urban post-and-rail over wall. A worm fence keeps cattle out of the orchard; a tight board fence discourages roadside predators.

Even if, like Jefferson, you were devoted to the new ideas of natural-seeming landscape gardening, fence-building was a necessity—and an expensive one—as long as you lived where there were still wild animals or where domestic animals were allowed to run free.

Peter Kalm observed that some farmers in Pennsylvania and New Jersey, foreseeing in the rapidly disappearing forests the end of cheap wood for fencing, were experimenting with hedges of privet, which is fast-growing if not completely livestock proof. Privet, interestingly, is still the hedge of choice for gardeners in the eastern part of this country, still prized in the land of mobility for its speedy growth. Although hedge-making was heavily proselytized by the horticultural press in the nineteenth century, it never really caught on as a method of agricultural enclosure, except for a brief flurry of interest in that spiny native, the osage orange, in the 1830s, which was ended by the invention of spinier barbed wire. As garden

Carolina. Stone walls seem to have been more popular in New England than elsewhere, and those used to enclose gardens seem to have been rather low but topped with fences.

But when did "Don't fence me in" gain the ascendancy over "Good fences make good neighbors"? It was really a matter of cattle and of livestock in general. As the landscape critic J. B. Jackson has pointed out, when Emerson had quoted that New England proverb approvingly, cows and pigs roamed freely in city and country.[9] The English novelist and travel writer Frances Milton Trollope was harassed by hogs in the streets of Cincinnati, and it was said that in the streets of New York and Washington you would meet as many pigs as people. The porcine brigades might be called the first city sanitation departments, but they were also turned loose on country roads. In 1852, Lewis Allen read a stern reproach to farmers for the practice in his pattern book, *Rural Architecture*:

enclosures, hedges had somewhat more acceptance; but even privet hedges take a certain amount of time, a good bit of labor, and some skill to make and maintain, three commodities that were often expensive and difficult to come by. Hedges did make sense as windbreaks in regions like the northern plains where trees and timber were scarce, and they were common there.

By the eighteenth century garden walls, generally of brick, had made their appearance in cities, and on some estates like Westover and Mount Vernon in Virginia. Philadelphia, founded in the late seventeenth century, walled in its gardens very early on and so did Charleston, South

What so untidy as the approach to a house, with a herd of filthy hogs rooting about the fences, basking along the sidewalk, or feeding at a huge, uncouth, hollowed log, in the road near the dwelling. It may be out of place here to speak of it, but this disgusting spectacle has so often offended our sight, at the approach of an otherwise pleasant farm establishment, that we cannot forego the opportunity to speak of it.[10]

By the middle of the nineteenth century in most of the northern half of the country, political pressure, particularly

from farmers who were tired of having their crops damaged by free-ranging livestock, had succeeded in forcing the passage of herd or fence laws that required the owners of said livestock to keep their animals under control. By this time, wild animals and Indians had been pushed far away from the white man's settlements, so fences were no longer needed for defense.

At this point, in the middle of the nineteenth century, from the horticultural press came a vehement attack on the whole idea of walls and fences. Andrew Jackson Downing, the great popularizer of the naturalistic landscape, wrote in *The Theory and Practice of Landscape Gardening*, 1841:

> Nothing is more common, in the places of cockneys who become inhabitants of the country, than a display immediately around the dwelling of a spruce paling of carpentry, neatly made, and painted white or green; a abomination among the fresh fields, of which no person of taste could be guilty. To fence off a small plot around a fine house, in the midst of a lawn of fifty acres, is a perversity which we could never reconcile, with even the lowest perception of beauty . . . there is never one instance in a thousand where any barrier is necessary.[11]

Frank Jesup Scott had studied with Downing, but he was also an Ohio real estate developer.[12] Since fences were expensive to build, a touch of commercialism may have tainted the rather pious message in his 1870 book, *The Art of Beautifying Suburban Home Grounds*:

> It is unchristian to hedge from the sight of others the beauties of nature which it has been our good fortune to create or secure; and all the walls, high fences, hedge screens and belts of trees and shrubbery which are used for that purpose only, are so many means by which we show how unchristian and unneighborly we can be.[13]

By contrast, Nathaniel Egleston seems simply a reformer and his proselytizing disinterested in *Villages and Village Life with hints for their improvement*, 1878:

> Nothing can be less tasteful than our common picket fence, for instance, with its stiff array of pikes set up as a barricade around our dwellings, as though every passing man or beast were accounted an enemy against whom we must entrench ourselves . . .which if removed, might give place to a beautiful sweep of lawn stretching down to the very edge of the travelled roadway and adding at once dignity and beauty to the dwelling.[14]

Action followed swiftly upon word. Two of the earliest planned suburbs — informally suburbs had existed around the northern cities ever since the seventeenth century — Llewellyn Park in New Jersey, begun in 1853, and Frederick Law Olmsted's Riverside, near Chicago, begun in 1868, were unfenced models that would be imitated right up to the present day, no matter how great the shrinkage in lot size. And it wasn't necessary to design a new community; fences came down on residential streets in cities and small towns all across America. Or, if they remained, following Downing follower Frank Scott's dictum that "*that kind of fence is best which is least seen, and best seen through*," they became low, decorative borders or open, and, figuratively speaking, transparent. The increasing availability of various kinds of iron and wire fences as the century wore on made this ideal easier and easier to achieve.

But what about privacy? All of these American writers and designers openly acknowledged their debt to both English theory and English practice, especially their admiration for the English lawn. But the walls around middle-class gardens did not come down in England, even though they had lost their defensive rationale far earlier than in the United States. As early as 1853, Lewis Allen in his notes to

Top left:
Where trees were scarce and rock expensive, hedges came into their own. The just married F. A. Pazandak — progressive farmer, photographer, and musician — ordered a pre-fabricated Craftsman-style house in 1917 from Sears Roebuck for his new farmstead northwest of Fullerton, North Dakota.

Top right:
By the late twenties the Pazandaks' home grounds outlined by shelter belts of trees and crisp hedges have become a green oasis in the farm's 1000 acres of tawny grain fields. There's an orchard in front of the porch and a rough side lawn occupied by poultry.

ROADWAY ACROSS HEAD OF LAKELET.

Adolescent herdsmen didn't always exercise firm control over their charges—witness this *Vicks Magazine* engraving—and hungry cows and pigs were a menace that kept both town and country gardens, as well as farm fields, fenced. Once herd laws were passed and enforced many fences came down.

In New York "piazza" was the common term for porches like those on the 1680 Billop House on Staten Island. The porches may have been added later, but some architectural historians feel New Yorkers extended and supported the projecting curved eaves customary in Flemish buildings very early.

the American edition of Charles H. J. Smith's *Landscape Gardening*, pointed out a difference in attitude that is more thoroughly examined by Sylvester Baxter in an 1890 issue of *Garden and Forest*:

> There is a strong contrast between European and American ideas as to the character and function of private grounds, be the area surrounding a house large or small. In Europe the idea is that of seclusion; in the United States it is rather one of inclusion. In Europe the space surrounding the dwelling is treated as an out-door extension of the dwelling itself; a high wall encloses it and so sacred is its privacy that the gaze of a stranger into its precincts is held as something to be guarded against almost as rigorously as actual trespass.... With us, the ground surrounding a dwelling is treated, in effect, as an intermediate territory; a transition between the freedom of the public way and the privacy of the household.[15]

Privacy was not a problem for the dweller in a forest clearing; more desirable was company that brought news, different experience, a chance to talk. To Mme de la Tour du Pin, who took refuge in the United States from the French Revolution, it seemed as if the first thing an American did after he had built a house in the wilderness was to hang out a sign to attract travelers.[16] The inn sign was a late development. Houses were built right at the side of the road and from the seventeenth century through the early nineteenth European travelers to the frontier reported that you would be housed and fed—and expected to pay—at whatever dwelling night befell you. The road, the street, represented sociability to people thinly scattered across the land.

It was in towns, however, that visitors first observed an institution that was a very significant factor in the open orientation of the American garden: the front porch. Just when it arrived on the scene and where it came from are still a subject of some disagreement, as we shall see. But both as architectural form and social custom it was well enough established in Burlington, New Jersey, by 1750 to attract Peter Kalm's attention:

Before each door is a veranda to which you ascend by steps from the street; it resembles a small balcony and has benches on both sides on which the people sit in the evening to enjoy the fresh air and to watch passers-by.[17]

In Albany, New York, according to both Kalm and Ann MacVicar Grant, the daughter of a Scottish officer who recalls her stay there between 1758 and 1768 in *Memoirs of an American Lady*, people spent almost the whole day on their porches or "open porticos," as she sometimes calls them, in fine weather. "Nothing could be more pleasing to a simple and benevolent mind than to see thus, at one view, all the inhabitants of a town . . ."[18]

As these quotations indicate, Europeans were not quite sure what to call this unfamiliar architectural element. Nor were Americans. "Portico" and "gallery" were sometimes used, particularly in the South. "Veranda" was more common and has remained current, but as a strictly architectural term. The real contenders up until the beginning of this century were "piazza" and "front porch." Piazza has a fascinating derivation. In the early seventeenth century the Italian word for open square was misapplied by the English to the Italianate arcade designed by Inigo Jones and built around two sides of the Covent Garden market. It quickly came to mean any space for walking or sitting covered by a pillar-supported roof on the open side and attached to a building on the opposite one. The building of piazzas on houses is mentioned in a Charleston ordinance of 1700, and for the next two centuries piazza was the name of choice all along the eastern seaboard. "Piazza" began to lose out to "porch" late in the nineteenth century as more Americans, both Italophile travelers and journalists, realized how much of a misnomer it was.

The porch, in the domestic architecture of the seventeenth and early eighteenth centuries, was a small vestibule into which the front door opened, and which also contained the stairs. Normally a room within the four walls of the house, occasionally it was built as an enclosed two story structure appended to the exterior. But sometimes the word was also used as a synonym for the open portico or gallery of a church or public building, so it is not hard to see how it gradually took on its American meaning: an open but roofed-over place to sit, attached to a house. Some writers used porch to denote a small sheltered space with benches on either side of the front door, as distinct from the larger piazza or veranda, but most used the terms interchangeably.

There are as many theories about the origin of the front porch as there are names for it, maybe more. Most architectural historians feel that in the southern part of the United States it was imported from the Caribbean, and indeed, many of the earliest settlers in the Carolinas were European planters from Jamaica and Barbados, and in Louisiana from the French and Spanish islands.

Both of these regions boast distinctive house types—the Charleston single house, the Louisiana raised cottage—fitted with piazzas. All the evidence indicates that piazzas were built earlier in the south than in the north, but there is a difference: southern examples were not built facing the street,

Engraved by William Birch in 1812 when occupied by an American general, Mr. Duplantier's Louisiana plantation house is typically encircled by verandas. This raised cottage style has been assigned a possible origin in the Caribbean to the south or in Canada to the north, or, just as likely, both.

at least in Charleston. There, one- or two-story verandas of the single house are set at right angles to the street and face a walled garden. On plantation houses they may face road or river, or both. Of course, one could say that in much of the South the road was the river, and if sociability was somewhat distant it was still a kind of sociability.

Architectural historian John Vlach feels the front porch really came by way of the Caribbean from Africa, where verandas are as common in house design as they are not in northern Europe. His comparisons between certain kinds of vernacular houses in Haiti and Louisiana do show a persuasive similarity.[19] However the plans of the principal floors of the Palace of Diego Columbus[20] built in Santo Domingo around 1510—well before Africans arrived in the New World—and Middleburg, 1699, the oldest frame house in South Carolina[21] are almost identical: a single line of rooms between parallel verandas. And the veranda—now considered a Portuguese word not an East Indian one as was long thought—is as characteristic of the folk architecture of northern Portugal and Spain as the patio is of southern Spain.

An unsigned article in an 1888 issue of *Garden and Forest* speculates that in the northern states the front porch evolved from the Palladian portico. In some of its forms it may have, but Kalm records the existence of porches before that style of portico came into use on this side of the Atlantic. The architectural writer Hugh Morrison suggests that the porch was a late eighteenth-century development of the traditional overhanging eaves of the farmhouses built by Flemish and Walloon immigrants to the New Netherlands and found on Long Island and in New Jersey.[22] But the verandas that Pierre van Cortlandt added when he remodeled his manor house near Croton-on-Hudson in 1751 are almost identical to those in several Brazilian plantation houses painted by the Dutch artists Frans Post and Albert Eckhout in the 1640s.[23] Verandas and porches may have been built earlier and spread more widely through the colonies than we know. They were usually constructed of wood even on masonry houses and

Right:
The verandas and ground-
floor galleries around
Pierre Van Cortlandt's
mid-eighteenth-century
manor house seem much
like those around a
Louisiana raised cottage,
but they have another
possible precedent.

Below:
A hundred years earlier, a
similar veranda appears in a
view of the Brazilian countryside painted by Albert
Eckhout during the Dutch
occupation and there was
considerable traffic between
New York and Pernambuco,
both outposts of the Dutch
West Indies Company.

most likely would have deteriorated faster than the fabric of the house.

Probably all these peoples and precedents contributed to the architecture of the front porch: People and especially merchants traveled and traded along the American coast and with the Caribbean. Shortly after founding New Amsterdam, the Dutch West India Company occupied the state of Pernambuco in northern Brazil and a handful of Caribbean islands, and there were certainly black slaves in seventeenth-century New York and New Jersey. Judging from paintings like *The Burgher of Delft and His Daughter* by Jan Steen and *Keizersgracht with the Westerkirk, Amsterdam* by Jan van der Heyden, seventeenth-century Holland also provided some precedent for the custom of sitting on a raised platform outside one's front door and conversing with passers-by. It was in the areas of Dutch settlement that the phenomenon of the front porch was first noted, as we have seen, and it was from these areas that it spread through the northern colonies, as these extracts from an exchange of letters in 1771 between the painter John Singleton Copley, then in New York, and his half-brother, Henry Pelham, in Boston, indicate:

> Copley writes: "I shall add a peazer when I return, which is much practiced here, and is very beautiful and convenient . . . "
> Pelham replies: "I don't comprehend what you mean by a Peazer."
> Copley answers: "You say you don't know what I mean by a Peaza. I will tell you then. It is exactly such a thing as the cover over the pump in your Yard . . . and 3 or 4 Posts aded to support the front of the Roof, a good floor at bottum, and from post to post a Chinese enclosure of

about three feet high . . . these Peazas are so cool in Sumer and in Winter break off the storms so much that I think I should not be able to like an house without."[24]

"These Peazas" had so proved their worth by 1841 when Downing wrote *The Theory and Practice of Landscape Gardening*, that he could recommend them without qualification.

> The obvious utility of the veranda in this climate (especially in the middle and southern states) will, therefore, excuse its adoption into any style of architecture that may be selected for our domestic uses . . .[25]

Almost without exception, every suburban or country house design in the multitude of architectural and gardening manuals of the nineteenth century incorporated a front or side porch. To the nineteenth-century American, "A country house without a porch is like a man without an eyebrow," as Donald G. Mitchell put it.[26] Less colorful but equally forthright was a *Garden and Forest* editorial of November 7, 1888:

> Nothing is more characteristic of American country houses, as contrasted with those of other northern lands, than their large covered piazzas. These have been developed in answer to as distinct and imperative a national need as ever determined the genesis of an architectural feature. . . . Certainly no really comfortable country home can exist in our land without a piazza. . . . How necessary it is we read in the fact that, when well arranged, the piazza always becomes the very focus of domestic life and social intercourse — as central a feature in summer as the parlor fireside is in winter.

What could be more natural than the placement of the most attractive part of your property, your garden, so it could be enjoyed from the porch where you spent your leisure and greeted your friends? That place was usually between the house and the street, at least in the north and middle west. Sylvester Baxter did admit that "possibly a minor motive may be the indulgence of a love of display" but found it "harmless in such a manifestation."

All through the nineteenth and early twentieth centuries the horticultural press poured forth plans for the front yard, designs for urns and flower beds to ornament it, and suggestions for vines to train up porch pillars, although some authorities recommended a well-kept lawn with a tree or two and a few shrubs as the most appropriate and tasteful treatment.

The American suburbanite, if he be something of a traveler, breathes a deep sigh of relief on returning from abroad, at the open, free-to-all charms of his own and his neighbor's home environments. The united stretches of lawn, the colored flower beds; the street, a sylvan avenue of arching elms, all to be viewed from a cool vine-decked piazza, with an opportunity to salute a passing friend: this is typically American, and in refreshing contrast to the walled grounds usual to many European homes, where custom has handed down notions of such exclusiveness that they must be shut off from the outside world with barriers of stone or brick 8 to 12 feet high, crowned with broken glass from which even the vines shrink![27]

As Charles Henderson's paean to the piazza was being published—*Henderson's Picturesque Gardens* came out in 1908—the engine of its destruction was taking shape. The affordable automobile would eventually do away with the front porch; the Model-T began to roll off Henry Ford's production line in 1909.

By 1927 Mrs. Francis King, in her advice on planning a garden, could say that:

Even the idea of the front porch is going from America now, especially since there are no beautiful horses to be seen longer on our streets, nothing but the sound and fury of the automobile . . .[28]

The smell didn't help either. Besides, automobiles went too fast for a casual exchange of greetings with porch-sitters. Family leisure activities moved to the back of the house and so did the garden, if there was a gardener in the household. Today the front porch survives as an institution only in rather remote regions, at resort hotels and Adirondack camps. Recent attempts at revival by architects and landscape designers have so far been defeated by the superior efficiency of air conditioning and the superior appeal of television. But the loss of this distinctively American architectural feature and the neighborly sociability that went with it did not bring about the loss of the distinctively American preference for an open front yard.

Like most American institutions, the unbounded front yard did not lack for critics. Novelist George Washington Cable's early twentieth-century objections were primarily practical: Neighborhood dogs and cats and unruly children continually laid waste to plants and discouraged gardeners. Later on, the landscape architect Fletcher Steele deplored its denial of privacy, and the design problems it created for the garden-maker. These strictures went unregarded even when post–World War II popular magazines pointed out that, by

walling or hedging their front yards, owners of small suburban lots could enlarge the range of outdoor activities available to them.

In a 1985 issue of *Landscape Magazine*, Christopher Grampp reported the attitudes he found in a survey of fifty homeowners in the San Francisco Bay area:

Some residents react angrily when neighbors fence their front yards. When his neighbor built a fence, Tim, a young attorney, was outraged: "I wouldn't construct a barrier, something that would detract from the neighborhood. I even dislike cosmetic fences. The neighbors

have done a nice job of improving their property, but they have closed themselves off from the world. You have a responsibility to keep your community looking decent, clean, and attractive. When their fence went up, the attitude throughout the neighborhood was negative. It cut into everyone's space, and a dimension of our vista was diminished. I find that negative."[29]

Tim's sentiments would be echoed in similar neighborhoods all across the country; even fences and hedges enclosing the backyard are frowned upon in some communities. Although it is almost never used and is probably seen more by passersby than by its owners, the open front yard retains its hold upon the American sense of fitness; and yet it was only a little less than a hundred and fifty years ago that the fences came down.

Piazza, porch, veranda, or gallery, the name might vary with the region, but almost every nineteenth-century house from mansion to cottage had at least one.

PART TWO ❦ CHAPTER TWO

The Vista
Garden

As long as the garden was separated by a fence or a wall from the land around it, the garden-maker did not have to concern himself about whether that land was flat or rolling or moun-tainous except as the topography affected the climate, the soil, and the drainage within the walls. Nor did he have to worry about what you could see from the garden, its attrac-tiveness or lack thereof, or its compatibility with his arrange-ments. All of these became essential considerations when, in Renaissance Europe, the design of gardens began to embrace views of the surrounding countryside. The garden-maker had to balance the demands of privacy and prospect, screen out unwanted views and frame desired ones, and bring together harmoniously the close at hand and the far away. It was garden design on a whole new scale.

It was also garden design that demanded from the design-er an imagination comfortable with complexity, an expanded range of skills, architectural and engineering as well as horti-cultural, and the ability to achieve variety and coherence in large compositions. Sometimes all the expertise was united in one person; many times the designer, who might have been an architect or a painter, a hydraulic engineer or a gar-dener, or just as often a gentleman amateur, functioned as the leader of a team of specialists. Amateur or professional, the makers of vista gardens saw their creations not just as pleasure grounds, but as works of art. They sought inspiration in the Classical authors, and consciously constructed imagi-native or symbolic representations of Greek and Roman antiquity, although the forms they created may, according to some historians, have been adapted from the gardens of Moorish Spain, transmitted through the Spanish Court at Naples.[1] They preferred to work with materials capable of producing large and long-lasting effects—stone, gravel, water, grass, trees, shrubs. Flowers and herbs and fruit trees might decorate these compositions—they very often did—but they were too small in scale and too ephemeral to count as essentials.

The Renaissance garden was no longer simply a place to grow plants. The intimate pleasures of scent and color, and shaded places to sit and walk, were no longer enough. Stronger emotions—wonder, exhilaration, surprise—were to be aroused, and the intellect stimulated. A garden might be arranged and furnished to tell a story or convey a symbolic message, or to play tricks on unwary visitors, like pavements that squirted water when stepped on. This was a major change. It opened a rift between the aristocratic and the ver-nacular garden—which prefigures what we now call the public and the private garden—that still persists. But it didn't happen all at once. In their first, Italian phase, the outward-looking gardens usually included walled spaces—*giardini segreti*—and beds for growing flowers, and because these gardens were almost always built on hillsides they could and often did frame vistas without totally abolishing walls and hedges. Italianate Renaissance gardens in England, built on less precipitous sites, utilized raised terraces, mounts, even tree houses to allow their inhabitants a look beyond the walls. Enclosures came down or were pushed to the side gradually, over a couple of hundred years, as the central axis and the view to the horizon gained control of the garden plan.

By the seventeenth century, at least in England, even the vocabulary was changing. The surroundings of the house were thought of less often as a garden than as a park, from the old word for a royal hunting preserve; or as a landscape, a word borrowed from the technical terminology of painting. "Gardener" came to imply craftsman rather than artist. The designer was called an "improver" or a landscape gardener. Landscape architect, as a professional title, would appear only in the late nineteenth century, but it is foreshadowed by the titles bestowed on André Le Nôtre in the seventeenth: In 1637 he took over his father's title of "premier jardinier du Roi au gd-jardin des Tuileries"; in 1643 he was "Dessinateur des plants and parterres de tous les jardins de S. Maj.," Louis XIII, and in 1666, "conseiller du Roi aux conseils et controleur général des bâtiments de Sa Majesté" to Louis XIV.[2] Despite this latter tribute to his architectural training and expertise, Le Nôtre never forgot his gardening origins. But it was a sig-nal that in the future, a thorough knowledge of plants would not always be considered of major importance in the educa-tion of a garden designer.

The villa gardens of fifteenth-and sixteenth-century Italy, the palace gardens of seventeenth-century France, and the country house gardens of eighteenth-century England were imitated, each kind in its period of ascendance, all across Europe and in the case of the latter two in North America as well. The Italian garden had to wait until the nineteenth century to make its influence directly felt on this continent. We usually separate the three great garden styles of post-medieval Europe — Renaissance Italian, French Formal, and English Landscape—but they can also be looked at as modifications of the vista garden as it encountered different terrains, national temperaments, political, social, and agricul-tural arrangements, and responded over time to changing fashions, scientific advances, and artistic ideals.

So much has been written about the difference between the geometric layout and architectural organization of the French style and the simulated natural forms and pictorial organization of the English style that they are usually consid-ered antithetical, but they really represent two different ways of applying the same principle: In both, the composition is controlled by the view or views to the horizon. Both rely on aerial perspective, which generally demands an east-west orientation for the main axis, and employs optical manipula-tion to shape space. And both can be and have been used to symbolize the political and economic strength of their own-ers. Right from the start the gardens of Versailles were consid-ered an eloquent demonstration of the power of Louis XIV. The English style was characterized by its literary champions as an expression of freedom; but one of its greatest artists, Humphry Repton, was quite explicit about the expression of social and economic dominance as a principle of "improve-ment" and a source of pleasure in landscape gardening:

> Appropriation. A word ridiculed by Mr. Price as lately coined by me, to describe extent of property; yet the appearance and display of such extent is a source of pleasure not to be disregarded, since every individual

who possesses anything, whether it be mental endowments, or power, or property, obtains respect in proportion as his possessions are known, provided he does not too vainly boast of them. . . . The pleasure of appropriation is gratified in viewing a landscape which cannot be injured by the malice or bad taste of a neighbouring intruder . . .[3]

Probably few owners on this or the other side of the Atlantic consciously saw their landscape-making as a power play, but in order to realize great vistas you had to own or to control the development of a large amount of land. However sincerely the impulse to creation sprang from love of the countryside and delight in artistry rather than from fashion following or status seeking, it took money or power and usually both to carry it to fruition. The first tries at French-style architectural vista gardens in early eighteenth-century America were made by colonial governors, who had the clout, or southern planters and northern merchants, who had the money. Governor Spotswood, a dedicated and normally generous gardener, made himself thoroughly unpopular with the Virginia Council, already unhappy about the amount of public money he had spent on the palace gardens, by cutting down some trees belonging to John Custis, an equally dedicated gardener, to extend a view.

Because it was only at the beginning of the eighteenth century that North American settlers were secure enough and rich enough to undertake the creation of large-scale pleasure grounds, what we call for convenience the French (or architectural) and English (or landscape) styles arrived on this side of the Atlantic almost simultaneously. Americans seem to have understood immediately the underlying similarity of principle. After the first two or three decades, gardens of both types were made throughout the century. Which was chosen seems to have depended on personal taste, with architectural order preferred in the frontier regions or close to cities. Many took elements from both styles and combined them, often retaining the enclosed garden as well, the first instance of the characteristic American response to new ideas in garden design.

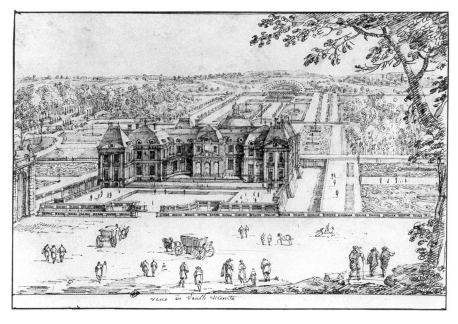

As always when it advanced into new territory, the vista garden was considerably modified in the New World; in its architectural form, it was drastically simplified. A complex organization of symmetrically balanced, carefully placed points of view and lines of sight was particularly well adapted to the rather flat countryside around Paris. Such intricacy did not work very well on the hilly, often rugged terrain of North America. Still more important, any extensive layout of the neatly clipped hedges, parterres de broderie, networks of precisely spaced trees, and elaborate waterworks shown in the garden books required a large pool of skilled labor to construct and maintain. Careful maintenance was critical. The shortage of skilled labor was endemic in America.

On the other hand, just because the terrain was more varied and dramatic, simpler means could produce spectacular results. Thomas Hancock boasted to a London seedsman in 1736 of his Beacon Hill garden that "its allowed on all hands

Lay a right-angle triangle over the plan of Middleton Place and the geometric structure of its 1741 landscape is clear. The central axis runs from the view down the Ashley River through what was the center of the house to the road from Charleston. The compartments of the formal garden laid out on a symmetrically balanced grid fill out the triangle.

the Kingdom of England don't afford so Fine a Prospect as I have both of land & water." Hancock's correspondence with James Glin, the seedsman, and his contract with one William Grigg for the construction of a garden on the "south side of a hill with the most beautifull Assent to the top" gives some idea of the way Americans adapted the ideas in early eighteenth-century garden books to their own situations.[4] Grigg obliges himself to "layout the upper garden allys. Trim the Beds & fill up all the allies with such Stuff as Sd. Hancock shall order and Gravel the Walks & prepare and Sodd ye Terras."

Hancock orders yews, hollies, and jasmine vines and asks for catalogues of "Curious Things not of a high price that will Beautifie a flower Garden" and "what Fruit you have that are Dwarf Trees and Espaliers" leading to the conclusion that his beds were shared by fruits and flowers. He also wants to know the price of "100 small Yew Trees in the rough which I'd Frame up here to my own fancy."

Of all the ornamental contrivances that filled the books, terraces and topiary—simple balls and cones for the most part—seem to have been the most popular with colonial Americans. Robert Beverley suggested as early as 1705 (in *The History and Present State of Virginia*) that, with Virginia's abundance of hills and streams, "the finest Waterworks in the World may be made, at a very small Expense."[5] As far as we know the suggestion was not taken up, even though all the books maintained that "fountains and Water-Works are the Life of a Garden." Very likely the needed hydraulic engineers were lacking. But if water was not made to dance and plash, it was caught in ornamental pools—"basons and canals"—and, in the form of lakes and rivers, was almost always a major feature of the vista. In eighteenth-century America rivers tended to be the major arteries of communication; most of the great estate gardens looked out on them. To their owners, with all the active river life to look at, fountains or cascades probably did not seem worth the expense. They certainly were not needed.

MIDDLETON PLACE

Middleton Place, on the Ashley River fourteen miles upstream from Charleston, South Carolina remained in the possession of the family that created it from the mid-eighteenth century until 1983. Then it was deeded to a not-for-profit foundation organized by its owner, Charles Duell, who still manages it: a remarkable continuity of ownership in the mobile United States. The garden has survived British raids during the Revolutionary War, the burning of the library and all but the guest wing of the house by Union troops during the Civil War, the loss of its economic base when emancipation made rice-growing unprofitable, the great earthquake of 1886, fifty years of neglect, and two centuries of changing fashions in garden design. What has not survived is any documentation about its origins.

By tradition, the garden was laid out in 1741, when Henry Middleton received the estate as his bride's dowry, and completed over the course of ten years, which seems confirmed by a bit of doggerel in the *London Gentleman's Magazine* for July 1753 in which it is mentioned.[6] There is also a tradition that the designer was British and professional without evidence to confirm or refute it. Whoever the designer, whether British or American, the garden is beautifully fitted to its surroundings.

The site is superb: a bluff overlooking the Ashley River just at the point where the river bends, describing an elongated S-curve perpendicular to the bluff. The house was built along the top of the bluff, and centered on the view down the river. Decoratively sculptured grassed terraces descend from a lawn in front of the house to a pair of Butterfly Lakes on either side of the garden's main east-west axis, which passes from the center of the river through the central hall of the house—now destroyed—out to the front gates on the road. The strict symmetry of the terraces and Butterfly Lakes at the core of the axis relaxes at the edges into a balanced composition adjusted to the topography, which argues for a skilled and confident garden maker. Gifted designers in the architectural style, Le Nôtre first and foremost, took advantage of inequalities in the terrain to create variety, and their designs, while measurably ordered, were not rigidly symmetrical. Unfortunately, this lesson was not grasped by most of their followers and some writers of garden books, who thereby left themselves open to Pope's scorn:

Grove nods at Grove, each Ally has a Brother,
And half the Platform just reflects the other.[7]

At Middleton Place, the terraced bluff juts out to the river like the prow of an ocean liner. On its south side, the land slopes down to a narrow lake formed by widening a creek, the Rice Mill Pond, beyond which rises a wooded hillside. On the north side a complex of geometrically designed paths and gardens occupies the high ground above flooded rice fields, filling an area roughly the shape of a right-angle triangle. The placement of the gardens proper to the side of the principal vista from the house rather than along it, although uncommon in European garden books seems to have been widely practiced on Southern riverside plantations. In Virginia, Westover on the James River and Prestwould on the Roanoke, to mention just two examples, also display serene turfed "falls" between house and river, with parterre flower gardens at one side.

The ornamental works at Middleton Place, as garden writers of the time would call them, include a bowling green, a wheel-shaped rose garden, a canal or reflecting pool, several secret gardens, and camellia allées. The different compartments of the garden today are not as elaborately worked out as the diagrams in *The Theory and Practice of Gardening*, and quite probably they never were, but they do display the diversity its author advocated:

> [I]f two Groves are upon the Side of a Parterre, tho' their outward Form and Dimensions are equal, you should not, for that Reason, repeat the same Design in both, but make them different within.[8]

Although time has softened its lines on the ground, the mathematical clarity of the original design is evident in the plan, and it is remarkable how little that design has been altered. The garden has indeed been enriched and added to in the more than two hundred years of its existence: The camellias for which it is famous only arrived in 1786 with the French botanist André Michaux, and according to Middleton

family tradition, two ancient specimens remain from his gift of four *Camellia japonica*. In the 1930s masses of red and pink indica azaleas were planted on the hillside above the Rice Mill Pond. Their blaze of color in March and April would probably startle an eighteenth-century garden designer, but who is to say that he would not have welcomed them had they been available to him.

The Azalea Hillside exemplifies the admirable balance between renewal of the eighteenth-century landscape and preservation of worthy additions from the nineteen and twentieth centuries achieved by Charles Duell and his grandparents, Mr. and Mrs. J. J. Pringle Smith, the restorers of Middleton Place after the years of neglect following the 1886 earthquake. Mr. Duell's reconstruction, over the past twenty years, of the stableyard and plantation street area with animals and activities suitable to an eighteenth-century rice plantation, was intended to interest and please the visitors who contribute to the survival of Middleton Place. Whether or not it accurately represents the original design in its details, bringing it to life was important in completing the restoration of the landscape plan, which like most in eighteenth-century America attempted to reconcile pleasure and productivity. Just as the flooded rice fields were unashamedly included in the principal vistas, the working heart of the estate was located near the mansion house, balancing the ensemble of ornamental gardens on the other side of the entrance lawn and drive.

The commanding vista down river, with the Butterfly Lakes in the foreground, has changed little since the eighteenth century, as long as you don't inspect the distant boat too closely. Then it would have been oar-powered, not motorized as it is today.

RUNDLET-MAY GARDEN

New Englanders are famous for being a conservative lot, so perhaps it is not surprising that when the newly prosperous merchant James Rundlet built what he called his Mansion House on the outskirts of Portsmouth, New Hampshire in 1806 he sited his house and composed his garden on terraces in the architectural style, by then thought to be rather old-fashioned. Yet, no hidebound traditionalist, he was one of the first in Portsmouth to equip his kitchen with the latest technology. The house itself, which, as far as we can tell, he designed himself with the help of excellent local craftsmen and perhaps a pattern book like Asher Benjamin's, is in the Federal style and up to date. The garden is not. Although New England merchants with more adventurous ideas had been experimenting with the new English landscape style of vista garden for some years — Theodore Lyman's The Vale in Waltham, Massachusetts, dates from 1793 — Rundlet chose to pattern his garden in the familiar grid of gravel walks and rectangular beds, and develop the acres surrounding it as a working farm. All the same, he bought poplar trees, very fashionable at the time, for that garden. As we will see again and again with American garden-makers, maintaining a consistent style doesn't seem to have interested him. Rundlet looked at all the options, old and new, open to him, then selected and combined those that best suited his purposes into a very individual design. That the garden also suited his descendants very well we can infer from the fact that it was loved and maintained by the family until they gave it to the Society for the Preservation of New England Antiquities (SPNEA) in 1971. The surrounding land has gradually metamorphosed into building lots, but the layout of the roughly

James Rundlet built his house and laid out his garden between 1806 and 1809 in the midst of farmland outside Portsmouth. His farms have long since been sold for house lots, but his mansion and home grounds have remained as shown on this 1812 plan although much of the vegetation has changed over the years.

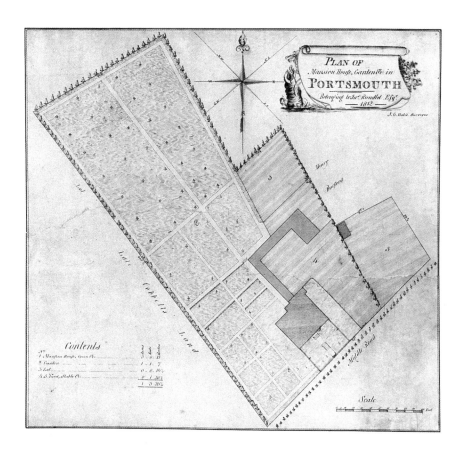

two-acre home grounds — house, stables, stable and service yards, garden and orchard — has remained as it was shown on a plan drawn in 1812.

Compared to southern plantations like Middleton Place or Mount Vernon, Rundlet's estate was quite modest, originally about thirty acres. Still, vista, which he would have called "prospect," was clearly very much on his mind. By the time construction was completed in 1809, or very shortly thereafter, Rundlet had acquired enough additional land so that everything he could see from his house, it was said,

belonged to him. The better to survey his possessions he set the house on a high turf terrace eight feet above what was then a country road. Indeed it may well have sat even higher in his day: Modern street widening and paving usually raises street and sidewalk levels. He could see his woods and fields extending across the road to a hill that came to be known as Rundlet's Mountain, and into the 1890s much of that land remained undeveloped.

Unfortunately no documents such as letters or diaries describing the building of the house and the shaping of the land have surfaced. What we have to go on, in addition to the plan, is a scattering of account books, ledgers, and memoranda of time spent by workmen on specific tasks.[9] The best guess we can make is that Rundlet took advantage of a small hill and extended it into a clearly defined terrace with rocks — his accounts show the purchase of a considerable quantity — and topsoil from the back of the lot. SPNEA horticulturist Gary Wetzel has found topsoil to be much thinner in that area.

On the east side, the terrace slopes down to the carriage

From the air, the sensitive adjustment of geometric plan to natural site, a high bluff sloping down to the river, suggests that the unknown designer of Middleton Place was highly skilled. The unusual and famous Butterfly Lakes testify that he was imaginative as well.

This page:
Terraces raise the house above street level, a common method of enhancing the dignity of large houses in or near cities in the eighteenth and early nineteenth centuries. It also gave owners more expansive views over the surrounding countryside or their own properties, as in Rundlet's case.

Opposite, top:
The view from the second story of the house over the garden, orchard, and grove of shade trees at the back of the property. Covered by a wooden arbor, the walk from the back door is flanked by one wall of the stable complex and on the other side by a bed of old-fashioned pinks.

Opposite, bottom:
Gravel paths divide the terraces at the west side and back of the house into a grid of grass-verged beds. Beyond the square devoted to peonies is one transformed by Rundlet's animal-loving grandson, Dr. James Rundlet May, into a cemetery for family pets.

drive leading to the stableyard. On the southwest or garden side of the house two additional levels, probably more clearly defined in Rundlet's day, laid out in rectangular beds descend beside and behind the house to the orchard, which rises gently to the northwest. Rundlet was a poor farm boy from Exeter, New Hampshire with an entrepreneurial flair that eventually made him one of Portsmouth's richest citizens; but judging from the beautifully executed diagrams in his geometry and trigonometry copy books, he also had a real sensitivity to mathematics and design. This gift is confirmed by his subtle adjustment of a gridded layout to sloping terrain and angled lot lines. That the beds are not in most cases exactly rectangular, and that he has slightly bent the axial path from the back door of the house to the back of the orchard is clear when you look at the plan. None of these irregularities are immediately noticeable as you walk in the garden or survey it from the windows of the house, but if you look for them you can see them.

Evidence of what was planted in the garden and orchard is fragmentary. Rundlet's accounts during the years he was building included payments for grapevines and rosebushes, pear and peach trees, poplars, plus several for unspecified fruit trees and just trees. They list purchases of wood for fences and gravel for paths and payments for their construction. A Memorandum Book for 1833–34 mentions apples, asparagus, potatoes, currants, and honeysuckles, and notes the time that workers spent gravelling and rolling paths, building steps, and turfing borders. This patchwork of evidence has lots of blank squares, but it strongly suggests that in his day, the garden held a typical vernacular mixture of fruits, flowers and vegetables.

With time came changes. But one of the beauties of a grid layout is that it can accommodate a variety of different plantings without changing character, providing those plantings do not seriously alter the vertical relationships among the sections. Sometime after the Civil War, Rundlet's animal-loving grandson, Dr. James Rundlet May turned one of the squares into a pet cemetery. His wife, Mary Ann Morison May, revitalized the orchard and replanted the garden with flowers. In the years of her stewardship, 1881 to 1936, there was no need to produce food at home, and every reason to plan a garden for pure enjoyment. The biggest change in this century was the gradual replacement of the open, sunny apple orchard in the back half of the property with a shady grove of forest trees—maple, butternut, ash, and black cherry—probably in an attempt to gain privacy. By the time Ralph and Gladys May inherited the property in the 1930s, houses plus a church and a school surrounded the garden, and Middle Street was a busy, noisy thoroughfare.

When Americans chose to create in the new "natural" or English landscape style they still operated on the principle that even a very grand and imposing landscape did not have to place its utilitarian support system at a distance from the house. This practical attitude characterizes the two best-known eighteenth-century American landscape gardens, Washington's Mount Vernon and Jefferson's Monticello. Both landscapes were developed over a long period of years with frequent interruptions when their creators were absent in public service. Jefferson was the more articulate about the need for adjusting the landscape garden's principles to American conditions, and about the ways in which this might be accomplished, although it is not clear how many of these ideas he actually carried out. Washington began earlier and worked in the more typically American fashion, that is from books, magazines, and his own ideas, without ever having seen, as Jefferson had, English examples or their French derivatives, and in the end achieved a more coherent and effective design.

A pair of spiral rose trellises, salvaged from now-vanished gardens, frame the steps up from the orchard, a third one serves as eye-catcher at the end of the path. Today's plantings are based on Mary Ann May's Colonial Revival rejuvenation of Rundlet's layout.

Mount Vernon's commanding site on a bluff 125 feet over the Potomac River gave George Washington a head start in creating his interpretation of the vista garden when he inherited it from his brother in 1754.

MOUNT VERNON

George Washington inherited Mount Vernon, where he had lived with his older brother after their father's death, upon the death of that brother's only child in 1754. He settled there on his marriage to Martha Dandridge Custis in 1759 when he returned from the French and Indian War, and began to enlarge his house, landscape his estate, and improve the productivity of his plantations. All of these projects he accomplished successfully in spite of all the years when he was absent and had to rely on never-too-satisfactory managers, usually relatives. The interruptions did take their toll in time. It was not until 1787 that the alterations to the house were finished, and he was still working on his landscaping when he died in 1799. But for a true gardener, a garden is never finished, and Washington was one. At sixteen, on his first surveying trip to the Shenandoah Valley in March of 1748, he wrote in his diary:

> Rode to his Lordships Quarter about 4 Miles higher up y. River we went through most beautiful Groves of Sugar Trees and spent ye. best part of y. Day in admiring ye. Trees and richness of ye Land.[10]

In the later diaries such bursts of enthusiasm are rare, but any gardener reading the steady, if laconic, lists of weather observations, seeds and fertilizers tried, plants bought and received, successes and failures noted, recognizes the presence of a brother.

Washington began the year 1760 by writing to friends for help in finding a gardener and a bricklayer, and in April "Planted out 20 young Pine trees at the head of my Cherry Walk."[11] But usually in the beginning practicality commanded priority: The walled gardens in their first, rectangular, configuration were constructed two years later according to the ledger. For the next few years the horticultural entries in Washington's diary record experiments in improving the soil, in grafting and planting fruit trees, and in trying different kinds of wheat, corn, flax, hemp and fodder crops. The experiments paid off. He developed a reasonably profitable mixed farming system and, unlike most of his contemporaries, was finally able to end his dependence on land-destroying tobacco, usually more lucrative to the broker in London than to the farmer in America.

In 1759 he had ordered Batty Langley's *New Principles of Gardening*, but without doubt he was aware already of the new ideas transforming garden design in England. Pope's

works were in his library and so were *The Spectator* and *The Gentleman's Magazine*,[12] much studied in the colonies as models for the writing of graceful prose. And, since connoisseurship in landscape gardening was considered one of the accomplishments of the complete gentleman one can be sure that the Virginia gentlemen who went back to England on business were careful to bring news of the latest fashions to their less-traveled neighbors. Washington liked being up to date and he went on buying gardening and farming books for the rest of his life. Among others, he owned those bibles of the eighteenth-century English-speaking gardener, Philip Miller's *Gardener's Kalendar* (1762 edition), *Gardener's Dictionary* (1763 edition), *The Universal Gardener and Botanist* by Thomas Mawe and John Abercrombie (1778), Uvedale Price's *An Essay on the Picturesque* (1794). W. Watts's views of *The Seats of the Nobility and Gentry* (1779), which includes many of Capability Brown's creations, would have given him the first visual evidence of the new style, but there seems to be no record of the date he acquired it.

Just as architectural historian Thomas Tileston Waterman could find no exact precedent for the magnificent piazza overlooking the Potomac where the family sat after their afternoon dinner, so Ann Leighton could find no specific precedents in Washington's book collection for the design of the grounds. But a considerably lesser intelligence than his would have noticed and weighed the discrepancy between the informality urged by the text and the formality shown in the illustrations of those books. And if he had not traveled in the Old World, he had in the New. In the piazza line he had been to Barbados and to New York — both piazza centers — before his marriage, but the one he built seems to be a truly original interpretation. Although he gives no descriptions, his diary for the first Continental Congress records visits to the Shippens and William Hamilton among other noted Philadelphia gardeners. Hamilton in particular was a practitioner of the landscape style and his estate, Woodlands, was much admired by Jefferson. However many sources he drew on, Washington digested what they had to offer and created his landscape to suit his own taste, situation, and resources.

His site was guaranteed to please the designer of a vista garden. Andrew Burnaby who traveled through the colonies in 1759 and 1760 noting many a "pleasing romantic scene," was impressed by it even before Washington started his improvements:

> The house is most beautifully situated upon a high hill on the banks of the Potomac; and commands a noble prospect of water, of cliffs, of woods, and plantations.[13]

Trees frame a vista of woods and fields rising to the horizon from the west front. The design seems less symmetrical than it really is because Washington matched trees in a mixture of species with varying tones and textures along the serpentine paths on either side of the Bowling Green.

The house, as landscaped by Washington, commands noble prospects from both sides. To the southeast—the view from the piazza—it overlooks the Potomac and the Maryland shore beyond; to the northwest—the view from the front door—it looks out to far away hills and woods. Was this the view he was creating when he "began to open Vistas throu the Pine grove on the Banks of H.[ell] Hole" in March of 1785? That it was important to his scheme is clear from his acknowledgment of the plan of Mount Vernon made and given him by Samuel Vaughan in 1787. He congratulates Vaughan, an English admirer on having

> described with accuracy the house, walk and shrubs except in front of the Lawn, west of the Ct. Yard. There the plan differs from the original; in the former you have closed the prospect with trees along the walk to the gate, whereas in the latter the trees terminate with the two mounds of earth on each side of which grow Weeping Willows leaving an open and full view of the distant woods. I mention this because it is the only departure from the original.[14]

If he extended his vistas to the horizon on both sides, Washington organized their foreground landscapes rather differently. On the western, entrance side the layout is symmetrical, and a very successful integration of carriage drive, plantation street, stableyard, and walled vegetable and flower gardens—the indispensable utilities of plantation life—with the lawns and shady walks of the pleasure grounds.

He arranged the approach from the Alexandria road so that the house was first visible in the distance, then disappeared from sight until horseman or carriage reached the West Gate. Then, after winding through groves of trees, the drive arrived at the bottom of the bowling green. From here a visitor could leave the carriage and walk to the house. For those who chose to continue on horseback or in a carriage the road looped around to the south and the house was again concealed until the visitor reached the stable road and the oval lawn before the front door. Visitors today, who walk straight up to the house, have less opportunity to appreciate Washington's artistry in combining the dignity that an architecturally balanced entrance layout conveys with the magnetism that comes with the landscape style's tantalizing succession of vistas.

The broad walks from the house to the gate, although precisely drawn in mirror image, are serpentine not straight—Washington had indeed studied his Batty Langley. They form a dignified approach without the stiffness of architectural-style allées. As planted, with a mixture of evergreen and deciduous trees on the lawn side, and on the other, what the eighteenth century would call a "shrubbery" of flowering trees and shrubs, these walks appear much more ordered in plan and from the air than they do when you move along them.

Contemporary observers characterized the walled gardens as neat and laid out in squares, the traditional plan. Washington also laid out walks in "the Wilderness and Shrubberies" which must have been delightful in May when

"The blossom of the Crab tree is unfolding, and shedding its fragrant perfume," The profusion of flowering shrubs that Washington collected to fill these sunny spaces was practical as well as ornamental: it helped to screen the sight and sound of plantation activities from family and visitors in the pleasure grounds.

On the river side, the grounds are laid out with the artless-seeming art of the mature landscape style. A broad lawn, protected from horses, cattle, and deer by ha-has (sunken fences) on both sides, sweeps from the piazza to the brow of the bluff. Trees and shrubs planted on the slope below form a low and irregular border to the Potomac in the middle distance and the shore beyond. One would think that the grounds on this side of the house were developed later; but this does not seem to be the case. The creation of the bowling green and serpentine walks, which apparently reflect design ideas from earlier in the century, is described in the diaries for 1785 and 1786. Yet in a 1776 letter to his cousin and estate manager Washington specifically requests an informal arrangement of the groves north and south of the house on the river side.

> …these Trees to be Planted without any order or regularity (but pretty thick, as they can at any time be thin'd) and to consist that at the North end, of locusts altogether. and that at the South, of all the clever kind of Trees (especially flowering ones) that can be got … these to be interspersed here and there with ever greens … to these may be added the Wild flowering Shrubs of the larger kind"[15]

Most of the trees and shrubs in his planting list were natives and the diaries show that Washington was always on the lookout for likely specimens as he rode around his plantations. But, like Jefferson and indeed most eighteenth-century gardeners, he was willing to try any plant from any part of the world, useful or ornamental, that might suit the soil and climate of Mount Vernon. The recently introduced weeping willow was a particular favorite. He maintained a "botanical garden" to try out seeds and plants sent by admirers from Europe, the Orient and other parts of this country, and visited nurseries as well as private gardens when he traveled. He was not always impressed with the former, chastising Bartram for inept design and disappointed by Long Island's Prince Nursery:

> These gardens, except in the number of young fruit trees, did not answer my expectations. The shrubs were trifling, and the flowers not numerous.[16]

It was a Hudson Valley nurseryman, Andrew Jackson Downing, who would become this country's first gardening tastemaker and secure truly national popularity for "modern gardening," that is, the natural style, in the early nineteenth century. Little remains of the gardens that Downing designed, but one estate that he very much admired and often wrote about has survived to show how the vista garden was interpreted in his day.

Opposite, top:
The two-story piazza or gallery—Washington called it both—shelters the interiors from the strong eastern sun and provides a cool space to sit in the afternoon and look at the river and the Maryland shore beyond the serene foreground landscape, a sloping tree-fringed lawn.

Opposite, bottom:
Flowers dominate this view of the Upper Garden, one of the two walled gardens screened from the Bowling Green by trees. Some early visitors called it a flower garden; but today it contains a more likely-for-the-period mix of fruit trees, herbs, vegetables, and flowers.

The Hudson River Valley has long been praised for the beauty of its views, and Montgomery Place enjoys one of the most splendid. The mansion, set on a high west-facing ridge, looks across the river to the Catskills, which that valley native, Andrew Jackson Downing, found "more beautiful than any mountain scenery in the middle States."

Opposite, below:
The estate began as a farm, purchased in 1802 by Janet Livingston Montgomery, which the family members who inherited it developed into much-praised pleasure grounds. To the west the land descends to the Hudson in gently graded but irregular slopes; to the north it declines precipitously through dense woodlands to the valley of the Saw Kill.

Above:
The most famous image of Montgomery Place depicts the North Portico, painted by Alexander Jackson Davis, the architect who designed it, in his first remodeling of the Federal-style mansion. Davis's imaginative outdoor room provided a cool and breezy space from which to enjoy summer sunsets.

MONTGOMERY PLACE

Montgomery Place, just north of Rhinebeck, on the east bank of the Hudson River began its transformation from farm to estate in 1802, when it was bought by Janet Livingston Montgomery, the widow of a Revolutionary War hero and a member of one of the valley's great landowning families. It descended in the same family until 1986, when it was acquired by Historic Hudson Valley, which is in the process of restoring it. The family, it appears, never threw anything away, thus providing documentation to delight a historian. Jacquetta M. Haley has brought to light the fact that Mrs. Montgomery not only continued to operate the commercial orchard already on the land but also started a commercial nursery in partnership with one James McWilliams in 1804 while she was building her Federal-style house and remodeling her landscape.[17] Montgomery Place, then, was from the beginning a working and at least partially self-supporting estate rather than a country retreat for someone whose work and whose money lay "in the crowded and busy haunts of men." It still is. But Downing's praise of the location's "accessible perfect seclusion" already foretells the way of the future.

Mrs. Montgomery, and in succession her brother Edward Livingston, his wife, daughter, and son-in-law, all had a hand in creating the country seat that Downing characterized in the 1849 edition of *A Treatise on the Theory and Practice of Landscape Gardening* as "nowhere surpassed in America, in point of location, natural beauty, or the landscape gardening charms which it exhibits." Two years earlier he had published a more detailed description in *The Horticulturist and Journal of Rural Art and Rural Taste*. Even if the rustic bridges, pavilions, and seats have long since vanished and the grounds probably can never be returned completely to their 1840s appearance, Downing's account, and Alexander Jackson Davis's accompanying illustrations, serve surprisingly well as a guide to the landscape of Montgomery Place. As one approaches from the land or east side, farm buildings and cottages — pleasant enough in appearance but not truly integrated into the design — and acres of orchards border the River Road.

Here is the entrance gate, and from it leads a long and stately avenue of trees, like the approach to an old

1. Entrance drive
2. Coach house
3. Mansion
4. Lake
5. Sawkill Cascades
6. Rough Garden
7. Ellipse
8. Herb and Flower Gardens

PLATE 2

Above:
Davis also painted the west front of the house from a path along the shore that Downing called the Morning Walk, in addition to the other illustrations that were engraved for Downing's lengthy description of the landscape in the October 1847 issue of *The Horticulturist.*

Below:
The lake formed by damming the Saw Kill seems much smaller today than as shown in this engraving after A. J. Davis. If he didn't exaggerate the size, it has simply silted up. The little temple has vanished, as have most of the ornamental structures that once dotted the landscape.

French chateau. Halfway up its length, the lines of planted trees give place to a tall wood, and this again is succeeded by the lawn, which opens in all its stately dignity, with increased effect, after the deeper shadows of this vestibule-like wood.[18]

Time has left gaps in the avenue, but the effect is as described, particularly if you walk; at automobile speed the wood barely has a chance to register. In Downing's day when you looked back at the East Lawn from the house you saw the Gothick Conservatory, the Flower Garden's "Bright parterres of brilliant flowers" and beyond them, the Arboretum. Only a few trees remain from the Arboretum, conservatory and garden are gone — probably too expensive to replace — and were when Charles Eliot visited Montgomery Place around 1889. For him, "from the point of view of design and general effect the substitution of the existing simple but well-framed lawn in place of the old garden and conservatory is by no means to be regretted."[19] The layout of the principal vista west across the Hudson remains much as Downing described it:

> …a large lawn waving in undulations of soft verdure, varied with fine groups, and margined with rich belts of foliage. Its base is washed by the river, which is here a broad sheet of water lying like a long lake beneath the eye. Wooded banks stretch along its margin … On the opposite shores, more than a mile distant, is seen a rich mingling of woods and cornfields. But the crowning glory of the landscape is the background of mountains. The Kaatskills, as seen from this part of the Hudson, are, it seems to us, more beautiful than any mountain scenery in the middle States.

"Characterized by simple, easy, and flowing lines" the grounds west of the house are a perfect example of what Downing meant by the beautiful in landscape design. He was even more enthusiastic about the parts of the estate that epitomized his definition of the picturesque and devoted considerably more space to them. There was the Morning Walk along the river:

> Deeply shaded, winding along the thickly wooded bank, with the refreshing sound of the tide-waves gently dashing against the rocky shores below, or expending themselves on the beach of gray gravel, it curves along the bank for a great distance. Sometimes overhanging cliffs, crested with pines, frown darkly over it; sometimes thick tufts of fern and mossy-carpeted rocks border it, while at various points, vistas or long reaches of the beautiful river scenery burst upon the eye.

"A feast of wonders to the lovers of the picturesque" was the Wilderness, the deeply wooded valley of the Saw Kill, with its rushing stream, cascades, and lake, that forms the northern boundary of the estate. Unlike the wildernesses in eighteenth-century landscape designs, which were deliberately if informally planted collections of small trees and shrubs, the Wilderness at Montgomery Place was truly native forest threaded with walks and embellished with native plants.

Rustic seats placed at strategic points along the Morning Walk and the Wilderness trails invited visitors to linger and were, Downing felt, important to the full enjoyment of "the natural charms of the locality." Downing, Davis, and indeed most nineteenth-century landscape designers were very concerned that garden structures, useful and ornamental, be suitable to the character of the landscape. Bridges, benches, and pavilions of bark-covered logs with thatched or mossy roofs were considered appropriate for the picturesque. The beautiful, on the other hand, called for just such a building as the pavilion "in the style of an Italian arcade" designed by Davis as the open-air north wing of the house.

Montgomery Place is not just large enough to support a harmonious combination of beautiful and picturesque landscapes in the natural style; it has absorbed with equanimity a series of gardens—the Rough Garden, the Ellipse, the Herb and Flower Garden—created in the 1920s and 30s by Violetta White Delafield, the wife of the owner, General John Ross Delafield, which have recently been restored.

Americans never seem to lose their appetite for vistas. Even today it is the high floors that command the high prices in New York skyscrapers and in J. B. Jackson's "imaginary average small town," Optimo City:

> Up on the heights beyond the Courthouse Square is the very finest part of Optimo. The northwestern section of town, with its tree-shaded streets, its view over the river and the prairie, its summer breezes, has always been identified with wealth and fashion as Optimo understands them.[20]

In his 1850 compilation of periodical articles from the previous decade, *The Western Farmer and Gardener*, E. J. Hooper maintained that:

> One of the principal features in this country is in laying out grounds attached to mansions built on knolls or high grounds; these are generally taken from land in its virgin state, and the object is an extensive view or landscape in connexion with a healthy location... perhaps no country in the world possesses better sites for residences of this kind than America.[21]

Few of these extensive view-directed landscape gardens still exist, and the reason why is clearly indicated in H. W. S. Cleveland's rather defeatist advice to his fellow practitioners a quarter century later in *Landscape Architecture as Applied to the Wants of the West* that when designing private estates one should make provision for subsequent subdivision and for possible changes in the character of the neighborhood.

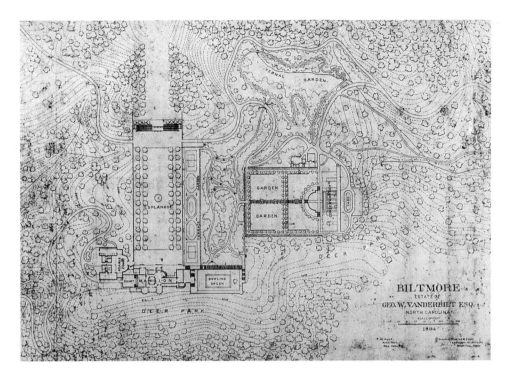

BILTMORE ESTATE

As Downing had foreseen in the 1830s, American dislike of primogeniture as a mode of inheritance would prevent the continuing development of large private estates by many generations of a family except in very rare instances. Add to this the progressive income tax, which he had not foreseen, and it is not surprising that few large-scale vista gardens have remained in private hands for more than a generation or two. Most that still exist have become public gardens.

This is really the case with Biltmore Estate, Frederick Law Olmsted's masterpiece in Asheville, North Carolina. Although it is still owned by the descendants of George Washington Vanderbilt, for whom it was designed, it is today, by economic necessity, managed as a public attraction with uncommon sensitivity to the spirit of its design.

It was the view from the bluff on which the house now stands that inspired Vanderbilt to buy his first 2,000 acres of cut-over, worn out farmland. In 1888 he asked Olmsted, who had long known his family, to look at the property and advise him on its development. Given the poor quality of the existing soil and trees, Olmsted replied:

> My advice would be to make a small park into which to look from your house; make a small pleasure ground and garden, farm your river bottom chiefly to keep and fatten livestock with a view to manure; and make the rest a forest, improving the existing woods and planting the old fields.[22]

For Olmsted, the creation of a forest had both private and public value. Managed for the production of timber it would be a good long-term investment for Vanderbilt. And in the proper hands it could become the first scientifically managed

The close-packed contour lines on this 1894 plan show clearly the mountainous character of the landscape at Biltmore Estate. This helped Olmsted isolate from the naturalistic composition he preferred the architectonic spaces called for by the architecture of the house and the requirements of the Walled Garden/Conservatory complex.

forest in the United States, an exemplary public service to both private and governmental owners. In following Olmsted's suggestion, Vanderbilt not only expanded the estate to 125,000 acres, but by hiring Gifford Pinchot, just back from European training in forest management, he launched the career of the man who would become the first head of the U.S. Forest Service. Pinchot's successor founded the Biltmore Forest School, the first of its kind in this country.

Olmsted's design for the pleasure grounds is a virtuoso composition of views, vast and intimate, displayed and withheld, architectural, pastoral and picturesque. For almost three miles the Approach Road winds upward through

Opposite:
From the air one can see how the gardens evolved from geometric to naturalistic as they gained distance from the house, and also the vista of river valley and distant mountains that inspired George W. Vanderbilt to buy the property, and that can be seen at ground level only from inside the house or from the South Terrace.

ravines clothed with native forest, enriched in Olmsted's day by exotic broad-leafed evergreens, many of them Japanese, to form a rich and intricate tapestry of textures. At every turn the scene changes, but the house remains invisible even though the planting is less dense than it originally was. Then in his words,

> the visitor passes with an abrupt transition into the enclosure of the trim, level, open, airy, spacious, thoroughly artificial Court, and the Residence, with its orderly dependencies, breaks suddenly and fully upon him. [23]

That residence, Richard Morris Hunt's 250-room evocation of a French Renaissance Château, clearly demanded an architectural landscape setting. Although such a design was not typical of Olmsted's work, he could produce one where he felt it was needed. He was well acquainted with the great French landscape gardens, and the Esplanade at Biltmore demonstrates how well he had understood Le Nôtre's art. Its surprise presentation is also testimony, as Charles Beveridge, editor of the Olmsted Papers, points out, to his belief that different styles of landscape design should be kept strictly separate.

Above:
The surprise at the end of the winding wooded Approach Road: trees and shrubs are held at bay by the sphinx-topped piers and gilded iron palisades, marking the formal entrance court. At left is the *Rampe Douce*, a structure of interlacing ramps in grand French style, between the Esplanade and the rising *tapis vert*.

From the slope above the *Rampe Douce* tulip tree allées flanking the Esplanade form a properly dignified approach to Biltmore House and conceal both the stable complex to its right and the principal view.

To the left as the visitor enters the "Court" is a high limestone wall pierced with fountain-filled niches and zigzagged with easy-to-walk ramps: a structure called the *Rampe Douce*. To the right, straight drives shaded on the outside by double files of tulip trees flank a rectangular lawn leading to the house. The trees conceal the distant mountains, and the vista back from the front door over the lawn and its low circular pool is a carefully contrived perspective of turf and trees rising to the east above the *Rampe Douce*.

The view that entranced Vanderbilt is only visible after one enters the house, or walks around it to the South Terrace, an extension of the foundation almost as large as the footprint of the house. From the terrace and its corner tea house the vista over the Deer Park to the lagoon and beyond to the mountains is breathtaking. But there was more on Olmsted's mind than vista when he persuaded Hunt and Vanderbilt to build such a terrace.

Attractive open-air apartments, so formed that they can be often occupied for hours at a time, with conven-

ience and ease in every respect, without the interruption of ordinary occupations or difficulty of conversation, are in deed indispensable in the present state of society to the preservation of health and cheerfulness in families otherwise living in luxury.[24]

Where the land sloped down south of the Esplanade, Olmsted laid out a French-inspired architectural terrace with shaped, stone-bordered pools set in turf. The panel of lawn nearest the house was used for lawn games, and benches sheltered by wisteria arbors along the north wall offered comfortable seating.[25]

On the next level down, sloping beds of shrubs and trees and patches of lawn form an irregular mosaic laced with serpentine paths. Sheltered on three sides, the Ramble or Shrub Garden was planned and planted to give the owners and their guests a pleasant place to walk out of the wind all year. It was intended to begin a progression of increasingly informal spaces as one moved away from the house, and from its east end a path led to a far more naturalistic space. The path

and progression still exist, but most visitors first visit the Walled Garden on the land directly below the Shrub Garden.

This square four-acre garden with its four-square beds, straight herbaceous borders, and Conservatory was originally designed not as one of the pleasure gardens but as part of the estate support system, supplying fruits, vegetables, and flowers for the household. Vanderbilt, however, wanted an ornamental garden, so the Walled Garden became primarily a flower garden, although the central grape arbor was kept.

There is a path to the bottom of the Vernal or Spring Garden from the Conservatory area of the Walled Garden, but to experience the succession of garden spaces as Olmsted planned them one should return to the Shrub Garden and take the path that leads east under a brick arch. Paths then lead down the slopes on both sides of a sheltered valley, colored in spring by forsythia, spireas, dogwoods, and redbuds, cool and green the rest of the year. From this valley paths descend to the roughly fifteen-acre Glen, a network of paths wandering through groves of trees and shrubs, along a

brook, and around wildflower meadows. It is now called the Azalea Garden and contains the native azaleas collected and given to Biltmore by Chauncey Beadle, who was hired in 1890 to oversee Biltmore's nursery, and eventually became superintendent of the estate, a post he held until his death in 1950. It is considered, according to William E. Alexander, Biltmore Estate's Landscape and Forest Historian, one of the most complete such collections in existence.

The early twentieth century saw a few more private estates composed at least in part around the view to the horizon; but from the last third of the nineteenth century onward Americans began to slake their thirst for vast vistas by creating State or National Parks to preserve the greatest ones of all—the Yosemite Valley, the Grand Canyon, Niagara Falls, the Adirondacks, the Great Smokies, the Badlands of South Dakota, and the Tetons of Wyoming.

In the Shrub Garden, paths wind through beds planted with shrubs, small trees and ground covers. Lawns and large trees play minor roles in this sheltered garden, which provides a continuous succession of color from spring through autumn.

Wilderness as Obstacle, Resource, Inspiration

The wilderness and the garden: the land as far as possible unaltered by the human hand and the land worked by the human hand into a form envisioned by the human mind. Symbols of two different attitudes toward the land, but not so opposed as one might think. Stewardship can encompass preservation and cultivation alike. The true conflict is with land seen solely as a producer of monetary profit, an attitude that often leads to short-sighted, slash-burn-and-strip exploitation. Alas, stewardship of the land is not a quality for which Americans are renowned, perhaps just because our land for so long seemed so big, even endless; so powerful, even fearsome. Yet, from the first European contacts, there have been those who saw the wilderness as an Eden to care for, and its defenders have often used the image of the garden to communicate its beauty, none more rapturously than John Muir in his essay "The Forests of Oregon":

> Around the great fire mountains, above the forests and beneath the snow, there is a flowery zone of marvelous beauty planted with anemones, erythroniums, daisies, bryanthus, kalmia, vaccinium, cassiope, saxifrages, etc., forming one continuous garden fifty or sixty miles in circumference, and it is so deep and luxuriant and closely woven it seems as if Nature, glad to find an opening, were economizing space and trying to see how many of her bright-eyed darlings she can get together in one mountain wreath.[1]

Similar images are woven through sixteenth- and seventeenth-century descriptions of the North American continent. Approaching the coast of North Carolina on the second of July in 1584, Captain Arthur Barlowe and his crew

> . . . smelt so sweet, and so strong a smel, as if we had bene in the midst of some delicate garden abounding with all kind of odiferous flowers, by which we were assured, that the land could not be farre distant.[2]

On the shore were grapes in such profusion "that I thinke in all the world the like abundance is not to be found," Barlowe reported to Sir Walter Raleigh.

But did the wild, spontaneous gardens of the North American landscape inspire or affect the kinds of gardens that would be created by Europeans? Early on, the wilderness certainly seems to have been viewed as something to shut out rather than welcome in, although individual plants might be hospitably received. Not all early explorers and settlers, probably not even the majority, saw the untamed landscape as a paradise. Reactions seem to have been somewhat contingent on the season of arrival. Cape Cod in November of 1620 was a very different proposition for William Bradford and his fellow Pilgrims:

> [W]hat could they see but a hideous and desolate wilderness, full of wild beasts and wild men? . . . which

way soever they turned their eyes (save upward to the heavens) they could have little solace or content in respect of any outward objects. For summer being done, all things stand upon them with a weatherbeaten face; and the whole country, full of woods and thickets, represented a wild and savage hue.[3]

John Winthrop and his better-prepared expedition reached Massachusetts in the spring, and his initial reaction was almost the same as Barlowe's, although it was the abundance of strawberries rather than grapes that impressed him.

Whether or not New England smelled like a garden, Winthrop and the Puritans, like the Pilgrims before them, had firmly fixed in their minds before they left England that they were going to find a "howling wilderness" and find it to their satisfaction they did. As self-consciously moral human beings bent on creating an exemplary and Godly society, they had to believe they were coming to unimproved land, which they would "subdue and make fruitful" according to the Lord's command. That the land was far from barren and untouched by human hands by the time they arrived on its shores they never seem to have recognized. Mostly they ignored, consciously or unconsciously, the evidence that the so-called savages did, in fact, have a successful system of crop-raising, and of game and forest management. Men like William Wood and Edward Johnson faithfully recorded Indian agricultural customs, but stopped short of acknowledging that these were as effective for the Indians' purposes as European ones were for theirs. Those purposes were very different; mutual incomprehension was total.

The Indians expected the land to produce sufficient food to meet their needs with enough surplus to serve as insurance against possible crop failures or shortages of game. While tribes or villages claimed territories, these were essentially political divisions. The idea that they could be sold for the exclusive use of a foreigner was as unimaginable to them as the idea that we could sell Long Island to another country to reduce the national debt would be to us! The Europeans, accustomed for centuries to land ownership as the source of money and power for church, state, and individual, expected the land to produce wealth. Satisfying basic needs was just the beginning; what was really wanted were commodities to sell or trade: what was under the land, or on it, or what it could be made to produce, or the land itself. Indians could not understand the English need for enclosure and title. The English could not—or did not want to—understand the environmental accomodations of Indian agriculture; in their eyes it did not wring maximum fruitfulness from the land.

Recreating the kind of agriculture, stock-raising, and horticulture that the settlers remembered and felt at home with was no easy task in New England's capricious climate and stubborn rocky soil. Nor was Virginia, in spite of its milder climate, much more hospitable to English farming practices. To compound the problem, many of the first colonists were artisans, merchants, and younger sons of aristocratic families

with little or no agricultural experience. Success came sooner in the middle colonies—New York, New Jersey, Pennsylvania—which had a greater percentage of experienced farmers among their settlers.

In addition, all the colonists were under continuous pressure to produce profits for the homeland investors who were financing the settlements but did not have very realistic ideas about the difficulties the settlers faced. No wonder most seventeenth-century adjectives for wilderness were pessimistic and pejorative.

Nature's garden to some, "daunting terrible" to others, and often both to the same person at different times, the American wilderness has elicited a mass of conflicting responses both as reality and as symbol. To the refugee from persecution or from poverty, and to the adventuring frontiersman it represented opportunity—a place to build a new society, a chance to start over—and at the same time danger—from savages and storms, wild beasts and new diseases. It was an obstacle: The forests were vast and difficult to break through, the plains seemed endless, the mountains forbidding, and the land, however fertile, required hard labor to clear and plow and plant. It was a resource of endless abundance to be exploited for minerals and fuel, for timber and furs, for food, medicine, and cash crops—corn, sassafras, tobacco, and ginseng. Yet there were those who did not see much profit in its vegetative bounty. One English explorer,

Ralph Lane, after a hazardous inland expedition from Roanoake in 1586, is convinced

> . . . that the discovery of a good Mine, by the goodnesse of God, or a passage to the South-sea, or some way to it, and nothing els can bring this Countrey in request to be inhabited by our nation . . . then will Sassafras, and many other rootes and gummes there found make good marchandise and lading for shipping, which otherwise of themselves will not be worth the fetching.[4]

Negative or positive, motivated by the need for survival or the hope for riches, early attitudes to the wilderness were overwhelmingly utilitarian, not surprising in an age that still believed unquestioningly that the world had been created for the benefit of man. Utilitarian attitudes die hard. Ask any conservationist.

Almost all of the American plants listed in the seventeenth-century English herbals are there because they are useful as food or medicine. Corn, beans, squash, and tobacco, as well as Virginia strawberries and persimmons, were soon sent to England. Settlers noted the plants the Indians used for healing, tried them out, and sent them home as well.

All through the eighteenth and most of the nineteenth century, naturalists, European and American, professional and amateur, roamed the mountains and valleys, forests and prairies, and even the deserts in search of new plants, and

By the time *Picturesque America* was published in 1894 tangled forests like these that J. M. Hunt depicted in the Adirondacks were considered scenic wonders. For early settlers they had just been obstacles.

The Western plains seemed not just trackless but endless and pioneers could never be sure how native inhabitants would greet them. Worthington Whittredge seems to have found a peaceable and friendly tribe.

those primarily for ornamental purposes. Whatever their background or training, they were above all observers, and they observed everything that their paths crossed: animals, Indian customs, soil composition, rocks, weather, waterfalls, and archaeological curiosities. What their efforts contributed to American gardens was eventually of major importance, but ironically, their discoveries were at first much more appreciated in Europe. While gardeners and garden-makers, botanists and botanic gardens, nurserymen and seedsmen begged Americans for native seeds and plants or sent their own plant collectors, Americans usually ordered from Europe and planted the seeds and bulbs, trees and shrubs that had furnished the gardens of their nostalgia. As the Philadelphia nurseryman Bernard McMahon wrote in his book of 1806:

> Here I cannot avoid remarking that many flower gardens, &c., are almost destitute of bloom during a great part of the season; which could be easily avoided . . . by introducing from our woods and fields the various beautiful ornaments with which nature has so profusely decorated them. Is it because they are indigenous that we should reject them? Ought we not rather to cultivate and improve them? . . . In Europe, plants are not rejected because they are indigenous; on the contrary, they are cultivated with due care; and yet here we cultivate many foreign trifles, and neglect the profusion of beauties so bountifully bestowed upon us by the hand of nature.[5]

McMahon's complaint was not new when he wrote it at the beginning of the nineteenth century, and it has been repeated right up to the present day. Yet it is hard to visualize a perennial border without phlox in summer or Michaelmas daisies in autumn, indigenous Americans both, even if they did go to finishing school in Europe. A good half of the flowers in Gertrude Jekyll's schemes for August and September borders originated on this side of the Atlantic, most in North America, a few below the equator.

Not surprisingly, the improvement and breeding of purely ornamental plants came rather low on the list of priorities in the new republic. The situation got better as the nineteenth century moved on, with hybridization encouraged by the horticultural societies, but even as late as 1880, judging from *Vick's Monthly Magazine*, American seedsmen and nurserymen tended to concentrate on developing improved fruits and vegetables, and to buy new varieties of flower seeds and bulbs from British and European sources.

This is not to say that the flora of the United States has lacked enthusiasts. If they have not been as plentiful as the indifferent, protectors have invariably come forth to restrain destroyers. Lady Jean Skipwith planted wild flowers in her garden at Prestwould in Virginia, Washington assiduously collected native shrubs and trees for his landscaping, and Jefferson's interest in and care of the plants gathered by Lewis and Clark are well known. The Reverend John Frederick Schroeder's exhortation to the Horticultural Society of New York in 1828 could have been spoken today:

Another object, far more interesting, invites your care. It is *the preservation and the culture of plants indigenous to our soil*. They are confided to your guardianship. But look around you; see them perishing in multitudes beneath the ploughshare and the axe. Certain species and varieties, which in old time adorned the verdant mantle of the earth, are to be found no longer. . . . We might find within this native circle, when possessed of suitable advantages for their *improvement*, the rarest and most estimable qualities, to please and benefit mankind.[6]

Protectors today would urge us to leave wild plants in the wild; but this is still a matter for debate, and indiscriminate collecting for quick commercial profit is a very different thing than collecting for propagation. Had the botanist John Bartram not carried back to his nursery cuttings of the tree he found at the mouth of the Altamaha river in Georgia and named *Franklinia alatamaha*, we would no longer have the late-summer blossoms and brilliant fall color of this highly ornamental native. It was never again seen in the wild after 1803.

The very abundance of the American wilderness suggests an explanation for the apparent lack of interest in native plants — and perhaps also for the native Indians' seeming indifference to ornamental gardening. When that wilderness is close at hand, just beyond the garden fence, and the uncultivated land offers carpets of strawberries in spring and more raspberries and blackberries than you can possibly eat in summer, why bother to cultivate them in the garden? As might be predicted, lists of the fruits grown in early American gardens almost never include strawberries, raspberries, or blackberries. When the hillside across the road is pink with mountain laurel or gold with California poppies, and you can easily cut as much as you like to fill your vases without diminishing Nature's spectacle, you save your garden soil and sweat for the useful, the rare, or the nostalgic. The pioneer point of view, both practical and appreciative, comes to life in *Land of the Crooked Tree*, U. P. Hedrick's account of growing up on a farm wrested from the forests of northern Michigan. His father was a dedicated and tireless gardener, but "Father's garden was wholly utilitarian. In it he grew plants to furnish food the year around and to add to our small supply of cash," according to the son, who was to become a great horticulturalist and horticultural historian.

We never had a flower garden on our farm in the early years. The best gardener in the world could not compete with Nature's gardens in the forest all about us . . . Even my prosaic father, when he walked in the woods, kept eyes and nose at attention for the beauty and fragrance of the good earth. . . . A favorite flower in our forests was *Trillium grandiflorum*, the great-flowered white trillium. It was as thick in our woods as quills in a porcupine's tail. . . . In Round Lake, a few miles from our farm, was a water-lily garden with which no planted garden of this flower in all the world could compete. The lake, more than a mile in diameter, was completely covered with the pinkish-white richly scented lily-like flowers, three inches in diameter, gloriously beautiful as a breeze rippled the sun-spangled pond. . . .[7]

Such scenes could be found all across the country. Archibald Menzies was dazzled by drifts of red valerian along the coast of what is now the state of Washington; whole hills and valleys "dressed in bloom" cheered Sarah Bayliss Royce's spring in an otherwise bleak mining camp on the California gold rush frontier;[8] and Fredrika Bremer was enraptured by her first sight of the tall grass prairie.

There in that brilliant light, stretched itself far, far out into the infinite, as far as the eye could discern, an ocean-like extent, the waves of which were sunflowers, asters and gentians. It was a really great and glorious sight; to my feeling less common and grander than Niagara.[9]

But did these fields of flowers provide a distinctive motif to the designers of American gardens then or now? In recent years, most definitely yes. And at every level. Think of the mail-order meadows in tins. There is some evidence that they did in the past as well, but it is not conclusive. Ann MacVicar Grant, describing the Albany gardens of her late eighteenth-century youth, offers the provocative observation that:

These fair gardeners too were great florists: their emulation and solicitude in this pleasing employment, did indeed produce "flowers worthy of Paradise." These, though not set in "curious knots," were ranged in beds, the varieties of each kind by themselves; this, if not varied and elegant, was at least rich and gay.[10]

Of all the mountain ranges westward-moving Americans would encounter the Rockies were the most intimidating; but images painted by Thomas Moran and others helped inspire the creation of national parks.

Lower left:
Jens Jensen was enchanted by
calm, slow-moving prairie
rivers like the Sangamon in
Illinois and found in them the
inspiration for a characteristic
feature that he often included
in designs for both private
gardens and public parks.

Lower right:
The "prairie river" on an
estate near Chicago designed
by Jensen is a pond, not a
river but its resemblance to
the real thing is uncanny.

Liberty Hyde Bailey's 1902 advice was unequivocal:

> What I want to say is that we should grow flowers when
> we make a flower-garden. Have enough of them to
> make it worth the effort. I sympathize with the man who
> likes sunflowers. There is enough of them to be worth
> looking at. They fill the eye. Now show this man ten
> square feet of pinks, or asters, or daisies, all growing free
> and easy, and he will tell you that he likes them.[11]

Some American garden-makers certainly have shared
Bailey's point of view. One can think of the swaths of brilliant
red and rose azaleas at Magnolia, near Charleston, the
prairie landscapist Jens Jensen's carpets of violets, and Beatrix
Farrand's hillside of forsythia at Dumbarton Oaks. In 1917
a Mr. Pifer who won a garden contest in Williamsport,
Pennsylvania, with a first-year garden of annuals that included a hundred-and-forty-foot-long front border consisting of
triple rows of six-foot-tall cosmos in pink, garnet, and white,
testified that:

> I am led to believe that whatever success my garden
> achieved was due to the fact that massed effects were
> used and that the flowers were grown in such
> profusion.[12]

European precedents for such opulent planting did exist:
England's "host of golden daffodils" and bluebell woods, if
originally a sample of Nature's largesse, became carefully
planned and cosseted effects in large gardens.

The one-color garden, planted with a variety of species
but all in tones of a single hue, is a notion usually credited to
the garden designer Gertrude Jekyll; but when, in her first
book, *Wood and Garden*, 1899, she describes a parterre
planted in tones of yellow and orange that she had seen
many years before, or discusses the subject more extensively
in *Colour Schemes for the Flower Garden* in 1908, she does
not claim originality: "occasionally I hear of a garden for blue
plants, or a white garden." The earliest descriptions of such
gardens in this country may be those of the American antiquarian and writer, Alice Morse Earle. In *Old Time Gardens*,
published in 1901, she devoted a chapter to "The Blue
Border" and in it mentions other single-color gardens, suggesting the idea as more suited to the small garden. She
begins another chapter, "The Moonlight Garden," with the
description of a white garden at Indian Hill in Newburyport,
Massachusetts, which seems to have been planted a generation before. The publication dates of the two books are close,
and Earle was an attentive but by no means submissive reader of Jekyll's first book, so perhaps one-color gardens were a
fashionable idea at that period on both sides of the Atlantic.

Or, perhaps all human beings like a sweep of color that fills the eye, at least once in a while.

Just as the European plantsmen were the first to appreciate the ornamental and edible riches to be found in the American wilderness, so were European travelers the first to see that wilderness as a source of inspiration. Niagara Falls was a magnet even in the pre-Rousseauian eighteenth century. No sooner had the country settled down after the revolution than the site was invaded by what seems a horde of memoir-writing tourists seeking wild romantic scenery and noble savages, their enthusiasm for the wilderness undampened by the difficulties of trying to make a living from it. That quintessential romantic, the writer François René de Chateaubriand, who traveled to America in 1791, asked

> Who can tell the feeling one has on entering these forests as old as the world, which alone give the idea of creation as it left the hands of God? The daylight, falling from on high through a veil of foliage, spreads through the depths of the woods a changing and mobile half-light which gives fantastic size to things. Everywhere we must climb over fallen trees, above which rise new generations of trees. In vain I seek some outlet from this solitude . . . the eye sees only trunks of oaks and walnuts which follow one upon another and seem to come closer together as they recede into the distance. I become aware of the idea of infinity.[13]

Chateaubriand's sensations have the shiver of the sublime. His English contemporary Thomas Ashe, who visited America in 1806, found a more cheerful sort of uplift.

> The peevishness and dissatisfaction, which before possessed me, were now compelled to yield to contrary sensations. The breadth and beauty of the river, the height and grandeur of its banks, the variation of scenery, the verdure of the forests, the murmur of the water, and the melody of birds all conspired to fill my mind with vast and elevated conceptions.[14]

The inspiration these travelers sought and found in the wilderness was of the intellectual or spiritual kind: none of them suggests trying to re-create wild scenes as a source of aesthetic pleasure. When Americans, especially the Transcendentalists, turned the romantic enchantment with wild nature into a philosophy, almost a religion, they too saw contact, generally solitary contact, with the wilderness as the essential source of moral, intellectual, poetic, and spiritual energy that was necessary to maintain the vitality of civilized man in an industrial age. Their rambles were a form of walking meditation. "Cities give not the human senses room enough," said Emerson,[15] but he and his fellow Transcendentalists were country-dwelling intellectuals with one foot in the town. The nature that inspired them was usually within walking distance of the village green. If all of them at one time or another dug in the garden or hoed a bean field, only Bronson Alcott appears to have been a truly enthusiastic gardener. Thoreau preferred nature as it is: "Gardening is civil

and social, but it wants the vigor and freedom of the forest and the outlaw."[16] If he usually seemed more interested in how the wilderness affected him than in the wilderness itself, he was quite aware that:

> There is just as much beauty visible to us in the landscape as we are prepared to appreciate — not a grain more. . . . A man sees only what concerns him. A botanist absorbed in the study of grasses does not distinguish the grandest pasture oaks.[17]

When he chose to observe his surroundings, his observations of both individual plants and landscape effects were vivid:

> Looking across this woodland valley, a quarter of a mile wide, how rich those scarlet oaks embosomed in pines, their bright red branches intimately intermingled with them! They have their full effect there. The pine boughs are the green calyx to their red petals.[18]

By celebrating the beauties of the wilderness and proclaiming its virtues for the civilized, the Transcendentalists in company with novelists like James Fenimore Cooper and Washington Irving, painters like Asher B. Durand, Frederic Edwin Church, and George Inness, and historians like Francis Parkman encouraged their countrymen to look at undeveloped land for what it was rather than what it could be made to produce. Working such a change in attitude was no easy task in a country where land speculation, as modern historians like Bernard Bailyn have shown us, has been the road to fortune from the very beginning. Not all Americans were or are converted; but enough were to set in motion a response to Thoreau's call for wilderness preservation. A generation later, Frederick Law Olmsted and his contemporaries would begin, with Yosemite, to create wilderness national parks, a truly American innovation. Their success was based on the argument that the natural wonders of this continent were cultural resources, the American equivalent of the castles and cathedrals of the Old World. As places of extraordinary beauty and monuments to the greatness of the nation they should be preserved for the inspiration and enjoyment of all people for all time. If asked, the majority of Americans would probably support this argument. Nevertheless, the parks are and always have been under attack from the exploiters, and only constant vigilance on the part of dedicated defenders has so far preserved them.

As young nineteenth-century Americans roamed the forests and climbed the mountains, their increased familiarity with and appreciation of the character of the indigenous landscape also worked a gradual change in the so-called modern or natural style of gardening.

Eighteen years before Thoreau presented the lecture that would be published as "Autumnal Tints," his contemporary, Andrew Jackson Downing, proposed in *A Treatise on the Theory and Practice of Landscape Gardening* an analogous planting scheme, "harmonious and beautiful as the rainbow," which combined the brilliant oranges and reds of the maple, the brownish purple of the ash and the yellow of the

Design inspiration straight from the wilderness: A cascade on the Blackwater River in West Virginia pours over stratified limestone typical of Ohio River Valley geology.

of beautiful scenery, to which his father was particularly sensitive, and to his own ramblings around the New England countryside as to his reading. His assistant and later partner, Charles Eliot, also, according to Eliot's father, "roamed the country roundabout and learnt it by heart."[19] Both Olmsted and Eliot had in addition some experience of English and continental gardens as a basis for comparison before they began their own careers; and both were very concerned that their designs derive from and be suitable to their environment, recognizing as Charles Eliot does in an article called "Anglomania in Park Making" that

> Within the area of the United States we have many types of scenery and many climates, but in designing the surroundings of dwellings, in working upon the landscape, we too often take no account of these facts. On the rocky coast of Maine each summer sees money worse than wasted in endeavoring to make Newport lawns on ground which naturally bears countless lichen-covered rocks, dwarf Pines and Spruces, and thickets of Sweet Fern, Bayberry, and wild Rose. The owners of this particular type of country spend thousands in destroying its natural beauty, with the intention of attaining to a foreign beauty, which, in point of fact, is unattainable in anything like perfection by reason of the shallow soil and the frequent droughts.
>
> I know too many of these unhappy "lawns.". . . the grass is brown and poor wherever the underlying rock is near the surface.
>
> Moreover, if the lawn were perfect and "truly English," would it harmonize with the Pitch Pines and scrub Birches and dwarf Junipers which clothe the lands around? No.[20]

Little by little, as they were able to convince their clients, designers like Olmsted, his son and stepson, and Eliot began to re-create in parks and even in some domestic settings characteristic visual effects from the local environment, and to employ indigenous plant material where it was feasible.

Still more vociferous in their promotion of native plant material were men of the next generation like O. C. Simonds, Jens Jensen, and Alfred Caldwell. These Prairie School landscape designers consciously studied the land around them and drew distinctive elements of their designs from its characteristic forms and flora: Jensen's waterfalls and prairie rivers are a good example.

There were even those like Professor Frank A. Waugh who felt the development of our great natural scenic resources to be "the special task of American landscape gardening." Waugh recognized that the national parks had to be managed to make their beauties accessible to the public, and as managed spaces they were indeed gardens on a very grand scale:

> Then when Niagara Falls and the Great Lakes, Pike's Peak, the Presidential Range, the Arizona desert, and the Father of Waters have received the fullness of scenic development, when they have been made the themes of great and adequate park projects, when they have

sycamore with evergreens like white pine and hemlock to take advantage of that distinctively American phenomenon, autumn foliage color. Like McMahon, Downing lamented America's neglect of its native plants in his magazine, *The Horticulturist*. He urged his readers to look at the land around them for design inspiration and advised them to choose for a country place, if at all possible, a site "naturally well wooded." As a youth he had thoroughly explored the Hudson Valley in both its wild and cultivated parts, and in his discussions of native trees he often noted particularly attractive wild plant combinations. Nature was to be improved by art, however, and as an "improver" he welcomed the introduction of exotic plants. However clear he was that they needed adjustment to American conditions, his design precepts were still stuck in British theory.

In its fundamentals the theory would not change, and successive generations of American landscape designers would read Loudon and Repton, Uvedale Price, and William Gilpin, as well as Downing, to learn the principles of naturalistic landscaping. However, Frederick Law Olmsted, one of Downing's most influential successors, attributed the formation of his vision as much to travels with his parents in search been set forth for human enjoyment, with all the help that art can give to the great achievements of nature, then surely we shall have so much distinctively American landscape architecture.[21]

The wilderness refined as a model for garden design gathered many influential supporters in the early twentieth century, but it was not to sweep all before it. New estate-creating money, even Waugh recognized, was more inclined to look to Europe or the Far East for inspiration, or to try a combination of many models; the small suburban garden got smaller and was increasingly paved over.

In recent years we have come to recognize that wilderness is more than just a source of forms and materials for the landscape designer. As early as 1864 the Vermont-born American diplomat, George Perkins Marsh, after careful study of the effects of human land use in this country and Europe over the course of history, concluded in his *Man and Nature: or, Physical Geography as Modified by Human Action*, that abuse of the environment had been a significant contributor to the downfall of past civilizations. Nature's resources were not unlimited, whatever his fellow countrymen might believe. Natural systems were complex and not really understood; and abused land did not and could not automatically heal itself if abandoned. In particular, he emphasized the effect of forestation on the control of water, and demonstrated that preserving native woodlands could prevent economically disastrous erosion, floods, droughts, and changes in climate.

Intense scientific scrutiny of the environment during the last twenty-five years has taught us a great deal more about the workings of ecosystems, and the costs and benefits of the many different ways we humans intervene in them, locally and globally alike. Environmentally sensitive citizens now realize how finite and fragile the wilderness is, its preserved remnants under pressure from tourists and developers, resource exploiters and industrial polluters, sportsmen and stockmen, and even nature-lovers, by the sheer weight of their numbers. Increasing danger to those remnants has brought increasing vigilance in their defense. Beyond that, it has stimulated greater attention to the potential of the indigenous plants and plant combinations — aesthetic as well as practical potential — for minimizing water, fertilizer, and pesticide use. The once-embattled householder trying to re-create a swatch of midwestern prairie or California chaparral in his suburban yard now often finds support from the local water authority as well as the local native plant society. If more and more garden-makers are trying to wean themselves from the gardener's usual tendency to fall in love with plants that need very different growing conditions from those he can offer, they are also learning that environmental probity does not have to deprive them of all the effects they cherish. Current experiments with the endemic grasses of the short-grass or dryland prairie, for example, may give lawns in dry climates a new lease on respectability.

Nor does environmental sensitivity dictate that designers must choose nature-based forms over architectural ones. The contest between the invented architectonic and the

rearranged natural for the allegiance of the American garden maker still continues, and probably always will. These are, after all, two fundamental approaches to organizing space in a garden and their respective appeals are deeper than the eddies of fashion.

Equally profound is our ambivalence in response to the competing claims of wilderness and civilization, as Alexis de Tocqueville, with his usual acuity, recognized:

It is this consciousness of destruction . . . that gives, we feel, so peculiar a character and such a touching beauty to the solitudes of America. . . . Thoughts of the savage, natural grandeur that is going to come to an end, become mingled with splendid anticipations of the triumphant march of civilisation. One feels proud to be a man, and yet at the same time one experiences I cannot say what bitter regret at the power that God has granted us over nature. One's soul is shaken by contradictory thoughts and feelings, but all the impressions it receives are great and leave a deep mark.[22]

Jensen carefully studied local rock formations before designing pools and cascades, and even experts sometimes find it hard to tell what is a natural formation and what is his construction. A case in point: the waterfall on the estate of K. D. Alexander in Spring Station, Kentucky.

The Picturesque Garden

For nineteenth-century Americans a modern garden was a garden based on Nature's forms and laid out in the firm belief that Nature abhors a straight line. Never mind that the Natural Style's theoretical literature and most influential European models had been created during the previous century, and that a good number of Americans had experimented with the style before the Revolution; on both sides of the Atlantic in the eighteenth century the proponents of naturalistic landscapes were the owners of large estates or the designers who worked for them, both before and after the war for independence. For most people, a garden was still a walled or fenced space divided along geometric lines. The idea of the naturalistic garden seemed a discovery, fresh and exciting, when it was set forth in the horticultural press that grew up in the 1820s as increasing prosperity provided funds and increasing immigration provided labor for garden-making. Particularly so, since this time the propagandists for the new approach directed their message to the middle class.

That message, too, was changing. If the idea of seeking the source of garden design in nature seemed revolutionary, it was also vague in the extreme. What kind of nature were you looking at? Pasture and farmland, or raw forest? Mountains or prairies? Marshes or deserts? Swift waters or placid? Pope's charge to "Consult the Genius of the Place in all" had left the way open to the creation of as many different kinds of nature-based designs as there were specific sites to be shaped into gardens. The next question—What kind of effect did you want to achieve?—was usually answered intuitively by the garden makers, and debated by the critics. The responses, visual and verbal, continued to evolve all through the eighteenth and well into the nineteenth centuries. Many English designers, professional and amateur, let their landscapes speak for them; some, like Repton, also took pen in hand; and a fair number of writers, Wordsworth among them, were both theoretical and practical garden-makers. Theoretical correctness was a serious matter if you believed, as most did in the eighteenth century, that there were truly objective standards of beauty and taste. Debates were heated, and not always polite. From our perspective many of the notions put forward by warring critics seem simply justifications for personal preference; but they did offer organizing principles other than the vista to the horizon for a designed landscape based on idealized natural forms. It is worth a brief look at some of these theories, because, after considerable adaptation to local circumstances, they had a great deal of influence on the way Americans shaped their landscapes, public as well as private. Although there was a certain chronological progression, new models, in real life, did not necessarily drive out the old: Different kinds of gardens were built in the same time span, and a good many garden makers combined ideas from two or three different models.

English landscapers, particularly the amateurs, tended to take their Nature filtered through the eyes of painters. Favorite of the early generations was Claude Lorraine, whose serene and golden Italian landscapes with their pastoral allusions and classical ruins had real appeal for gentlemen brought up on the classics and polished up on the Grand Tour, an appeal to which classically educated Americans were not immune. At one period Jefferson seriously considered embellishing the Monticello landscape with temples and grottoes in the best Claudian manner and Washington hung engravings of Claude's landscapes on the walls of Mount Vernon.

By mid-century several gifted landscape gardeners, or "improvers" as they were often called, had developed a style that depended for its interest on the play of light and shadow on the distilled contours of the English countryside. While an occasional temple or tower was still built to anchor a view, elaborate literary or political messages were less and less part of the program. Then, toward the end of the century, garden critics began to find the flowing lines, smooth lawns, still waters, and tree-framed horizons of these pastoral landscape gardens boring, if beautiful. To stimulate their admiration, a landscape had to offer variety, irregularity, surprise. They invented a category called The Picturesque and distinguished it from both of the accepted sources of aesthetic pleasure: The Beautiful and The Sublime. Some sought inspiration in another seventeenth-century painter, Salvator Rosa, famous for dramatic scenes of rocky mountains and twisted trees, others in what they imagined was Chinese practice. In 1794, the principal theorist of The Picturesque, Sir Uvedale Price, summed up its characteristics:

> I think, however, we may conclude, that where an object, or a set of objects, is without smoothness or grandeur, but from its intricacy, its sudden and irregular deviations, its variety of forms, tint, and lights and shadows, is interesting to a cultivated eye, it is simply picturesque . . ."[1]

The idea of the Picturesque had a special appeal for the increasingly fashionable Romantic outlook, but a landscape — even in a painting — had to appeal to more than the cultivated eye in order to satisfy the Romantic sensibility. It had to touch the emotions. René-Louis de Girardin, friend of Jean-Jacques Rousseau and creator of the Picturesque garden at Ermenonville where the philosopher spent his last days, had already suggested in 1783 that the garden-maker call on the services of both a painter and poet in designing his landscape so that its details would have "a character which speaks to the imagination and the heart; an effect often wanting in very fine pictures, when the painter is not also a poet."[2]

The landscape garden in its Picturesque form was highly exportable. Price emphasized that the Picturesque had "no connection with dimensions of any kind" and could be found in many kinds of sites. The substantial land-holdings required by English pastoral landscape gardens were economically feasible because the acres of gently contoured green grass provided grazing, the lake or streams water, and the trees shade for the livestock central to the agricultural system. The belts of woodland that ringed them could be managed to provide salable timber and a variety of game. When a country estate was neither profitable agriculturally nor a source of political power, such grand sculptural compositions usually demanded too much expensive labor to keep up, even if the land could be assembled. The noblemen and the rich bourgeois who created the new *jardins anglo-chinois* near Paris in the late eighteenth century were content to develop their country places on a rather less generous scale. So, too, were prosperous American merchants and manufacturers forty years later. Even slave-owning plantation owners in the American south were unlikely to divert any great number of workers from agricultural production to the maintenance of extensive pleasure grounds. As a passionate gardener and Maryland plantation owner's wife, Rosalie Stier Calvert, wrote in 1804, "The work necessary to grow tobacco employs the negroes every day of the year."[3] Her illuminating letters to her equally horticulturally-minded family in Belgium are sprinkled with complaints about the difficulty of getting a competent gardener. She planned on a generous scale and hired the artist William Birch to create a landscape design for her, but a lithograph of Riversdale in 1827 showing the tree-studded north lawn suggests that the grounds around the house were of moderate extent.

Girardin went so far as to suggest that vistas weren't needed and that limitations could be a blessing:

> The larger the house is, the more open space it requires in the general outline, and consequently much is given up of what produces pleasure in the detail. A small house, on the contrary, can take advantage of every thing; distance may even be given up entirely, or it may easily be made without going beyond the territory, since it is very possible to produce one in a wood, by lights happily managed — a landscape merely of wood might

The exiled Joseph Bonaparte created an influential garden in the Picturesque Style, French version, at Point Breeze in Bordentown, New Jersey between 1817 and 1841. In Karl Bodmer's 1832 painting, trees obscure most of the grounds except the belvedere. Clearly visible: the throng of townspeople and travelers made welcome by Bonaparte.

In 1824 a Belgian horticulturist, André Parmentier, established a commercial nursery in Brooklyn, New York, and laid out part of its grounds in the Picturesque Style with curving tree-shaded walks and rustic *fabriques* (garden structures and seats) to promote his skills as a landscape designer. It worked. His career was brief but successful.

Parmentier had built a rustic lookout pavilion in his garden and the idea was much copied in the early nineteenth century. Log and twig structures were considered ideal for Picturesque landscapes, more finished masonry ones, like this elaborate design by Samuel Sloan, for Classical or Pastoral ones.

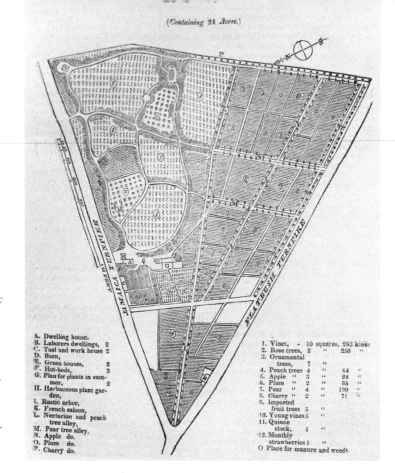

(Containing 24 Acres.)

A. Dwelling house.
B. Laborers dwellings, 2
C. Tool and work house 2
D. Barn,
E. Green houses, 2
F. Hot-beds, 3
G. Plan for plants in summer, 2
H. Herbaceous plant garden,
I. Rustic arbor,
K. French saloon,
L. Nectarine and peach tree alley,
M. Pear tree alley.
N. Apple do.
O. Plum do.
P. Cherry do.

1. Vines, - 10 squares, 263 kinds
2. Rose trees, 2 " 250 "
3. Ornamental trees, 7 "
4. Peach trees 4 " 64 "
5. Apple " 3 " 24 "
6. Plum " 2 " 85 "
7. Pear " 4 " 190 "
8. Cherry " 2 " 71 "
9. Imported fruit trees 5 "
10. Young vines 5 "
11. Quince stock, 1 "
12. Monthly strawberries 1 "
O Place for manure and weeds.

in fact be sufficient, and procure much nearer home an endless variety of delightful recesses, glades, and shady walks. In this, as in all things else, what advantages for mediocrity![4]

When the naturalistic garden made its come-back on the American scene it added to already assimilated English ideas a large dose of inspiration from French interpretations of the picturesque, wrought and written. Girardin's friend, former neighbor, and fellow romantic gardener, Joseph Bonaparte, solaced his post-Waterloo exile by creating a Picturesque park on the banks of the Delaware near Bordentown, New Jersey. Bonaparte's hospitality to his neighbors and to travelers ensured that his landscape was often described; contemporary plans and paintings show it to have been a simplified version of the *jardin anglo-chinois*, with a restrained number of evocative structures, or as the French called them, *fabriques*. Still more influential was André Parmentier, a Belgian-born landscape gardener and a member of a distinguished European horticultural family. Parmentier arrived in 1824 and immediately started a nursery in Brooklyn, offering fruit trees, vines, ornamental trees and shrubs, roses, and a variety of flowers on a twenty-three-acre site laid out to show off his skill as a landscape designer. It worked. Parmentier was commissioned to design, plant, or furnish plans for gardens from Canada to the southern United States. Andrew Jackson Downing considered Hyde Park on the Hudson, which Parmentier had laid out for Dr. Hosack "one of the finest specimens of the modern style" and credited "M. Parmentier's labors and examples as having effected, directly, far more for landscape gardening in America, than those of any other individual whatever."[5] Since only traces of his gardens have survived, we have to take Downing's word for their

quality, but Parmentier's short article "Landscapes and Picturesque Gardens," which was published both in Thomas G. Fessenden's *The New American Gardener* and in his own nursery catalogue, has survived, as has a description and plan of the nursery, and together they give an idea of his approach.

An aspect of Parmentier's design that would have been particularly appealing to practical Americans was the combination of orchards and vineyards with winding paths, rustic arbors, and unexpected vistas. Of necessity, his nursery was an ornamented farm; but such combinations were characteristic of the French Picturesque style. Girardin, wishing the romantic garden to please more than the sight, had included orchards, vineyards, pastures, and happy farmers in his vision of "moral landscapes which delight the mind," and among the *Plans Raisonnés de toutes les espèces de Jardins* published by landscape architect Gabriel Thouin, in 1820 were several such landscape plans as well as more detailed layouts of orchards and kitchen gardens specifically intended for insertion into picturesque parks and gardens.

Girardin's writings and Thouin's designs were very much admired by John Claudius Loudon, the energetic Scotsman who dominated British horticulture and garden design in the first half of the nineteenth century. Loudon's biographer, Melanie Simo, notes that his 1831 design for the Birmingham Botanical Garden, although more complex, seems indebted to one of Thouin's plans combining kitchen garden and pleasure grounds, a plan that he published in his *Encyclopedia of Gardening*.[6] As well as a designer of private estates, public parks and suburban gardens, Loudon was an inventor, and an agricultural and social reformer. Most important, he was a writer and publisher of horticultural books and magazines with correspondents both on the Continent and in this

country. His publications did much to introduce the French
rendering of the Picturesque to the English-speaking world,
more through its influence on his own thinking than because
he made a point of its distinct traits.

A great admirer of Loudon, and one of his American correspondents, Andrew Jackson Downing, in his turn, adapted
Loudon's principles of modern landscape design to circumstances on this side of the Atlantic. Like his mentor, Downing
was both a practicing landscape designer and a prolific
writer. In addition he was the son of a nurseryman and for
some years, in partnership with his brother, a nurseryman
himself. Downing's interpretation, set forth in words, plans,
and pictures in three books and many magazine and newspaper articles, would do much to shape American taste for the
rest of the century.

For Downing natural scenery provided the designer of the
"modern" landscape with two models — the Beautiful and
the Picturesque, "the beauty characterized by simple and
flowing forms, and that expressed by striking, irregular, spirit-
ed forms." He admitted that the natural landscape could also
express Grandeur and Sublimity but these, he felt, were
beyond the creative powers of the landscape gardener who
could only "respect them where they exist in natural landscape which forms part of his work of art."

The Beautiful and the Picturesque had equal value as
artistic expressions in Downing's eyes. Each was the idealization of a particular kind of terrain. The designer's choice
would be determined by the nature of the site, with the
implied corollary that if the owner had a strong preference
for one or the other model he should choose a site that lent
itself to the desired treatment.

On a large estate, Downing conceded, the terrain
often permitted a combination of the Beautiful and the

119

Top:
As a mature designer, Downing successfully blended the Beautiful and the Picturesque at Matthew Vassar's estate, Springside, just outside Poughkeepsie, New York. In this view of the newly landscaped pleasure grounds painted by Henry Gritten in 1852, there's a glimpse of the

Hudson River beyond the entrance lodge to the right, but it is incidental. The real attractions for those moving along the paths and carriageways are within the boundaries, shifting scenes composed of trees and grass accented with pools, fountains, or an occasional building like the conservatory to the left.

Above:
The pleasure grounds are hidden by trees in this view of the working part of the estate, which takes in the walled kitchen garden, the Cottage (visible in the center), and the complex of farmyards and buildings in the foreground.

Picturesque. The ability to blend them into a harmonious whole was, for him, the highest test of a landscape designer's artistry. Montgomery Place was one that he held up as an example, but it was oriented to the view, and the two landscape expressions were clearly separated. In contrast, at Springside, the forty-four-acre estate that he laid out for Matthew Vassar just outside Poughkeepsie, he skillfully wove together episodes of the Beautiful, the Picturesque, and the utilitarian. The site, a partially cleared farm, would seem to have called for a purely picturesque design according to a description by Vassar's biographer, the historian Benson Lossing:

> Much of it was in a state of natural rudeness. Wooded knolls rose above tangled hollows. Springs gushed out from oozy little hill-sides and formed rivulets.[7]

However, when Downing was first commissioned by Vassar in 1850 he was asked to develop the property as a rural cemetery, if subscribers materialized, or as a private estate if they did not. Robert M. Toole, a landscape architect who has carefully studied the history and remains of the landscape, believes that this double program led Downing to use the knolls scattered over the shallow valley as picturesque accents and smooth out the rest to create a calm and harmonious landscape more appropriate for a cemetery.[8] By 1851 the property was clearly intended as a private estate. It was nearly finished when Downing was killed in 1852, and later that year Vassar commissioned four views of the estate from an English painter. As these paintings make clear, Springside represents a major shift of emphasis in the design of a painterly landscape based on natural forms. The view beyond is no longer in control. What is important is what is within the boundaries.

After Downing's death Matthew Vassar himself completed the design and planting of his blend of pleasure grounds and working farm. Benson J. Lossing, described Springside as it appeared in 1867 in considerable detail. From this account, Vassar added more statues and ornamental structures than the landscape's designer might have liked, but on the whole he seems to have shared Downing's vision.

Today, some roads and paths are still discernable, but what is left of the developed landscape is overgrown and of the dozen or so buildings designed by Downing, only the porter's lodge remains. In its heyday Springside's walks and drives led to meadows and fields of grain, and "gentle eminences . . . without trees or shrubs and enlivened by a herd of fine Devonshire cattle," as well as wild spots "in which art has refrained from interfering with nature."[9]

Even in its present ruinous state Springside demonstrates that every advantage was taken of the hilly site and the possibilities for varied effects that it offered. In spite of his vast admiration for English lawns, Downing had harsh words for those who begin gardens or lay out suburbs by cutting down trees, ripping out rocks and leveling all the character out of a piece of land, actions that he said express love of power not love of beauty. From his day to ours, some have listened but many, sad to say, have not. Unlike English theorists, many of whom saw one or another model as an abstract ideal to be followed in all cases, Downing treated the Beautiful and the

Picturesque simply as standards of comparison for analyzing the forms to be found in the local environment, and, as he gained experience, he became increasingly convinced that his countrymen should root their gardens in their own countrysides.

> Let us take it then as the type of all true art in landscape gardening—which selects from natural materials that abound in any country, its best sylvan features, and by giving them a better opportunity than they could otherwise obtain, brings about a higher beauty of development and a more perfect expression than nature itself offers. Study landscape in nature more, and the gardens and their catalogues less,—is our advice to the rising generation of planters, who wish to embellish their places in the best and purest taste.[10]

He himself was a careful observer of his surroundings and extoller of the virtues of native trees and plants, but he did not feel that the landscape designer's palette had to be limited to natives. This was the period when plant-hunters such as David Douglas in the American West and Robert Fortune in China and Japan, to mention only two, were discovering plants by the hundreds. How could plant-lovers not be enticed by this tide of introductions? Downing, like Loudon before him, certainly was, particularly early in his career.

> The *beau idéal* in Landscape Gardening, as a fine art, appears to us to be embraced in the creation of scenery full of expression, as the beautiful or picturesque, the materials of which are, to a certain extent, different from those in wild nature, being composed of the floral and arboricultural riches of *all climates*, as far as possible; uniting in the same scene, a richness and a variety never to be found in any one portion of nature[11]

Downing explains most clearly his manner of reconciling exotic plants and the native landscape in a long passage on planting the shores of created lakes or ponds. The planting should be modeled on the layers of the native woodlands, "with trees of different heights and sizes, and underwood and shrubs of lower growth." Such a composition might, for example, duplicate the eastern spring's tender green canopies of oak and maple and hickory lighted up by the white blossoms of understory dogwoods rising above mountain laurel or native azaleas with carpets of white trillium covering the forest floor. Downing proposes a long list of suitable native plants for each layer and suggests the addition of graceful native vines. If properly executed and softened by time this man-made scenery "will not be much inferior to those matchless bits" of the natural landscape; but for him there is a still higher level:

> A more striking and artistical effect will be produced by substituting for native trees and shrubs . . . only rare *foreign* shrubs, vines, and aquatic plants of hardy growth, suitable for such situations.[12]

Top:
At the left in Gritten's view from the approach road is the garden façade of the Downing-designed house or Cottage, as it was called, screened from the stable and coach house by the Knitting Knoll, one of several rocky tree-covered knobs dotting the site.

Above:
The fenced flowerbed beside the steps on the east façade of the Cottage and the kitchen garden contain the only herbaceous plants in Gritten's paintings. More vistas of the Hudson come into view from the painter's position, but they are vistas from cow pastures. The open circle on the knoll at right was for a soon-to-be-built summerhouse.

In such a scheme European or Oriental primroses might replace the notoriously hard to propagate trillium; brilliant red and pink and magenta asiatic azaleas and rhododendrons, the delicately tinted native species; the English hawthorn or the pawlonia, the dogwood. As for trees, however, most of the large exotics in his annotated list of ornamentals are wisely recommended for use as isolated specimens near the house rather than for integration into a picturesque woodland.

Exotic plant material was not the only embellishment permitted to the nineteenth-century naturalistic garden. French Picturesque gardens, in particular, had been filled with *fabriques* — vases, greenhouses, summerhouses, seats, bridges, fountains, prospect towers, pagodas, and tents. In adapting this kind of ornamentation to the middle-class garden, there was the danger that the owner might be tempted to cram into a two-acre landscape all the temples and pavilions and urns and statues and seats and inscriptions admired in a two-hundred-acre one. Downing was well aware of the risk of such a jumble and peppered his discussion of these ornamental features with warnings to use them with discretion and only in appropriate places. He seems to have been fairly sparing of them in his own designs but many Victorian gardeners showed little restraint.

Ideas of how a landscape is to be abstracted and idealized and of what constitutes suitable or pleasing embellishment for it, whether public park or private garden, tend to change with each generation. Downing's enduring contribution was to encourage Americans to look to their own landscape for the structure and spirit of their gardens.

MAGNOLIA PLANTATION

The best known and most spectacular of nineteenth-century American picturesque gardens, Magnolia Plantation on the Ashley River near Charleston, South Carolina, dates from Downing's day but whether its creator was familiar with his contemporary's writings is not known and probably never will be.

The land on which the plantation was established in the late seventeenth century was given by Stephen Fox, an immigrant from Barbados, to his daughter upon her marriage to Thomas Drayton, Jr., another Barbadian settler. Eleven generations later it is still in the hands of the same family.[13] Little pre-Civil-War documentation, written or pictorial, exists. Magnolia's history was not of the kind that promotes archives. It was inhabited only for a few months in the spring, one stop on the yearly circuit of Drayton plantations and houses. The gardens and "venerable mansion" were mentioned but not described by John Davis, a young Englishman who spent a year, 1798–99, as tutor with the peripatetic family. The original mansion burned down a year or so later. Its replacement was built to the south and east, off-axis from the entrance allée of ancient live oaks. That house in turn was burned in the Civil War, and the present one erected on its foundations. Add to this condensed narrative several severe earthquakes and hurricanes and one can see why most of our information comes from family tradition, not plans, or diaries, or bills from nurseries and seedsmen.

In the March 13, 1889 issue of *Garden and Forest* a Charleston correspondent, who signs his column simply S., says that in the early years Magnolia's grounds were laid out on the land side with an oak-bordered meadow, and on the river side with a spacious lawn, specimen oaks and magnolias, and box-bordered paths. S. then goes on to describe the creation of the gardens as we know them today.

> In 1841, when the present proprietor, the Reverend J. G. Drayton, D. D. — then a young man with health, to all appearance, shattered beyond hope — returned to the home of his ancestors, he found the great trees, and besides them only some dimly outlined walks, a few specimens of Gardenia, Calycanthus, *Illicium anisatum* and some wild shrubs on the border. . . . He knew little about plants then and less about work, but since that day his own hands have done most of the planting which has made his garden famous the world over, in some of its features . . . in 1848 he planted the first Camellias and Azaleas of his remarkable collection. . . . Of Camellias there are some 300 varieties, many of them seedlings of his own raising. The plants, too, are remarkably large, strong and floriferous . . . The Azaleas are quite as numerous and equally remarkable for variety, vigor and size. There are probably 150 distinct kinds, with individual specimens from ten to fifteen feet high and fifteen to twenty feet in diameter.

Since John Grimke Drayton had been educated for the ministry in England and in New York City he was probably aware of the fashion for picturesque landscape design before he took over his inheritance. We don't know how much interest he had in gardening before doctors told him that his only hope of regaining health was physical work in the open air. What he had seen, what he had read, are also mysteries; but what he produced is the kind of garden his contemporary Downing was calling for.

The fame of Magnolia's spectacular azaleas and camellias has obscured its importance as perhaps the earliest American garden design truly derived from the distinctive features of its environment, that marshy slice of the Atlantic Plain known as the Carolina Low Country. Dr. Drayton's romantic garden is an idealized swamp, much of it built on abandoned rice fields. The lakes that anchor the informal plantings and network of paths were formed originally by damming a tributary stream to make reservoirs for flooding the rice fields. Now, dyed black by tannin from the towering native bald cypresses that grow in their shallows, they mirror their surroundings with burnished clarity. Enormous, ancient native trees — magnolia, live oak, cypress (*Taxodium distichum*) — form the canopy. From their branches hang swags of wisteria, banksia, and Cherokee roses, and Carolina jasmine as well as soft gray tresses of Spanish moss, that epiphytic member of the bromeliad family that has become an emblem of the romantic South. Native dogwoods in the understory are

Contributing as much to the distinctive character of the gardens as the native magnolias are the equally native bald cypresses that dye the water black in the lakes along which they grow. The white lattice bridge over Big Cypress Lake dates back to Dr. Drayton's day.

almost overtopped by the robust Indica azaleas and camellias, exotics previously confined to northern greenhouses, for which Dr. Drayton found a perfect setting.

Curving paths, nearly at water level, follow the Ashley River shoreline, weave through banks of shrubbery, skirt clearings in the woods, and wind around the lakes, revealing an ever-changing series of pictures. The straight walks remaining from the original garden—one to what is left of the formal parterre, a pair flanking the strip of lawn between house and river—have been so softened by the luxuriant shrubs and vines that they fit harmoniously into the prevailing woodland quality of the garden. Magnolia is a garden, not of long and dramatic vistas, but of poetic images and great strokes of brilliant color.

As the flowers mentioned indicate, Magnolia was designed to peak in the spring—February, March, April—before the family escaped sometime in May to the interior highlands for the summer. In 1870, Dr. Drayton, his financial resources depleted by the Civil War, opened the gardens to the public to help pay for their survival. Their fame spread quickly and by the turn of the century Baedeker had placed Magnolia on a par with the Grand Canyon and Niagara Falls.

In the mid-1970s, the present owner, Drayton Hastie, realized that the spring season alone could not draw enough visitors to sustain the gardens in the late twentieth-century economy, and set out to turn them into a year-round attrac-

tion. Recognizing that tourists in vast majority want to see color in a garden, he has planted to ensure that every month has a display of flowers. And he has planted in broad sweeps of color as his great grandfather did. He has also added gardens of a very different kind—a Biblical garden, a maze, an herb garden—but on the periphery where they do not clash with the mood of the woodland.

To amuse small children, notoriously impatient with gardens where they can't pick the flowers, there is a petting zoo in part of the former meadow, occupied by a greater selection of animals than the sheep that were "nibbling in the meadow" in 1889. To the north of the gardens proper, wooded highlands and salt marshes along the river are managed as a wildlife sanctuary. Hastie has constructed boardwalks and trails to allow nature lovers to experience the eerie beauty of this wild landscape and its equally eerie inhabitants, among them the anhinga and the alligator. For those who don't care to be on the same level as the alligator, he has built a viewing tower that cannot be seen from the garden. In addition to its intrinsic interest, the sanctuary offers a rare chance to compare an improved and an unimproved landscape.

In the last decades of the nineteenth century and the early years of the twentieth, professional landscape designers, particularly in the Middle West, made a concerted effort to root their designs in the characteristic landforms and vegetation of the region in which they were working. Easterners had not always seen Mid-Western prairies as either poetic or

picturesque, and it is ironic that the man who Frank Lloyd Wright would call Chicago's "native nature poet," and "a true interpreter of the peculiar charm of our prairie landscape" was born in Denmark and came to know that prairie landscape as a young adult in 1886. Over the next sixty-five years the designs of Jens Jensen and those of his older and younger contemporaries, O. C. Simonds and Alfred Caldwell would become widely known as the Prairie School of landscape architecture. Jensen's rapid rise from park-sweeper to foreman to designer to park superintendent to Superintendent and Landscape Architect for Chicago's West Park System is a classic American success story, and his dedication to the Middle-Western landscape displays a convert's equally classic passion.

Sunday and holiday excursions made by Jensen and his wife to the wild woods and meadows, in those days right at the end of the trolley lines, taught him the beauty and growth habits of the native flora, and "to love the native landscape for its contours and physical aspects as well as for its plant life." As the years went by, these excursions ranged farther afield and Jensen was often accompanied by the pioneer ecologist Henry Cowles and his students. He could base his compositions of native plants on a better understanding of ecological processes than was available to predecessors like Downing and Olmsted, who also drew design inspiration from the forms of nature. Yes, he made some mistakes in the light of what we have learned almost a century later; but he understood that sensitive maintenance was just as necessary with natural plantings as with architectural or horticultural ones and also recognized that many imported species might run wild and elbow out more attractive native ones.

Jensen's private clients gave him great freedom to express his mature design philosophy:

> It has become my creed that a garden, to be a work of art, must have the soul of the native landscape in it. Each type of landscape must have its individual expression. . . .
>
> But in trying to make a garden natural we must not make the mistake of copying Nature. . . . Copying Nature is only one step removed from copying another garden. Art idealizes; it is creative, and a reproduction is only a reproduction, no matter how fine and noble the model is. The landscape garden must have a dominant thought or feeling in it, just as a great painting must have a dominant thought in it. To me, that feeling should be spiritual; it should be love for the great out-of-doors, for the world that God made. Such a garden will be a shrine to which one may come for rest from the strife and noise of the man-built city. It will have in it the mystery of the forest, the joy and peace of a sunlit meadow, the music of a laughing brook, the perfume of flowers, the songs of birds, the symphony of color in tree and shrub.
>
> And the elements one works with are the contours of the earth, the vegetation that covers it, the changing seasons, the rays of the setting sun and the afterglow, and the light of the moon. [14]

The gardens at Magnolia Plantation near Charleston represent the brilliant enhancement of a South Carolina Low Country swamp. In 1841, the Reverend John Grimke Drayton began creating the lakes and planting the Asiatic azaleas and camellias that would turn his already 150-year-old family plantation into a world-famous picturesque garden. Beyond this azalea-fringed pool is a glimpse of the native woods and marshlands remaining on the 500-acre estate.

In this aerial view of the Edsel and Eleanor Ford estate in Grosse Pointe Shores, Michigan the entrance road is first hidden in a grove of trees, then it briefly crosses the lawn, Jens Jensen's stylization of a prairie meadow, and proceeds to the house along the shore of a lagoon created from Lake St. Clair. To the south it offers occasional glimpses of the lawn and trees, to the north views of Bird Island, the wildlife refuge Jensen created by building up and planting a sandbar. Just visible are the wheel-shaped rose garden at left and the farm complex top right, both isolated by trees from the painterly landscape.

THE EDSEL AND ELEANOR FORD GARDEN

If Nature was to be abstracted and idealized, with each type given individual expression, then the woods and steep ravines on the suburban Chicago estate of the Julius Rosenwalds or the rocky slopes of the Edsel Fords' summer place in Maine called for a very different kind of abstraction than the almost flat peninsula that constituted the Fords' Grosse Pointe property. The latter, now open to the public, is one of the best preserved of Jensen's private landscapes. Like his architect friends, he saw the prairie as a harmony of horizontals, and designed Gaukler Point, as it was sometimes called, in that spirit, although the site was in fact not on a prairie but on the shore of Lake St. Clair, smallest of the Great Lakes.

To express the spirit of a place he selected a few elements and used them at times in rhythmic repetition, at times in sweeping masses. He composed the groves at Gaukler Point primarily with American elms, silver and sugar maples. To them he added his favorite horizontally branched native trees — the crabapple, the dogwood, and the hawthorn — both as individual specimens and as a transitional layer

between the lawn and the taller trees. Usually in his forest plantings he used these more generously, as they normally grew, in clumps at the meadow edge or as underwood beneath oaks and maples, and then on the ground beneath them spread wildflowers in broad masses of a single species—trillium or phlox, or violets, a special favorite. According to Robert Grese, the more open planting at the Ford estate was the result of security concerns at the time it was created.[15]

"Light and shadow and their distribution during the entire circle of day and night are important fundamentals in the art of landscaping," Jensen wrote in *Siftings* and the more often you visit one of his gardens, the more you realize how sensitively he has observed the movement of the sun at each site and in every season. Jensen very much admired the paintings of George Inness, so it is not surprising that he often arranged his lawns as paths to the rising or to the setting sun. These may be on a very grand scale as is the one at the Ford estate or little more than lanes of varying width opened into the woods. Shrubs and trees with vivid autumn foliage

like sumacs, dogwoods, and sugar maples he placed at just the point where backlight from the setting sun could double the brilliance of their colors. At the Ford Estate, the house, designed by Albert Kahn, is situated at one end of a long lawn, the domestic abstraction of the prairie meadow, but on an axis angled to exploit just such an effect. Jensen loved the silhouettes of bare deciduous trees and the shadow patterns they made on the snow, considered evergreens unnecessary for winter interest, and rarely employed them unless the owner specifically asked for them or they already existed on the property, as they did at the Fords'.

His landscapes don't reveal all they have to offer from any one viewpoint. For example, he almost always made the entrance roads to private houses curve through shadowy groves before ending them in a sunlit lawn at the house. At Gaukler Point the drive is tree-flanked on both sides at the enterance, crosses the lawn giving a glimpse of the house at the far end, and then makes a long loop through trees before arriving at the front door.

Jensen's landscapes are even more inviting to explore on

Jensen found numbers of silver maples on the property and worked them into his design, supplementing them with sugar maples and elms, all indigenous. In autumn they pave the lawn with golden leaves.

Above:
The view to Lake St. Clair on the opposite side of the house from the meadow. Jensen loved the strong silhouettes of bare deciduous trees and the calligraphy of the shadows they cast on snow. He rarely planted evergreens, but kept them if they were already on the land.

Opposite:
The swimming pool is tucked into a patch of woodland near the lake. Around it drifts of native *Trillium grandiflorum* and *Mertensia virginica* cover the ground under clouds of dogwood blossoms in the spring.

foot. He wound paths through the wooded borders of his lawns so that you can enjoy the sunlight but walk in the shade. Large lawns and small sun spaces alike curve around peninsulas of trees and shrubs in such a way that you can't tell just how far they really extend, a technique also used by Frederick Law Olmsted to create mystery and anticipation. Sequences of light and shade pull you forward; paths narrow and wrap around you, then open into clearings or turn to offer unexpected views; grades and curves and steps feel comfortable to the body, and there are places to stop, sit, and enjoy the patterns and colors of bark and foliage, the fragrance of flowers, the songs of birds that have been enticed with plants they like.

To provide both a nesting place for wild birds and shelter for the family's boats, Jensen took a sandbar in the lake at the northwest corner of the Fords' property, built it up with material dredged from the harbor area, and planted it—this time in his usual style—with a dense mixture of trees, shrubs, and wildflowers. Today it seems as if it had always been there, and in truth, by turning sandbar into island he simply put nature on fast forward. Such sandbar-based islands frequently arise over time in Michigan lakes.

While he firmly believed that for the most part gardens "should be planted with the trees and shrubs and flowers that are native to the surrounding landscape," Jensen gave his clients flower gardens when they wanted them. Most did. His flower gardens, like the Fords' rose garden, were laid out geometrically, but he tucked these little oases of order into the woods where you come on them as a surprise at the end of a path. He justified this seeming contradiction by recalling a garden he had seen near Berlin in his youth:

> Then one lovely summer day I was rather surprised, when wandering through the woodlands beyond these English parks, to meet a little garden enclosed within the deep shadow of the forest. This garden was architectural in its layout, but, nevertheless, it had a certain sense of freedom, more in keeping with the life of the people than the French copy. This little garden left an impression upon my mind that has never been entirely forgotten.[16]

If clients had an interest in gardening it was natural for them to want such flower gardens, in which they could express some of their own ideas. Jensen had no objection as long as these gardens did not encroach on or interrupt the sweeping lines of the overall landscape design. There, only Nature's changes were to be permitted.

Here and there along the stepping-stone paths that thread through the nine-acre property, the Ohmes built stone benches into mossy hillsides or tawny rock formations.

OHME GARDEN

In 1929, the year that the Fords moved into their Grosse Pointe estate, a garden designed to embellish a very different kind of landscape was about to take shape in the state of Washington. Herman Ohme, who had grown up in Illinois, and Ruth Orcutt, who came from a local pioneer family, married and bought forty acres to start an orchard in the Wenatchee Valley. Those acres included an agriculturally useless dry and barren bluff. But that bluff offered spectacular vistas of the Columbia River, the orchards on the valley floor, and the Cascade Range. To the Ohmes it seemed like the perfect place for their house, but the Great Depression had dried up sources of mortgage money, so they stayed in the property's existing house and climbed up to enjoy the view at the working day's end. If house building had to wait, they decided, they could at least start making a garden. Both had enjoyed hiking in the Cascade Mountains to the west of the river, and the mountains became the inspiration and the source of materials for their creation.

To turn their sagebrush-covered, treeless slopes into what today appear to be evergreen glades among mountain meadows and pools, the Ohmes had to overcome a major challenge. The site had the right topography and it was well furnished with the kind of granite outcrops that characterize the region's alpine lakes and meadows. What it did not have was water. The Wenatchee Valley is on the dry eastern slope of the Cascade Range, and its famous apple orchards would not exist without irrigation channeled from the Wenatchee and Columbia Rivers. Lacking water, the bluff did not have a single tree when they started. Undaunted, the newly married couple drove up to the mountains on weekends, dug up ferns and wildflowers, seedling trees and bushes, and brought them back in the rumble seat and on the running boards of their Studebaker coupe. Then they drove up a truck filled with five-gallon milk cans of water and hand-watered their transplants. Their dedication paid off: Gradually trees and ground covers replaced the sagebrush. Eventually they were able to pump irrigation water from their orchard up to the

site using pipes salvaged from demolished buildings in the town. Today the irrigation and sprinkler system is more refined and its mechanics are carefully concealed, but it is still essential to the garden's survival.

The garden grew slowly. The Ohmes, who did not consider themselves either horticulturists or designers, worked without predetermined plans but clearly, judging from the result, with innate artistry. They built stepping-stone paths, some quite precipitous, with flat rocks that they trucked up from the banks of the Columbia and then hauled into place on an old army stretcher. When a dam drowned that source of flat stones they split rocks on a nearby mountain with a wedge and sledgehammer. The two of them did all the work themselves, calling on the aid of a mule only for very heavy-duty work like moving large rocks, leveling some areas for lawns, and carving out a swimming pool for themselves and their two sons. They cut logs in the mountains to build seats and rustic shelters for which they hand-peeled cedar bark for roofing. After work and after harvest, they planted, watered,

To capture the spirit of a mile-high alpine meadow on the wet western side of the Cascade Mountains on a bare and rocky bluff only 1200 feet above sea-level on the dry eastern side, Ruth and Herman Ohme had to bring down evergreens, and carry up water from their orchard in Washington's Wenatchee Valley below until they could build an irrigation system. It took them and their sons sixty years, but they succeeded gloriously.

dug pools, moved rocks, laid paths, and built benches and fireplaces. "You couldn't hire me to do that," Herman said, "It was a labor of love."

They intended the mountain landscape they were creating only as a retreat, "a nice backyard," for the family, but people in the valley had noticed the two-acre green oasis on the brown hillside. They came up to look, were enchanted with its beauty, and put pressure on the Ohmes to open it to visitors. Finally in 1939, the family gave in. They set an admission charge to help pay for the extra maintenance, hoping that it would keep people away. That backfired: it attracted more visitors. Finally they decided to lease out their orchard and devote themselves to the garden, gradually doubling its extent. In 1953 one of their sons, Gordon, took over management of the garden, modernized the irrigation system, and expanded it to nine acres, its present size. Then, after sixty years of commitment, the family's ownership came to an end. Gordon developed a rare and terminal illness, which left him unable to keep up the garden. To preserve it, he sold it in 1991 to the State of Washington Parks and Recreation Commission. Today by agreement with the Commission it is a park operated and maintained by Chelan County.

Photographs of the Alpine Lakes Wilderness region of the Cascades, above and to the west of the garden, show that the Ohmes truly captured the spirit of these mountain meadows. But they didn't always use the same plants to do it. They did succeed in establishing many of the conifers that frame and accent views and slopes. As in the wild, Douglas firs, Pacific silver firs, Western red cedars, and mountain hemlocks provide cool shade. It is the open areas that required substitutions. According to Michael Short, the manager of the garden, the Ohmes started out with wildflowers brought down from the mountains. But they found that many denizens of mist-veiled meadows at 3000 or 4000 feet above sea level did not thrive on sunnier and drier slopes at 1200 feet. Nor did the patches of level lawn they wanted, although not large in relation to the whole, have precedents in the mountains. It took a considerable amount of trial and error to achieve the effect they were aiming for. Today, the ground covers include saxifrages and Sagina—also called pearlwort—the principal one being creeping thyme, within which sedums and dianthus have taken root. The most brilliant color is contributed by tufts of ajuga and phlox. A ground-hugging native phlox is common in the area, but most of those in the garden are nursery-bred cultivars. The season of color lasts from April through June. The rest of the year the garden offers a variegated mantle of greens studded with tawny rocks and parted here and there by pools reflecting the bright blue sky.

However much their garden respects the rugged character of its site, the Ohmes planned it for human enjoyment, and the elements that promote such enjoyment play an important role in its design. The stepping-stone paths, which add up to very nearly a mile, make it considerably easier to negotiate the steep slopes. At the same time they represent a dynamic organizing force, pulling the eyes—and the feet—through space. Does that path up the hill lead to a spectacular panorama of snowy peaks? Or to an evergreen grove that invites quiet contemplation? Stone benches, strategically

placed, provide places to rest, but they also serve as sculptural accents along the paths. Rustic pavilions for shelter from sun and rain have a long history as practical ornaments for natural gardens. The lodges built by the Ohmes continue the tradition, but with special touches of humor. And the patches of level lawn offer reassuring places to stand while adding a brilliant note to the tapestry of greens.

The garden seems unchanged from the days of the family's ownership when you compare photographs taken over the last fifteen years, a tribute to the stewardship of the state and county. Still, as Michael Short points out, the trees keep growing and adding shade so pruning is ongoing and thinning sometimes needed. Some groundcovers invade territory where they are not welcome and have to be weeded out and restrained. Most exciting, the staff is researching and reintroducing wildflowers that had once been in the garden but vanished, such as the rare *Lewisia Tweedyi*, which is found only in the Wenatchee Mountains and in the Walathian mountains of British Columbia.

COBAMONG

Great granite boulders thrusting up from the soil are as characteristic of the New York and New England landscape as they are of the Cascades. And like the Ohmes, Ted Nierenberg has turned to advantage the granitic skeleton of his Westchester property. For more than forty years he has been adding and removing, thinning, pruning, arranging and rearranging trees and shrubs and plants to produce a very personal landscape that perfectly fulfills Downing's ideal of "uniting in the same scene, a richness and a variety never to be found in any one portion of nature." Yet this tapestry of color and texture appears at first glance to be a natural Northeastern woodland through which someone has skillfully woven paths and then into it carefully dropped a house.

Tall granite outcrops embrace a roughly ten-acre lake in the glacier-carved rock basin that forms the site of Nierenberg's garden, which he calls Cobamong, an Algonquin word meaning "beautiful hidden valley." That had been just the name of the lake when he bought the property, a prophetic one. The land had once been cleared for pasture, but when he found it in the 1950s the lakeside slopes had reverted to a typical second-growth tangle of wild grapevines, poison ivy, brambles, and trees young and old. Some trees were good, some of poor quality but all too packed together. Nierenberg quickly decided where the house would go, but did not rush to start construction. For his choice of property to fulfill his dream of a woodland garden its vegetation needed a lot of editing. His patient pace allowed him to develop a profound understanding of the land, its rocks, its soils, its drainage patterns, its moods at different times of day and in different seasons. And for him and his wife and children to find the views and perching places they liked the best. In the meantime he developed at his home a veritable nursery to grow the plants he would need when the time came to carry out the plans taking shape in his imagination.

At the heart of Cobamong is the lake, mirror and magnet, drawing the eye at almost every turn as you walk along the paths. Often they hug the shoreline but even when they veer off into the woods or climb a ridge, a shimmer of blue glimpsed between trees will soon pull you back to the lake and its magical reflections. The glacier gave Nierenberg a good start at creating an interesting shoreline, scooping out coves, exposing bedrock, and dropping boulders in what seem to be strategic spots. He hasn't hesitated to do a bit of rock moving himself; but primarily he has built on nature's foundation with his choice and placement of plants to enhance its varied characteristics. In one place he goes for more drama, in another more delicacy. He will lay bare one rock ledge, fringe another with shrubs; almost smother an outcrop with ferns, endow another with just enough earth to support one sapling. He has become adept at training trees to lean out over the water, having learned by trying that straight-trunked specimens planted at a steep angle would curve gracefully after a few years. His leaning trees soften the line where land meets water and their leaves add a layer of color and texture to views across the lake.

As Cobamong is a garden of paths through a forest, it is a garden you must move through to experience. There are only two long views: one from the house to the end of the lake and the other back to the house. While they can be beautiful, they reveal little of the garden's riches. These are to be found in the progression of scenes, intimate or expansive, all along the paths and beyond every turn they take. That Nierenberg, as gifted a photographer as he is a gardener, called a book of his photographs *The Beckoning Path: Lessons of a Lifelong Garden* is entirely appropriate. Mark Kane, who wrote the book's text, explains in some detail how Nierenberg engineered the paths with the help of Henry Malewitz, an experienced horticulturist who has worked with him from the beginning.[17] They are mostly narrow, like Indian trails that oblige you to walk single file and like those trails the surface is duff. Nierenberg and Malewitz fitted stones together to bridge streams and swampy areas and built steps across steep slopes with stones or logs. Remarkably in this age of supposedly labor-saving machinery, they used only wheelbarrows and hand tools — harder on the worker, perhaps, but not damaging to the land.

What catches the visitor's attention along the trail may be a tree-trunk whose peeling bark is near enough to touch or a distinctive leaf or a branch of flowers reflected in the lake. An appealing but elusive scent or the murmur of a waterfall may draw one forward. The surprise around the corner may be a clearing filled with wildflowers or one spectacular Japanese maple. The balance between in the distance and up close, open and sheltered, has been so attentively orchestrated that it seems completely natural.

Nierenberg has layered his plantings just as they would be in the native forest. From moss and ground-covers only three or four inches high rise taller bulbs and perennials, shrubs, and understory trees, with canopy trees towering over all. But he has by no means limited his plant palette to indigenous species. Dawn redwoods from China, Douglas firs from the Pacific Northwest, bald cypresses and magnolias from the Southeast are only a few of his additions to the oaks, maples, ashes, beeches, and white pines that originally canopied the site. Natives and exotics co-exist at every level in fact: native

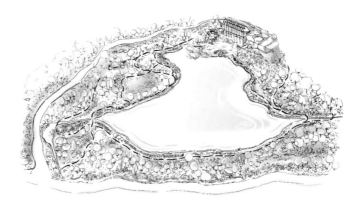

Retreating glaciers scooped out the valley and carved the granite ledges around it; Ted Nierenberg's landscaping made it live up to its Indian name, Cobamong, "beautiful hidden valley." In his woodland garden threaded with paths the only really level space is the lawn below the house, where the paths begin and end.

With each season the landscape takes on a different mood and coloration: delicate and pastel in spring, cool green in summer, a blaze of color in autumn. Winter snows douse the color, but bring their own special beauty.

A little brook ran down the hillside and naturally attracted water-loving plants. Building on nature, Nierenberg laid interrupting stones to shape waterfalls, enriched the ferns and wildflowers with taller azaleas and rhododendrons, and planted a cascading Sargent yew at the top of the slope.

azaleas with Exbury hybrids, native rhododendrons with yakushimanums, mountain laurels with andromedas and euonymus.

Nierenberg is a demon researcher. Wherever he goes he looks at gardens. If a plant interests him because he's seen it in someone else's garden or been told about it, he will consult every available authority to learn about its habits, likes, and dislikes. If he thinks it will thrive in his garden he will track down the nursery that does the best job of growing it. Yet his is not a plant collector's garden. Each species, each cultivar has been chosen because it contributes to a visual effect he wishes to achieve. The redbuds, cherries, and crabapples add a froth of pink to the white tracery of dogwoods and shadblows native to the Northeastern spring. The mixture of native, exotic, and hybrid rhododendrons gives Nierenberg a

In summer Cobamong is a tapestry of greens with just a zest of blossom color. Nierenberg chose the site for the house, which was designed by his friend Jens Quistgaard, early on, but started work on the garden well before it was built.

Come autumn the fiery hues for which northeastern forests are famous paint native maples, oaks, birches and dogwoods. Added trees from other parts of this country and from Asia help create displays of color even richer and more brilliant than nature's — as well as longer lasting.

longer season of bloom to compose with. Sourgums, sourwoods, sweetgums, and ginkgos add fuel to autumn's blaze of color. True enough, as Dr. Kim Tripp of the New York Botanical Garden says, "there are points of plantsmanship here and there." But even these rarities, beyond intriguing the connoisseur, contribute to the design as beautifully placed surprises.

Given the amount of space at his disposal, Nierenberg could plant for broad strokes of a single color more often than he does. His technique is more subtle. Trees grouped to provide a wash of blossom or leaf color in one place reappear singly or in pairs as accents not too far away. A bank of rhododendrons that in late summer contributes a swath of a single texture in one shade of green, offers a blend of harmonious pastels when in bloom. Just as the garden rewards attentive observation, it requires attentive observation both to compose and to maintain. Any garden does, of course, since plants may grow too big, reach the end of their life span,

succumb to frost, drought, or disease. Often such changes are less immediately apparent in a naturalistic garden. Nierenberg doesn't need to worry about Nature's changes getting out of hand. His photographs constantly monitor them. And they sometimes stimulate him to make his own changes.

It is not necessary for a designer to have a canvas as large as did the garden-makers in this chapter; but historically such landscapes have provided the inspiration. We will see in a later one that it is even possible to create a picturesque idealization of a local landscape on a small town lot.

Early spring brings color back in a shimmer of white, pink, yellow, and pale green. Beyond the foreground screen of blooming Yoshino cherry and bare branches, steps ascending the hill across the lake are just visible. On steep slopes Nierenberg eased the climb by anchoring long-lasting locust logs across the path and filling in earth behind them.

Democracy, Miniaturization, and

In the early decades of the nineteenth century, American writers, especially New Englanders, liked to picture the United States as a country without extremes of wealth or poverty, views echoed by European visitors like Frances Wright and Alexis de Tocqueville. A particularly persuasive native observer was Timothy Dwight, clergyman, politician and president of Yale. His posthumously published *Travels in New England and New York* was intended to defend his country against what he considered foreign misinterpretation, but his own calls for more country cemeteries and city parks, and less wasteful exploitation of the forests anticipated concerns that would become widespread later in the century. Still, after his yearly travels between 1795 and 1805, he assessed the social condition of the northern states with some satisfaction.

> Great wealth, that is, what Europeans consider great wealth, is not often found.... But poverty is almost unknown. Comfortable subsistence is enjoyed everywhere, unless prevented by peculiar misfortunes or by vice.... A succession of New England villages, composed of neat houses, surrounding neat schoolhouses and churches, adorned with gardens, meadows, and orchards, and exhibiting the universally easy circumstances of the inhabitants, is, at least in my own opinion, one of the most delightful prospects which this world can afford.[1]

In our day, historians have been quick to point out the less than total accuracy of the portrait and consider it at best an idealization. But it was an idealization that could pass for reality because it did reflect the nation's unprecedented economic and social mobility and the political and social power of its very large middle class. The irony is that in those same years accelerating industrialization—"honorable to the industry and the ingenuity of my countrymen" in Dwight's opinion—was laying the foundation for very apparent economic inequalities at the end of the century.

Idealization or not, the conviction that individual American fortunes tended to be moderate, and to be dispersed within a generation or two was accepted by most nineteenth-century horticultural writers—almost all of them northerners—and shaped the kind of guidance they offered to beginning landscapers and garden-makers. Donald Mitchell put it succinctly in 1867:

> In America, we must count upon divisions and subdivisions of property. Great ancestral estates will nowhere be long ancestral. Our republican mill grinds them sharply. Hence we lack, and must always lack that artistic dealing with country estates which can count upon oneness of proprietorship for an indefinite period of years. Better to admit this in the beginning, and let our landscape art take its form accordingly...[2]

This landscape art may have derived its ideal form from the great landscaped English estates, but the design suggestions as well as the advice published in the horticultural press represented a drastic miniaturization of the individual estate. Even the exceptionally large percentage of Montgomery Place's four hundred acres devoted to ornamental purposes, which A. J. Downing considered "second to no country estate in America," was humbled by its counterparts in England—the two thousand acres of landscaped grounds at Blenheim, the thousand at Mt. Edgecumbe, or the eight hundred at Petworth.

Rich city businessmen seeking country property were admonished not to take on more land than they could care for. They were warned that experienced gardeners were expensive, if indeed they could be found, and that farming was not an amateur sport. Large land holdings were not a source of political power as they were in England, and when cultivated by the inexperienced were more likely to drain than replenish the bank balance. Land frankly acquired for speculative subdivision was another matter and the source of many American fortunes, but rarely did the purchaser attempt to use it as interim pleasure grounds, or give it any artistic finish.

The most expansive designs in the pattern books for country-house pleasure grounds did not pretend to develop more than fifty acres, and that very rarely. Most were clearly intended for suburban villas and labeled as such. These usually included winding drives, lawns, and "naturally" grouped trees and shrubs, and a lake or pond as well as a barn and barnyard, kitchen garden, orchard, and occasionally, a small greenhouse; all on properties ranging from three to twelve acres. Much simpler plans were offered for city lots, but they were still based on the same painterly design principles. Downing, who personally admired large and lavish estates, was quite aware that his readers were far more likely to need help with city or suburban lots.

> ... even in the small area of a fourth of an acre, we should study the same principles and endeavor to produce the same harmony of effects, as if we were improving a mansion residence of the first class.... The man of correct taste will, by the aid of very limited means and upon a small surface, be able to afford the mind more true pleasure, than the improver who lavishes thousands without it, creating no other emotion than surprise or pity at the useless expenditure incurred...[3]

Shrunk to fit a quarter-acre lot, the English landscape garden did not have much pictorial quality left. Some of the plans on paper might have worked on the ground if they had surrounded a modest four-room cottage, but Americans more often set a good-sized house on that quarter-acre lot. Nineteenth- and early twentieth-century residential neighborhoods are full of great big houses on little tiny lots. Under

Spiritual Uplift

those conditions, the most successful landscaping generally belongs to wiser homeowners who stayed with the more geometrical architectural style of garden design. Admittedly the gardening tastemakers of the period paid lip service to the idea that architectural layouts were better suited to small house lots; but they didn't show any plans for them. Not fashionable.

Eventually the painterly garden in miniature did achieve successful simplicity as a swatch of lawn bordered by lines of "shrubbery swinging in and out in strong, graceful undulations,"[4] a pattern proposed by novelist George Washington Cable in 1914. Depending on the size of the yard and the interest of the owner, the borders will be thick or thin and be planted with flowers and shrubs or shrubs alone, and the lawns would or would not be punctuated with a "well-situated tree or two." Gardens are still being made on these design

hard work. They really wanted to popularize gardening and garden-making and not just because they loved gardens themselves. Gardens, they earnestly believed, performed important social functions.

Some were concerned about the social consequences, if unchecked, of "The spirit of unrest" so characteristic of the nation. That this restlessness provided energetic men to tame the wilderness was an unmitigated benefit at the time, especially, in Timothy Dwight's eyes, because without the wilderness, such malcontents, impatient with law, religion, and taxes, would destroy orderly society. Downing, although he admired and quoted Dwight, hoped, on the other hand, that gardening would charm men "to one spot of earth" and give an insignificant bit of soil "such an importance in the eyes of its possessor, that he finds it more attractive than countless acres of unknown and unexplored 'territory.'" For Dwight it

Although Poestenkill is in northern New York State near the Vermont border it epitomizes the kind of orderly, well-kept but unpretentious New England town that nineteenth-century democratic reformers held up as an ideal to Americans.

principles and in the hands of a sensitive designer, amateur or professional, can be very attractive.

There was some disingenuousness to all the talk of democratic moderation. Downing in particular deplored the universal desire of the newly rich to show off, compounded by the tendency of the less rich to imitate all excesses on the cheap. Over and over he and his fellow tastemakers stressed that simplicity, not ostentation, was the essence of elegance. Their strictures were not meant to deter the creation of gardens. On the contrary, they simply intended to make sure that beginning gardeners did not take on more than they could handle successfully and throw down their trowels in disgust. Nineteenth-century garden writers, unlike some twentieth-century ones, never pretended that gardening did not require attention, care, and a certain amount of plain

was the possession of that spot of earth that worked the charm.

> It is however to be observed that a considerable number even of these people become sober, industrious citizens merely by the acquisition of property. The love of property to a certain degree seems indispensable to the existence of sound morals.[5]

Downing took the contemporary growth of horticultural societies as evidence "that the Anglo-Saxon love of home is gradually developing itself out of the Anglo-American love of change." This was wishful thinking: If horticultural societies and love of property have continued to flourish since Downing's day, so has love of change.

An early twentieth century example of a naturalistic garden successfully adjusted to a smallish suburban lot. The placement of the conical conifers that anchor curving beds of flowers and shrubs, aided by the rising ground, makes it hard to tell just where the lawn ends and the back boundary begins.

A hundred and sixty years later it is difficult to see any necessary relationship between sound morals and a community settled in one place for generations, but love of change still has its critics. Nineteenth-century moralists feared the violence and lawlessness of the frontier. Their twentieth-century counterparts rebuke the movers for running away from violence and lawlessness in the cities — escaping to the suburbs or the Sun Belt — rather than staying put and trying to find solutions.

Cities did not get good press in the nineteenth century either. Thomas Jefferson's anti-urban bias was widely shared. Born with the century, Bronson Alcott at thirty-nine found cities ugly and complained that "The city does not whet my appetites and faculties."[6]

There was general agreement that farmers were the backbone of the republic and that without a steady infusion of healthy young people from the countryside, cities would lose their admitted vitality. Most northeasterners realized that farming wasn't much of a paying proposition in their region, but few were as frank about it as the Reverend Henry Ward

Beecher, the renowned preacher who doubled as a popular gardening columnist: "Money is the one manure which the farm greedily covets." By the second decade of the century abandoned agricultural land was reverting to forest in many of the original colonies. If the agrarian ideal of the healthy, moral, outdoor life were to be achieved by a large part of the population, it would have to be achieved in small towns and suburbs: the farm miniaturized into a garden.

A magazine editor, Thomas Green Fessenden, observed in his very popular book, *The New American Gardener*, that:

Horticulture, as respects ornamental gardening is one of the most innocent, the most healthy, and, to some, the most pleasing employment in life. The rural scenes which it affords are instructive lessons, tending to moral and social virtue; teaching us to "look through nature up to nature's God."[7]

According to the horticultural press there was nothing to impede the spread of gardening throughout the country since the homeowner could make a fine show of color in less than an eighth of an acre without having to spend more time and effort than even a working man could afford. Just as important as the idealization of the small garden in giving gardening opportunities to city workers of quite modest means was the development of inexpensive mass transportation. Railroads and trolleycars, and, in some cases, steamships and steam ferries made living outside of the tightly built core of the city affordable in time and money. Railway and streetcar companies actively promoted suburbanization by buying and developing tracts of land around big cities. Downing approved of dispersal to the countryside as healthy but deplored as missed opportunities the grids of fifty-foot lots that made up most such subdivisions. This kind of planning, in his eyes, just created more of the "graceless villages" that disgraced the American countryside outside of New England. Downing felt deeply that attractive surroundings were very important and not just for the aesthetic pleasure of the observer:

> ... when the affections are so dull, and the domestic virtues so blunt that men do not care how their own homes and villages look, they care very little for fulfilling any moral obligations not made compulsory by the strong arm of the law.[8]

The badly built houses and unkempt yards and streets that he believed indicated uncivilized inhabitants had been a major concern for Timothy Dwight. He brought up the subject repeatedly in his *Travels*, and one of these passages, a long one, was reprinted by Downing in an editorial in *The Horticulturist*. In essence their point was that "the perception of beauty and deformity ... is the first thing which influences man to attempt an escape from a groveling, brutish character." In most people, according to Dwight, this perception could only be awakened by contact with good houses, good clothes, and good manners, "what may be called the exterior of society." To those who found this a strange argument from a minister and college president who, they thought, should be upholding the virtues of plain living, Dwight replied

> There are virtuous cottages still, though their number is now, and always has been, less than it has been supposed by the fancy of the poet and the novelist. ... But the debate is not between cottages and palaces, nor between poverty and opulence; it lies between taste and the want of it, between grossness and refinement.
> In these letters you may observe that only a single style of building and living has been particularly commended, viz., that which is neat, tidy and convenient.[9]

Refinement, for these Puritan descendents, was a suitable and attainable ideal for the citizens of a republic, particularly one in which literacy was practically universal and in which real, grinding, imprisoning poverty, they believed, did not exist.

The higher social and artistic elements of every man's nature lie dormant within him, and every laborer is a possible gentlemen, not by the possession of money or fine clothes — but through the refining influence of intellectual and moral culture.[10]

The believers in this vision of true democratic refinement would probably be horrified at the turn their ideal has taken over the past hundred and fifty years. As restated by George Washington Cable, it was ready to become an underpinning for consumer society:

> Almost any good American will admit it to be a part of our national social scheme, I think, — if we have a social scheme, — that everybody shall aspire to all the refinements of life.[11]

For all their faith in the positive moral effect of the fine arts in general and gardening in particular, nineteenth-century social critics were quite aware that they would have to sell the idea to their fellow citizens, many of whom saw no useful purpose in creating attractive surroundings unless there was money in it. One quite effective strategy was to emphasize the importance of such an environment for children. Downing quoted an "eloquent appeal" from a New Hampshire farmers' club report:

> If you would keep pure the heart of your child, and make his youth innocent and happy, surround him with objects of interest and beauty at home ... adorn your dwellings, your places of worship, your school-houses, your streets and public squares, with trees and hedges, and lawns and flowers, so that his heart may early and ever be impressed with the love of Him who made them all.[12]

Children were not only to grow up in a beautiful environment, they were also to help create it and thus learn the value of work. Fessenden among others made a special point of flower gardening as an improving and amusing pursuit for young people, heavy on the improving:

> Let them be instructed, that nothing valuable is to be obtained or preserved without labour, care, and attention — that as every valuable plant must be defended, and every noxious weed removed, so every moral virtue must be protected, and every corrupt passion and propensity subdued.

Henry Ward Beecher's sisters, Catherine and Harriet, authors of that very Christian household manual *The American Woman's Home*, also considered gardening a desirable domestic amusement for children, especially girls, who could be "led to acquire many useful habits." Among these were early rising, active participation in household work, orderliness, and neatness.

Beecher's own genuine love of flowers shines through essay after essay — "no man should have to walk more than twenty paces to find a flower." — but alas for the moral, he was not to be trusted with his friend's wife.

Beecher seemed to aim a lot of his horticultural advocacy at the less advantaged: "[A]nything which shall increase the knowledge and skill of the *plain people* in the management of flowers will be a contribution to the public welfare." Others proposed community gardening and garden contests as a way of assimilating immigrants into American society, and were taken up by companies like National Cash Register and towns like Northampton, Massachusetts. Still others addressed a more highly educated segment of society, thus the Reverend John Frederick Schroeder to the members of the New York Horticultural Society:

> We are engaged in the promotion of an object suited to man's highest earthly destinies.
> It is calculated to afford the *intellect* abundant themes, to which a patriarch's long life might with unceasing gladness be devoted . . . it is replete with the animating pleasures of discovery, and the calm delights of contemplation . . . it can act upon the *heart* with a benignity, that has power to allay the angry passions of the breast; it can promote our peace on earth; and it can fill us with pure sentiments and holy breathings.[15]

The horticultural writers were just as convinced as the Transcendentalists of the spiritual benefits to be found in direct contact with nature, even if they tended to prefer nature "with her hair combed," as the author of an 1852 architectural pattern book, Lewis Allen, put it, and hands-in-the-soil exercise to solitary rambles in the forest. The far-sighted, like Frederick Law Olmsted, recognized that cities were here to stay and would only become larger and more crowded. Olmsted truly valued the cultural opportunities that only cities could provide, but he was equally concerned about making the experience of nature available to everyone, especially those who for whatever reason could not leave crowded urban centers. His friend and mentor, Downing, campaigned vigorously for city parks. To convince skeptics that there was a popular thirst for such open spaces he pointed out the weekend crowds that thronged the new garden cemeteries like Mount Auburn near Boston, Green Wood in Brooklyn, Laurel Hill in Philadelphia, and Spring Green in Cincinnati. Created in the 1830s and '40s, these had been

Above, right:
The cottage ideal illustrated in the April 1878 issue of *Vick's Magazine*. The accompanying poem celebrated a woman's love of flowers that led to a "cottage quaint of cultured grace" replacing a farmer's "squalid hovel" and its weed-infested yard.

Lower right:
A section devoted to "Botany for little folks" and other horticultural activities for children was a regular feature in *Vick's Magazine* during the late 1870s in response to the prevalent ideas that such interests were important for their religious development.

Benevolent and social feelings could also be cultivated by influencing children to share their fruits and flowers with friends and neighbors, as well as to distribute roots and seeds to those who have not the means of procuring them. A woman or a child by giving seeds or slips or roots to a washerwoman or a farmer's boy, thus inciting them to love and cultivate fruits and flowers, awakens a new and refining source of enjoyment in minds which have few resources more elevating than mere physical enjoyments.[13]

For their brother the love of gardening was both a source of "pure satisfaction" and a sign of virtue.

> But if a man that loves flowers, and loves them enough to labor for them, is not to be trusted, where in this wicked world shall we go for trust? A man that carries a garden in his heart has got back again a part of the Eden from which our great forefather was expelled.[14]

OUR YOUNG PEOPLE.

intended as places for the quiet contemplation of mortality in the midst of nature, not as the settings for Sunday picnics which they had become. Parks would provide fresh air, spaces for exercise and musical entertainment, and for bringing all social classes together in the enjoyment of natural beauty. The cemeteries had come into being through private subscription; public parks would have to be created by public taxation although contributions by individuals would be welcome supplements. The problem, as Downing saw it, was that

> [W]hile no men contribute money so willingly and liberally as we Americans for the support of religion, or indeed for the furtherance of any object of moral good, we are slow to understand the value and influence of beauty of this material kind, on our daily lives.[16]

Change moral to humanitarian and the sentence could have been written today. This may very well be why American nature-lovers and park and garden sponsors from the beginning of the republic onwards have addressed their appeals for money and legislation to the utilitarian rather than the aesthetic sensibilities of their fellow citizens. The argument that an attractive environment makes better citizens has considerable validity. There have been several quite convincing studies showing the psychological benefits, even the healing quality, of pleasant surroundings, particularly natural ones, and it very often turns out to be true that people will cooperate with their neighbors to protect and care for a building or a park or a tree that they find pleasing to look at. But not always. Human nature doesn't seem to be as perfectable as the nineteenth century thought it was and we would still like to believe it is.

By the late 1850s Downing and his fellow promoters of city parks had won their battle, selling public and politicians alike on the usefulness of parks in improving the health—mental, moral, and physical—of city dwellers. Their faith that one good example would be instantly imitated was also vindicated. The success of Olmsted and Vaux's Central Park inspired a wave of park-building in towns and cities all across the country, once the Civil War was over. And with Frederick Law Olmsted, Calvin Vaux, and their contemporaries like H. W. S. Cleveland, Robert Morris Copeland, Charles Eliot, and Jacob Weidemann, landscape architecture became firmly established as a profession in the United States. Although these men would spend almost as much time designing private estates as they did public spaces, they saw their profession as having a social and environmental mission and they were not shy about proclaiming it in books and magazine articles. The same vision has continued to motivate some part of the profession ever since, one legacy of the nineteenth century's conviction that artistic, or at least tidy, cultivation of the land was a force·for moral and social betterment.

Indeed, that conviction has indelibly tinted the American attitude toward gardens and gardening. We still tend to think that the person who neglects his yard probably neglects his children. This is not necessarily so, but the belief that helping slum-dwellers to clear vacant lots and turn them into com-

munity gardens will make the participants more constructive citizens has usually proved valid. The problem with the gardening-is-good-for-you approach, then and now, is that it often carries with it more than a whiff of condescension — keep them in the garden and out of the tavern — and so provokes resistance among independent spirits. Could this be one reason why the popularity of gardening has risen and fallen with such regularity in this country over the last two hundred years?

When you love gardens, and feel that both the results and the process of gardening truly lift your own spirit, sharing your enthusiasm without seeming to preach takes tact and sensitivity. There are encouraging signs that in the present surge of interest in gardening, enthusiasts have recognized the problem. In particular, those who consider horticulture a possible remedy for social and educational problems are learning to muffle the moral overtones. Horticultural programs for schoolchildren emphasize experiment and intellectual stimulation; for prison inmates, practical job opportunities. Support groups that aid and encourage community gardeners in poor inner-city neighborhoods stress the sociability and pleasure of the activity, the flavor and beauty of the results.

Many of today's social activists, planners, and designers are even beginning to share Timothy Dwight's belief in the power of private property to promote social responsibility. It seems to be that a house of one's own on one's own land, no matter how small, remains a fundamental and energizing dream for most Americans.

Home grounds treated with the dignified simplicity that A. J. Downing advocated for the non-gardening home-owner at 77th Street and Broadway. Mayor of New York during Central Park's early years and a Tammany Hall Democrat, Fernando Wood had some run-ins with the reform-minded Olmsted, but made a signal contribution by fighting off attempts to take away some of the park site for residential development.

Revivals and
New Patterns

Today, minus the vine-veiled pergola that formerly enclosed it, the south end of the garden at Hamilton House opens on a serene vista down the Salmon Falls River.

Even in this country that part of the nineteenth century that loosely coincides with the reign of Queen Victoria is usually called the Victorian Age. As far as the arts are concerned, it might as accurately be called the Age of Revivals: Classic Revival, "Gothick" Revival, Romanesque Revival, Renaissance Revival, Rococo Revival, Colonial Revival. Curiously, in a time when new knowledge, new technology and new materials were transforming their fabrication, architecture and the decorative arts resolutely turned their eyes to the past for design inspiration. That the results would never have been recognized by the style being revived was a matter for self-congratulation not embarrassment: The very differences represented progress.

In the world of gardening, the first revival was the *parterre de broderie* of the eighteenth-century pattern books. And it was revived to fill a gap in garden design. The modern or natural style as transmitted to the United States by the horticultural press was formed from grass, water, trees, and shrubs and made little provision for the display of flowers in either of its modes, Beautiful or Picturesque. Writers were concerned with emphasizing the contrast between the structure of the two styles: the "modern" based on abstractions of natural forms, and the "ancient" on architectural ones. Flowers were rarely discussed. But most people, gardeners or not, like flowers. The sole exception may be landscape architects, or at least the purists among them.

During the eighteenth century, in fact, there weren't many purists among English landscape gardeners, as they were then called. After long and careful study of plans, paintings, correspondence, and nursery bills, Mark Laird has established that even Capability Brown, considered the master of the grass-woods-and-water landscape, arranged borders of flowers and flowering shrubs along paths in parts of the pleasure grounds.[1]

Shrubberies, groves of trees, and shrubs flanking the lawns in front of the principal facades of a mansion provided family and friends with shaded places to walk and enjoy the scents, sounds, and colors of the garden but left open vistas to the park and its grazing animals beyond the ha-ha, or sunk fence. Often, shrubbery paths were edged with seasonal flowers planted in graduated lines. On some estates, Laird notes, strollers might even find orderly flower gardens tucked into secluded spaces within wildernesses, as shrubberies were sometimes called.

Not all planters integrated flowers into their schemes. Groves were abstractions of natural phenomena and blended smoothly into the undulating belts and clumps of trees that defined and accented the park. Flower gardens were plainly a result of human ordering. Moreover, it was not easy to keep them in attractive bloom all year at that time. Some gardeners kept favorite flowers in a traditional walled and sunny enclosure, often a kitchen garden where they shared space with fruits and vegetables, and kept that enclosure away from the house, hidden from view with belts of trees and shrubs. George Washington used both strategies at Mount Vernon, collecting flowering trees and shrubs for groves and wilderness, and planting flowers and vegetables in separate walled gardens. Only after settlement had pushed out wild animals and fence laws restrained domestic ones in the nineteenth century did those Americans landscaping a large piece of property concern themselves with integrating flowers into a naturalistic design.

In the meantime, English garden theorists and designers were returning flower beds to their former position directly beneath the windows of the house. They had come to feel that some degree of architectural treatment of the immediate surroundings of the house was not only more convenient for its inhabitants but also made a better visual transition between house and park. By the 1790s Humphry Repton and his contemporaries had brought back the terrace and with it, flowers, planted in shaped beds based on the knot garden or the parterre. Whereas the creators of the Elizabethan knot garden or the seventeenth-century *parterre de broderie* had relied on trimmed evergreen foliage — box, santolina, artemisia, lavender — in various tones of green to outline their patterns and filled them in with pebbles, coal, and brick dust as often as they did with blossoms, the early nineteenth-century designer colored his patterns exclusively with leaves and flowers: spring bulbs followed by annuals and perennials. The development of the new flower parterre is usually ascribed to a new availability of long-blooming summer flowers from South Africa and South and Central America, but a little research turns up the fact that quite a few of these — *Impatiens balsamina* and *Celosia* from the Far East, the misnamed African and French marigolds from Mexico, nasturtiums from Peru, cannas from South America, for a few examples — were available all through the seventeenth and eighteenth centuries. And in both centuries, the French had experimented with the idea of the flower parterre. Louis XIV had scented flowers placed in the beds under his bedroom window at Trianon. He even had his parterres planted overnight so that his family could enjoy a stroll among spring bulbs in January, a courtesy that depended on greenhouses and a legion of skilled gardeners.

Early nineteenth-century garden-makers really saw flower parterres as a way to show off flowers, and the more new flowers that became available, the more they had to show off. Geometric layouts were dismissed as obvious and lacking in variety by the theorists of the Natural style, but those who love flowers would agree with Repton's opinion as expressed in *The Theory and Practice of Landscape Gardening*: "Variety in a flower-garden is derived from the selection and diversity of its shrubs and flowers."

According to the garden books, there were basically two ways to lay out a flower garden. The more traditional way was to compose it of beds separated by gravel paths and edged with foliage plants suited to clipping, like boxwood, or with tiles or stones. In these beds the flowers — perennial and annual, tall and short — were mixed to the owner's taste. Even before the Philadelphia Centennial Exhibition of 1876, which is often considered the genesis of the Colonial Revival, the old-fashioned flower garden, which it purported to restore, had plenty of supporters like Anna Warner, whose popular *Gardening by Myself* was published in 1871. The other option, cutting the beds into a ground of green turf, was considered more modern and was preferred by many,

The flowerbeds around the west lawn and the oval beds next to the house at Monticello, laid out according to Jefferson's 1812 revision, are simple shapes cut into the turf, representing a very early example of the massed-color plantings that would become common later in the century. He made no attempt to keep all beds in bloom all the time.

particularly after the lawnmower, which simplified maintenance, became widely available in the 1850s.

Designers in the early years were not as concerned about creating flat and even patterns as were their successors later in the century; but they were concerned with something that had not really bothered gardeners before: the sight of earth between the plants in a flower bed. This was a subject on which nineteenth-century garden writers — not just Downing and the Americans, but William Robinson and Gertrude Jekyll later on — were often fanatical:

> In a hot climate, like that of our summers, nothing is more unpleasing to the eyes or more destructive to that expression of softness, verdure, and gayety, that should exist in the flower-garden, than to behold the surface of the soil in any of the beds or parterres unclothed with plants.[2]

Downing did not get this particular notion from his mentors Repton or Loudon. Repton doesn't bring up the subject although his watercolors of flower gardens do show the beds solidly filled with leaves and flowers. If this passage from *The Suburban Gardener and Villa Companion* published in 1838 is any indication, Loudon took a rather negative view of the idea:

> ... one principle of planting must never be lost sight of; that is, distinctness, or the keeping of every particular plant perfectly isolated, and, though near to, yet never allowing it to touch, the adjoining plants ... we should never for a minute think of recommending what may be called the picturesque in flower-planting, either for a flower-garden or for flowers in borders. We except, however, creepers and low plants, and perhaps plants gener-

ally, where the object is to produce one dense mass of any particular colour; because this object cannot be effected without allowing the plants to cover the whole bed.[3]

Dense masses of color for us are a hallmark of Victorian style, but they took a while to gain popularity. Even then they had to compete with the botanical fascination of plant collecting. Downing, who liked what he called the new English style of one-color plantings both for their coverage of the soil and their "breadth of effect," had to admit that most flower-lovers had a passion for novelty and variety and that the *mingled* flower-garden was more popular.

One of Loudon's planting lists for a front-garden flower parterre included eighty-six different genera of perennials and another, thirty-six species of perennials and thirty-eight of bulbs, chosen to "show how much botanical interest a very small garden may afford." Many of these were low-growing but not all: lilies, delphinium, oriental poppies, mallows, monarda, and coreopsis had a place. Also, flowering shrubs were often included in these beds and borders. They could be kept on the low side by pegging down the branches or by selective pruning and had the advantage of remaining green after flowering. Repton welcomed devices for adding height to the flower garden:

> ... above all, there should be poles or hoops for those kinds of creeping plants which spontaneously form themselves into graceful festoons, when encouraged and supported by art.[4]

But garden-makers in England and America didn't just revive the parterre, they took it apart and used its elements, the shaped beds, separately or recombined in brand new

Above:
Taking elements from classic parterre patterns, Victorians added other shapes and recomposed the whole in unpredictable ways. The free-wheeling assembly in Wade Hampton's South Carolina garden is subdued compared to some. In the deep South, swept earth formed a more typical background for flower beds than turf.

Right:
John Claudius Loudon invented the term "gardenesque" to label Victorian landscapes displaying a collection of specimen plants and trees. With restraint in choice and generosity in spacing, such design can mature gracefully; but it very often became a jumble, as in this engraving from Frank J. Scott's *Beautifying Suburban Home Grounds.*

ways. Jefferson's flower gardens at Monticello offer a good example of this turn-of-the-nineteenth-century practice. He cut oval flower beds into the lawns on both the east and west fronts of the house and bordered the gravel walk around the west lawn with narrow beds. All were planted with different combinations of flowers and flowering shrubs, which were arranged to give color through the seasons. Nearly two-thirds of the roughly one hundred species he grew were the familiar flowers of the European garden; but he supplemented them with wildflowers from the surrounding countryside, some of the new western species brought back by Lewis and Clark, and whatever of the new exotics from South Africa his friend and seedsman, Bernard McMahon, could supply him.

Jefferson's simple round and oval beds were soon joined in gardens by arabesques and teardrops, crosses and crescents, motifs taken from oriental carpets and amoeba-like shapes of unknown origin. One of these might be tucked individually into the curve of a path or several strung out to border its edges. Arranged in such a way, fancifully shaped beds planted with a sensitive eye for color and texture could give color and interest to the walkways of even a small garden and still allow a coherent design.

Passionate interest in new and exotic plants does not necessarily or often produce good garden design. It is the individual plant that fills the eye of the planter, not the effect of the whole. As Frank J. Scott rather ruefully admitted in *The Art of Beautifying Suburban Home Grounds,*

> When once the planting fever is awakened, *too many of both are likely to be planted*, and grounds will be stuffed rather than beautified.[5]

The plans and engravings that illustrate his book do not bear out the restraint advocated in his text. Lawns tend to be dotted with single specimens of exotic trees and shrubs, each placed to display its individual character, and quite a few flower beds have wandered away from their moorings. These are often joined by a miscellany of other ornamental escapees from the architectural garden like vases, urns, arches, tripods, fountains, garden seats, and garden houses. The passion for novelty underlying much of this clutter was fed by the increasing ability of manufacturers to produce furnishings and ornaments for the garden as they did for the house in styles hybrid or pure at prices within the budget of the middle-class homeowner.

In the same way, the passion for new and exotic plants was nourished by the continuous introductions of the plant-hunters and by the increasing skill of horticulturists in growing and hybridizing them to create forms with larger and more colorful flowers, neater and more compact growth. New technology also played a role: Loudon's invention in 1817 of the curved metal glazing bar, and the ridge and furrow technique that some years later would be developed so brilliantly by Joseph Paxton revolutionized the design of greenhouses. The entire structure, roof and sides, could now be glazed. With all this available light, plants from the tropics, or any part of the world, could be grown in Britain and America. And with the development by Dr. Nathaniel Ward of what was essentially a portable greenhouse, the Wardian case, plant collectors could count on bringing their finds back alive. The greenhouse or conservatory soon became a fashionable adjunct to the estates of the wealthy on both sides of the Atlantic, and Downing saw no reason why "cottages of more humble character" in this country could not enjoy the possession of small greenhouses or "plant cabinets" if their inhabitants were truly interested in plants. There is little evidence that humble houses went in for greenhouses, but interest in exotic plants there certainly was. Caroline Kirkland offers evidence in her memoir-thinly-disguised-as-novel, *A New Home . . . Who'll Follow* as she describes loading a wagon to move her family's possessions from the

relatively civilized Detroit of the late 1820s to her new home on the forest frontier:

> A convenient space must be contrived for my plants among which were two or three tall geraniums and an enormous Calla Ethiopica.[6]

Topiary work also made a come-back: Scott was particularly fond of creating living gateways and summerhouses using everything from hemlocks and hawthorns to elms and apple trees. One of the problems of the period's horticultural writers was that in trying to make readers aware of all the possibilities available to them, they appeared to encourage those readers to try them all. There were plenty who didn't need much encouragement, as photographs from the middle of the century indicate.

The naturalistic landscape was for most of the period considered the proper setting for the dwelling; for small lots Downing suggested grass and trees "and a knot of flowers woven gayly together." Lawn and trees were the essentials, flowers were add-on decorations and this was a time when abundant decoration was popular. Frank Scott's plea for discretion would be repeated and paraphrased for a quarter-century:

> Imagine bits of lace or bows of ribbon stuck promiscuously over the body and skirt of a lady's dress. 'How vulgar!' you exclaim. Put them in their appropriate places and what charming points they make! Let your lawn be your home's velvet robe, and your flowers its not too promiscuous decorations.[7]

Downing located his flowers on the terrace under the parlor windows, but in the last half of the century the knot of flowers took shape as a circle of bright-hued annuals cut into the front lawn. Massed color and bedding out, the technique for achieving it, had arrived. To be effective, massed flower beds need a rather large number of plants of even, compact growth and consistent, abundant, long-lasting color, which can be provided either by flowers or foliage. Often the first flowers in a bed would be daffodils or hyacinths or tulips, bulbs planted in the previous autumn and lifted after they finished flowering to be instantly replaced by the long-blooming summer bedding plants. This can be achieved, with luck and cooperation from the weather, by sowing the seeds of annuals directly into the soil after the danger of frost has passed, letting them grow up around the bulbs, and

> as they grow, keep them rigorously within bounds; clip and train and fasten back, and let nothing stray over the limits by so much as a bud. A geometric garden must have military line-and-rule precision[8]

Anna Warner cautions her readers that this will take time, attention, and patience, and should be undertaken only by those who have all three in abundance. For herself, she preferred the old-fashioned garden. A more reliable system that could produce a longer period of bloom was to start annuals

or tender perennials from seeds or cuttings indoors and then plant or bed them out as soon as the weather was favorable. You could as an alternative buy your plants from a nursery or florist. This, too, had its drawbacks: A frequent complaint about massed beds was that inexperienced homeowners would plant up their beds from the florist's stock without any idea of what those plants required in type of soil or amount of moisture. The instant effect might be attractive, but after a month or so of neglect—no deadheading, no pinching back, no watering—all that was left was a depressing tangle of dead and straggling plants. Massed bedding required a lot of maintenance. In spite of Downing's approbation, this major contribution of the Victorians to the garden maker's bag of tricks did not catch on quite as fast in this country as it had in England, perhaps because we could not boast of so many well-trained professional gardeners who "love such beds because they show how skilfully they can grow and trim their plants." Mariana Griswold van Rensselaer, like most serious landscape critics at the end of the century, disliked pattern-beds as they were usually employed, and went on to observe that "owners love them because—well, I fear simply because they are showier than anything else." Mrs. van Rensselaer was fair-minded enough, unlike many of her contemporaries, to concede that such beds could be

> artistic whenever they look as though they belonged in the place where they lie; and this leads us to the fact that they are especially artistic when they look as though this place belonged to them—as though it had be prepared for them and could not rightly be filled with anything else.[9]

She felt that their proper use was on architectural terraces and in urban spaces too small to support trees or shrubs, and that they usually disfigured anything in the naturalistic style, front lawns and public parks alike. One wonders how she would respond to the spectacularly crowd-pleasing effects created today with the massing technique by the expert horticulturists at public gardens like Longwood or Disney World.

It is really not surprising that the biggest promoters of the bedding-out system were nurserymen—Downing himself, Joseph Breck, James Vick, and above all Peter Henderson. But in addition to the horticultural journals such popular magazines as *Godey's Lady's Book* published patterns for flower beds with suggested planting lists, and architectural pattern books routinely placed circular beds in the foregrounds of their perspective engravings. And circular beds duly appeared in front of workman's cottages, suburban villas, country mansions, and farm houses from New England to the Middle West.

Massed beds did not have to be brilliantly colored, but they often were, simply because most people like bright colors. Elias Long was not alone in observing that in public parks in this country and abroad,

> the parts devoted to these showy arrangements of flower are those among all competing ones in interest, that are the most constantly thronged by admirers.[10]

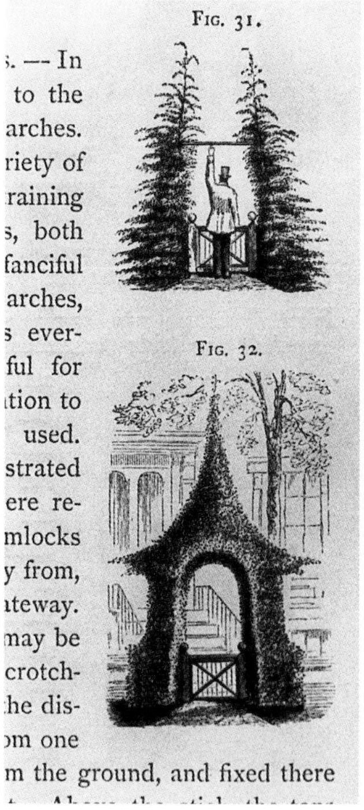

FIG. 31.

FIG. 32.

s. — In to the arches. riety of raining s, both fanciful arches, s ever- ful for tion to used. strated ere re- mlocks y from, ateway. nay be crotch- he dis- m one m the ground, and fixed there

Above, top:
Scott also had a passion for topiary. If the instructions that he gave his readers for training the gateway arch illustrated really worked, the results would have been amazing—and unlike any topiary seen before or since.

Above, bottom:
This even more fanciful arch required, according to Scott, a complicated system of twisting together two weeping elms, then grafting on them Scamston elm (a mysterious cultivar) and growing it on for ten years.

Above:
The scroll pattern for a carpet bed from Peter Henderson's 1875 *Gardening for Pleasure* comes with the warning that it requires a vast number of plants less than six inches high, and the suggestion that the design be worked out first with colored papers.

Above, right:
At the entrance to a city house, a carpet-bedding scheme perfectly suited to its location: Two tones of clipped foliage form a simple pattern on the central cone of heaped earth outlined at its base with narrow rings of contrasting foliage. Low, neatly edged beds of what look like white begonias circumscribe the outer edge of the design.

Right, below:
Peter Henderson recommends achieving masses or ribbons of color based on the normal height of certain plants, warning that some may need pinching to keep them in line. In his diagram the cone slopes from a six-foot canna through rings of colored foliage plants to a less-than-six-inch lobelia.

James Vick suggested that if you were tired of *scarlet fever*, you could try working with softly shaded succulents like sedums, echeverias and mesembranthemums for more subtle effects. Nor did the beds have to be all one hue. Quite often they were laid out in two- or three-color designs: The star was a favorite. Another popular variation was called ribbon bedding. This could refer to stripes of color bordering a path or drive, or a shaped bed planted in concentric rings of different colored plants of different heights. In *Gardening for Pleasure* Peter Henderson suggests a scheme carried out for the most part with foliage plants. The majority of these plants originated in tropical or subtropical Africa and South America, and one argument advanced by the enemies of bedding out was that even when you tried hard to care for them some exotics just did not thrive. Liberty Hyde Bailey sums up the attitude of those who believed in growing what

grew naturally in the opening chapter of his often reprinted book, *Garden-Making*, and says it is the best advice he can give a beginner.

A patch of lusty pigweeds, growing and crowding in luxuriant abandon, may be a better and more worthy object of affection than a bed of coleuses in which every spark of life and spirit and individuality has been sheared out and suppressed. The man who worries morning and night about the dandelions in the lawn will find great relief in loving the dandelions.[11]

A wide variety of effects could also be achieved by the placement of the beds. Long, narrow beds laid out in a scroll or similar running design could be placed, like the carpet borders they resembled, to frame a stretch of lawn. Or beds could be packed together to create carpet bedding, so called because the effect was thought to resemble the richness of an oriental rug. A well-documented arrangement of this sort has been restored by the Society for the Preservation of New England Antiquities in Woodstock, Connecticut.

ROSELAND COTTAGE

Once Henry C. Bowen had built himself a fortune in New York City, he built himself a summer house, Roseland Cottage, in the small northern Connecticut town where he was born. The bright pink Gothick cottage could have come straight from the pages of Andrew Jackson Downing's *Cottage Residences* or *The Architecture of Country Houses*, but it was in fact designed by Joseph C. Wells, the British-born-and-trained architect of the First Presbyterian Church on West 12th Street in Manhattan and the Plymouth Church in Brooklyn, and built about 1846. It is quite likely that the architect also had a hand in the design of the parterre garden next to the house but this is not documented. What is documented are its plants. In 1850 Henry Bowen placed an order with Dyer's Nursery in Brooklyn, Connecticut for fruit trees, perennials, and "600 yards of dwarf box edging." That same dwarf English boxwood—after drastic but rejuvenating pruning—still borders the same twenty-one beds.

However overgrown and weed infested, the fact that this garden remained on its original site gave Rudy Favretti, the well-known landscape historian and restoration specialist, a head start when SPNEA commissioned him to prepare a rehabilitation plan after buying Roseland Cottage from the Bowen family in 1970. In addition to the 1850 order there were "survivor" plants in the garden and an unusual number of period photographs, family scrapbooks, and newspaper descriptions to show how the garden had looked from 1850 until the 1920s. Bowen had been an early supporter of the Republican Party, and remained an influential political figure. His spectacular Fourth-of-July parties drew presidents and cabinet members, as well as distinguished orators like Henry Ward Beecher and Oliver Wendell Holmes to Woodstock. They also drew the attention of the national press.

The east front of Roseland Cottage with its twin verandas looks out to the Woodstock village green, separated from it by a narrow lawn, a low fence, and a double file of sugar maples flanking the road. The green, planted and maintained by Bowen, along with the broad lawn on the north side of the house serves as the landscape setting considered necessary for such a villa-cottage at mid-century and as a park for the town. If the line of street trees, another amenity provided by Bowen, is not exactly in harmony with Picturesque landscape ideas, it does not represent as much of a barrier to the view from the house to the green as one might think. And street-tree planting was considered at the time to be one of the best improvements that a civic-minded citizen could make to his town.

The roses that once climbed up the latticework summerhouse at the garden entrance are still in place, but the summerhouse itself disappeared between 1905 and 1915 along with the lattice fence that surrounded at least three sides of the garden. The present summerhouse, a miniature Greek

Top:
A conical bed on the same model as Peter Henderson's but less rigidly geometric ornaments the lawn of the Francis Robinson Drake homestead in Northampton, New Hampshire. Attractive punctuation: the evenly spaced caladium leaves around the base.

Above:
A watercolor portrait of Roseland Cottage in Woodstock, Connecticut perhaps painted by its architect, Joseph C. Wells. The subdued color of the house is inaccurate. Documents and paint layers show that Henry C. Bowen painted his house from the beginning the same bright pink that it is today. Was it just too loud to suit an English architect?

temple of wooden pillars framing lattice panels, was added by one of Henry Bowen's sons in the 1920s at the opposite side of the garden. Beyond the flower garden to the south is an orchard and to the west a large barn.

If the arrangement of the parterre is typical — two sets of beds separated by gravel paths and centered on circles on either side of a long oval pointed straight at the front door — the planting is unexpected. The central oval is a massed bed of geraniums arranged ribbon-style in bands of pink, white, and red, and there are massed beds of snapdragons, petunias, begonias, and sedums: so far, the epitome of traditional carpet bedding. But in the bed of sedums there is a good-sized Japanese maple, visible in a 1901 photograph. Another photograph from the same year shows a large rhododendron in one of the beds west of the center oval. It is still in place along with a large rosebush in another shaped bed. In fact most of the beds on the west are filled with flowers in a wide variety of heights: mixed perennials — delphinium, dianthus, aruncus, coreopsis, iris, lilies — as well as biennials like hollyhocks and several different kinds of annuals. Although it would probably have horrified most garden theoreticians of the mid-nineteenth century, the combination of massed and mingled styles of planting works; the garden has great charm at ground level and still provides an effective pattern from the second-story windows. Archival photographs suggest that such a mixture of planting styles was quite common practice in this country except on large estates or in public parks, where staffs of trained gardeners could provide the kind of precision maintenance that ribbon and carpet bedding ideally required.

With such maintenance ribbon beds can even be effectively executed in well-chosen perennials, as they were in a now vanished mid-twentieth-century garden near Minneapolis, Minnesota. In all probability the inspiration for the beautifully proportioned small rose garden next to a big 1920s summer cottage was French. Its designer, the Harvard-trained Minneapolis landscape architect Edmund Phelps, who had spent part of his childhood in Paris and served in the French army during World War I, was a lifelong francophile.[12] On one of those brilliant green lawns for which Minneapolis is known, five circular beds filled with pink roses were spaced around a central stone basin that once held a fountain, and then a sea of white begonias, the garden's only annuals. Curvy beds of mixed perennials, mostly in tones of white, pink, and yellow, and shrubs bordered the lawn, backed on two sides by white lattice panels wreathed in clematis and honeysuckle and set off by a screen of evergreens, including arborvitae. At the back there was a lacy white wire settee from which to contemplate the flowers and the view.

A LONG ISLAND GARDEN

In 1966, the last garden designed by Umberto Innocenti was carved out of a wooded site on Long Island for a client who had grown up on the estate and loved it. She just wanted to add the kind of Italianate outdoor spaces or "rooms" for which he and his firm, Innocenti & Webel, were famous, in order to accommodate her generation's more outdoor-oriented family life. She coaxed Innocenti out of retirement and worked with him for a year to redesign the entire property, creating, among other spaces, a sunken swimming pool garden bordered by espaliers and formal flower beds, a walled terrace garden, and a hidden "English" garden in the woods.[13] On the breakfast terrace, all-of-a color tulips fill central, corner, and border beds in a geometric layout accented with ilexes and clipped boxwood. Standard and bedding lantanas replace the spring tulips for the rest of the flowering season.

In the English Garden, a real *giardino segreto* enclosed by tall hedges, the plan is circular and the bedding-out more complex. A gravel path circumscribes a slightly raised central bed and is in turn circumscribed by a flower border, which is punctuated by three antique English oak benches. A pair of tall, perfectly conical Alberta spruces anchors the central bed. In spring all the beds are ablaze with tulips planted in irregular blocks of color, sensitively interwoven to create a brilliant but not garish mosaic. For a final touch of spring poetry, flowering cherries veil the sky with soft pink blossoms.

The summer bedding scheme, which stays in place until October, presents a still more intricate mosaic of colors and textures carved out with annuals plus some old-fashioned carpet-bedding staples — coleus, dusty miller, begonia. Although the owner has gardeners and a greenhouse to raise the bedding plants for her garden, she believes in using "everyday plants, in abundance and in many varieties." Her

luxuriant beds contain nothing that is not readily available from garden centers across the country.

The garden provides a long season of pleasure for its owners; but it also requires careful — and expensive — maintenance. The soil is carefully monitored and replaced with fresh topsoil every three or four years, which pays off in healthy plants and reliable color, and in some ways is easier than maintaining a perennial border: Beds can be dug and soil improved without having to work around existing plants. It is also one way to turn the limited choice of annuals in garden centers to advantage, if you can go in with an open mind and meet the challenge of creating an attractive scheme from the colors they happen to be selling that year.

Carpet bedding in its day was a very modern adaptation of the old parterre. But almost as soon as it arrived the last of the revival styles, which would persist into the mid-twentieth century, was taking shape. Like the contemporary Arts and Crafts movement in England, which took its inspiration from Medieval and Renaissance gardens, the Colonial Revival was a reaction against the stiffness of proper Victorian planting and even more against its unresolved conflict between the attempted naturalism of the landscaping and the blatant artificiality of bedding out. In addition, taking inspiration from the so-called grandmother's gardens of the eighteenth century seemed more appropriate for Colonial-style houses and even for newly fashionable shingle-style and Queen Anne villas. But the late nineteenth century visualized the dooryard gardens of the eighteenth with Victorian eyes. Even such a knowledgeable critic as Mrs. van Rensselaer speaks of "freely growing flowers in rectangular box-edged borders, after the old colonial scheme." Boxwood borders did have a place in some southern gardens of the eighteenth century, but not even in all of them. Letters and diaries do tell of daughters carrying slips of box from their Virginia birthplaces to their new homes in Kentucky and Tennessee. Washington did plant some box at Mount Vernon. Jefferson did not grow it at Monticello, and the majority of so-called colonial boxwood

Opposite, top:
Most of the parterre makes no pretense at the flat color massing called for by contemporary writers. Large and woody specimens — a rhododendron, a rosebush, even a Japanese maple — pop up from low blankets of annuals in some beds. Mixed perennials of varying heights stuff others. The pattern traced by the box edging holds the design together.

Opposite, bottom:
In true bedding-out style, massed geraniums pack the central oval bed in the parterre at Roseland Cottage. The latticework fence and summerhouse are gone, but vigorous rosebushes still flank the entrance to the garden.

Above:
Constant pinching, clipping, and deadheading are critical to the success of ribbon and carpet bedding. White begonias, the only annuals in this Minnesota garden designed by Edmund J. Phelps lap the sculpture in the central stone-ringed bed. Pink Dainty Bess roses encircled with well-trimmed *Nepeta mussinii* fill all five beds in orbit around it.

A different interpretation of bedding out informs the hidden garden designed by Umberto Innocenti on a Long Island estate. Tulips — singles, doubles, Darwins, and lily-forms, early to late — blaze in blocks arranged so that the green of the about-to-blooms or the just-finished-blooming doesn't spoil the picture. Once the last fades, all are removed.

Above:
An intricate mosaic of common annuals takes over the garden and lasts until October. Ground huggers like marigolds, begonias, impatiens, and ageratum stay on the edges and often overflow into the path. Taller-stemmed varieties like cosmos and blue salvia crowd the center around the two conical Alberta spruces.

Opposite, top:
Frances Benjamin Johnston's photograph of the terrace at the Gamble House in Pasadena, a refined—and revered— example of Arts-and-Crafts architecture, demonstrates that Greene and Greene paid as much attention to the foliage textures as they did to the brick patterns of the steps and the polished wooden framework of the sleeping porch.

Opposite, bottom:
Charles Fletcher Lummis walked to California after graduating from Harvard and fell in love with the Southwest. In true Arts-and-Crafts style, he built El Alisal, his Southern California house, himself out of boulders hauled from the nearby arroyo and con-fined his garden-making to cutting paths through the wildflowers on his land.

turns out to have been planted in the 1830s and 40s. Further-more, boxwood seems to have played no role in New England gardens, according to careful researchers like Ann Leighton. This is hardly surprising since today the only boxwood that will overwinter there without burlap or plastic wrappings is Korean, which arrived in this country in the nineteenth century.

Susan Fenimore Cooper's descriptions of the cottage gardens of Cooperstown in upstate New York are a more accurate representation of the colonial garden as it moved west with the frontier.

Potatoes, cabbages, and onions are grown here by every family as first requisites. Indian corn and cucumbers are also thought indispensable. . . . Peas and beans rank next in favor: some of each are generally found in the smallest gardens . . . the light green leaves of the lettuce are seen every where. There is usually a pumpkin-vine running about the corn-hills. . . . Sometimes you find squashes, also, in these small gardens, with a few toma-toes, perhaps; but these last are difficult to raise here, on account of the occasional frosts of May.

Flowers are seldom forgotten in the cottage garden; the widest walk is lined with them, and there are others beneath the low windows of the house. You have rose-bushes, sun-flowers, and holly-hocks, as a matter of course; generally a cluster of pinks, bachelor's buttons, also, and a sweet pea, which is a great favorite; plenty of marigolds, a few poppies, large purple china asters, and a tuft of the lilac phlox. Such are the blossoms to be seen before most doors.[14]

Susan Cooper goes on to describe the vines — scarlet runners, morning glories, and hops — that shade the windows, and explains that few fruits, with cherries the most common exception, are grown in the gardens because strawberries, raspberries, currants, and gooseberries grow wild in the woods, and peaches and grapes are so easily obtained by railroad from gentler climates. The one essential ingredient of colonial gardens not mentioned in this description comes up elsewhere in *Rural Hours* — a remark that country people ignorant of the names of flowers did know those of herbs and simples — so we may be sure that the latter were also grown. It is true that Cooperstown in 1848 could not really be called a frontier settlement, but in frontier Michigan a decade earlier Caroline Kirkland had described, and herself planted, gardens of the very same kind, although with a somewhat different mixture of specific vegetables and flowers.

What the real vernacular American dooryard garden or grandmother's garden offered the Colonial Revival was the mixture of annuals and perennials, old-fashioned favorites and new introductions, the same kind of inspiration that the English cottage garden gave to the Arts-and-Crafts gardens of Gertrude Jekyll. Both were attempts to recreate what was thought to be the environment of an earlier and nobler time, in contrast to both industrial blight and new-rich ostentation. Although in principle Arts and Crafts can be considered a revival, its proponents varied in their attitude to past styles. The Mission Revival gardens of California, which will be examined in a subsequent chapter, and the walled gardens of Charleston and Savannah were intended to replicate those of earlier periods albeit in highly romanticized form. For many Arts and Crafts garden makers, what counted was fidelity to the flora and geology of the region in the materials used, fine craftsmanship in their use, and close attention to the needs of the garden owners.

A prime example of this approach is the garden at El Alisal, the house that Charles Fletcher Lummis built for himself, mostly by himself. It consisted simply of paths cut through the native vegetation. Although Lummis was a transplanted easterner, he called California wildflowers "The Carpet of God's Country" in a magazine article and expressed his disdain for properties "lawnmowered to eternal smugness."[15]

Most American members of the movement were quite prepared to admit ideas and techniques from any quarter. In the Middle West the influence of the Scandinavian crafts tradition has been little explored except for the work of Jens Jensen and the Saarinen family. It may have been more extensive than we realize. Particularly in the West, designers

Below, left:
In its exuberant heyday the Colonial Revival garden at Hamilton House almost hid the genuine 1785 Georgian mansion in South Berwick, Maine that it was created to enhance. Only the roof and chimneys are visible in a 1929 photograph by Paul Weber. On the recommendation of Sarah Orne Jewett, Mrs. George Tyson and her step-daughter, Elise, bought the house in 1898 to save it and asked their renovation architect, Herbert Browne, to design the kind of garden they felt such a beautiful house should have.

Below, right:
Later the Tyson ladies had a small cottage built beyond the main flower garden, using beams and paneling from a demolished eighteenth-century house. Its walled garden with brick paths, lilacs and old-fashioned flowers, is very much Arts and Crafts, as this Paul Weber photograph demonstrates.

Right:
Gertrude Jekyll's lavish perennial plantings were added to the Colonial Revival program by American garden writers like Mrs. Francis King. Her now vanished garden at Orchard House in Alma, Michigan, her laboratory for the advice she offered her readers, reflects Jekyll's ideas; but its layout is that of a traditional American town garden.

found a great deal of inspiration in Japanese carpentry and stonework. The terrace plantings at the Greene brothers' Gamble House in Pasadena come immediately to mind.

Arts-and-Crafts and Colonial-Revival designers fashioned their gardens from hardy plants — not necessarily native ones — informally arranged against a strong architectural background of walls or hedges or, especially in this country, fences. Tropical plants were for the most part sent back to the greenhouse, or planted in pots as movable accents. And the garden-maker's skill was focused on the creation of harmonious groupings of colors and textures to give the garden interest all year long. Information and admonition passed back and forth across the Atlantic with increasing frequency as the nineteenth century drew to a close. Herbaceous borders adapted to local conditions began to appear in American gardens. Wilhelm Miller and O. C. Simmons, two pillars of the Prairie Landscape school knew William Robinson. Frank Lloyd Wright admired Robinson and Gertrude Jekyll and visited their gardens, as did Beatrix

Farrand. Most of the influential American garden writers like Mrs. Francis King, Louise Beebe Wilder, and Elizabeth Lawrence corresponded with Jekyll and acknowledged her influence: She was an extraordinary colorist.

Similar principles did not necessarily produce the same results in both countries. Much that thrived in England's damp and mild climate wilted in America's extremes of drought and flood, heat and cold. Even when the flowers were similar, the layout and character of the garden sites were different in this country. In the most common plan rectangular beds faced each other across a central path that ended with an arbor or a garden bench. Sometimes rectangles of lawn edged with flowers replaced the beds of flowers. There was another path around the perimeter and this was often bordered by narrow beds along the fence or hedge. The Colonial-Revival garden was particularly suited to small or medium-sized lots and suburban backyards. When it did appear on a large estate, it was usually one self-contained element in an anthology of different garden styles, a

After Elise Tyson Vaughan bequeathed Hamilton House to SPNEA in 1940, the fences, pergolas, and other wooden garden structures succumbed to age and winds and were removed. The arch aligned with the eastern façade of the house has just been replaced and others are scheduled for rebuilding in the garden's on-going reconstruction.

A sundial hedged in by
clipped arborvitae marks
the center of the path that
leads from the east door of
the house through an opening in the euonymus hedge,
crosses the garden and passes in front of the cottage.
This view, taken before the
installation of the arch,
shows the young hedge of
spirea, which will be backed
by a taller one of arborvitae.

Victorian legacy that will be explored in a later chapter.

The prim, box-edged beds that gave order to the seemingly casual drifts of flowers in Colonial-Revival gardens did not appear as often in Britain. Americans identified them with a romanticized eighteenth century although they were really Victorian simplified. They had no such resonance for the British. Americans were quite ready to admit some Italian touches into the Colonial-Revival garden and indeed to use a little bedding out, too, if it seemed to solve a problem. Good examples are the garden that Ellen Shipman designed in the twenties for Chatham Manor, a genuine eighteenth-century house across the Rappahanock from Fredericksburg, Virginia, and the earlier one that Emily Tyson and her stepdaughter, Elise, created at Hamilton House in South Berwick, Maine.

Historians and preservationists have long been scornful of Colonial-Revival gardens, particularly those at Colonial Williamsburg. They found these gardens too neat, too prettified and full of wrong-for-the-period plants. It is true that Arthur Shurcliff based his designs on gardens in Fort Royal, Virginia, and Newburyport, Massachusetts, particularly the Brockway garden, which he had studied in the 1890s.[16] He was convinced that the Newburyport gardens dated from the eighteenth century,[17] whereas present-day garden historians have found that they could not have been created before 1841. Shurcliff himself is a perfect example of the link between Arts and Crafts and Colonial Revival. He grew up in a family that prized handwork, belonged to the Boston Society of Arts and Crafts, and was an accomplished woodworker. He and his wife, also a woodworker, built their summer house in Ipswich almost completely by themselves and made all of their own furniture.[18] A weathered wooden farmhouse-like building added onto over the years, surrounded by fenced and walled gardens, and nestled into the landscape, the house made no pretense at Colonial Revival style. It was pure Arts and Crafts.

In recent years, Colonial Revival has come to be accepted as a style in its own right, and recognized as worth study. It is an adaptation to its era, with deep roots in American garden tradition. Amateur gardeners with small spaces can still find in its rather free adaptations of geometric order useful ideas for organizing collections of native plants as well as the more expected herbaceous perennials.

The Arts-and-Crafts tradition, too, is alive and thriving, and not just in the revived interest in the gardens of Jens Jensen and O. C. Simonds but also in the care for fine workmanship apparent in the designs of many contemporary landscape architects.

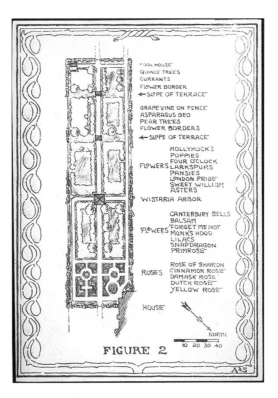

FIGURE 2

The gardens of Colonial Williamsburg are what most people immediately envision as Colonial Revival style. Arthur Shurcliff, their designer, intended them as authentic re-creations of eighteenth-century town gardens, but the boxwood parterres in his models like the Brockway garden in Newburyport, Massachusetts actually date to the 1840s.

Laid out in a pattern similar to one of the Brockway parterres nearest the house on this plan, the dwarf boxwood hedges of the Greenhow tenement garden in Colonial Williamsburg encircle a topiary of Yaupon holly shaped like one from an English cottage garden.

The Femininity of Flowers and Women in

Start investigating women's role in the design of American gardens and you find a finely chequered pattern with all kinds of contradictory opinions, not to mention incompatible assumptions and confusing evidence. In a 1937 address tracing the development of landscape design in this country J. E. Spingarn found it a decidedly negative one. Spingarn's assessment—"the deep-seated prejudice that flowers are the special province of women was an American limitation from the outset."[1]—is surprising for a professor of comparative literature, a former president of the NAACP, and an expert grower and exhibitor of clematis. It would not have surprised the band of talented women who entered the landscape design profession at the beginning of the twentieth century: they had often encountered just such an attitude. Nor did they let it go unchallenged. Ellen Shipman as quoted in a 1938 *New York Times* article seems to be answering Spingarn directly:

> Until women took up landscaping, gardening in this country was at its lowest ebb. The renaissance of the art was due largely to the fact that women, instead of working over their boards, used plants as if they were painting pictures and as an artist would.[2]

However obvious the connection between women and flowers—what poet has ever resisted comparing feminine beauty to one or another kind of blossom?—it is not at all sure that women always held a monopoly on flower growing. Gilbert Imlay found floriculture to be a passion of both sexes in late eighteenth-century Kentucky.[3] In my own family the flower garden absorbed my great-grandfather's horticultural attention; great-grandmother grew the vegetables. If Spingarn meant that flower gardening's identification with women made men reluctant to enter the field, that doesn't quite fit the facts either. For example, the horticultural societies that proliferated from 1818 onward were all founded by men. Women occasionally appear among the exhibitors, but most of the prizes for breeding and raising flowers go to men. In fact, Spingarn's declaration would have been news, though not unwelcome, to most early nineteenth-century horticultural writers, who were vociferously exhorting women to go out and work in the garden. Had he read further in Fessenden's 1828 *New American Gardener*, he would have found that the passage he quoted for support— "such is the laudable taste of the fair daughters of America, at the present day, that there are but comparatively few, that do not take an interest in a flower garden"—was essentially a piece of propaganda. Fessenden goes on to proselytize:

> The cultivation of flowers is an appropriate amusement for young ladies. It teaches neatness, cultivates a correct taste, and furnishes the mind with many pleasing ideas. The delicate form and features, mildness and sympathy of disposition, render them fit subjects to raise those transcendent beauties of nature, which declare the "perfections of the Creator's power."[4]

Fessenden was clearly a believer in the better-honey-than-vinegar school of persuasion. Downing was more forthright:

> *What is the reason American ladies don't love to work in their gardens?*
>
> It is of no use whatever, that some fifty or a hundred of our fair readers say, "we do." We have carefully studied the matter, until it has become a fact past all contradiction. They may love to "potter" a little…
>
> Honestly and ardently believing that the loveliest and best women in the world are those of our own country, we cannot think of their losing so much of their own and nature's bloom, as only to enjoy their gardens by the *results* like the French, rather than through the *development* like the English.[5]

Henry Ward Beecher was almost hectoring:

> Everyone knows to what extent women are afflicted with nervous disorders, *neuralgia* affections as they are more softly termed. Is it equally well known that formerly when women partook from childhood, of out-of-door labors, were confined less to heated rooms and exciting studies, they had comparatively, few disorders of this nature …
>
> Now we are not quite so enthusiastic as to suppose that floriculture has in it a balm for all these mentioned ills. We are very moderate in our expectations, believing, only, that it may become a very important auxiliary in maintaining health of body and purity of mind.[6]

Right:
Log-cabin life did not preclude such amenities as afternoon tea for pioneer women in turn-of-the-twentieth-century North Dakota. The owner of this log house has made a good start on landscaping it. In front of the door a swept-earth yard contains at least two planting beds, and beside the house shrubs border a remarkably neat lawn scattered with trees.

Garden Design

As one reads nineteenth-century horticultural books and periodicals, it is hard not to conclude that if women didn't have a taste for flower gardening already, men were determined to push them into it. What is missing are the women's own voices. They would eventually be raised.

Historians have assumed without much question or much supporting documentation that when Europeans first settled in this country women planted and tended the gardens while men tilled the fields. The assumption is probably accurate, but not the whole story. That in a frontier situation gender-specific roles were far from fixed is indicated by the much-better-documented experience of westward moving pioneer families. When help was needed in the fields, women came out to plough or plant or bale; when it was needed in the garden, men lent a hand with the digging, hoeing, and weeding.

It would not be at all surprising that women did try to make their yards pleasant as well as productive. You would want to spend every minute that weather allowed in the garden if you lived in the seventeenth century. The dwellings, even those of the prosperous, were small in size, the windows were few and very small; but the households — an extended family and its servants — might number more than thirty people!

Plants and flowers meant more than beauty to pioneer women from the seventeenth to the twentieth: They were a link to the past and an often-distant childhood home. *Pioneer American Gardening*, Elvinia Slosson's 1951 compilation of essays from garden club members across the country, is filled with accounts of the seeds and bulbs and cuttings carried to Kentucky by brides from Virginia, to Oklahoma by Choctaw and Chickasaw women on the Trail of Tears, to the Middle West by farmwives from upstate New York. Many of the stories were local traditions but enough documentation can be found in local historical societies to confirm the truth of the practice, and one writer, Beth Mattocks, tells of her family's journey to Colorado:

> My own mother crossed from Pennsylvania alone in a covered wagon with her seven little children in 1870 to join my father. I have a pot of maidenhair fern in my window, which she brought with her on this journey. The plant has been divided year after year, but can, I am sure, claim to be an early pioneer…[7]

Writing about "Agriculture in the Dakotas" in the same book, Margaret H. Davidson quotes a letter to her mother from the wife of missionary Stephen Return Riggs, who came to the Dakotas in 1837:

> The Indians, the babies, the chickens and mice seem leagued to destroy the flowers, and they well nigh succeeded.… Shading our family room are Alfred's morning glories and a rose bush … a shoot from this wild rose is seven feet high, the growth of a single season, and is laden with buds! You may wonder why I bestow

any of my precious time on flowers, but the principal reason is that I feel my mind needs some such cheering relaxation.[8]

Mrs. Riggs clearly gives the lie to those who claimed that no American ladies gardened in the early nineteenth century. She also demonstrates that flower growing can be a pleasurable activity even for those whose daily lives are physically demanding. In a survey of the leisure-time activities of farm women in the North Central states, conducted from 1927 to 1932 as part of her doctoral dissertation, Lucile Winifred Reynolds found gardening second only to reading in popularity. More than ninety percent of those surveyed enjoyed gar-

dening, defined as work with flowers, shrubs, and the house lawn. Differences were slight among those aged 35–44, 45–54, and over 55, and non-existent between those whose formal education had ended in the eighth grade or earlier and those who had graduated from high school or gone on to college.[9] This data, although limited, casts some doubt on a common theory that flower gardening is strictly a middle-class or upper-class pursuit. It is just the latter groups that write about it.

Not all contributions to the design of gardens are made by designers. Botanists, horticulturists, and sellers of plants and seeds also have considerable influence. By the mid-eighteenth century women were active in all these areas and some were acknowledged even then. John Bartram, the most important American botanist of the day, numbered several among his correspondents. In 1756 he exchanged seeds and botanical notes with his "Respected Friend Jane Colden" who lived on 3000 acres seventy-five miles north of New York in the then-wilderness of the Catskills. Jane Colden was unusually well educated for an eighteenth-century woman and her botanical interests were encouraged by her father, a polymath who was a distinguished botanist himself as well as Lieutenant-Governor of New York. Her plant discoveries led two British botanists to petition Linneaus to name one of

The plants on either side of the young woman standing outside her sod house around 1900 appear to be thriving, but those in the rock-bound bed indicate just how hard it was to make a garden in the dubiously named Meadow, South Dakota.

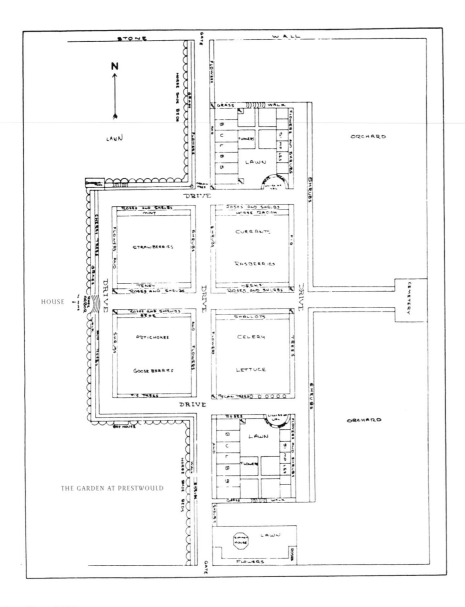

THE GARDEN AT PRESTWOULD

By the last years of the eighteenth century some women, upper-class, well-educated, and in the South, were designing or influencing the design of larger and more elaborate estate gardens. They may well have done so earlier: records are lacking. We have Eliza Lucas Pinckney's description of a Middleton garden, but we don't know what her own looked like. After returning from her stay in England between 1753 and 1758 she wrote friends there about modernizing it and about her pleasure in it but, alas, did not describe it.

> I love a garden and a book, and they are all my amusement, except I include one of the greatest businesses of my life, (my attention to my dear little girl) under that article. A pleasure it certainly is to cultivate the tender mind, to teach the young Idea how to shoot.[13]

Although Lady Jean Skipwith was born in Virginia, her family returned to Scotland when she was twelve. There she received most of her education, an exceptionally good one: she assembled a large personal library and was familiar with Latin, not a common female accomplishment. She returned to Virginia when she was thirty-eight and two years later married her elder sister's widower, Sir Peyton Skipwith, the only American-born baronet. Lady Jean was a passionate gardener and her garden still exists in skeletal form at Prestwould in Mecklenburg County, Virginia. The Skipwiths built their house between 1794 and 1795 on a high bluff just below the confluence of the Dan and Staunton rivers that forms the Roanoke, moving to the ten-thousand-acre plantation in 1797. The land slopes down from the house to the river in turfed falls, and originally presented a view of three islands. On one of these Lady Jean had a wildflower garden, and on another an orchard. Today the islands are gone, submerged when the Roanoke was dammed to form the Buggs Island Lake, and the view of the water is masked by second-growth forest along the shore.

The five-acre garden on the level of the house and east of it was laid out in 1801.[14] Lady Jean and Sir Peyton probably designed it together. Family papers in the Earl Gregg Swem Library at the College of William and Mary demonstrate that he was as devoted to growing vegetables as she to growing flowers and fruit. We have a very good idea of what grew in it and in her wildflower garden. Like Thomas Jefferson she was a dedicated list maker, and we can consult a number of her plant lists and cultivation notes. Any gardener will sympathize with such headings as "Bulbous Roots to Get when in my Power" or "Shrubs to be Got when I can." She recorded Latin as well as common names when she could find the former in Miller's *Gardener's Dictionary*. When a flower was not in Miller she said so and that was often the case with wild ones. What we don't know is exactly what she planted where.

When Rudy Favretti, who is often considered the dean of American restoration landscape architects, undertook the garden's restoration in 1980, he found sufficient traces of beds and paths on the ground to confirm the accuracy of the layout—100-foot-square beds with broad paths between them—published in Edith Tunis Sale's *Historic Gardens of Virginia*. In addition the garden house, traces of the conserva-

Lady Jean Skipwith's Virginia garden is one of the few early estate gardens planned and planted by a woman for which actual physical evidence exists, plus detailed notes and lists of its plants. It was laid out to the left of Prestwould House along the top of a ridge from which the land drops steeply to the Roanoke River. A modern copy of a plan in Lady Jean's unpublished journal shows its distinctive scalloped border of "horseshoe beds" and her summerhouse.

them for her as "the first lady who has so perfectly studied your system. She deserves to be celebrated."[10] Linneaus did not comply.

Bartram exchanged plants and seeds with Martha Daniel Logan of Charleston, the enterprising daughter of Governor Robert Daniel, who conducted a flourishing nursery business from her garden and wrote what is considered the first horticultural book, *A Gardeners Kalendar*, published in this country. No bound copies have ever been found. Either they were thumbed to dust by gardeners grateful for advice based on local not English experience or *A Gardeners Kalendar* always took the form of newspaper columns. It was reprinted for years in *The South Carolina Gazette* after its 1752 debut. Martha Logan's business was not unique: In 1774 six of Boston's eight major seed retailers were women.[11]

Another skillful Charleston gardener, Elizabeth Lamboll traded bulbs, plants, and seeds with Bartram. The nature of their correspondence offers a clue as to our paucity of detailed information about seventeenth- and eighteenth-century women gardeners: Mrs. Lamboll's husband, Thomas, wrote all the letters.[12] He made it very clear that the gardening expertise was hers, but left us to wonder why she didn't write herself. Was it lack of education or lack of time? One suspects both.

tory, and some plants and trees had survived. That interpretive plan based on one in the Skipwith family's possession suggests plantings of some flowers and vegetables for some of the beds; but Favretti did not try to follow these, since it would have a created a very labor-intensive garden with little labor available. Rather he used ground-cover plantings to outline the location of the parterres and re-create the shape of the unusual horseshoe beds that edge the garden on the side nearest the house.

Sir Peyton died in 1805. Lady Jean continued to garden and to manage the plantation with great success until her own death in 1826. Her daughters, Helen and Selina, carried on her horticultural interests and modeled their own gardens at Tallwood and Estouteville on the design of Prestwould.[15] Her attempts at systematically recording her experience in growing plants could benefit only her family because they were not published until the twentieth century. The same is true of the detailed diaries kept from the 1830s to 1896 by Martha Turnbull of Rosedown Plantation in Louisiana. But these hard-working ladies prefigured the way in which American women would make their first big impression on the gardening world: as authors.

Such exceptions notwithstanding, the overall landscaping of a property is usually credited to men in the eighteenth century, but the garden seems to have been considered a woman's domain and, according to Anne MacVicar Grant, "no foot of man intruded after it was dug in the spring." Mrs. Grant, who grew up in Albany, New York, between 1758 and 1768 as a British officer's child, noted the link between gardening and child-raising as nurturing occupations in memoirs written many years later. That both have usually been performed by women is a commonplace for us: it seems to have surprised her.

I must observe a singular coincidence; not only the training of children but of plants, such as needed peculiar care or skill to rear them, was the female province. . . .

I think I yet see what I have so often beheld both in town and country, a respectable mistress of a family going out to her garden, in an April morning, with her great calash, her little painted basket of seeds, and her rake over her shoulder, to her garden labors. These were by no means figurative . . . A woman in very easy circumstances, and abundantly gentle in form and manners, would sew, and plant, and rake incessantly.[16]

Ellen Shipman's elaborate 1924 Colonial Revival garden commissioned by Colonel and Mrs. Daniel B. Devore for Chatham Manor stands in vivid contrast to the modesty of a genuine eighteenth-century garden. For the 1771 Georgian mansion above the Rappahannock overlooking Fredericksburg, Virginia, Shipman included her trademark overflowing perennials in the firm architectural layout.

Above:
Martha Brookes Hutcheson placed great emphasis on the importance of axis in designing a landscape and relating it to architecture. A plan of her own garden at Merchiston Farm (now Bamboo Brook Outdoor Education Center) in New Jersey, which shows that for her axial organization did not preclude curving roads and paths adjusted to the site's topography.

Right:
Describing Hillwood, the complex of gardens on the Long Island estate of Marjorie and Edward F. Hutton, for *House & Garden* in 1924 Marian Cruger Coffin wrote: "The flower garden is the central feature and from its two axes the skeleton of the scheme develops." Her design, photographed by Mattie Edwards Hewitt, is a charming fantasy attuned to the Tudor-style mansion.

Mrs. Grant lists the vegetables that qualified as garden material and, as we noted earlier, describes the layout of the flower gardens, which she does attribute to the women. She then goes on to say that "To the Schuylers this description did not apply; they had gardeners, and their gardens were laid out in the European manner." Just what she considered to be the "European manner" in 1768 is a mystery, but this observation offers a clue to when and why pottering replaced serious gardening for middle-class women, at least for a time, along the eastern seaboard. With the commerce and industry that brought widespread prosperity to the early nineteenth century came a widespread thirst for refinement, a development analyzed in fascinating detail by Richard L. Bushman in his 1992 book, *The Refinement of America*. What better model to emulate, thought well-off farmers and businessmen, than the old-line landed families like the Schuylers and De Lanceys in matters of superior culture or polish? They failed to recognize that these families themselves were often trying to emulate European ideals irrelevant to this country. Unfortunately they seized on the less desirable and more superficial aspects of aristocratic behavior, among them disrespect for work. Schooling that focused on parlor accomplishments and social graces did not do much to prepare their daughters for running a household. It often takes a couple of generations for men and women to realize that true refinement does not preclude physical labor. Just what the arbiters of taste like Downing were trying to tell the new middle class. The urge for refinement, which could strike both sexes, was paralleled and reinforced by increasing suburbanization and by the cult of domesticity of which women were denoted the priestesses. Catherine Beecher and Harriet Beecher Stowe summed up its credo in their dedication to *The American Woman's Home*:

TO THE WOMEN OF AMERICA IN WHOSE HANDS REST
THE REAL DESTINIES OF THE REPUBLIC AS MOULDED

BY THE EARLY TRAINING AND PRESERVED AMID THE
MATURER INFLUENCES OF HOME, THIS VOLUME IS
AFFECTIONATELY INSCRIBED.

The Beecher sisters, like their brother, were very much in favor of physical work by ladies, whom they defined as women "of education, cultivation and refinement." They argued that "Cultivated women, who are brought up to do the work of their own families, are labor-saving institutions. They make the head save the wear of the muscles."[17] While their book does contain very good ideas for simplifying household work, it is rather ironic that two women who seem to have had little talent for domesticity themselves were promoting a submissive domestic existence for their peers.

Well before the Beechers took pen to paper, basic education for both men and women was nearly universal in this country. Women had acquired the intellectual training needed to become writers and readers. And the time, at least middle-class and upper-middle-class women, who could afford help. Most of the early efforts are suspiciously akin to Downing's "pottering" about the garden. Such books as *Flora's Lexicon* by Catherine Waterman published in 1840 and *The Poetry of Flowers and Flowers of Poetry to which are added A Simple Treatise on Botany and A Copious Floral Dictionary* by Frances S. Osgood, published in 1853 are curious mixtures of literary quotations, the language of flowers, and simplified explanations of the Linnean system. While Osgood introduces her "Treatise on Botany" with the statement that "The study of botany is one of the most interesting and delightful pursuits in the whole range of science" she devotes only twelve pages to it. The rest of its two hundred seventy-six pages are given over to the meanings of flowers, with quotations, anecdotes, brief bits of history, and colored plates. It is telling that amid such parlor-table trifles, Almira Lincoln Phelps's straightforward scientific manual *Familiar Lectures on Botany*, first published in 1829, was reprinted

continually for the rest of the century. Downing himself edited for the American market Jane Loudon's down-to-earth *Gardening for Ladies and Ladies' Companion to the Flower Garden* in 1843 and it went to three editions, even though it was too British to be completely useful.

Then in 1871 came Mrs. S.O. Johnson's *Every Woman Her Own Flower Gardener*, and in 1872 Anna Bartlett Warner's *Gardening by Myself*, the first freshet of what would become by the century's end a stream of books grounded in hands-on experience in which women gardeners shared their successes and failures, likes and dislikes, opinions about color and design. Unlike some later authors who could afford help, Anna Warner had to garden all by herself. Her father had lost his fortune in one of the century's financial panics. She and her older sister Susan retreated in 1837 to the remaining family property, Constitution Island below West Point, and supported themselves by writing books, mostly uplifting moral tales for adults and children. Anna, the gardener of the two, also contributed to the household by selling vegetables, and followed up the success of *Gardening by Myself* with the thinly fictionalized *Miss Tiller's Vegetable Garden and the Money she made by it.*

Gardening by Myself introduces what will be the characteristics of most garden books and articles by women for the next sixty years: The tone is conversational; the opinions are personal and definite but not preachy; the advice is both detailed and sound. Most important, the book is addressed to small-town and suburban gardeners not to professionals or estate owners. The recent reprinting of Mrs. William Starr Dana's *How to Know the Wildflowers* (1893), Celia Thaxter's *An Island Garden* (1894), Alice Morse Earle's *Old Time Gardens* (1901), and Helena Rutherfurd Ely's *A Woman's Hardy Garden* (1903) testifies to the value of their observations and the quality of their writing. These women might not have thought of themselves as professionals, but the level to which they had educated themselves as gardeners makes the word amateur seem off the mark.

In fact the last quarter of that century saw educated women straining against the cult of domesticity to find outlets for their talents and energy. Even if not engaged in the struggle for women's rights, they were quite prepared to become professionals, whether or not their husbands, if they had them, approved. It was the time of pioneering entrepreneurs like Lydia Pinkham and journalists like Nellie Bly (born Elizabeth Cochrane) and Ida Tarbell, whose career choices took real daring. Writing and gardening were more

socially acceptable pursuits for women and provided a somewhat easier path to personal self-expression. For some, as for Anna Warner, the real driving force remained economic necessity. For others it was truly a matter of choice, as it was for Mariana Griswold Van Rensselaer, who was this country's first critical writer on landscape design after Downing and is still one of the most illuminating. She came from an old-money New York City family, as did her husband, a mining engineer. According to a letter quoted by David Gebhard in his introduction to *Accents as Well as Broad Effects*, a compilation of her writing on art, architecture, and landscape, Schuyler Van Rensselaer was not very supportive of her writing career.[18] Aside from refusing any regular position with a magazine in deference to his wishes, she continued to write, her first published article "Optical Illusions as Affecting Architecture" appearing in *American Architect and Building News*, the first American professional architectural journal in 1876. After his premature death in 1884, her writing provided an important supplement to her somewhat modest private income. She contributed to the first issue of *Garden and Forest* in 1888 and continued to write both signed and unsigned pieces for the magazine as long as it existed. *Art Out-of-Doors*, published in 1893, made an even greater contribution to American garden and landscape design, one that still repays careful reading. It is not a how-to book, as she says in her Preface:

All I have wished to do is to say a friendly word to the public on behalf of gardening as an art . . . simply to

Ruth Bramley Dean designed large estate gardens often working with her husband, architect Aymar Embury II; but her writing was directed primarily to the owners of suburban lots. Her own Long Island property validates her advice to keep the garden and its furnishings in scale with the house and to provide sheltered spaces to sit, with something interesting to look at.

Long before she turned her talent to making gardens for movies, Florence Yoch's fine sense of theater was evident in estate gardens like Il Brolino in Montecito, California, created for Mary Stewart in 1923, and photographed in luxuriant maturity by Jessie Tarbox Beals. On the top terrace a classical exedra, scaled to the mountains behind it, backed a fountain like one at the Villa Medici in Rome. The off-center tree was intentional: It appears in Yoch's earliest sketches.

plead the cause of good taste by showing why this art should be practised and judged as are arts of other kinds.

To pick just one among the many observations that demonstrate the clear-sighted soundness of her judgments is hard, but all designers to my mind should post this one where they can see it every day:

> The only right theory is that no theory is always right— that good sense and good taste must dictate the specially appropriate solution for each special problem.[19]

Art Out-of-Doors was published too soon to include consideration of the talented women who became fully professional landscape designers at the turn of the century, but Van Rensselaer was careful to point out in a chapter added to the 1925 edition that there were fourteen women members of the American Society of Landscape Architects, of which she became an honorary member in 1926. She also mentioned that she had heard praised two landscape design schools for women only. These were, in order of founding, The Lowthorpe School of Landscape Architecture and Horticulture for Women in Groton (1901) and the Cambridge School

of Architectural and Landscape Design for Women (1916) both in Massachusetts. In between came the Pennsylvania School of Horticulture for Women in Ambler (1911), which she did not mention, perhaps because of its concentration on plants rather than design.

No landscape architecture schools for either men or women existed when Beatrix Jones opened a landscape design office on the top floor of her mother's New York City brownstone in 1895. Harvard and MIT would begin their programs in 1900, a year after Jones, known today as Beatrix Farrand, her married name, joined ten other professionals, including John Charles Olmsted, Samuel Parsons, O. C. Simonds and Warren Manning to found the American Society of Landscape Architects. Farrand had educated herself in horticulture by studying with Charles Sprague Sargent at the Arnold Arboretum and in design by traveling and examining gardens both in this country and in Europe, among them Gertrude Jekyll's Munstead Wood. European travel would be a formative force for most women who entered the field at the turn of the century as it had been for the senior Olmsted and his sons, Charles Eliot, and Charles Adams Platt. Of Farrand's contemporaries, only Ellen Shipman learned her craft in this country, visiting Europe for the first time as a mature artist at sixty. In fact foreign tours before, during, or after university study have continued to be important in the education of landscape architects to the present day, but usually they are considered supplementary rather than basic.

Farrand opened the door, and other women pressed through it, many of them citing her example as their inspiration. Martha Brookes Brown talked her way into the MIT program (Harvard did not admit women) in its first year and Marian Cruger Coffin in its second one. Both had to have intensive tutoring to make up for the lack of mathematical and scientific training in their earlier education, and both had very clear ideas of what they needed to learn from their courses. As Rebecca Warren Davidson reports in her introduction to the recent reprint of Martha Brookes Brown Hutcheson's *The Spirit of the Garden*, Hutcheson (better known by her married name) was dissatisfied by the amount of horticultural information offered at MIT and supplemented it with lectures at the Arnold Arboretum and work with local nurseries.[20] She left before finishing the course, and opened her practice in Boston in 1902. Coffin, who did graduate, also took courses at the Arboretum and studied drafting with an architect.

All of these women belonged to upper-class families and through their social connections came the first commissions that kept them going while they established their reputations. Of course, many young architects and landscape architects even today get their first independent jobs from family or family friends. But for these women it was crucial: They could not start out working in established offices, which simply refused to hire them. Ellen Biddle Shipman, who made a late start at forty-one, was one who did have the benefit of an apprenticeship, working in association with Charles Adams Platt for about ten years before starting her practice in 1920.[21] It was her only training. The knowledge of plants and their behavior, which would be a hallmark of her designs, she learned on her own. Platt and his wife summered in Cornish, New Hampshire, the artists' colony where Shipman and her husband, Louis, an aspiring playwright, came to live in 1894, and the two couples became friends. Cornish was a fertile source of inspiration for anyone interested in gardens, containing well-publicized ones by, among others, Augustus Saint-Gaudens and his wife, the Thomas Dewings, the Stephen Parrishes, their son, Maxfield, and the Platts. When the Shipmans' marriage fell apart, leaving her to support herself and three children, Platt, who admired the flower garden she had created for herself, asked her to join his office. Her primary role was to develop planting plans for the numerous commissions that came his way after he gave up painting for landscape architecture and architecture, but he encouraged her to learn all aspects of garden design.

Rose Standish Nichols was another Cornish resident whose landscape design career benefited from Platt's advice and early encouragement. Nichols then went on to patch together a study of horticulture and design in Cambridge and New York, in England and France. After her return she acquired her first commission in 1904.

Those women who came along a few years later could count on a certain amount of in-place educational structure. Ruth Dean spent 1908–10 at the University of Chicago and then worked for Jens Jensen before setting up her practice in New York. Elizabeth Lord and Edith Schryver both studied at the Lowthorpe School before joining forces in Salem, Oregon. Washington-based Rose Greely went to the Cambridge School, as did Lucile Council who would become a partner in 1925 of Florence Yoch. The California-born Yoch, who was the principal designer of the team, had tried programs at the University of California and Cornell before settling on the University of Illinois. In 1918, after supplementing her college studies with extensive travel in Europe, a practice she and Council would continue for the rest of their lives, she established herself in southern California.[22]

All this talent, motivation, and resourcefulness might not have been enough, had there not been a market for landscape and garden designs. Fortunately these women came on the scene at a time of exuberant economic growth, and those who profited from it did not even have an income tax to limit their spending. In truth, the income tax when it came did little to restrain estate creation in what is called "The Country Place Era." The tycoons and their wives who had been exposed to European gardens realized that they needed more than the services of the usually untrained local nurserymen if they were to have grounds to be proud of. Women designers were particularly successful in working with women, whether they were clients in their own right or the wives of clients. Not only did they take the time to listen to a client's wishes, but they also understood the love of flowers that would lead a Clara Ford to plunk an inappropriate flower garden down in one of Jens Jensen's carefully designed meadows. They were hands-on gardeners themselves, but they were also skillful designers who knew how to integrate those flowers into a pleasing plan. Unfortunately, when it

Top:
After completing courses in architecture and landscape architecture at the Cambridge School, Rose Ishbel Greely settled in her hometown, Washington, D. C. Given her belief in marrying the styles of house and garden, her precise courtyard design for Ruth Hanna McCormick Simms's Georgetown property suggests a Georgian or Beaux-Arts house.

Above:
In 1932 Annette Hoyt Flanders's landscape plan for "the Play House" on the Charles E. F. McCann estate in Oyster Bay, Long Island won a gold medal from the Architectural League of New York (Ruth Dean and Marian Coffin were previous winners). Classic closure for an allée, a circular temple backed by a curve of hedge terminates the main axis from the Play House.

came to public work, the male establishment turned women's plantsmanship, attention to detail, careful observation of local conditions, and sensitivity to clients' wishes into the argument that they did not have the breadth of vision or technical capacity to work on a large scale. Even Guy Lowell, who had allowed women to enter the MIT program he had designed shared this attitude:

> A woman will *fuss* with a garden in a way that no man will ever have to patience to do. If necessary she will sit on a camp-stool and see every individual plant put into the ground. I have no hesitation in saying that where the relatively small garden is concerned, the average woman will do better than the average man.[23]

It's amusing to note that the gardens by Lowell illustrated in *Pioneers of American Landscape Design* are very fussy in comparison to the spacious and dignified work of his pupils, Coffin and Hutcheson. Shipman and Farrand among others responded to attitudes like his by employing only women when they could afford to staff their offices with associates.

When women did manage to land public commissions, their attentiveness paid off in designs that needed little later alteration, unlike drawing-board schemes, which often do. For one example, Farrand, in designing open spaces and courtyards at Princeton and Yale, first studied where students actually walked between buildings before laying out paths, and where they liked to sit before placing benches.[24] The other argument, that they would not be able to supervise contractors and workmen, was quietly demolished by their success in creating estate gardens, albeit with a certain amount of difficulty. Still only a very few women had a chance to design or collaborate in the design of large-scale public projects, and even when they did, often went unrecognized. Such was the case with Marjorie Sewall Cautley, the majority of whose commissions were for parks and housing developments. She was the landscape architect for Sunnyside Gardens in Long Island City and the new town of Radburn in New Jersey. Only Clarence Stein and Henry Wright are usually credited with the design of these famous 1930s model housing developments; until very recently she has rarely been mentioned. Genevieve Gillette in Michigan received more recognition for her work in conservation, low-cost housing, and park design, but she is less known than most of her male contemporaries. It must be said that landscape architecture is still not a profession whose practitioners of either gender enjoy high name recognition. Since landscapes and gardens are living, growing works of art they tend to change beyond recognition or disappear unless they are consciously maintained. Without evidence it is hard to evaluate individual contributions or celebrate accomplishment.

Because so many country estates have vanished, we have little more than scattered photographs to tell us about the personal approaches of many first-wave women landscape designers. But based on these and on the gardens that still exist, all of them worked within a convention characteristic of the period: geometrically organized spaces near the house moving out to naturalistically organized ones on the perimeter. Particularly in the flower gardens, but also in paths and steps, they modified European-inspired Beaux-Arts eclecticism with ideas from the Arts-and-Crafts and Colonial Revival movements. In terms of planting design Gertrude Jekyll was a major influence, but most also placed a lot of emphasis on the use of native plants wherever possible. The luxuriant blends of perennials that fill to overflowing crisply articulated parterres give their gardens a look that seems distinctively American. That these are very high-maintenance designs was generally of no concern to them or to their clients. Immigration reached one of its peaks in the period and garden workers were easy to come by.

Small gardens were not usually part of their professional practice but that did not signify a lack of interest. On the contrary, these landscape architects made up a very important strand in a web of garden-minded women who shared their enthusiasm, interests, and energy. They wrote books on design and articles for magazines like *House & Garden* and *House Beautiful*; they gave lectures and sometimes taught courses. They encouraged the assignment of pioneer women photographers like Frances Benjamin Johnston, Jessie Tarbox Beals, and Mattie Edwards Hewitt to record their work. And they joined garden clubs. Most garden clubs were formed in the years right after 1890, although Susan Davis Price has identified a Ladies Floral Club founded in 1869 in Austin, Minnesota[25] with an agenda very similar to that proclaimed by the first umbrella association of individual clubs, The Garden Club of America in 1913.

> The objects of this association shall be to stimulate the knowledge and love of gardening among amateurs, to share the advantages of association, to aid in the protection of native plants and birds, and to encourage civic planting.[26]

Garden Clubs are rarely given proper acknowledgement of their influence on landscape design. To sample some accomplishments of Garden Club of America members: lobbying crucial to the creation of the National Arboretum and passage of the Billboard Control Amendment to the 1956 Highway Act, buying and donating 4,220 acres of redwoods to the state of California, endowing a fellowship in Landscape Architecture at the American Academy in Rome. In 1930 and 1934 it published under Mrs. Luke Vincent Lockwood's editorship the two volume *Gardens of Colony and State*. Never mind that the different states' entries are uneven and that some of the scholarship is badly out-of-date, it was a milestone and remains an invaluable record for the garden historian. The GCA created another invaluable record when it started to collect photographs of members' gardens, a collection that now forms the core of the Smithsonian's Archives of American Gardens.

In 1928 the Garden Club of Virginia, another umbrella group, organized garden-visiting as an extremely successful yearly fundraiser for the preservation of historic gardens and it has continually worked to raise research and restoration standards. In this they followed the path blazed in the 1850s by Ann Pamela Cunningham and the Mount Vernon Ladies

Association who bought, rehabilitated, and have maintained it to ever-higher standards of scholarship. Another association, The National Federation of State Garden Clubs, formed in 1929, produced its own historical documentation in 1951 with *Pioneer American Gardening* edited by Elvinia Slosson. It has paralleled and sometimes cooperated with the educational and environmental activities of The Garden Club of America.[27]

Another strand of garden-club-connected tastemakers in the period was plaited from journalists and garden writers. Frances Duncan wrote articles for magazines like *Century* and *Scribner's*, and became the first garden editor of *The Ladies' Home Journal*.[27] Louisa Yeomans King, who always identified herself as Mrs. Francis King, was a founding member of both The Garden Club of America and the Woman's National Farm and Garden Association. She wrote nine books and countless magazine articles, edited a series of books on the Little Garden and lectured constantly, never failing to impress upon her audience the importance of employing a professional landscape designer whenever possible. She considered Gertrude Jekyll her mentor, and with her own well-known garden in Alma, Michigan as laboratory, did a great deal to adapt Jekyll's principles to American realities. So did another garden club member and prolific garden writer with an acclaimed garden, Louise Beebe Wilder, several of whose books have recently been republished. They are only two out of dozens.

The 1929 crash and subsequent depression forced some designers to retrench, but barely affected others. Florence Yoch, for example, found new and very prosperous clients in the motion-picture industry and eventually a new challenge as well: the design of garden settings for movies. World War II produced a real upheaval and in its aftermath a considerable setback to women as professional landscape designers. During the conflict, understandably, everyone focused on vegetables and Victory gardens. The Cambridge School closed when the Harvard Graduate School of Design admitted women in 1942. In 1945 the Lowthorpe School was absorbed by the Rhode Island School of Design. The Pennsylvania School kept going a bit longer, but in 1958 bowed to the postwar pressure on women to return to domesticity and merged into Temple University. Little by lit-tle the earliest professionals died out, and while talented replacements appeared—Nelva Weber, Marie Berger, and Alice Recknagle Ireys come to mind—their numbers were smaller and they received less publicity. For one thing, interest in gardening went into a steep decline, and magazines reduced their coverage, responding to reader surveys. The reasons for gardening's fall from grace are not completely clear but do include the anything-to-save-labor attitude that pervaded the country in the 1950s and early 1960s. No matter how clean and livable their designs, female landscape architects were also reproached for what critics saw as an old-fashioned approach. True, they were not producing work as innovative as that of Rose and Eckbo; but they were producing what their clients wanted and most clients are conservative. Thomas Church after all suffered the same criticism for responding to his clients' desires.

Only the garden clubs continued to thrive, serving as outlets for the managerial abilities of well-educated married women barred by social pressure from joining the workforce. According to the National Council of State Garden Clubs, membership peaked between 1959 and 1961, hit its lowest point in 1981, and has rebounded to some degree in the last few years, but with a difference. Today women have flooded into the professions, and men have joined the garden clubs. Meetings and classes are held in the evenings to fit the schedules of their mostly working members.

Almost the same timetable applies to women's reentry into the landscape profession. In 1983 seven percent of the ASLA's members were women, in 1992 eighteen percent were, and members probably represent no more than half those working in the field, many of whom head their own firms. Leaf through several years of *Landscape Architecture*, the journal of the ASLA, and you find that women, in addition to residential design, are doing historic and environmental restoration; park and corporate land design; land use and water management; city and regional planning. They may be supervisors in the National Parks or Fish and Wildlife Services, city park administrators, or corporate executives. And there are several on the cutting edge of design: like them or not, Martha Schwarz's Bagel and Davis Gardens represent a very different vision of the garden, and not one that could be called particularly feminine.

Even a quick survey of women's roles in the making and keeping of gardens indicates that they did nothing to inhibit and a lot to promote the development of American landscape design. The culprit that Spingarn should have pointed at, if there truly is one, is the ingrained American bias for the utilitarian. It is hard to teach appreciation of garden and landscape design as an art—not to speak of proper respect for its practitioners—to a public suspicious of anything that doesn't make money or can't be put to use immediately. Now that they have become full members of the landscape design profession, one can only hope that women continue to embrace those qualities that were once turned against them and convince their male colleagues to follow suit. Those who take the time to study the physical requirements of a site in real depth, and, just as important, listen to the desires and concerns of those for whom a design is being made, stand a much better chance of creating a landscape that is sustainable, that will be cared for, than those who impose ideas from the top down.

The Lure of
the Exotic

Preceding page:
Beyond the Bourn Gate lies one of the most evocatively Italian vistas at Filoli, an allée of fastigiate Irish yews marching up to the highest point in the gardens. Called the High Place, the semi-circular seating space at the top offered William Bowers Bourn II a view of Crystal Springs Lake, which had prompted him to locate his estate in the valley.

Left:
Time has both simplified and added a new richness to H. H. Hunnewell's pioneering Italian garden. In the lakeside landscape the stone balustrade along the lake and some of the evergreen topiaries remain as evidence of its inspiration; his specimen conifers have matured into a grove of textured greens.

Americans have never hesitated to rifle other cultures for objects or ideas that pleased or interested them or that they thought might be useful. Even Ralph Waldo Emerson, who so often exhorted his fellow countrymen to rely on their own instincts and observations, found foreign forms and ideas stimulating. The point was to assimilate the principles, not imitate the results. When, during her visit in 1850, Fredrika Bremer asked him

> whether he considered the intellectual culture of the New England States to have attained its acme. . . "by no means," replied he; "there are at this time a number of Germanisms and other European ideas, nay even ideas from Asia, which are now for the first time finding their way into the life of the mind, and which will there produce new developments."[1]

At the end of the nineteenth century American garden-makers, owners, and designers alike seemed to feel in need of new inspiration. Like Emerson they looked both to Europe and to Asia; but within those continents, they looked to Italy and Japan, rather than to Germany and India, as he had. For those who were most comfortable with geometrically ordered surroundings Italian Renaissance gardens offered a more sophisticated and showy range of possibilities than the simple four-square layouts and picket fences of vernacular gardens. And Italian gardens were more receptive to the still-popular bedding-out patterns than the landscape style. For those who preferred the latter's stylization of natural forms but had difficulty adjusting its sweeping contours to small suburban and town lots, Japanese gardens suggested solutions.

Americans, particularly New Englanders, had been flocking to Italy since the beginning of the republic, but it was art and antiquity that drew them, and for a long time few took much notice of Italian villas and their gardens. Catharine Maria Sedgwick, a well-connected New England writer of popular novels, was one of the earliest who did, perhaps because she came equipped with introductions to their owners on her tour in 1839. In her letters—ostensibly addressed to relatives but really intended for the press—she described several gardens but not in the detail one would like. Her response to them was ambivalent. She visited most of the important villa gardens around Lake Como, and found many "to which nature, climate, art and wealth have given the last touch of perfection." Later, in what seems an about-face, she criticized Roman gardens for torturing instead of obeying nature with their topiary, wall-like hedges, and "coloured stones and flowers in arabesque patterns." What appealed to her and to the romanticism of her age were the softened edges of age and neglect:

> I am not sure I should not steal away from the faultless beauty and perfection of adornment of an English nobleman's park, garden, and conservatories, to wander over the old Mattei Villa on the Coelian Hill, ruined and abandoned as it is, with its ragged berceaus, its untrimmed rose hedges, its broken-nosed statues, and its vineyard, as it now is, broken and sere, for from its high-swelling grounds you have an unbroken view of the mountains that half girdle Rome.[2]

Despite her somewhat positive feelings for "the ancient school of landscape gardening" as her contemporary Andrew Jackson Downing called architectural gardens, English naturalistic landscaping would continue to dominate American thinking for the rest of the century. Even the Italian garden created by H. H. Hunnewell on his Massachusetts estate was just one element in a landscape laid out mostly on naturalistic lines. Apparently he did not visit the gardens on Lake Como that his tiers of topiary so resemble until after he had created his own in the 1850s. He lined up his fancifully clipped trees on six terraces linked by a long flight of steps descending to a lake. For him the use of topiary was a way to cope with a slope too steep for flowers, and he tailored the trees so they would not fill out too much and obscure the view.[3] Hunnewell's Italian Garden was much admired—he was very generous in allowing the public to visit—but it does not seem to have produced imitations right away.

In the late 1880s Italian-inspired gardens began to appear on the estates of well-traveled collectors such as Isabella Stewart Gardner in Brookline or John T. Morris and his sister Lydia in Chestnut Hill. Like H. H. Hunnewell they treated the Italian garden as one style among many in their anthologies of garden styles. Such compilations of exotic gardens as expressions of the collecting instinct in landscape design will be examined in more detail in the chapter on collectors' gardens.

At about the same time, architects started to design the gardens as well as the houses for country estates. That they turned to geometrically ordered landscapes is not surprising. Such landscapes are architectonic by nature, and they can be carried out with a very small vocabulary of plant materials. Some early landscape designs by architects trained in Ecole des Beaux-Arts principles like McKim, Mead & White and Carrère & Hastings are based on French interpretations, strictly symmetrical if much simplified. Charles A. Platt played an important role in redirecting designers of formal gardens to the study of Italian Renaissance and Baroque villa gardens. He had also studied in Paris, but painting and etching were his chosen fields. According to his biographer, Keith Morgan, it was there that he came to reject picturesque expressiveness in favor of a balanced classical harmony ultimately derived from Greek and Roman examples, just as did the student architects, many of whom he knew.[4] He had visited Italy in 1886, and the gardens he designed between 1889 and 1891 for himself and for a neighbor in Cornish, New Hampshire, show that he had assimilated the Italian Renaissance approach to garden design, and could adapt it successfully to American landscapes. But when he wrote the magazine articles after an 1892 tour that he expanded into his influential 1894 book *Italian Gardens*, Platt still considered himself a painter.

By the time he studied them most of these gardens were not only neglected and overgrown—obvious from his photographs—but also had undergone many design changes. That he was aware of this is clear from the text. For the most part he chose to photograph details or evocative corners. He was very taken with the flower gardens. While not truly accurate historically, they were typically made up of geometric box-edged beds overflowing with flowers. That combination would become characteristic of his gardens. Only in the cases of Villa Lante and Villa d'Este did he discuss the overall layout, but that he had paid close attention to the plans of all the villas he discussed is clear from his work, as we shall see.

Really detailed analysis of Italian villas and their gardens came ten years later with Edith Wharton's book of that name. The book's highly atmospheric illustrations by Maxfield Parrish don't do much to explain the structure of the gardens. That was the task of the text. Wharton started off by dismissing flowers as important elements in the planning of the Renaissance garden.

> The Italian garden does not exist for its flowers; its flowers exist for it: they are a late and infrequent adjunct to its beauties, a parenthetical grace counting only as one more touch in the general effect of enchantment.[5]

In this, she was only partly right. Modern scholarship has established that flowers were important to the rich and powerful princes of church and state for whom these gardens were created. Theirs was an age when plant introductions from the Middle East, Asia, and the Americas were proliferating and they competed to get and grow such exciting novelties as tulips, crown imperials, lilacs, marigolds, and tuberoses.[6] Wharton was correct in that the flowers did not dictate the arrangement of the flower garden, one of the three standard parts of the villa landscape along with the orchard and the park. The flower garden was laid out in clear geometric divisions, which were outlined with clipped herbs like santolina, lavender, rosemary, or myrtle, and the flowers planted within the divisions. It is difficult to say just how the flowers were arranged, but it's unlikely that the compartments were packed with blossoms, bedding-out style, or overflowing with perennials as they often were when Platt saw them. The rarer bulbs were probably sparsely planted so that they could be admired as specimens: prints and paintings from the fifteenth well into the seventeenth centuries show this kind of planting. There is also evidence that sometimes more common flowers like violets, pinks, and roses grew loosely in beds along with herbs. With clearly defined compartments in place, owners and gardeners could try out different ways of planting, confident that the garden would always have strong pattern to satisfy the eye.

For Wharton, Italian gardens demonstrated that enchanting effects could be created using only stonework, water, and evergreens. With just these three elements, she contended, the country house architect of the Renaissance had found a timelessly successful way of responding to what she saw as the challenge of the garden with a view:

> [H]is garden must be adapted to the architectural lines of the house it adjoined; it must be adapted to the requirements of the inmates of the house, in the sense

of providing shady walks, sunny bowling-greens, parterres and orchards, all conveniently accessible; and lastly it must be adapted to the landscape around it.[7]

Wharton embraced the classical values of clarity, restraint, and proportion in the design of landscapes just as she had promoted them earlier in *The Decoration of Houses*, which she wrote with Ogden Codman, Jr. She disliked intensely the clutter and confusion of Victorian interiors, and undoubtedly responded in the same way to the same characteristics when they appeared, all too often, in Victorian gardens. For whatever reason, perhaps personal temperament, she seemed unable to see the virtues of even the best naturalistic designs. Yet, she did realize that woodland played an important role in Italian gardens. Except in some urban locations these architectonic gardens were carved out of natural forests and those forests were a calculated part of the total landscape design, whether they were considered hunting parks or simply shady places to walk; enhancing backgrounds or sources of surprise enlivened with hidden pools or statues. When they didn't exist on the site they were planted, sometimes in rather stiff boscos (groves) but just as often in freely composed mixtures of trees and shrubs.

Most often laid out on hillsides, villa gardens offered American designers a couple of lessons. One was a variety of arrangements whereby a splendid display of wealth and power could also include spaces of privacy and charm. The other, the diversity of ways in which a geometrically organized and strongly axial layout could be fitted onto very uneven terrain. Many of these gardens were composed of terraces arranged symmetrically on either side of an axis running through the house from front to rear. In one direction the axis directed the eye to a panorama of the countryside; in the opposite direction it focused on a statue or pavilion on the hillside above the house. This had been the most influential model for other countries in the seventeenth and eighteenth centuries, but it was far from the only one. Even with a strictly symmetrical layout, the most important view might lie at an unemphasized diagonal to the main axis. The terrace divisions might stray from the orthogonal to adjust to the lay of the land, or walled gardens, symmetrical within, shoot off at odd angles. In some cases, as for example at the Villa Gamberaia in Settignano and the Villa Medici in Rome, the major organizing axis ran parallel to the house. Along it were arranged the different garden "rooms," usually on different levels connected by stairs or ramps. This axis might be terminated at either or both ends by vistas, or a variety of views presented from one or all of the different gardens. Even if the major landscape panorama lay on a cross axis, that cross axis might not be emphasized in the organization of the garden, and the view deliberately withheld as a surprise.

FAULKNER FARM

Within a few years of the publication of *Italian Gardens* Charles Platt had transformed himself from painter to architect and landscape architect, professions for which he turned out to have great gifts. In 1897 he received his first major

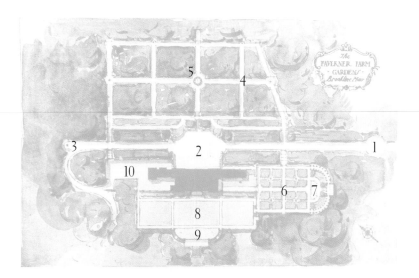

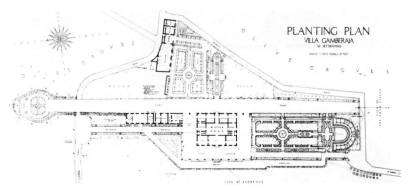

Above, top:
Faulkner Farm Plan:

1. Entrance drive
2. Parking court
3. Juno sculpture
4. Bosco
5. Temple
6. Italian garden
7. Pavilion and pergolas
8. Back terrace
9. Semicircular lookout
10. Service court

Above, middle:
The plan of the Villa Gamberaia in Settignano may not have directly suggested that of Faulkner Farm, but it is a good example of an Italian garden structured like it along an axis running across a hillside perpendicular to the principal views.

Above:
A reflecting pool backed by curved pergolas extending from a central pavilion terminates the geometrically balanced flower garden. In later photographs flowers overstuff the beds and the Faulkner Farm flower garden became an often-copied model of the Italianate style.

landscape commission, the design of the grounds for the Charles F. Sprague estate, Faulkner Farm in Brookline, Massachusetts. Mr. and Mrs. Sprague were well-traveled and very familiar with Italian villa gardens. It is highly likely that this influenced their choice of Platt as landscape designer, and they may well have suggested certain details.[8] Their original choice, the Olmsted firm, had led to no meeting of minds.

The Spragues' recently built house was set high on the side of a hill. Platt adjusted the entrance drive to bring it straight through the walled entrance court parallel to the façade of the house. A giant statue of Juno gave the drive a visual terminus, though the actual roadway made a turn down the hill to the farm and the service court on the northwest side of the house. Platt treated the drive as the organizing axis for his design. Like the long central path at the Villa Medici in Rome, this drive governed the disposition of the different gardens and groves above and below it. In both gardens the major views are from the cross axes, but these are subordinated within the garden to the horizontal terraces.

Opposite the house at Faulkner Farm, steps lead from the forecourt up the hill to a temple on the wooded crest from which you can see Boston in one direction and a panorama of the countryside in the other. As at the Villa Medici and several other villa gardens, a grid of broad paths overlays this thickly planted version of the grove or bosco, but nature provided the height for the vista. Platt did not have to build a mount for his temple as the Medicis did.

Screened from the road by trees, a grass terrace on the same level as the house extends to the southeast. From the terrace, steps descend to the walled flower garden. Quartered by gravel paths, with each quarter again quartered around a marble wellhead, the garden in its heyday brimmed with flowers. At the far end a semicircular composition of pavilion and curving pergolas embrace, a reflecting pool. Down another level is a spacious turf terrace that runs across the back of the house and reveals a broad panorama of farm, field, and forest. Another semicircle, this time of balustrades and benches, edges the massive retaining wall that supports these lawns. Although Platt's plan shows similarities to that of Villa Gamberaia, it is not a reproduction of it. There seems to be no evidence that he had visited that particular villa, but, as Keith Morgan points out, he could easily have seen the plan in one or another book, and in any case he had seen other gardens organized along axes parallel to the house. The most likely scenario is that Platt drew upon many of the gardens he had visited for inspiration. The pavilion bears a strong resemblance to one at Villa Lante, and Phoebe Cutler finds echos of Villa Borghese in the upper garden.[9]

The Faulkner Farm landscape was highly influential. It was published and praised as soon as finished in *Harper's Weekly Magazine* in 1899. *House & Garden* devoted two articles to it in 1901, the magazine's initial year. Other magazines and books followed suit. Where there was criticism, it was generally criticism of the Italian architectural and sculptural fragments it contained. That the artifacts would be mistaken for the art was always the danger in looking to the past or another culture for inspiration. Many creators of country house gardens, designers and clients alike, made that mistake. Platt did not, even though he loved the artifacts.

Broad panels of green grass and pale gravel paths with a few well-placed artifacts form a clean-lined, symmetrical composition at the rear of the mansion. From the wide rectangular turf terrace a semi-circular viewing platform rimmed by balustrades and benches tops the massive retaining walls.

Below:
A few mature trees remained on the site when Charles Platt first built his house in Cornish, New Hampshire pasture. When this family photograph was taken, the contouring of the land to frame the views and create terraces was just beginning. The house has grown larger, the piazza now has a flat roof and the landscape has changed dramatically.

Today the house appears to have been tucked into a forest, but that forest is Platt's creation, following the example of Renaissance garden makers for whom a forest or bosco was as integral a part of a landscape composition, as were a flower garden, sheltered living spaces, and clipped trees like the hemlocks that flank the steps.

CHARLES A. PLATT'S OWN GARDEN

In better condition to show how sensitively Platt could orchestrate the elements of the Italian garden and integrate them with the American landscape is his own garden in Cornish, New Hampshire. The layout, which does not have the kind of architectural reinforcement that characterizes his commissions, demonstrates his mastery with great clarity. Revitalized by his grandchildren, the planting is much simpler now than it was in his day, but the garden is no less beautiful and livable.

The house, garden, and studio appear to have been set into a forested hillside according to the best Italian tradition, but that forest was created by Charles Platt. A family photograph of the newly constructed house shows a bare hill — formerly a sheep pasture — with a few scattered trees, one by the door a remnant of a long vanished apple orchard. Over the years massed plantings of hardy shrubs and native trees have grown to wrap the house, the garden, and the meadow in a rich green stole that opens to frame a view of the Connecticut River valley down the hill. Platt selected his site so astutely that he had a choice of views. The valley view,

particularly poetic at sunset, he aligned with the garden's major cross-axis, which he further aligned on the piazza at the western end of the house. The view of Mt. Ascutney, on which most of his neighbors focused, Platt hid behind a grove of pine trees. Only after the visitor walked across the lawn and into the grove did the majestic mountain come into sight. There Platt placed a slate table around which family and friends could gather for afternoon tea in the piney shade.

The house is set on a turf terrace parallel to the hill and below its crest. Just inside the entrance gate, a steep right-angle path hedged on both sides branches from the gravel walk along the front of the house and turns up the hill to the studio. Steps from the temple-like piazza — the Platts have stayed with the old American word for veranda — lead down to the garden terrace. Below this terrace additional steps descend to the lawn. Another path and steps, aligned with the back of the piazza, lead downhill to a tennis court hidden in the woods. The layout of the garden terrace and its flowerbeds varied over the years but resembles that at Faulkner Farm.

Nothing better demonstrates the strength and soundness of the original design than the success with which it has accommodated alterations made to it by changing family circumstances, time, and nature. After the death in 1933 of Platt, and in 1953 of his wife, Eleanor, who had lived there year round, the terraces were turned to lawn. The family members who had inherited the estate found it impractical to maintain horticulturally demanding gardens, since they could come only on weekends. The hurricane of 1938 destroyed much of the pine grove, revealing Mt. Ascutney. Fortunately a few trees were left to punctuate the horizon and separate the mountain view from that of the river valley. Platt's grandson, another Charles Platt and an architect in New York, his wife, Joan, and other family members undertook a rejuvenation of the garden in 1990 with help from William Noble. They don't call it restoration and quite rightly so. Not that there isn't documentation. There is an abundance. But it shows that the gardens were always changing when Charles A. Platt himself was alive. Rather, Mr. and Mrs. Platt and their cousins have re-created an atmosphere that feels right historically but makes sense for the present. Turf now covers much of the garden terrace for both practical and sentimental reasons. But all around the lawn are borders brimming with the same kind of old-fashioned flowers that once filled the original beds.

The plan of the flower garden bears a striking resemblance to a basilica's nave, aisles, transept, and apse. It must have been a favorite with Platt. Even the walled vegetable garden at Cornish repeated the overall shape but with simpler divisions. And Platt used variations of such a plan for gardens on estates like Faulkner Farm, Maxwell Court, and Woodston. In a 1903 article for *House & Garden*,

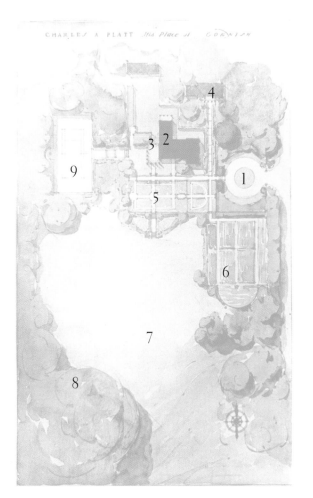

Left:
Platt Garden Plan:

1. Entrance circle
2. House
3. Piazza
4. Studio
5. Terrace flower gardens
6. Vegetable and cutting garden
7. Lawn with view to river
8. Grove facing Mt. Ascutney
9. Tennis court

Below:
From the path above the main terrace Mt. Ascutney is clearly visible today thanks to some tree-clearing by the 1938 hurricane. Platt had deliberately hidden it behind a grove of artfully pruned pines, a surprise to be seen only by those who entered the grove.

"American Garden-Craft from an English Point of View," by Edward S. Prior, M. A. (who appears to have been an art historian specializing in the Middle Ages), considers the basilican approach a distinguishing characteristic of American gardens:

> The details of disposition vary, of course — a court or 'narthex' may precede the 'nave.'. . .Often there is the square 'chevet' in place of the semi-circular. But generally the layout presents the unity and proportions of a church-plan rather than the connection of a series of courts and chambers which constitute most frequently the English manner of plan.[10]

This basilican plan certainly had plenty of precedents in Italian gardens; but it also appears in American gardens of the eighteen-thirties through the eighteen-sixties. It is particularly common in town gardens, most probably as a response to the narrow frontage and great depth of the lots. In many of these, the "apse" was represented by a summerhouse, a garden seat, or a grape arbor, rather than the architecturally powerful casinos, pergolas, or exedrae designed by Platt and his fellow Italophiles. Indeed, Prior remarks that at Faulkner Farm "the architect rather crowds out the gardener." An unfair judgment since the garden was new and the plantings, always luxuriant in Platt's gardens, had not had time to grow up.

Another distinctively American feature for Prior was "the constant use of pergola and piazza." These were just not suited to the English climate and "became the damp abode of beetles and spiders" whereas in the hotter drier American summer they provided delightful places for outdoor living:

> Indeed the country house gains a charming addition when it can throw out piazzas and colonnades and so embrace within its arms flower gardens, fountains, and set courts. And esthetically what a valuable connecting link such additions make between the stolid, smooth permanence of the masoned structure and the vegetable raggedness of the surroundings!

Piazzas were already in place, but the Italianate pergola would be as enthusiastically adopted by Colonial Revival and Arts-and-Crafts designers as it was by those of the Beaux-Arts persuasion. Gustav Stickley, promoter of Arts and Crafts, was also a promoter of the pergola, especially in rustic form; and by the first decades of the twentieth century it had made its way into the small suburban garden. American garden-makers, as usual, were picking up elements from the Italian garden — pergolas and balustrades — and adding them to their design vocabulary.

Is there really any difference between this ingrained American habit of gathering ideas from different periods or cultures and the turn-of-the-century stylistic program we call Beaux-Arts Eclecticism? There are reasons to think there is, although they are very much related. Fashion plays a role in both, whether it simply calls attention to a new-to-the-designer idea or fuels that very human desire to be up-to-date and "with it." When Washington, Jefferson, and their con-

At its eastern end the main terrace steps up two levels to a semi-circular lawn. Flower borders backed by shrubs and a simple white wall take the place of the pavilion and pergola at Faulkner Farm, but the division of the ground plane is almost the same. The mood is very different: charm in Cornish, stylishness in Brookline.

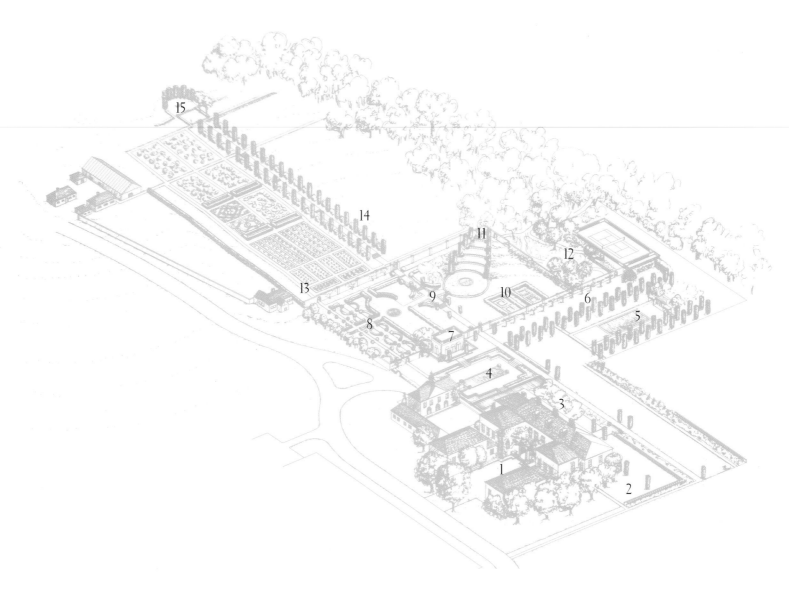

temporaries went about domiciling the then-modern landscape style in this country, they made a place within it for the older enclosed four-square garden. The latter was retained not because it was historical but because it was a practical necessity. Like American garden-makers earlier and later, they selected from the repertory of garden features those they felt would solve the problems at hand, practical or visual. No one claimed theoretical justification for the choices. Beaux-Arts Eclecticism came armed with theory, architects' theory. Reginald Blomfield's justification in *The Formal Garden in England* is unequivocal:

> The formal school insists upon design; the house and the ground should be designed together and in relation to each other; no attempt should be made to conceal the design of the garden, there being no reason for doing so, but the bounding lines, whether it is the garden wall or the lines of paths and parterres, should be shown frankly and unreservedly, and the garden will be treated specifically as an enclosed space to be laid out exactly as the designer pleases.[11]

Although Blomfield was engaged in a vituperative battle with William Robinson over the latter's brand of natural-

ism—he detested naturalism of any kind—his favored models were the architectural gardens of sixteenth- and seventeenth-century England rather than their Italian or French antecedents. Since the Ecole des Beaux-Arts considered all past styles open to imitation, but had little interest in exact replication, American architects and landscape architects of that persuasion didn't hesitate to blend elements from Italian Renaissance, English Georgian, French Baroque, Medieval, and Hispano-Mauresque—any or all—in their houses and estate gardens. Longwood and Nemours, two du Pont gardens in the Brandywine Valley, were, unsurprisingly, mostly French in character. And Florida could boast the fantastic gardens of Vizcaya, in which Italian, French, and Spanish elements combined to tame subtropical vegetation. Whether or not such mixtures resulted in a unified work of art really depended on the talent of the garden maker, his understanding of the principles behind the surfaces of the different historical styles, and his ability to convey that understanding to his clients. The dangers of consciously mining the past for ideas lay in the creation of rigidly historical assemblages unrelated to the surrounding landscape or to the lives of the homeowners, and in a tendency, particularly in the schools, to think that solutions to garden design problems were to be found *only* in past practice.

FILOLI

Bruce Porter, who created at Filoli, near San Francisco, one of the most original and appealing estate gardens in the early twentieth-century eclectic manner, had little or no exposure to academic dogma. Porter—painter, poet, critic, and versatile designer—was a very respected member of the Bay Area arts community. From available biographical information he seems to have educated himself mostly by traveling in Europe. Apparently he did study painting in Paris, but with whom or for how long remains a mystery.[12]

Porter was exceptionally fortunate in having as his client a man who was not only very rich but also appreciative of the native landscape and truly interested in the process of creating a garden. William Bowers Bourn II was the son of a well-off New England merchant who came to San Francisco in 1850 and bought a gold mine, which made him even better off. The younger Bourn grew up in San Francisco, attended Cambridge University in England, and knew many of the great English and Irish estate gardens. Upon returning to San Francisco he took over management of the mine, increasing its productivity, and proved to be an even more sure-handed entrepreneur than his father. He built the Greystone Winery in St. Helena, was president of the San Francisco Gas Company, and in 1908 bought the Spring Valley Water Company and the Crystal Springs Lake, one of the reservoirs in the San Andreas Rift valley east of the Pacific Coast Range. It was this latter purchase that led to the creation of Filoli.

Bourn fell in love with the valley, which he found similar to the landscape around the Lakes of Killarney, where he had bought an estate, Muckross, for his daughter and her Irish husband. He decided to build himself a country estate on the shore of Crystal Springs Lake. It turned out that he could not, even though he owned the lake. Because the lake supplied water to San Francisco its shoreline could not by law be turned to private use. Eventually he was able to buy land at the southern end of the valley. As the site for his house he carefully selected a low knoll on the eastern slope of the valley, from which he had a vista north to the lake and west to the top ridge of the mountains. To design the house Bourn commissioned Willis Polk, the San Francisco architect who previously had designed his townhouse and a country house near the mines. Polk offered nineteen different designs in a choice of styles from which Bourn selected a simple dignified English Georgian mansion in Flemish-bond brick with a Spanish tile roof.[13] The name Bourn created for his estate was compounded of the first two letters of *fight, love, live* drawn from a favorite maxim: "Fight for a just cause, love your fellow men, live a good life."

The long axis of the house ran parallel to the valley floor but above and to the east of it. Apparently Polk's office had sketched out a conventional formal garden extending into the valley on both sides of a cross-axis centered on the house. This Bourn rejected. It would have compromised his view of the lake and interrupted the long sweep of the oak-dappled valley to the north. He and Polk then asked Bruce Porter, a friend of both in 1916, to plan the garden. Bourn found

Porter's approach to landscape design sympathetic and their collaboration was long and successful.

Although he acknowledged that most of his art training was in Europe, Porter in an essay on art and architecture in California made clear that European—or Oriental—ideas were not to be copied literally. The American spirit was to weave them into the texture of American life. "The tradition of European art is preserved and yet it is translated into a new refinement and delicacy, indicative of a new choice and new predilections."[14]

Porter preferred a formality that extended a house's sense of shelter into the gardens around it. The old Mission gardens for him had a "rightness of design" adjusted to the land and he felt that there was "common sense in directness of passage, and economy in orderly rather than haphazard planting." But he also loved the native California landscape and believed that gardens should be contained:

> The tendency of the great place is constantly to increase, rather than wisely to limit, the area of cultivation; lawns encroach upon woodland; flowers incongruously appear where they do not belong; the place gets out of hand…[15]

The designed landscape at Filoli makes up twenty-seven acres of an estate comprising somewhat more than six hundred. Although the gardens—sixteen acres—are walled, the walls are visible only in a few places. Trees and shrubs of colors and textures that blend into the native vegetation beyond conceal the boundaries. Paradoxically, the highest point in the garden, and the place from which Bourn could enjoy his cherished view of Crystal Lake to the north is at its southernmost end. Porter developed a garden plan based on an axial path that runs parallel to the house from that high spot and ends with a view down the valley at the northern end of the broad terraces that form a podium for the house. This spine links the complex of gardens that branch from it on both sides, but it changes character as it moves through them. From a semicircular seating area, The High Place, it descends in wide flat turf panels with brick steps between them to the Bourn Gate of the Walled Garden, where it narrows and becomes a brick walkway. After descending through the Walled Garden it widens upon passing the Filoli Gate, runs between the Sunken Garden and the Bowling Green, and continues along the garden façade of the house on what is called the Lawn Terrace. It makes a right angle turn at the northern end of the podium and passes beside the house to the entrance drive. A less obvious but parallel axial path extends from the hall of the house along the eastern edge of first the Sunken Garden, then the Walled Garden and the Panel Gardens, ending at the end of the working gardens.

Porter used columnar Irish yews, *Taxus baccata* 'Stricta', in a variety of configurations as a way of defining his layout. The shapes are Italian-inspired, the yews themselves were grown from cuttings taken at Muckross House. Yews flank the path to the High Place, as an allée of cypresses

Trees play a major organizing role at Filoli. A double file of Irish yews on the north side of the Bowling Green balanced on the south side by the Walled Garden wall and a line of pleached London plane trees pulls the eye straight to the autumn-gilded Camperdown Elm and to the native woods beyond.

would in an Italian garden. This allée ends at the Walled Garden. Within the Walled Garden yews edge the five terraces that rise to what is called the Wedding Place in the southwest corner. These forced-perspective terraces, on a diagonal axis between that corner and the Summer House, are Porter's dynamic solution to an eleven-foot change in grade between the Woodland Garden — entered from the Wedding Place — and the rest of the Walled Garden. In the original plan a double file of yews separated the Bowling Green from the Lawn Terrace and created an east-west axis. This axis plus the yews in pairs that mark the steps to the garden entrance of the house and in triplicate mark the northern end of the principal axis emphasized the interlocking Ls of the terraces that opened to the valley in a very modern way. Later, when the swimming pool was added, another double line of yews at the outer edge of the Lawn Terrace was planted to shelter the pool. This new allée curtailed the breadth of the valley view; but did not substantially alter the basic structure of the design.

From the gardens already named it is clear that Filoli offers a diversity of garden rooms or perhaps better, garden experiences — in fact, so many that it seems much bigger than it is. But a consistent use of a limited number of defining materials — clipped box and yew hedges, brick walls, stone

balustrades, wrought-iron gates — and well-thought-out but often unexpected relationships among the different parts gives the garden as a whole a feeling of unity. In the same way, inspiration or motifs from different countries and styles are woven together so that their different origins seem simply accents in an overall conception. Detailing of walls, gates and summerhouse links these to the English Georgian architecture of the house.

A rich and varied spectrum of plants offered another source of pleasure. In this realm, Porter and Bourn were assisted by Isabella Worn, a San Francisco florist and plantswoman who was locally famous for her imaginative combinations of colors and textures. In addition to broad strokes of brilliant color in the parterre beds and the abundant terra-cotta pots, flowering cherries, wisteria, and azaleas light up corners in spring giving way to clematis, climbing roses, trumpet vines, and morning glories in summer, and Japanese maples, ginkgos, and Virginia creepers in autumn.

After Mr. and Mrs. Bourn died in 1936, Filoli was purchased by William P. and Lurline Matson Roth. Isabella Worn continued to work with Mrs. Roth, a dedicated horticulturist particularly interested in rhododendrons, camellias, and magnolias. She added many more flowering trees and shrubs to the gardens as well as some of the first Dawn

The Chartres Cathedral Window Garden is a colorful fantasy that doesn't really look like a stained glass window, the key to its success. The intricate pattern of clipped boxwood and holly represents the leading, the massed pink and white petunias the glass, with standard roses supplying needed vertical punctuation.

Olive trees sheared into drums flank the swimming-pool pavilion framing a golden honey locust and mark the southern corners of the Sunken Garden, their gray foliage echoed by cushions of clipped germander. Pots and borders of pink petunias, tubs of lavender and white Japanese iris contribute soft-hued accents.

Redwoods, *Metasquoia glyptostroboides*, planted in this country after their seeds were brought back from China in 1948. She also built the swimming pool and it was her idea to shape the olive trees that she placed to flank the pool house, and the entrance to the Summer House as drums, an unusual and effective touch.[16] Beginning in 1975, Mrs. Roth donated the house and gardens and eventually the entire estate of Filoli to the National Trust for Historic Preservation. Today it is operated by Filoli Center, a non-profit foundation, for the National Trust.

Many eclectic estate gardens of the country place era were more literal in their adaptations of European styles than Filoli. Or they seem so because the derivative architectural elements of the design make a stronger visual impact. A detailed examination of the role of Italian stonemasons who immigrated in large numbers to the United States at that time would probably be very illuminating in this context. Their craftsmanship and its availability may well have pushed owners and landscape architects toward a preference for Italian models. Even designs that are really French in derivation were often referred to by contemporaries as Italian, possibly because of the stonework.

CASA DEL HERRERO

At Casa del Herrero in Santa Barbara, the basic layout, given architectural detailing of a different character, might easily be classified as French or Italian rather than Hispanic. Even more than Filoli, this is a garden in which the owners had as much influence on the design as the professionals involved. Ralph and Carrie Steedman, who were originally from St. Louis, did considerable research in service of their desire to conjure up a Spanish estate. For the house, they chose an architect, George Washington Smith, who was known to be fond of the style. Ralph Steedman made a six-week trip to Spain in 1923 during which he photographed and sketched ideas, all the while bombarding Smith with suggestions. His visit was particularly rewarding because he met and was advised and accompanied by a couple who were recognized experts on Spanish architecture and design. Arthur and Mildred Stapley Byne would continue to work with him and buy for him as the garden developed. Steedman was himself a craftsman and an accomplished metalsmith. He had no hesitation in consulting experts like horticulturist Peter Reidel, but Steedman's seems to have been the deciding voice.

As laid out by the original landscape architect, Ralph Stevens, the grounds followed a pattern typical of the era: architecturally ordered gardens close to the house set in a naturalized landscape laced with winding paths and drives. The principal axis was perpendicular to the house, with the familiar basilica-form lawn sloping down to the south. Smaller enclosed gardens to the east and service courts to the west were arranged along a cross-axis through the house. This basic structure remained, as did some of the tropical planting for which Stevens was known, but the Steedmans, working with landscape architects Francis Underhill and Lockwood de Forest, Jr., made considerable changes to the entrance and the gardens around the house. In place of the gently curving entrance drive they contrived an arrangement of walled courtyards. East of the house they arranged a progression of enclosed gardens: the Spanish Patio, the East Garden, the Exedra, and the semicircular Rose Garden. At the back of the house they replaced Stevens's semicircular turf terrace with a rectangular arrangement of brick terraces flanking a square lawn. From it a band of broad paved steps led down to the south lawn, which ended in shady garden rooms on two levels. Below these and to one side they added a cactus garden.

Spain was in the details: The Motor Court's octagonal fountain and its black-and-white pebble-mosaic modeled on paving at the Alhambra; the tiled fountains in the Spanish Patio, the south garden rooms, and especially the typically Moorish eight-pointed star set in the terrace lawn; the complex of tile-lined conduits and pools in the steps below it; the colorful tiled benches and wall of the Exedra; and the arcaded wall of the East Garden, which appears to be a clipped hedge but is a masonry wall covered in creeping fig. To see the origin of many of the garden's details one has only to open the Bynes' 1928 *Spanish Gardens and Patios*.

Beaux-Arts designers focused on Europe and didn't attempt to integrate Chinese or Japanese ideas in their garden designs. It's understandable since Oriental gardens, however stylized, were based on the abstraction of natural forms. Plants from the Orient were another story, as we've seen at Filoli. The similarity between many Japanese species and native American ones intrigued botanists as soon as the first dried herbarium samples came back from Commodore Perry's expedition in 1853–54. Then in 1861, George Rogers Hall, a New England physician turned trader who was living in Yokohama at the time sent a shipment of Japanese plants in Wardian cases to a friend in Boston. The next year, Hall himself brought to the Parsons Nursery on Long Island another collection of plants that included *Magnolia kobus*, *Magnolia stellata*, hinoki, and sawara cypresses, zelkova, Japanese maples, and wisteria. Popularity came immediately to Hall's treasures. After Americans saw the Japanese garden at the Centennial Exposition in Philadelphia and subsequent ones in 1893 and 1894, Japanese gardens, too, became prized features on the estates of those who collected gardens in different styles.

In the meantime two men who were to write the first significant books on Japanese gardens in English reached Japan. In 1877 both were invited to teach at the Imperial University by a nation determined to learn Western technical and scientific skills. One, an American, Edward S. Morse, was an entomologist; the other, an Englishman, Josiah Conder, an architect. Morse's book was motivated by his desire to record the traditional arts of architecture and gardening before they were altered by Westernization. His *Japanese Homes and Their Surroundings*, published in 1886, focuses on small city gardens and is more descriptive than analytical. Conder offers a more comprehensive and penetrating view of Japanese garden art. He considers public parks and imperial and monastery gardens as well as private ones, and examines the different styles and the theory of their composition. Conder's observations were not published in book form until 1893 with *Landscape Gardening in Japan*; but they had appeared in 1886 in the *Journal of the Asiatic Society in Japan*. In 1889 Mrs. Van Rensselaer excerpted and explained them for the readers of *Garden and Forest*. She noted similarities between Japanese and European practice, like the incorporation of the surrounding landscape, known as "borrowed scenery," and the dissimulation of boundaries to increase the sense of space; but pointed out that there were traditional historic or symbolic meanings attached to certain elements and compositions to which non-Japanese could not respond. Her analysis of the essential aesthetic difference between the two approaches was succinct and enlightening:

> The Japanese…never desires anything but a strictly natural effect; but he is content that it shall be suggested rather than displayed. The elements before him are valued less for themselves than for their power to act upon his imagination and recall the forms of beauty which they typify rather than reproduce. We demand in a natural garden that it shall be a beautiful passage of scenery. The Japanese demands that it shall suggest a beautiful passage of scenery.[17]

Above:
From a typically Moorish pool inlaid in a square of lawn on the south side of the house water flows down a runnel interrupted by a diamond-shaped pool, disappears beneath the lawn to resurface at the bottom in the central fountain in the Fern Garden. Clipped eugenia hedges wall in the *tapis vert*, which follows the natural slope of the land.

Right:
As the plan makes clear, the layout of the gardens at Casa del Herrero in Montecito, California is quite Italian. Only the courts or patios to the east and west of the house have a real relationship to the customary spatial divisions in Spanish gardens.

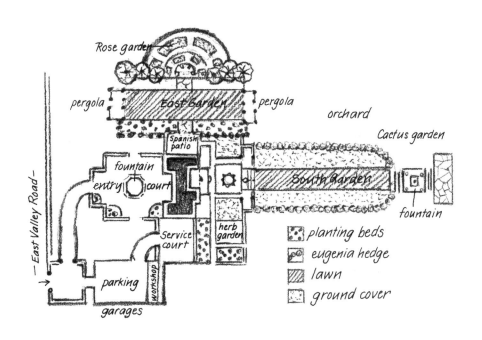

Rose garden

pergola   East Garden   pergola

orchard

Cactus garden

Spanish patio

fountain

entry   court

South Garden

fountain

Service court

herb garden

planting beds

eugenia hedge

lawn

ground cover

parking   Workshop

garages

— East Valley Road —

Americans, at least in the beginning, did not try to construct the large hill-and-water or stroll gardens characteristic of palaces and monasteries, although one writer, Clay Lancaster, does report the building of one by William Verbeck in upstate New York around 1888, but Verbeck had grown up in Japan.[18] Nor did Americans attempt the small, dry-stone Zen gardens for meditation. The preferred model was the tea garden or its miniaturized version, the courtyard garden. It could be adapted to a small city yard as well as to a suburban lot, and appreciated on purely aesthetic terms: no knowledge of tea-ceremony customs or symbolism needed. In fact, a tea pavilion in Japanese style made a very attractive summerhouse, even if the rest of the garden showed little inclination in that direction. To some it was the exotic artifacts that really mattered. F. Maude Smith suggested stone lanterns, bridges, and gateways as "Artistic Japanese Features for Gardens and Country Estates" in a 1907 issue of *House & Garden.* He — or she — was particularly taken with two-story Temple Gates used as studios or sitting rooms. Almost

as an afterthought came the suggestion that a garden with Japanese architectural features should include bamboos, wisteria, and pines.

Critics who sympathized with Arts-and-Crafts ideals were very much drawn to the careful workmanship in Japanese gardens, but they warned their readers to learn from the Japanese and not try to imitate them, as tastemakers always do, and their advice was ignored for the most part, as it usually is. Nor were they always consistent. Gustav Stickley in discussing what may be done with water and rocks in a little garden praised the Japanese approach, but was emphatic that:

> We need no temple lanterns or images of Buddha in this country, but we do need the kind of garden that brings to our minds the recollection of mountain brooks, wooded ravines and still lakes, and while it takes much thought, care and training of one's power of observation and adjustment to get it, the question of space is not one that has to be considered, and the

Tiles for the paving and the octagonal fountain in the center of the Spanish Patio were imported by Ralph and Carrie Steedman from Spain and Algeria. On the opposite side of the arcaded wall coated in *Ficus repens* is a tiled exedra centered on the eastern side of the East Garden behind which the Rose Garden is hidden.

Blue and white flowers fill the borders of the East Garden at Casa del Herrero, another *tapis vert* running from the tiled seating area at the northern end to a pergola at the southern one. The palms, evergreens and citrus suggest the variety of trees that will thrive in California's Mediterranean climate.

expense is almost nothing at all.

The thing to be most avoided is imitation either of the Japanese models from which we take the suggestion for our own little gardens or of the scenery of which they are intended to remind us.[19]

Unfortunately for his message Stickley chose to illustrate his remarks with photographs of John Scott Bradstreet's Minneapolis garden, which is well furnished with lanterns plus a Buddha. Stickley's excuse was that garden "might have been picked up in Japan and transported bodily to America." Bradstreet had, in fact, visited gardens on many trips to Japan and, equally important, possessed the talent needed for a reasonably successful recreation. Stickley felt he had to show his readers what a Japanese garden was like if they were to draw inspiration from it. Suburban homeowners were captivated by the idea. In 1906 *House & Garden* reported that in California one group of homeowners copied Japanese gardens, another Italian gardens, and a third adapted eastern dooryard gardens to California's much wider choice of flowers. The fourth and largest, as one might predict, settled for a palm tree — or a banana — or two on the lawn.

American versions of Japanese gardens have been made all through the twentieth century, with or without the help of

Japanese consultants, though a few were re-christened Chinese during World War II. The stream of books on the art of the Japanese Garden and how it could be adapted to this country, which began with professor Morse in 1886, has done nothing but increase in both quantity and quality ever since. With the coming of color photography these books are able to convey, as the earlier ones could not, the atmosphere and the emotional power of Japanese gardens.

One of the many important contributions that color photographs have made to the repertory of American garden designers is the appreciation of moss. Even before those who went to Japan saw it in situ they had been enthralled by it in books. True, Americans had been able to see the beauty of moss as a ground cover in dense forests like those of the Adirondacks. It was a different story when it appeared around houses, as it often does when the soil is too acid or trees spread too much shade or compete too vigorously for grass to survive. It became a weed. Inspired by the Japanese, garden-makers have now begun to encourage moss.

Japanese gardens radiate a serenity that is very hard to resist. It was meant to be so. They were created to slow their viewers down and put them in touch with nature; to cleanse the mind of daily concerns and encourage meditation and "elegant play." They cast their spell with strong design: sensi-

tive proportions, dynamic asymmetrical balance, simplification — a paring down to essentials of line, shape, texture, and color. They are composed to give pleasure in all seasons. But even very small ones do not yield up all their interest from one vantage point. There is always the sense that something else is just around the corner, a touch of mystery that prolongs fascination.

Rocks are quite literally the foundation of the Japanese garden, both physically and spiritually. In sum, according to T. Kaori Kitao, an art historian, one "may be created without flowers, grass, ponds, streams, mounds, paths, and even trees and shrubs, but a Japanese garden cannot exist without rocks."[20] In Japan, rocks are prized not only for beauty but for energy and presence as well, and they embody a multiplicity of myths, meanings, and metaphors. Happily we do not have to share their complex reverence for rocks, a difficult feat, in order to learn from Japanese usage. Acknowledged or not, the ways that American designers shape and lay out stepping stones and use rocks as accents have been profoundly affected by Japanese examples. We have also learned from them how to turn gravel or pebbles to decorative effect, sometimes drawing fairly obviously from their traditions but very often using these materials in gardens that show no other trace of Japanese influence.

Far left:
Josiah Conder, an English architect, went to Japan to teach Western design but fell in love with its gardens and wrote one of the earliest analyses of the principles on which they were based. This illustration from his *Landscape Gardening in Japan* shows a small garden belonging to a merchant at Sakai, a design that Americans found very appealing.

Near left:
Edward S. Morse's 1886 *Japanese Homes and Their Surroundings* is filled with his sketches of Japanese houses, gardens, and their furnishings, giving Americans detailed documents of traditional, everyday Japanese design. In addition to this stone lantern and footbridge, illustrations show paving patterns, fences, gates, and summerhouses.

Below, left:
That the garden Arts-and-Crafts merchant John Scott Bradstreet built for his house in Minneapolis resembles the merchant's garden in Sakai is not too surprising since Bradstreet had visited gardens with Conder during his many trips to Japan. But as photographed around 1918 it could not be called serene or artifact-free.

THE JAMES ROSE GARDEN

That a gifted designer could spend a considerable amount of time in Japan, immerse himself in Japanese culture, practice Zen Buddhism, yet produce gardens that are truly American is brilliantly demonstrated by the mature work of James Rose. Stone plays a large role in his designs. At times he may use it in ways that suggest Japanese stonecraft: stepping-stones in a pool or a dry stream of pebbles. But that dry stream exists to solve a drainage problem, not to symbolize a river nor to provide a decorative accent although in fact it does both as well. There is an angularity in the shaping of Rose's ground planes, pools, and steps that owes more to Cubism and Constructivism than to the Japanese aesthetic. Also unJapanese is his very successful integration of the swimming pools and spaces for outdoor entertaining and other activities Americans love.

According to Dean Cardasis, Associate Professor of Landscape Architecture at the University of Massachusetts and Director of the James Rose Center, "Nothing made Rose madder than to suggest that he did Japanese gardens." At one point, Cardasis relates, "a distinguished Japanese architect and scholar who had met Rose in Japan came to visit him at his house in New Jersey. 'I didn't know you had a Japanese house,' said the man with some surprise. Rose simmered a while, then said 'But you are an architect and a scholar, you must know that this is not a Japanese house.' 'That's not what I meant,' his guest replied, 'What I meant is that your house has the spirit of a Japanese House, its relationship to the land.'"[21] One hopes the famously testy Rose then took the remark as a compliment. Although he protested too much, it echoes his own thinking:

> Can we not wrestle with our own esthetic problems in terms of our own natural landscape? This is precisely what the Japanese have done so successfully. A solution cannot be bought or transported successfully. It must be elaborated on the home grounds, so to speak, until something appears that could not possible fit any other place in the world because it so perfectly belongs right here and right now.[22]

However important esthetic considerations were to Rose as an artist, he was as much concerned with bringing his clients and the spaces they lived in—their houses, gardens and environment—into a meaningful, joyful relationship. A garden needed privacy, he felt. But you didn't have to enclose it with high fences or walls or hedges. You could conceal what you didn't want to see or want others to see with carefully placed screens or baffles "in successive planes throughout the property with open spaces between them." These planes could be created with trees or shrubs or they could be built. With such an approach to enclosure Rose could develop overlapping and interlocking spaces that would accept a variety of activities, create a sense of movement, and make even a quite small lot seem expansive. This is certainly the case in his own New Jersey house, where indoors and out are inseparably interwoven. How Rose managed to outwit suburban setback and fence-height rules to build what he has likened to a small village, makes entertaining and illuminating reading in his books, *Creative Gardens*, and *The Heavenly Environment*. Now his very personal dwelling houses his archives and operates as a research center in landscape architecture.

Early in his career, Rose had been as interested as his fellow modernists in contemporary materials, particularly translucent ones like fiberglass, which he often used in variations on shoji-panel screens. And he made a point of using common and inexpensive ones like railroad ties, painted plywood, bamboo blinds. That all were impermanent was unimportant: plants grew and died, people's needs and desires changed. In addition, they encouraged experiment. "His own house was a continuing experiment in the creation of space," Cardasis says, "in finding the edges that shape space. A material like fiberglass that is translucent can change the perception of space." What a garden was made of was incidental in Rose's eyes:

> A garden is an experience. It is not flowers, or plants of any kind. It is not flagstone, brick, grass, or pebbles. It is not a barbeque or a Fiberglas screen. It is an experience. If it were possible to distill the essence of a garden, I think it would be the sense of being within something while still out of doors.[23]

Considering how swiftly and enthusiastically Americans embraced the garden art of Japan, and how deeply some of its techniques and principles have penetrated our thinking about garden design, it is surprising how little interest we seem to have had in the garden art of China. Doubly surprising because Chinese theory and practice had such a profound influence on the Japanese. Our trade with China has a much longer history than that with Japan; we have always loved Chinese porcelains, Chinese silks, and Chinese wallpaper; and our gardens are filled with Chinese plants.

One possible reason is that most China traders did not see Chinese gardens. Auguste Duhaut-Cilly, a French ship captain who visited Canton in 1829 reported that the Chinese were so unfriendly that Europeans and Americans avoided going ashore unless absolutely necessary.[24] Nor did the inhabitants welcome scholars. Edward Morse, who followed up his book on Japanese homes with a visit to China at the end of the century found himself faced with rudeness, hostility and contempt at every turn. Only a few Chinese who had studied in the United States really tried to help. And as he was there in February he wasn't much impressed by the gardens, only city ones, that he saw. Morse was a fair-minded man, and acknowledged that the Chinese had real reasons for their dislike of Westerners. Still he didn't find it a pleasant place to visit. His book did not sell well.[25] American missionaries seem to have roamed more freely about the country, but essentially they were there to change the Chinese way of living and thinking, so they were unlikely to develop an interest in the gardens. Nor were they likely to have seen any of the large and elaborate Imperial or noble gardens.

In the seventeenth and eighteenth centuries the more flexible missionary priests like Père Attiret, and the employees of French and Dutch East India Companies gave the

West most of its information — not always accurate — about Chinese gardens, supplemented by the few Chinese of high rank who visited France and England. As letters and reports trickled back to Europe in the eighteenth century, they fueled a passion for *chinoiserie* in all the decorative arts, not just in gardening.

Most of the impact on garden design was decorative — picturesque pagodas, pavilions and bridges strategically dotted around both landscape and architectural gardens — although Chinese and Western landscape gardens had many principles in common. According to Ji Cheng, author of *Yuan Yi* or *The Craft of Gardens* written between 1631 and 1634:

> Making use of the natural scenery is the most vital part of garden design. There are various aspects such as using scenery in the distance, near at hand, above you, below you, and at certain times of the year.[26]

Proponents of the landscape garden would have agreed wholeheartedly with this statement, and with his contention that the "most important element in the layout of gardens is the siting of the principal buildings" and that "the primary consideration is the view." Note that he speaks of buildings, not building. And, in fact, the largest part of his manual is devoted to the construction of houses, bridges, pavilions, covered walkways, doors, windows, paving, and artificial mountains. According to the distinguished Scandinavian scholar, Osvald Siren, "A Chinese garden without buildings to divide, surround, or complete it is simply inconceivable."[27]

This is where the English in particular part company with Ji Chen. Yes, there were a few temples and grottoes in their landscape gardens — fewer as time passed — but their pleasure grounds were designed to include agricultural use. For both practical and emotional reasons the fundamental components of English landscape gardens were grass and trees. Trees interested the Chinese to a degree, grass not at all. Their fundamentals were rocks and water. Large landscape gardens in China were strictly for the pleasure of their royal or noble owners. Along with palaces, a variety of buildings to shelter a variety of activities ranging from contemplation and study to drinking games dominate their design.

In countries like France and Sweden, where the naturalistic gardens of the eighteenth century lacked an economic component, Chinese ideas had much more influence. The French, in fact, called their versions *jardins Anglo-Chinois*, and furnished them with a variety of *fabriques*, including Chinese pagodas. Americans followed French practice in endowing landscapes with structures, but these were usually rustic in character and rarely betrayed more than a hint of Chinese inspiration. In a way, most of what we could learn from Chinese landscape design on a large scale came to us already simplified and adapted either by Japanese or Europeans.

Chinese scholar's gardens like those for which the city of Suzhow is famous seem to have had even less resonance for us. The complex system of interlocking courtyards, zigzag walkways, open pavilions, and closed rooms packed with changing vistas grew out of equally complex customary household arrangements, and was perfectly suited to them.

Right:
Inside his house in Ridgewood, New Jersey the inspiration James Rose found in Japan is obvious, but the angular pool outside the window owes as much to the shapes in early twentieth-century art as it does to Japanese stonecraft. Rose was a master at integrating house and garden for a climate that did not permit year-round outdoor living.

Below:
The flat, broken, irregularly stacked rocks that form a smaller pool in his garden suggest the kind of Constructivist compositions Rose admired. The hemispherical metal fountain basin must also have been a favorite: It turns up in several of his landscapes.

True, courtyard or patio gardens had a history in parts of this country, but their layouts were far simpler. Even the Mormon polygamists never seem to have tried such an architectural program for keeping their multiple families in one compound.

American courtyard gardeners did share the custom of growing flowers in pots; but have always found it hard to appreciate the features that meant most to their Chinese counterparts: the incredibly intricate rocks displayed individually as sculpture or piled into miniature mountains. The Chinese revere rocks as much as the Japanese and for many of the same reasons it seems; but the Chinese taste for fantastic, baroque forms like the famous wave-carved Lake Tai rocks is not easily acquired by Americans.

What does have some appeal are the framing devices that both arrest and beckon the eye, the shaped doors and windows like the circular so-called Moon Gate; but in American gardens they have not played the crucial compositional role they do Chinese scholar's gardens. The way such framing devices govern the design is hard to understand from photographs. Those who have not been to China can get a good sense of their role by visiting a carefully researched example like the New York Chinese Scholar's Garden in the Staten Island Botanical Garden, or the Classical Chinese Garden in Portland, Oregon. New York's newly constructed garden was designed by Zou Gongwu, China's leading scholar in the

area of classic garden design, assembled and fabricated in Suzhou, shipped to New York, and erected by Chinese artisans.[28] As one moves around the garden, walking and sitting and looking, the relationships between rocks and water, rocks and plants, and plants and architecture are very satisfying when one concentrates only on the image within a frame: a tracery-filled window, a conventional doorway, or one shaped like a leaf or a circle, or perhaps two trees. After a while it becomes clear that the garden was designed to be experienced sequentially, as a series of framed pictures that shift subtly or disappear as the viewer's position shifts. Try to look at it as a whole and the composition seems to fall apart or become confused. Respect the framing and it is magical.

Garden makers in this country began to experiment with some of the shaped doors and latticed windows at the beginning of the twentieth century but American resistance to walling, in small suburban yards and gardens meant that Chinese features usually appeared only on fairly large estates. One Chinese-flavored garden, for which we now have only documentary evidence, was designed by Beatrix Farrand in 1914 for Willard and Dorothy Straight's estate in Old Westbury, Long Island. Farrand had not visited China, and never would, although she would again adapt Chinese ideas to American desires and conditions in a later and more complex garden for Mr. and Mrs. John D. Rockefeller, Jr. That the

Straights wanted a Chinese presence in their garden was understandable. Although they had originally met in this country, it was in China that they came to know each other, fell in love, and spent the first year of their marriage. In Willard Straight, Farrand had a first-class source of information on Chinese gardens. He had spent ten years in the Orient with only brief visits to the U.S. and Europe as, among several roles, a diplomat and the representative of a consortium of American bankers. He spoke Chinese and had traveled widely in China, Manchuria, and Korea, with his pencil and sketchbook always at the ready, it seems. He had originally wanted to be an architect and clearly had real talent as an artist. If most of the drawings reproduced in biographies of Straight by Herbert Croly and Louis Graves[29] are of people, there are enough of temples and gates to demonstrate that he had observed these carefully.

It was temples and gates that Farrand adapted to give a touch of China to what was otherwise a formal flower and swimming-pool garden. The brick wall enclosing the flower garden was pierced by Moon gates, not to be used as entrances but to frame views of the landscape beyond the garden. The arbors that faced each other in the center space between garden and swimming pool were temple-like structures in wood, as were the two summerhouses at the end of the pool. In at least one design for the flowerbeds, a

Rose's garden continually changed because he was always experimenting with interlocking spaces and different kinds of barriers—solid, transparent, and semi-transparent—like the four different panels that make up this harmonious assembly of solid wall and woven fences.

Walls, windows, gates, and pavilions are crucial in Chinese garden design, so it is not totally inappropriate that these are the elements most often picked up by Westerners. Beatrix Farrand adapted them very successfully to flavor a symmetrical and very unChinese layout in the Long Island garden she created for the Willard Straights.

Opposite page:
To shape the landscape at Innisfree in New York's Dutchess County, the Walter Becks looked to Chinese landscape paintings, and set out to fashion a similar succession of scenic passages. Lester Collins, who had visited China before joining forces with them, completed the design, giving the lake a central unifying role by clearing its shores.

very un-Chinese but very American notion, she harmonized the two by laying out beds in a fretwork pattern.

INNISFREE

Like Beatrix Farrand, neither Walter nor Marion Beck ever visited the Far East. Yet when they began to create a garden on 950 acres near Millbrook, New York in 1930, they took the same path as did Ji Cheng in the 1630s. Ji Cheng began as a painter before creating gardens and writing the earliest known manual on Chinese landscape design. Walter Beck was a painter who had become fascinated with Oriental painting and made a profound study of its compositional techniques. It was to Chinese painting that he and his wife turned for inspiration in creating Innisfree, just as a Chinese garden maker would have done. Ji Cheng continually refers his readers to specific paintings for ideas. Osvald Siren sums up the relationship:

> Especially characteristic of Chinese garden art is its intimate relation to painting. It was in very large part the great painters who created the typical gardens in China, and in this they were inspired by ideas similar to those which found expression in their painting.[30]

After careful study of copies of the famous scroll in which the poet and painter Wang Wei (A.D. 699–761) described and illustrated his garden, Beck concluded that in a Chinese garden one moved as in a scroll from one to another of a series of enclosed designed spaces. He called these spaces "cup gardens" not a term found in the *Yuan Yi*. In her book, *The Chinese Garden*, Maggie Keswick called them "space cells." The Chinese seem to take such enclosures for granted

and find no need to name them, although enclosure — natural or man-made — is critical to their landscape designs.

Beck was not interested in creating a Chinese garden as such; he simply felt that Chinese design principles were particularly appropriate for laying out his garden in the natural enclosure that was to be its site. The most obviously Chinese element is a carefully carved circular window that marks the opening of a hillside cave. It frames, not a garden view or a few carefully composed plants, but a pair of stones that appear to be shouting at each other if not actually fighting. Rocks and water were the defining elements of the garden. Beck shared the Oriental love for rocks, and for their arrangement; his wife was the horticulturist of the team. Rocks were plentiful on the property, and there was a large lake. To the lake's tranquility Beck and Lester Collins, the landscape architect who began advising the Becks in the 1940s, added movement and sparkle with streams, fountains, and waterfalls. Collins, who had studied gardens in China and Japan, took over the care of the garden after Beck's death and oversaw its transition to public space after Marion Beck's death in 1959. He more than doubled its size, clearing the shores of the lake, which had been densely wooded, and endowing it with the unifying role that the river plays in Wang Wei's painting. Collins "wove Beck's gardens into the fabric of a total landscape," using paths and berms to conceal and reveal a series of pictures like those in a Chinese scroll.[31]

Recently there has been a renewal of interest in Chinese approaches to landscape design, as it has become possible for more Americans to visit the country and study the gardens first hand. Such studies will probably provide ideas; but it is likely that exact replication will be left to museums and botanical gardens.

One of the few overtly
Chinese passages in the
landscape, the meandering
stream in the Meadow,
resembles similar streams
built to play a game in which
a cup of wine was floated
to guests seated along the
banks, who were to compose
verses on a subject set by the
host and recite them in time
to take a sip from the cup as
it passed.

Mobility, Fashion, and the Role of the Press

The trait that observers, foreign and home-grown, first seize upon as typically American is the ease with which we pull up stakes and move. Move across the street, across town, across the country. Move in search of better land, a better job, a better climate, a better neighborhood, a better dwelling. The Census Bureau did report in 2000 that mobility had slowed: only 16 percent of the population moved the previous year as against 20 percent during the 1950s and 60s, a decline that many demographers feel reflects the aging of the U.S. population. Even if it does represent a trend and not a blip, the numbers — more than 43 million — are still astonishing to foreigners.[1] There is a good case to be made that this national restlessness has been a stronger influence on the kinds of gardens we make than the absence of primogeniture. Attachment to a particular place remains rather shallow-rooted, and mobility is still deplored by many social critics, who don't appreciate the power new surroundings give an individual to live the way he or she wishes. One may move to pursue economic opportunity or develop a talent, but one also may move simply to escape the burden of conforming to family or neighborhood expectations.

When we move away from home, most of us don't reject everything about that home. We take along objects that have meaning for us, memories of pleasures, and ideas of the way our surroundings ought to look and feel and smell. The image of a garden that we keep in the back of the mind may not be that of our parents' garden, but it is usually one we formed as children. The trees and flowers in it are those we loved then. Even in this age of aircraft and automobiles, people and possessions are more easily transported than plants, but that has never kept us from trying. Pioneers carried seeds, and nursed cuttings and plants in their wagons. Today we are more likely to order replacements for our favorites from nurseries or seed catalogues. Whether or not they will grow happily — or at all — in a different environment is another story. We have far more information on a plant's requirements in terms of temperature, soil, and rainfall at our disposal than did the pioneers but most of us still succumb to nostalgia and try to grow what we grew up with rather than what really belongs around our new home.

The pattern is not a new one: seventeenth-century settlers, with little advance information to go on and most of what they did have inaccurate, quite naturally brought with them what they thought they would need. On a practical level, they very swiftly learned to grow the corn, squash, and beans of the Indian

diet along with the herbs, fruits, and vegetables to which they were accustomed; but they organized their plantings, agricultural and horticultural, along customary lines. This was not always the best solution. Indian fields with corn, beans, and squash all growing together looked messy to Europeans but in fact needed less weeding and caused less erosion than the plowed furrows they favored. For what we would call gardens indigenous inhabitants seem not to have offered models. The northern Europeans — English, Dutch, Swedish, German, French — who settled along the Eastern Seaboard had little choice but to follow those from their homelands.

The Spaniards who had a century earlier moved into Florida and into the Southwest duplicated their own Mediterranean design traditions, as they would again in California towards the end of the eighteenth century. Their gardens were enclosed and unseen from the street. The pattern had variations. The 1586 map of St Augustine illustrating Sir Francis Drake's attack on the settlement shows houses lining the streets with the centers of the blocks empty. In a late eighteenth-century map the centers are divided up into fenced or walled gardens, but Albert Manucy's examination of early records turned up only a few mentions of patios or patio walls. In what he calls the St. Augustine Plan, the house with its loggia or sheltered porch faced a fenced side yard with its narrow end abutting the street. To enter, one passed through a gate in the fence and then through the main entrance in the loggia.[2] Such an arrangement is very like that of the eighteenth-century Charleston single house and may have had a Caribbean origin, since many settlers in both cities came from the islands. In the Southwest sometimes rooms surrounded the patio on all four sides, sometimes a combination of rooms and walls. The ground plane was paved or made of packed swept earth, practical in both subtropical Florida and the arid West. These walled or fenced

gardens harbored varying amounts of vegetation, mostly planted in pots, and a variety of activities, mostly work-related.

Richard Westmacott's recent studies of African-American yards and gardens in rural Georgia, Alabama, and South Carolina have brought to light a different kind of design built from a swept-earth surface.[3] The gardens he has examined surround houses and are arranged for both enjoyment and work. They are places for children to play, for friends and family to gather and talk or eat. They may be used for washing clothes or preparing and cooking food. Some space may be given to raising chickens or pigs. How many plants and trees they are furnished with depends on the interest of their owners. Some are jungly, some are sparingly planted but ornamented with objects. Sometimes plants are arranged in beds, but more often they are planted in containers, usually recycled ones. The arrangements may look haphazard and undesigned to those accustomed to different traditions, but they were deliberately composed by their creators.

Westmacott speculates that this kind of garden design was brought here from Africa. His theory seems supported by the gardens he studied, but swept-earth yards next to or in front of white-owned houses were mentioned by early nineteenth-century visitors to the rural South, although they are apparently rare today. In gardens "attached to town houses and modest country cottages in Georgia," according to historian Catherine Howett, "the clean 'swept yard,' with paths of sand or compacted clay (frequently salted to prevent the emergence of grass) surrounding a simple pattern of planting beds, was a dominant regional convention."[4] Many early gardens created by American immigrants to California combined tamped-earth walks and sitting spaces with raised flowerbeds. This suggests that swept earth as ground plane is an instinctive and sensible response in regions that don't lend themselves to turf raising.

Cities that were planned as cities from their founding at the end of the seventeenth or beginning of the eighteenth centuries followed European urban precedents. In Philadelphia and New Orleans, for example, houses were built right to the edge of the street. The gardens were in back or at the side and concealed by high walls or close fences. If the spatial organization was similar to the Mediterranean patio, the planting was not. Vegetation was plentiful but geometrically organized. Philadelphians in particular were noted botanists and plant collectors, and many soon fled the constraints of city lots to create spacious villa gardens on the outskirts.

Given the diversity of settlers' backgrounds and the equally great diversity of the climates, soils, and vegetation in this country, one might expect each region to have evolved a distinctive design style over the last three or four hundred years. It hasn't quite worked out that way. Certainly you can find recognizable differences among gardens in different parts of the United States. Differences in vegetation ensure it. An allée of live oaks dripping Spanish moss does not look the same as an allée of American elms, even if the layouts are identical. Yet, as you travel across the country, you find many more similarities than differences among gardens on both

coasts and everywhere in between. Had your travels taken place a hundred and fifty years ago, you might have made the same observations. That famous American mobility has tended to handicap the development of local plans and plants into gardens of strong regional character, although it is not the only force at work, nor does it always act directly.

Where there were local design traditions, locals tended to stay with them, at least in the beginning. Newcomers often had very different ideas. In New Orleans, for example, inhabitants of the older quarters, mostly of French or Spanish descent, tended to re-create the house forms and enclosed patio gardens in the new suburbs they built as the city expanded. The Yankee entrepreneurs drawn to the city as a trading base after the Louisiana Purchase, on the other hand, only occasionally adopted the local layout. In their best-known suburb, the Garden District, developed in the 1840s, they set their houses — Greek Revival, Italianate, or Gothick — in the middle of lawns and gardens. In plan these gardens might have come from a good residential neighborhood almost anywhere in this country, and over time this arrangement modified or replaced the creole tradition in much of the city. It was the climate that gave and still gives the city's gardens the specific regional character described by Suzanne Turner:

> A direct result of the size and speed of vegetative growth is that most New Orleans gardens are shaded. The plant palette thus relies to a great extent upon shade-loving evergreen plants, particularly ground covers and shrubs. Related to this reliance upon evergreens and the scale of the vegetation is the quality of light filtered through the branches of mature trees. A remarkable chiaroscuro effect dances across the ground plane producing a vast

Above:
Californians tend to refer to their swept-earth ground planes as "hardpan." This patio is roofed by a truly monumental grapevine.

Opposite:
A swept-earth yard in the South with plant containers sunk into the ground. Dorothea Lange's caption for her 1937 Farm Security Administration photograph reads "Home of Negro landowner, Greene County, Georgia. This man has owned his land since 1913. He has raised ten children here."

Residence of J. J. FAIRBANKS

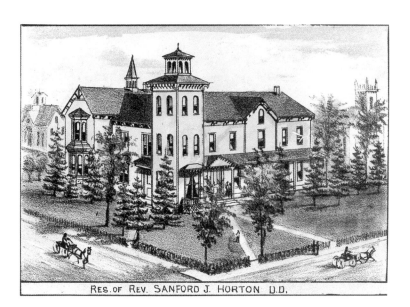

RES. OF REV. SANFORD J. HORTON D.D.

RES. OF Wᴹ AMBROSE, AUBURN.

range of greens that are subtle and refined. And even more ephemeral than the light is the fragrance. The atmospheric quality intensifies the sense of smell when the air is nearly palpable, especially when filled with the aroma of floral blossoms.[5]

Nostalgia has more appeal for expatriates; novelty for homebodies. Even after living on this side of the Atlantic for two or three generations, most colonists were still devoted to the daffodils and tulips, the roses and lilies of Europe. Europeans were hungry for the pine trees and rhododendrons, the lady's slippers and sunflowers of America. They even imported poison ivy![6] For its brilliant fall color, of course. Unsurprisingly, by the beginning of the eighteenth century a brisk transatlantic exchange was under way. But the more East-coast Americans filled their gardens with old-world favorites, the more these favorites furnished the nostalgic gardens of their children as they fanned out beyond the Appalachians.

Nostalgia, at least in the early years, wasn't the only motivation. As long as the United States remained primarily agricultural, homesteaders sought out new lands to reproduce the kind of farming they were accustomed to. Southerners who could afford it re-created the plantation economy based on slave labor, or if they were stockmen, the open range. Northern farm families tilled their own land and fenced their livestock, assisted by hired hands when needed. All raised or tried to raise the crops they understood. The same with gardens. The plants that had been in their families' gardens were the plants pioneers knew how to grow. Their neighbors usually were newcomers as well and as unaccustomed to local conditions as they were.

Garden magazines of the nineteenth century are filled with both queries from gardeners settling in new-to-them territory as to what they can grow, and reports on what has or has not been successful for them. A correspondent in Vermillion, Kansas writes James Vick, seedsman and proprietor of *Vick's Illustrated Magazine*, in 1878 telling him of her success with her lawn, dahlias, and roses; but regretting that she "had to give up the old home loves here, the Pansies, Daisies and Primrose." Nevertheless she still intends to try growing them when the trees she has planted give more shade. In his reply Vick cautions that she probably won't have much luck. This exchange of views, successes and failures was equally valuable to the nurserymen/publishers and the garden-makers. Early on, most of the former were based in the East and had little direct knowledge of Western conditions. Established customers who shared their experiences were a big help in responding to future customers.

Pioneers also brought to the attention of nurserymen attractive plants they found growing wild. The Kansas correspondent also asks if he knows a rich blue prairie flower she calls October Beauty, which she thinks might make a good garden flower. Vick seems to know about it and warns that the Blue-fringed Gentian is "a true wild flower and does not take readily to civilization."[7] Like the lady in Kansas, many Americans saw the beauty of their native flora. As wildflower enthusiasts have learned to their sorrow, a tree or a flower dug from the forest and transplanted to the back yard too often dies.

It takes dedication, patience, and considerable expertise on the part of nurserymen to domesticate wildlings. They must first figure out how to propagate, then, if successful, invest space and money in growing sufficient stock, and finally inspire potential customers with their own enthusiasm and build a market. Particularly in the case of ornamentals, it was simply easier and more profitable to import seeds, bulbs, and plants until late in the nineteenth century. Given their popularity there, even American natives could be grown more efficiently in England. Talking about *Kalmia latifolia* that enthusiastic American horticulturist Henry Winthrop Sargent observes that:

> [A]lthough the mountains in our neighborhood abound with them, we have found it less expensive to import plants from England, raised from seed, at 15 cents apiece, than to transplant the native habitants of the mountains with their long straggling roots.[8]

Today regional nurserymen working to sell native plants would find themselves in sympathy with fellow nurseryman Downing's own earlier exasperation as he tried to build a market for American trees: "[I]f people ignore oaks and ashes, and adore poplars and ailantuses, nurserymen cannot be expected to starve because the planting public generally are destitute of taste."[9]

In the case of oaks vs. poplars, it is not just natives vs. exotics. It is also slow growth vs. fast growth. Mobility encourages that very human desire for instant results, and here the critics have a point: the fastest solution is not always or even often the best one. Fast-growing trees tend to be brittle, short-lived, invasive, or some combination thereof. But people who don't expect to stay in a house more than a decade aren't likely to plant a noble burr oak that takes twenty years to grow fifteen feet. Or to take a shorter span, sod can be laid in a few hours; but a lawn grown from seed, which takes three or four months, is healthier and better looking in the long run. In periods of great economic prosperity there are always people who are willing to pay for overnight lawns and the transplanting of full-grown oaks. The rest of the population tends to rely on fertilizers and fast growers.

In his early years Downing himself had been more interested in exotic plants, and he admitted that he really had not appreciated the beauty of native trees until he saw them in their full beauty grown as specimens in England. He attributes his late conversion to the human tendency to undervalue what is nearby and familiar. Conversely, it often takes time for people to appreciate an unfamiliar landscape and its flora, even those trained in horticulture and landscape design. Many Americans from the East, including Olmsted and Cleveland, at first found the prairies flat and monotonous compared to the hills and forests they had grown up with. Scandinavians like Fredrika Bremer and Jens Jensen, who responded immediately to the distinctive beauty of the Middle-Western plains, seem to have been exceptions.

What never entered the mind of either James Vick or the
gentian-loving lady from Kansas was the possibility of considering the surrounding prairie or a swatch of it as "the garden"
and enjoying its flowers in their wild state. Not surprising.
Even today, when prairie restoration has its passionate devotees, there aren't all that many Thoreaus who can find more
beauty in a wild bog than in a well-kept yard. If the lady had
made a wild garden, she would not have received the compli-
ments she reports from neighbors and passersby on her lawn
and flowers.

Making a garden that everyone recognized as a garden
was a way to create community, to be accepted by your
neighbors. And moreover to ensure that you would be identified as American whether you had just immigrated from
Europe, or from another part of this country. But how could
you tell what your new neighbors would recognize as a garden? You looked to newspapers, magazines, and books for
guidance.

Observers from Tocqueville onward noted the omnipres-
ence of newspapers and the fact, astonishing to many, that
the inhabitants of a newly built village in a forest clearing or
on a prairie crossroads were quite as aware of current news —
and current fashions — as those in long established cities.
Pockets of primitivism did exist. Education and high culture
were far more a matter of class in the South, and knowledge
gained by wealthy plantation owners on trips to European
and Northern cities didn't appear to trickle down to their less
fortunate neighbors. The kind of ignorance and illiteracy that
Olmsted encountered in the backwoods South and reported
in *The Cotton Kingdom* was rare in the regions populated by
pioneers from the Northeast where at least some degree of
universal education was the norm. It was from the Northeast,
as well, that most of the founders of newspapers and writers
of books were drawn.

The words of the press were as influential in spreading the
garden design ideas of the Northeast across the continent as
the Yankees who swarmed to settle it. The journalists of the
horticultural press in particular believed they had a mission
to increase the knowledge and, just as important, improve
the taste of their readers. Not for nothing was the monthly
edited by Downing titled *The Horticulturist and Journal of
Rural Art and Rural Taste*. If the dooryard garden with its mix
of flowers, fruits, and vegetables was the first model for the
pioneer garden it was not long before the "lawn and trees
with a little knot of flowers" recommended by Downing and
followers like Frank Scott replaced it.

In the nineteenth century, just as it is today, the American
horticultural press was part of a pan-European network. As
soon as it was founded in 1829 The Massachusetts Horticultural Society ordered a subscription to John Claudius
Loudon's *Gardener's Magazine*, the major British journal.
The reports of nineteenth-century travelers criss-crossing the
ocean went back and forth among American and European
magazines. Books and their authors followed the same pattern. For example, the English radical politician, William
Cobbett, wrote *The American Gardener* in 1823 based on his
experiences farming in the United States, but clearly
European in viewpoint. Then, back home in 1829 and run-

ning a seed farm, he published *The English Gardener*.
Downing corresponded with Loudon, and his own books
were well known in England. Along with practical information on planting and transplanting, fertilizing, and pest control, the horticultural magazines contained news from
around the world. By following *The Horticulturist* in 1847 and
1848 you could find out who won prizes for what at major
horticultural society exhibitions; learn how to build a
hydraulic ram or a Wardian case; visit famous gardens like
Montgomery Place in the Hudson Valley or the Jardin des
Plantes in Paris; keep up with the latest advances in
hybridization of stone fruits and berries; weigh into the argument over the best strawberry varieties; note the successful
introduction of the tea plant from China into India and the
Gloriosa lily from Japan into Europe and America; and even
enjoy an occasional spoof directed at horticultural fanaticism. And you would have been up to date on the latest garden fashions in England.

It's not just hard to draw a line between fashion and news;
how do you distinguish between a fashion that will develop
into a long-term trend and one that is simply a brief infatua-
tion? Journalists striving for material to fill their pages didn't
bother to try. The 1878 and 1879 issues of *Vick's Illustrated
Magazine* offer a look at some of the fashions that swept
across the American gardening world in those years. To give a
new look to the "bedding" that he said has been fashionable
for many years, the editor suggested carrying out the designs
in plants with large and striking leaves such as cannas, rici-
nus, caladiums, and coleus accented with dahlias and
gladiolus. This fashion for the subtropical look in northern
gardens — with a wider palette of plants to choose from —
reappeared in the 1990s. Plants grown indoors can't really be
called a fashion: They seem always to have been with us. But
the way they are displayed does have its fads.

Rockeries were a fashion correctly attributed to the English and started by visitors to the Swiss Alps who wanted to recreate in their own gardens the habitat of the alpine plants they had fallen in love with. The examples shown in *Vick's Magazine* strike a contemporary viewer as awkward and ineptly sited: parlor rockeries, rockeries cut into a lawn, rockeries beside a house. But this was a fashion that would eventually grow out of its absurdities. As fanciers of alpine plants learned more about their requirements, they adapted or created more harmonious and natural-seeming settings. Rock gardening has endured as a specialty, albeit a very demanding one. It has tremendous appeal for born collectors and lovers of miniatures. But the rockery craze also taught non-specialist garden makers to see that rocky outcrops, common in much of this country, could be turned into assets if suitably and sensitively planted.

Whether it was coincidence or increasing confidence, in the years after the 1876 Centennial Exposition American designers for the first time began consciously examining regional characteristics and trying to express them in their work. Most of them were familiar with and influenced by the ideas of the contemporary English Arts-and-Crafts movement, which advocated rooting architectural and landscape design in local materials and building traditions. As Ruskin and Morris had looked to medieval England for inspiration, East-coast designers looked to eighteenth-century America.

In the Middle West there wasn't much past to look to. To forge a regional style, designers there really had to study the land around them. That's just what Chicago architects and landscape architects did in the 1880s. The result was what we call the Prairie Style. The most distinguished landscape architects, Ossian Cole Simonds and Jens Jensen, were friends and collaborators of the style's much better-known architects, among them Louis Sullivan and Frank Lloyd Wright. Wilhelm Miller, who publicized the work of Simonds and Jensen in the magazines *Country Life in America* and *The Garden*, set out the principles of the style in a University of Illinois Bulletin, *The Prairie Spirit in Landscape Gardening*.[10]

> The prairie style of landscape gardening is an American mode of design based upon the practical needs of the middle-western people and characterized by preservation of typical western scenery, by restoration of local color, and by repetition of the horizontal line of land or sky which is the strongest feature of prairie scenery.

What Miller seems to have meant by "the restoration of local color" is the use of native plants; but Simonds, Jensen, and later Alfred Caldwell also studied and adapted local landforms, rock strata, and waterways for their landscapes. And when they had commissions in other parts of the United States, they made serious efforts to reflect the local environment and flora in their landscape designs.

That gardens large and small in the Southeastern part of the country continued to seem regional and exotic to visitors was less a function of conscious regionalism than one of distinctive and exuberant vegetation. In the long period of economic disarray after the Civil War, not many could indulge in passing garden fads and fancies. They stayed with the kinds of garden designs they already had, mostly geometric or nineteenth-century picturesque. And Nature was ready to spread green luxuriance over their gardens. Natives—live oaks, magnolias, and ferns—and Oriental imports—camellias, oranges, and Cherokee roses—thrived in the heat and humidity that characterizes most of the lowland South.

Although a few years behind Middle Westerners, Californians did make an effort at the end of the nineteenth century to come up with an approach to layout and planting that would reflect local conditions. California regionalism divided itself naturally into two branches along historical and climatic lines. Arts-and-Crafts attitudes were an important component of the experiments in both branches. In Southern California, journalists, most of them easterners who had come to find health in the sun, sought to create a way of life that would make the most of its climate. For inspiration they looked to its Spanish and Mexican past of missions and ranches, and to the classical architecture and vegetation of the Mediterranean. They wanted houses planned for outdoor living. They embraced the patio but romanticized it and filled it with flowers. Hispanic settlers, particularly those from Northern Mexico had been accustomed to the careful husbanding of water necessary in an arid climate. Flower-filled patios, extensive orange groves, and too many of the Mediterranean planting schemes devised by promoters of regionalism demanded more water than Southern California could supply and led to diversion of water from considerable distances for irrigation. But there were some who understood the importance of drought-tolerant planting in the creation of a true regional style. Kate Olivia Sessions, who was born and grew up in the San Francisco Bay area and founded her San Diego nursery in 1885, used native plants in many of her designs. In addition, she searched out and grew a wide variety of drought-tolerant species from similar climates around the world. Perhaps the most vigorous promoter of California

House plants are always with us but their display changes from generation to generation. A modest conservatory, really a glassed-in porch, from *Vick's Magazine* demonstrates the Victorian penchant for training vines around windows and ceilings.

wildflowers was an Englishman, Theodore Payne, who came to Southern California in 1893. He sold them in his nursery, planted them in the landscapes he designed, and lectured and wrote on the necessity for preserving them.

Northern California had a somewhat greater supply of water, but even there hot, dry summers rendered the lawn-based designs of the East inappropriate, as Frederick Law Olmsted had pointed out in the 1860s. Sharing Olmsted's assessment, several transplanted easterners imbued with Arts-and-Crafts ideals, like Charles Keeler, a Bay area poet, and his friend, the architect Bernard Maybeck, tried to set out guidelines for gardens to suit the region. In his 1904 book, *The Simple Home*, Keeler first considers the ways in which placement of the house on the lot could be adjusted to provide space for a garden, paying particular attention to the hillside lots, so frequent locally. A garden in the natural style, using only native plants, offers "a purer sentiment, a more refined love of nature undefiled" he finds, "but such a garden needs room." In the land of the giant sequoias, lots of room, and, as he points out, even smaller native trees on a small lot will tend to shade out colorful flowers and make the house gloomy. So many exotics thrive like weeds along the coast to San Francisco and much farther north in interior valleys that they can easily be introduced into naturalistic plantings. He suggests that garden makers study the way in which Italians and Japanese structure their gardens, not to imitate but to learn from them because such prodigal growth needs discipline to be truly pleasing.

As to the precise form which this new garden type of California should assume, it is perhaps premature to say, but one thing is vital, that at least a portion of the space should be sequestered from public view, forming

a room walled in with growing things and yet giving free access to light and air. . . . My own preference for a garden for the simple home is a compromise between the natural and formal types — a compromise in which the carefully studied plan is concealed by a touch of careless grace that makes it appear as if nature had unconsciously made bowers and paths and sheltering hedges.[11]

In his emphasis on designing the garden as a room — "the extension of architecture into the domain of light and life" — Keeler prefigures the California gardens of the forties and fifties that would do much to shape suburban gardens across America. The proponents of a California regional style seem more welcoming to exotics than the Middle Westerners; but in fact the latter were less dogmatic about using native plants in action than they were in words. When he wanted a certain texture in a Chicago garden Jensen pruned ailanthus low as a substitute for native sumac, which could not tolerate the polluted air of the city. And around his own house in Door County, Wisconsin, he planted some of

the old-fashioned garden flowers and shrubs, such as the lilac, hollyhock, oleander, geraniums — plants that the white man has carried with him wherever he has gone and that have become through the centuries household pets, just as the dog and the cat are.[12]

At the beginning of the twentieth century it seemed as if a series of regional gardening styles would take shape across the country at both estate and suburban house-lot scale. The country was prospering; interest in gardens and gardening was growing fast; landscape architecture had established itself as a profession; and a freshet of magazines devoted to the design and furnishing of houses and gardens had come on the market. *Country Life in America, The Garden Magazine, House & Garden, House Beautiful*, offered something new to their readers: They were copiously illustrated with photographs. At least in early issues these periodicals made an effort to report on gardens all over the country, and many of their writers enthusiastically supported attempts to root American garden design in the country's native landscapes. But there was a rival point of view in the land that was to deprive these attempts of the kind of support they really needed to prosper: clients with money. While a few early twentieth-century tycoons, like Henry Ford, continued to patronize regionalist designers, more tried to model their country places on European palaces or villas.

How much of this turn of taste was instigated by socially striving clients and how much by architects trained in Classical — that is, French or Italian — design either at the Ecole des Beaux-Arts in Paris or at American design schools that imitated its methods is hard to tell. During the nineteenth century what had started as a trickle of Grand Tourists in the previous one gradually swelled to a torrent. As usual, the trailblazers were the intellectuals — artists, scientists, scholars, writers — seeking, not just inspiration, but advanced technical training not then available in this country. For example, when Henry Hobson Richardson and Richard Morris Hunt went to the Ecole des Beaux-Arts in the 1840s they were well in advance of the first American architectural school that would be established at MIT in 1865. The artists were soon followed by the rich and restless. By the mid-1840s, a thousand Americans a year were arriving in Rome;[13] by the end of the century, few newly minted millionaires were willing to forgo the social cachet conferred by an Italian tour or a winter in Italy. They admired what they saw and

wanted it back home. Perhaps they recognized instinctively that the great Italian Renaissance gardens had been created to please and to demonstrate the power and the riches of the new-made tycoons of that period, the cardinals of the church, and the rulers of the city states.

Little by little the selection of material in the magazines tilted toward the European- oriented preferences of their East-coast editors and publishers, who were far more likely to present compositions featuring pergolas, balustrades, urns, clipped hedges, and dressed stone stairs. It didn't take long for the Italian garden to become a symbol of nouveau-riche pretension especially for many garden-makers who really gardened. Typical is Mabel Osgood Wright, who in her popular 1901 garden book was already poking fun at her neighbor's "good showy Italian garden."

> You wouldn't believe what our Italian garden cost, with digging out and filling in. My dear, we had to fill up thirteen feet deep in one spot, and piping the water for the pools, and after that the engine to run the fountain, and the electric plant to light up at night. For of course the trees are so young yet that there's no shade, and it's perfectly impossible to go out there in the daytime.[14]

Later, the Lady of the Italian Garden, on being told that the best way to make the garden look as you want is to do the pruning yourself is horrified:

> But my dear woman, It's impossible! Me stand out in the sun! Me cut flowers to give away! It would ruin my social position.

Meanwhile, at a popular level, the lawn embellished with trees had consolidated its hold on the front yard all across the nation with foundation planting gradually replacing the trees

or supplementing them. This development, by now too deeply embedded in American attitudes to be called a fashion, will be examined in more detail later. In the back yard what happened depended for a long time on the interests of the individual householder. It did not always become a garden. Some used it as a children's play yard first. For others it was a dog run. And, if many horticultural books of the early part of the century are to be believed, the majority used it for drying clothes, housing trash cans, and woodpiles.

The garden-design fashion that would take over the back yard in the last half of the twentieth century started in California. Not surprisingly designers and householders living in a region where it was possible to spend time out-of-doors all year began to think of gardens not so much as places for quiet contemplation and the enjoyment of nature but as settings for a wide range of activities. True, many big estates had been arranged to accommodate large-scale entertaining and active sports ever since the middle of the nineteenth century. But trying to insert such spaces into a suburban garden was a new idea, one that was quickly picked up by magazines in the 1920s and 30s. After the wartime

pause of the early forties, the California garden and the California ranch house became desired models for both the builders and the inhabitants of new suburbs throughout the country. Perhaps the chief proselytizer was *Sunset Magazine*, which deliberately restricted its circulation and content to the western states, but national magazines, *House Beautiful* in particular, weren't far behind.

When the house lot was large enough it could contain a swimming pool, even a tennis court, and provision for some outdoor cooking—barbecue, after all, was a western tradition—as well as such traditional garden features as flowers and trees and even a vegetable plot. Reduce the lot size to that in most post-World War II suburbs and something had to give. The tennis court was an obvious deletion. The swimming pool held its own, even in regions where it was unusable for half the year. The barbecue pit was a must. It was the plants that retreated. A tree or two for shade, a small patch of lawn, and a few annuals or potted geraniums were often all the vegetation in a yard that was more than half paved or

With time came skill, and by the beginning of the twentieth century garden makers had learned how to arrange and plant rocky sites naturally. An attractive example: the New Jersey garden of Mr. and Mrs. J. W. Sherer.

bricked or boarded in the name of low maintenance. During the middle decades of the century it seemed as if the more leisure time people gained, the less time they wanted to spend on taking care of their houses and grounds. If anything required physical labor, and gardening certainly did, it was not considered an appropriate use of leisure time.

As always in this country there were counter currents. Men and women who found delight and satisfaction in gardening did not cease to exist, even though their numbers didn't seem to be increasing. Some landscape designers and garden-makers, particularly in California and the Southwest, still searched for ways to create gardens that truly reflected the local environment. Many landscape architects in the post-war generations had absorbed the new ways in which twentieth-century painters and sculptors shaped space and composed forms. Among the general public, interest in gardening would begin a major comeback in the last quarter of the century, with cooking as an important energizer. Leaf through the magazines of the 1960s, 1970s, and 1980s and you

first see herb gardens, then vegetable gardens, and finally a resurgence of ornamental horticulture in many forms. Plants started to win back the yard as considerable numbers of Americans discovered that gardening itself was an enjoyable activity. For inspiration they turned to England. Gertrude Jekyll's books were reprinted in the early 80s, contemporary British gardening writers found an eager audience, and the herbaceous border again became the height of fashion. It soon became clear, just as it had to U. S. gardeners at the beginning of the century, that English ideas and planting plans needed considerable adjustment if they were to perform creditably in this country.

During the same years, mounting scientific evidence began to erode the optimistic and well-promoted American confidence that you could grow anything anywhere given enough water, fertilizers, and pesticides. Perhaps you could, but you might be dismayed by some of the consequences. Efforts to create environmental sensitivity have continued ever since, but progress is slow and setbacks are persistent. It

is true that we still have much to learn about what really constitutes sound ecological practice, and even among scientists there are conflicting viewpoints.

In a way, the environmental movement has exposed the limitations of the power of the press to change ingrained habits. Some environmental writers, organizations, and journals are so confrontational and advocate such extreme measures that they alienate many who would truly like to act responsibly. On the other hand, popular journals in general offer up a buffet of opinions, and rarely make clear the risks involved in quick and easy solutions. Television is little better and rarely takes up such subjects. Only consider the front lawn. In the 1950s *Sunset*, the influential West-Coast magazine, campaigned for the enclosure of the front yard on the grounds that it was wasted space, which, given privacy, could be used for family living. The idea gained only spotty acceptance. More recently the lawn has come under attack in books and magazines for its water-guzzling and its depend-

ence on toxic chemicals and polluting fertilizers. Yet it shows no sign whatsoever of disappearing.

Trying to think ecologically does create design problems: Nature is messy and human beings like order around them. At the same time, ecological thinking represents a powerful incentive to root the design of a garden or landscape in the natural characteristics of its region. The problem is not insoluble, in spite of the dedicated gardener's apparently overwhelming desire to grow just those plants that don't belong where he or she lives. The flora at our disposal is rich enough that suitable alternatives can be found. Designers who are skilled enough can reconcile nature's drift to complexity and humans' urge for legibility. The important goal is not to create a regional style so much as to make what people like and like to live with compatible with and respectful of regional conditions.

The fashionable Italian garden didn't take long to move to the suburbs where it became a symbol of ostentation. But within the first ten years of the twentieth century it was rescaled for the small backyard. This restrained example will seem less lonesome when the evergreens behind the pergola have grown into a solid hedge.

The Collector's Garden

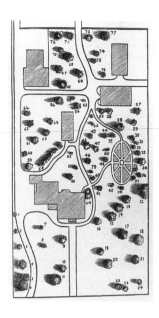

It would be surprising if the collecting passion did not find expression in domestic pleasure grounds, but in this country, at least, that passion did not really have a shaping influence on the design of those grounds until the middle of the nineteenth century. In earlier periods, the idea that a garden might be laid out primarily to display a collection to best advantage doesn't seem to have crossed the minds of garden-makers. The princes of Renaissance Italy, who went to great lengths to secure samples of all the new horticultural treasures coming from the Near East, planted them in the same kinds of beds that they filled at other times with familiar herbs and flowers. And in the eighteenth century, the English enthusiasts who bombarded Bartram with orders for new American plants laid out their "American Gardens" in the fashionable style of their period. The new introductions added variety and color and extended the blooming season, but essentially they were enhancements, not determinants, of design. In both periods, many garden owners were also sculpture collectors, but usually they placed their acquisitions for symbolic impact or to tell a story, terminate a view, mark an opening, or enliven a glade rather than designing their gardens as galleries for their sculpture collections. But, if their sculptures were particularly ancient and valuable,

they might build garden pavilions or casinos to display them in a semi-outdoor setting. Elisabeth MacDougall, whose specialty is Italian garden history, does make a case that a court of the Belvedere created by Pope Julius II and part of the Villa Medici were designed to display sculpture as art; but admits that for the most part sculpture was simply used as garden decoration.[1]

Both of these periods share with the last half of the nineteenth century two of the characteristics that the historian Kenneth L. Ames has identified as shaping the impulse to make gardens for collections.[2] Like post-Civil War America, Renaissance Italy and eighteenth-century England saw a striking expansion of wealth accompanied by an equally striking expansion of knowledge, knowledge both of the natural world and of the art of the past. But in the nineteenth century new technologies raised the impact of these expansions to far higher level. Steamships and railroads made travel easier and opened up hitherto rarely explored parts of the world. More people could travel to more places; the intrepid could travel still farther. Photography enlightened and tantalized the stay-at-homes and supplied the travelers with *aides-memoire*. True tycoons could do even better: They could buy and bring home almost any artifact that appealed. To

bring back plants needed somewhat more expertise, but that, too, was forthcoming. Scientific organizations, commercial nurseries, and rich enthusiasts sent expeditions and competed to grow, hybridize, and improve plants from every part of the world.

Ames points out that the passion for collecting took on a particular form at the time: the anthology, which he defines as "a group of examples selected to create a reasoned survey of some range of materials." He notes that the late nineteenth century saw the invention of the world's fair, a proliferation of museums, and of department stores, all of them expressions of the anthology-making impulse. The term "arboretum," strictly speaking a collection of trees but often loosely used to identify a variety of botanical or horticultural collections was, according to the *Oxford English Dictionary*, first used in 1838. From the 1840s into the early twentieth century the creation of arboreta was high on the agendas of landscape designers like Downing and Olmsted and plant lovers like Henry Winthrop Sargent, H. H. Hunnewell, John and Lydia Morris, and Henry Shaw. An arboretum represented more than just a display of the owner's wealth and knowledge. It had value as a scientific experiment. Hunnewell planned his pinetum to test the hardiness of conifers and identify all the species that would survive in Massachusetts. It was educational. In an arboretum the general public — many private ones were opened often to the interested — could learn to identify trees, observe their habits of growth, and see the beauty of rare species or those rarely available commercially. Assembling such a collection was extremely expensive, maintaining one even more so. No wonder most private arboreta, like the ones developed by the Morrises in Philadelphia and Henry Shaw in St. Louis had to go public to survive. Or that some of the most successful — the Arnold Arboretum in Boston, the Strybing Arboretum in San Francisco — were conceived as public works from the start.

You need a lot of land to plant a respectable collection of large trees, and such an assemblage lends itself particularly well to a painterly landscape design if attention to color and texture goes right along with attention to cultural needs and the space is well modeled. Since the individual components of the collection form its main attraction, a long vista rarely serves as the organizing principle for its layout. A collection garden is more likely to be planned as a series of vignettes that make it easy to focus on special plants but are linked together to make a satisfying whole. The interests of art and of science also need to be carefully balanced. Grouping all the members of one family together for comparison may not work aesthetically. Labels, which need not be obtrusive, will solve that problem. A map helps, too. Even if a garden is not intended for public viewing, most collectors like to keep track of their prized possessions.

KRENITSKY GARDEN

That the space and financing available today for the creation of arboreta is almost always found in parks or botanical gardens hasn't stopped individuals from collecting trees. Gardens may have been miniaturized, but so have trees. The garden that Tom Krenitsky created on a third of an acre in Chapel Hill, North Carolina demonstrates just how effectively a collection of dwarf trees can be composed in a small space. Krenitsky didn't start out as a collector of dwarf conifers. He investigated them because he wanted a garden that would be interesting all year long. As he says, a lawn was an obvious solution, too obvious. Also lawns don't keep their looks in long southern summers. Dwarf conifers appealed but before he could plant anything he had to divide the space. He liked the idea of island beds threaded with gravel paths because they would offer a variety of viewing points, but found they needed some order. The solution was provided by the site itself. A row of tall oaks between the back of the house and the open space of the garden formed a gentle curve that fit the long curve of an ellipse.[3]

With the help of a mathematically inclined neighbor Krenitsky traced out an ellipse with a graveled path around it, emphasizing its outline with evenly spaced English boxwood. An overlay of free-form paths leading into the center of the ellipse and trailing through the rest of the space softened the

Page 211:
Log slices stacked into what Balthazar Korab calls crankshafts, thrust up from a bed of different hosta cultivars arranged by his wife, Monica, the plant collector of the pair

Opposite, top:
On the 1879 plan of a city tree-collector's landscape in *Vick's Magazine* the seventy-nine numbered specimens include fifty-nine different species of trees and shrubs plus two flower vases and two peony plants. All this in a less-than-two-acre space which also hosts the house, a cold grapery, a forcing house and conservatory, a hothouse, stables with carriage room, and a seventy-five-foot-long oval "flower plat."

Opposite, bottom:
With so many windows overlooking it, Tom Krenitsky's North Carolina garden needed year-round interest. His solution, dwarf conifers, soon turned him into a dedicated collector. He planted soft-textured cultivars like glaucous *Juniperous procumbens* 'nana' or *Thuja occidentalis* 'Rheingold' in groups to set off and organize bolder specimens.

Above:
Seasonal color changes were unexpectedly great, and Krenitsky worked to maintain the summer harmony shown and still take advantage of cultivars like *Thuja occidentalis* 'Sudworthi' and *Chamaecyparis pisifera* 'filifera aurea' that are dramatic in winter. The result: a richly textured tapestry produced by discipline and ongoing rearrangement.

Mexican Barrel cacti, *Echinocactus ingens,* roost in a bed of aloes with high-rising panicles of bright red blossoms and some spiky yuccas. More and taller yuccas back up the robust kalanchoes with their rosettes of fleshy blue-green leaves.

design, but he felt that the garden needed some kind of architectural element to balance the house, which dominated the eastern side of the garden. Seemingly on cue, the demolition of a neoclassical mansion in town gave him salvaged materials with architectural character. These he assembled into a five-sided structure that he could fit into the southwest corner of the garden like a corner cupboard. The stage was set. Furnishing it with dwarf conifers soon aroused collecting instincts dormant since childhood and the quest for rare specimens was on.

> The extensive natural diversity of conifers, very ancient in the evolutionary scheme of things, has been augmented by man so that the designer has an amazing range of height, texture and form with which to work. The range of colors is also surprising: blues, purples, golds, yellows, whites, grays, silvers, and, of course, varying shades of green.
>
> The temptation of planting one of each variety was great and that is exactly how I began. But soon I was forced to choose between a collection and a garden.[4]

Fortunately, dwarf conifers grow very slowly so Krenitsky had plenty of time to work out a harmonious balance. As a general principle he placed larger varieties around the edge of the garden, smaller ones in the central part. In the island beds he reversed the pattern, with medium-height trees toward the center, lower and smaller ones next to the paths. He also had to adjust his plants according to their cultural requirements. Pines, cedars, junipers, and spruces as well as all gold and yellow cultivars put on their best show in full sun. The more shade-tolerant hemlocks, yews, false cypresses, Japanese temple cedars, and firs could go closer to the high canopy of the oaks. When the conifers were young ground-covers with blue or white blooms carpeted the space between them. As the conifers grew, the ground covers retreated to the edges of paths and to rock outcroppings.

Change was a constant in this garden, Krenitsky found. Conifers really do look different in the different seasons, so the course of a year provided even more variety than he had anticipated. He also found that he was developing strong likes and dislikes. With some it was a matter of placement; others didn't work anywhere. Also, most dwarf conifers are not really dwarfs. They are just very, very slow growing, and when really settled in will start transforming themselves into large trees and threaten both the scale of the garden and the plants around them. So, no matter how cherished, they too have to go. Krenitsky's experience has led him to feel that "the best approach is to plant a wide variety at first and let a combination of time, cultural conditions, and personal taste do the selection and the blending."

His garden has matured very successfully, but Krenitsky now feels the need of a larger canvas, so he has sold it and is starting a new and expanded one out in the country.[5]

HUNTINGTON DESERT GARDEN

Collectors' gardens do seem to have a large appetite for land. Take the Huntington Desert Garden in San Marino, California. It started small. In fact it wasn't even on Henry E. Huntington's original agenda for the development of his estate. But if he was passionate collector of rare books and art, William Hertrich, his landscape designer, ranch foreman, and eventually estate superintendent was an equally passionate collector of plants. Cacti were particular favorites. He had been born in Germany and trained in Austria, where cactus and succulents were and are more popular than in the United States, and he persuaded his reluctant employer, who had had an uncomfortable run-in with a cactus as a young man, to allow him to start a small cactus collection on a dry and barren hillside.[6] He began with about 300 plants and embarked on collecting expeditions, first to nearby California deserts, then to Arizona, and then to Mexico. The garden grew to three acres.

Desert gardens, called "Arizona Gardens," were fashionable features on Southern California estates in the early decades of the twentieth century, so Hertrich could supplement his own collecting activities by trading with other collectors or buying from them, or even, occasionally, buying their collections. As the garden developed, Huntington caught his enthusiasm and took great pride in the increasing fame and scientific stature of the collection. More acreage was added, more expeditions made, more varieties of desert plants from more parts of the world included.

Today the Desert Garden displays in its twelve acres more than 4,000 species. It is an almost other-worldly landscape that takes full advantage of the extraordinary shapes, textures, and colors of succulents and cacti. It does not look like a real desert, and was not intended to. However great its scientific importance, it is even more magical as art. To weave plants with such strong personalities and powerful forms into a concordant design is quite an accomplishment.

In his recollections Hertrich says little about how or why he composed his plants the way he did, but the current Curator of the Desert Garden, Joe Clements, sheds a good deal of light on the process by which the garden was created.[7] Hertrich started by lining up river-washed boulders to delineate the beds, always working with the slope, since efficient drainage is essential to the health of desert plants. In early photographs the cacti are small and the beds sparsely planted indeed, but they soon grew up and out and filled in the space. And once Huntington was convinced of the collection's importance, he ran spur lines into the cactus garden, top and bottom, so really big specimens could be brought in. It's no small help to a plant collector to have a railroad magnate as employer.

According to Clements, Hertrich always based his plantings on relationships he saw in nature, but they had to please his eye as well. And with limited space and an increasingly extensive collection, he had to pack his beds; nature could spread out. Some beds are geographical, for example those called the Baja and the California Beds. But he found as have his successors that strict adherence to geography is too limiting aesthetically. Only the most tender and fragile ones displayed in the Conservatory are arranged according to strict scientific standards.

A certain amount of redesign was needed when the estate was turned into an educational institution, The Huntington Library/Art Gallery/Botanical Gardens, after Henry Huntington's death. The beds had been small and the paths narrow. To accommodate visitors Hertrich laid out a walk 1,100 feet long and ten feet wide through the garden and along it built an irregular chain of rockeries with desert lava rocks. These new beds brought the plants closer to the eye of the beholder. Raising the plantings also helped maintain good drainage, and subsequent curators and gardeners have continued to construct raised beds when changes had to be made. And as in any garden, change and replacement is a continuing process. Maintenance is especially tricky and time-consuming: Just imagine weeding a cactus bed. Frost and disease claim victims, as does old age. Many desert

plants live to a great age, blossom once, and die. They may weigh a ton or so and sport vicious spines as well, but they must be removed for, as Clements says, they make a garden seem shabby. Out in nature they would not be so noticeable.

As the name attests, the Huntington Botanical Gardens, like many large estates of the period, are a collection of gardens, most dedicated to plant families—cycads, camellias, roses, palms. Each garden is effective in itself but they are not related to each other in a coherent plan. This is not surprising: They were developed piecemeal as land became available, or Huntington and Hertrich's interests developed or changed. Many anthology gardens came into being this way. Owners would drop into their overall landscapes different kinds of gardens as they were attracted to a style on their travels or in a book or magazine, often hiring a different designer for each one. Each or several might be successful, but the juxtapositions weren't always graceful, and coherence was many times sacrificed to variety.

Spiky and spiny, smooth and hairy, cacti and other succulents have textures as varied and forceful as their forms. William Hertrich, the original designer, and his successors at the Huntington Desert Garden have done a masterly job of placing zanies like the snaky Argentinean cactus *Trichocereus thelegonus* to pep up their compositions.

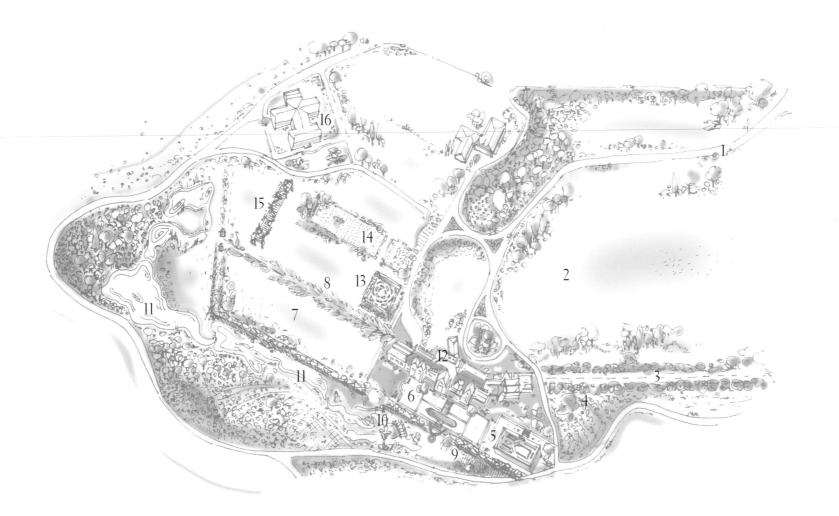

Above:

Stan Hywet Garden Plan:

1. Main Drive
2. Great Meadow
3. Plane Tree and
   Rhododendron Allée
4. Dell
5. Walled English Garden
6. West Terrace
7. North Lawn
8. Birch Allée
9. Perennial Border
10. Japanese Garden
11. Lagoons
12. Breakfast Room Garden
13. Rose Garden
14. Cutting Garden
15. Grape Arbor
16. Conservatory

STAN HYWET

It doesn't have to be that way. A garden of garden styles can be welded into a work of art. A splendid example is Stan Hywet in Akron, Ohio, designed between 1911 and 1928 by Warren Manning for Franklin Augustus Seiberling, founder of the Goodyear Tire and Rubber Company, and his wife, Gertrude. Manning, the son of a highly respected Massachusetts nurseryman, was already a well-trained plantsman when he went to work for Frederick Law Olmsted in 1886 at the age of 26, and in a short time he became the firm's plant designer for major projects like the Columbian Exposition and Biltmore. He left to start his own office in 1896 and soon had a nationwide practice very much like that of the Olmsteds.

When Seiberling had assembled 3,000 acres of farmland just outside the city on which to build a country estate he hired Manning to design the grounds even before he selected an architect for the house. In this Seiberling was an unusually wise client. Manning was able to place the house, and then work with the architect to take the greatest advantage of the site's distinctive characteristics. The approximately 100 acres to be developed as the home estate were well endowed. The sandstone ridge was the highest point in the area and offered expansive views. There were good orchards, and forests on two steep slopes, dry at the top and watered by springs at the base, allowing for varied understory plantings. In addition, Manning wrote to Seiberling after assessing the site,

The feature that will give the estate its greatest distinction is the old quarry. Roughly this may be described as a great, irregular pan, with one side a perpendicular rough wall face, capped by an old Peach orchard, some trees of which should be saved. The other sides of the pan are irregular, steep earth piles that were stripped from the original surface.... The bottom of this pan is nearly flat sandstone rock, with a thin surface of soil or no soil. Deep channels and pits have been broken through the bottom of the pan...and in some of these are springs that seem to be permanent and cold enough for trout.

In this great irregular pan are conditions that will make for a unique garden.[8]

This was the feature that gave the estate its name. The Seiberlings had early shown a preference for an English-style house, so it is quite in keeping that they called it Stan Hywet Hall after the Middle English for stone quarry. Allowed a free hand, Manning would have developed the whole quarry level as a naturalistic garden with a mixture of native and complementary exotic plants, and somewhat more than half did take that form. One senses from his letter that he foresaw a good deal of give and take before the estate took its final shape. When clients are both interested and knowledgeable, that give and take makes for a more successful result. Both

Mr. and Mrs. Seiberling were intimately involved in the planning. After they settled on an architect, Charles Schneider, the Cleveland area representative of a New York architectural firm, they took him to England to study authentic models for the mansion they wanted. The house that resulted is a very pleasing evocation of a Tudor manor adapted to an early twentieth-century way of life.

What is brilliant is its relationship to the land, and that is Manning's doing. The house bends to follow the angle of the sandstone ridge at its central and highest point, which offers spectacular views of the Cuyahoga Valley to the west. Continuing along the top of the ridge allées of trees extend the axes of the house in both directions. To the north an allée of birch trees ends in a pair of tea houses offering splendid vistas across a lagoon; to the south an allée of plane trees underplanted with rhododendrons ends at the treetops of a forested slope. These emphasize the line of the escarpment, anchor the house to it, and tie together the varied garden spaces.

Manning, like Olmsted, considered gardens and landscapes different design categories with different goals. A garden was contained and intimate, a landscape expansive and related to the whole of its surrounding environment, which might well include farms and orchards as well as woods and streams. At Stan Hywet he set the gardens the clients wanted within his definition of a landscape, organizing them as a progression of distinct spaces near and referring to the house but on different levels provided by the topography of the site.

In the best pastoral landscape style the estate drive begins at the southeast corner of the property and winds up through the remains of an orchard alongside a tree-studded lawn to the front door. At the south end of the house it descends from the ridge passing what is called the Dell, a natural amphitheatre, on the left and the first garden level, on the right. This level, just below the ridge, is home to the Walled English Garden, the West Terrace, and the North Lawn, all architectural in character. The flower-filled Walled English

In the area that had been a stone quarry, the Japanese Garden and Lagoons form a picturesque naturalistic composition of trees and pools of water laced with paths and a pleasure drive as the landscape architect, Warren Manning, intended. He prized the water and its reflections as foreground to the view of the distant landscape below and beyond.

Garden was planned as a quiet retreat for Mrs. Seiberling. Manning was never quite happy with its planting, and in 1928, at his suggestion, it was successfully redesigned by Ellen Shipman, whom he considered the best designer of flower gardens in the country. The West Terrace with its rectangular grass plots and oval pool was to be a setting for entertaining, as well as a suitably simple foreground for a spectacular vista. More vistas opened from the large North Lawn which allowed plenty of room for the sports and games of the six Seiberling children as well as for party overflow.

From this level the estate drive goes on down to loop around the quarry level, which hosts another south-to-north succession of gardens, which become progressively more painterly in character. From the Perennial Garden, a Jekyllesque herbaceous border, paths lead to the Japanese Garden, and the Lagoons. The latter wrap around the north end of the ridge and make up a path-laced landscape of ponds and trees that takes advantage of the old quarry in the way that Manning originally envisioned. In addition, there is a small garden off the breakfast room on the other side of the house that looks out on the shrub-ringed Elliptical Garden, shaped by the service drive, as it branches from the estate drive. A geometrically laid out Rose Garden lies north of the service drive as do the Cutting Gardens and a Grape Arbor, all that remains of the support gardens that kept the estate in vegetables, fruits, and flowers. A lot of different visual and kinetic experiences to harmonize into a whole! And a lot of vegetation and structures to care for.

Stan Hywet today comprises just seventy acres, the home grounds, of the original 3,000, 2,000 of which are now Akron parkland. The remainder was sold for development. The break-up has been well handled, and the views of the countryside that meant so much to Manning and the Seiberlings are still beautiful. Much credit is due to preservation-minded volunteers who banded together to form a foundation, with support from the family, and save the house and gardens after Frank Seiberling's death in 1956. Over time the volunteer foundation became more and more professional, although much of the maintenance is still done by volunteers. It became clear that a good deal of restoration was needed: Disease had felled chestnuts and elms; other trees and shrubs had grown rampant, obscuring the design and blocking the views; time and weather had taken their toll on stone and brickwork; and some colorful flowerbeds planted to please the public were badly sited. In 1983 the foundation hired Child Associates of Cambridge, Massachusetts to develop a master plan. Susan Child and her associates—first Peter Hornbeck, then Douglas Reed—found themselves with a real research job. As she has written:

> All but two of Manning's 380 plans for the estate were lost. What remained was the structure of the landscape design in depleted condition, approximately 350 early photographs of the estate, taken between 1911 and 1928, and over one hundred letters between Manning and Seiberling from the same period.[9]

Fortunately the letters were very detailed, some of the Seiberling children were still alive to add their memories, and in 1988 the plan for the Great Lawn was found. One of the first steps in restoring the design was also one of the most significant: Reopening the vistas gave the grounds back their grandeur. Restoration continues as money becomes available. Some of it is infrastructure, necessary but unseen, but a most visible step came with the restoration of Ellen Shipman's design for the Walled English Garden. The trees around it had grown so much that from 1950 to 1991 it had to be planted as a shade garden. In the latter year, Shipman's plans and plant lists were found and the decision was made to remove enough trees that it could again become a flower garden. This has been successfully accomplished, and Stan Hywet today is a testament to the artistry of Manning and Shipman, the sensitivity of the Seiberlings, and as well the commitment of the foundation to the never-ending process that is caring for a garden.

Sculpture has had a place in the garden at least since Roman times in Europe. In fact, from the Renaissance on "garden sculpture" was a distinct category—The Four Seasons, Pan, Pomona, herms, and terms are only a few examples—deliberately created to ornament gardens. Also, one has to consider the Lake T'ai rocks in Chinese gardens as sculptures, even if they are meant to symbolize natural forces, and don't represent gods, humans, or animals. And what about the rocks in a Zen garden like Japan's Ryoanji? But on the whole, sculpture has been treated as punctuation, like urns and jars and obelisks, rather than as the driving force in the design of the garden. But hard and fast categories are hard to establish in this realm. Consider topiaries. They are living plants that humans have carved, clipped, or trained into arbitrary shapes. Formed geometrically they may serve as decorative accents like those on William Paca's terraces, or be assembled into a self-contained garden like those at H. H. Hunnewell's. The same with representational topiary; one pair of birds frames the view at El Brolino in Santa Barbara; everything from giraffes to armchairs is gathered in the garden called "Green Animals" near Newport, Rhode Island. These creatures and Hunnewell's trees certainly did determine the design of the garden. They are living sculptures rooted in the earth: You can't move them around.

Almost as difficult to move around are the large, often gigantic pieces that have engaged the talents of many twentieth century sculptors, who intended them for large public spaces. Where is a private collector going to put them? Where else but out of doors? Such was probably the impetus for the gardens designed as outdoor galleries for sculpture that began to appear in this country after the 1930s. Americans may have pioneered the idea: The only such private outdoor collection that this author has been able to find antedating Brookgreen Gardens in South Carolina is sculptor Carl Milles's own garden outside his studio in Stockholm. The dates are close but no one seems to know whether Archer and Anna Hyatt Huntington were aware of it when they began to create Brookgreen gardens in 1930. Archer

Huntington came from the same railroading dynasty as Henry Huntington, whose California gardens we've already examined. His wife, Anna Hyatt, was a well-known, prize-winning sculptor. Initially it was for the sake of her health that the Huntingtons investigated the South Carolina Low Country. They ended up buying four once-flourishing rice plantations, and assembling a 9,100-acre tract near Pawleys Island. This became their winter retreat until Archer Huntington's death in 1955. Making a garden for the display of Anna Huntington's large and energetic sculpture was probably in their minds from the start, and soon they began buying the work of other American figurative sculptors and enlarging and revising the gardens to form appropriate settings for them. Their patronage was a genuine lifesaver for many artists during the Depression. From the beginning the garden was open to the interested public, probably not very numerous while they were living at Brookgreen as it was not easy to reach. But the garden was set up as a non-profit foundation to ensure that the public would continue to be welcome.

From the 1950s right through the present, outdoor galleries for modern sculpture with at least some horticultural elements have steadily multiplied. Collectors, public and private, have taken a variety of approaches. James Rose carefully composed interlocking platforms for the Alan Wurtzburgers' collection to set up a complex conversation among the sculptures, the geometric garden beds and pools, and the Maryland woodlands around them. Other collectors have chosen to place their pieces in pastoral or picturesque landscapes. When the sculpture looks as if it really belongs in just that place, natural and man-made forms create a dynamic counterpoint. Too often, alas, the pieces look as if they had been dropped wherever there was room. Given the earth-moving equipment at our disposal, the land can be reshaped to marry sculpture and setting. But then shaping the land can become an end in itself, making the land the sculpture: Land Art. The creations of men like Robert Smithson and Michael Heizer occupy hundreds of acres, even square miles. Such works of art clearly come down outside any definition of garden.

KENNETH DAYTON GARDEN

That both sculptured land and a collection of sculptures can effectively coexist within the normal dimensions of a house lot is demonstrated by the house and garden of the Kenneth Daytons in Minneapolis. At once dwelling place and work of art it is a collaborative creation by a landscape architect, George Hargreaves, and an architect, Vincent James, with significant contributions by James Carpenter, an artist and designer specializing in architectural glass, and the still more significant guidance of the owners. For years the Daytons had enjoyed living at Lake Minnetonka, outside of town. When they decided that they wanted to be closer to the vibrant cultural life of the city they sold that property and bought three-quarters of an acre overlooking Lake of the Isles very near downtown. Well known as discerning collectors of cutting-edge contemporary sculpture, the Daytons are equally committed to modern architecture and landscape

design: Their former house had been designed by Romaldo Giurgola and landscaped by Dan Kiley. After a careful search they chose James for their new one and hired Hargreaves at Kiley's suggestion. Independently, both men had been exploring the interweaving of designed structure and designed landscape and welcomed the owners' desire for a truly collaborative project. For Hargreaves, most of whose recent practice has been concerned with large-scale site reclamations like Candlestick Point Park in South San Francisco, the project was particularly appealing because it was small enough to allow real hands-on execution.

The site was challenging. It sloped steeply down from the street. There were city setback regulations, views to the lake to capture, and the need to keep the house from blocking the neighbors' views. There was another challenge: the sculpture collection, which had been spread out over twelve acres in the country. Once the designers had had a chance to study the land and think about what the Daytons wanted, the couple invited them to a two-day design retreat.[10]

Positioning the house was a quick and early decision. There weren't a lot of choices. All agreed that the right place was somewhat more than halfway down the slope. And all agreed that the retreat's two days of concentrated study of plans and design ideas helped them forge a common vision to guide the working out of the final design. Important as the collection was in everyone's thinking, the clients made the point that while sculpture would inhabit the landscape, the landscape was not to be designed primarily as a series of settings for specific pieces.

Hargreaves' own sculptural contribution is, however, very site specific. Three tapering pyramidal mounds molded of lawn-covered earth spill down the slope between street and paved entrance court. Nailed to the land by a row of littleleaf lindens across the top and another along the driveway edge they energize the space and accentuate the playfulness in two sculptures by David Nash, constructed from branches of a tree felled on the Daytons' country estate. Their placement seems inevitable. So does that of all the sculpture on the property; yet placement came relatively late in the process. Owners and architects worked with wood-and-canvas models to determine the siting of each piece.

For all its apparent rigor, the landscape offers a rich variety of spaces. Hargreaves and the Daytons tend to think of them and their inhabiting sculptures as forming a circuit. At street level a sequence of three courtyards leads to a self-contained apartment on the house's second floor. The first is furnished with a quincunx of crabapples and a bench by Siah Armajani and hedged with euonymus. The second, fenced and hedged, houses mechanical equipment; the third forms a simple entrance court for the apartment. From the upper walkway along these courtyards, stairs descend beside the house to the ground plane on which the house and lawn rest. To the right is James Carpenter's *Periscope Window*, marking the house's second floor-landing. To the left is a raised terrace defined by limestone walls on two sides. A fence above the north wall, an arborvitae hedge above the east wall ensure privacy. A double allée of honey locusts marches the length of the gravel surface, framing Peter

Recently restored to Ellen Shipman's 1921 plan, the Walled English Garden is typical of her designs: luxuriant beds of perennials in pastel shades filling out a firm architectural framework. Eventually the espaliered pear trees will grow up to soften the contrast between the brick walls and the herbaceous borders.

Plan of the Kenneth
Dayton Garden:

1. Pyramidal mounds with David
   Nash sculptures
2. Quincunx of crabapples with
   Siah Armajani sculpture
3. Mechanical equipment
4. Entrance to apartment
5. Raised terrace with honey
   locusts, Peter Shelton and
   Ellsworth Kelly sculptures
6. Richard Serra arc sculpture
7. Alpine currant ha-ha
8. Joel Shapiro sculpture
9. South terrace with Scott
   Burton and Richard Long
   sculptures

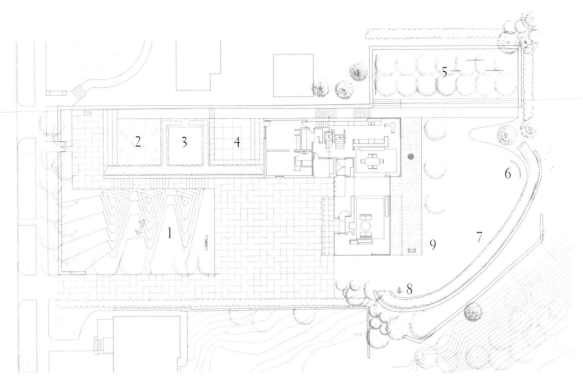

George Hargreaves's *Earth
Waves* turns the steep slope
between the street and the
Kenneth Daytons' house into
a sculpture across which
dance two more sculptures,
David Nash's *Standing
Trunk + Limb* and *Ferndale
Ladder*. Providing a street-
level entrance to the second
floor, the terrace, to the right
of the stairs, is divided into
three courtyards.

Shelton's *snakearm* at its northern end. Within the trees stand the white cut-metal shapes of Ellsworth Kelly's *Untitled (Triptych)*. A clipped arborvitae hedge closes the space on the south and makes a subtle textural transition to the grove of spruce trees that supply a background for Richard Serra's *Garden Arc* at the edge of the lawn.

In a departure from the orthogonal lines that delineate the other spaces, a dark gray concrete containing wall curves out from behind the Serra to inscribe an elliptical lawn. To cope with the twelve-foot drop beyond the edge of the wall Hargreaves pulls a switch on the ha-ha, or sunk fence. The three-foot-wide and two-foot-deep trench between lawn and wall is intended not to keep animals out, but people and pets in. Planted with alpine currants trimmed flush with the lawn, its darker green and contrasting texture also underscore the curve and help pull the eye toward the view of the lake. If you follow the sweep of the lawn past Joel Shapiro's *Dancing Man* and the western end of the house, a narrow corridor leads you back to the entrance court. If you walk toward the house instead you find a terrace along the south façade shaded by maples that hosts Richard Long's *Small Green Stone Circle* toward the eastern end and Scott Burton's *Six Part Settee* at the western one.

The interpenetration of house and landscape achieved by the designers' collaboration is not a static one. The house can change from a transparent pavilion through which the landscape seems to flow to a snug, inward-looking space appropriate to Minnesota's twenty-degrees-below-zero winters, a transformation in which Carpenter's expertise played a major role. But no matter how many layers of glass, louvers, and curtains cover the window-walls, his *Periscope Window* captures and projects leaves, branches, and the changing sky, ensuring that the out-of-doors is never totally excluded. Planting choices mark the changing seasons with color. In the spring come flowers — crabapple blossoms, tulips, and daffodils. Summer is a tapestry of greens. In autumn the euonymus justifies its common name, burning bush, by turning scarlet. Winter in Minnesota is a reliable provider of snow, which reshapes as well as recolors the landscape and retreats with a flourish, melting on the south side of Hargreaves's mounds before it does on the north.[11]

Both the Daytons' garden and their collection tap into the current of modern artistic endeavor that seeks meaning in the reduction of forms to their elemental geometry. Such an approach usually produces results that suggest stability and permanence. But it need not be solemn, and, as the Daytons demonstrated, it can be sparked with wit.

The view across the south terrace, anchored by Scott Burton's *Six Part Settee*, shows how transparency and opacity interplay in house and landscape. Ellsworth Kelly's *Untitled (Triptych)* lurks in the linden trees on the raised terrace, and Richard Serra's *Garden Arc* marks the start of the retaining wall that gives the house and lawn a level platform.

The turned over skeletons
of lilac bushes, victims of a
devastating ice storm, seem
to be fleeing across the snow
that has almost buried the
lines of log slices.

KORAB GARDEN

Witty juxtapositions are just as characteristic of a very different Middle Western garden, one energized by the equally fertile modern aesthetic that celebrates flux and transience, and calls to attention the expressive potential in found objects. In Balthazar and Monica Korab's Michigan garden, land forms, the relations between land and sculptures, and the sculptures themselves are always subject to change.

A distinguished architectural photographer, the recipient of an AIA Gold Medal for his work, Balthazar Korab is an architect by training, having studied both at the Polytechnicum in his native Budapest and the Ecole des Beaux-Arts in Paris. His modeling of the land, still in process, was basically motivated by a love of undulating hills, he says. When the Korabs bought their four-acre piece of relatively flat farmland in 1970 it was "burned out, neglected, underbrush-filled with a few groups of mature trees, scattered incoherently. We worked around all of it with no set plan." [12] As a practical matter, berms help protect his family's privacy from encroaching developments, its peace and quiet from increasing traffic noise. When the Korabs settled there, Troy, Michigan was a crossroads farmland town; today it is a fast-growing Detroit suburb. But more compelling is the exhilaration Korab finds in shaping and reshaping land. As he says himself, "When I'm directing the bulldozer or rolling rocks, I understand how Michael Heizer gets his kicks."

By creating rolling hills on almost flat land he was not making an arbitrary statement: There is a good bit of hilly country nearby. The Korabs carefully planned their remodeled landscape to seem natural, and it does. There were some deciduous trees, mainly maples, on the property, according to Monica Korab. "Mostly they weren't where we would have liked them to be, but we worked around them." In addition there were three centenary Michigan white pines. These are cherished. Mrs. Korab has been known to build fires near them in a sleet storm to melt potentially branch-breaking ice. They went on to plant the same kind of white pines in quantity and placed them from the beginning to underline the sweeps of molded earth.

Like the pines, much of the rest of the flora comes from the surrounding countryside. "As the bulldozer was fast turning farm and woodland into suburbia," Korab says, "I was often just a step ahead with my shovel to dig trees, bushes, and wildflowers." Not every plant is native. But all have been in the area so long that it seems peculiar to call them exotic. If there is any latent tendency to plant collecting in the partnership, it dwells in Monica Korab. In addition to being cheerleader, critic, and sounding board for her husband, whose garden she insists it is, she also seems to be plant-nurturer-in-chief. At one point she was devoted to lilies. Now her enthusiasm has transferred to hostas, "all those wonderful colors of green, and they really thrive here."

Changes in landforms and plantings don't happen all that frequently. Changes in the placement and configuration of what one could call found-object sculptures — Korab calls them markers — may, and often do, take place with every change of season. He sees them as "visual anchors in the landscape, endowed sometimes with a tongue-in-cheek sym-

Korab created his newest berm when the highway department cut into his land to make a turning lane. The wildflower meadow the Korabs planted on it stopped traffic. The seed mixture, although not completely native, was formulated for the region by a company affiliated with Michigan State University.

Balthazar Korab's bulldozer-made rolling hills are backed by a forest of Michigan white pines planted to set them off, in tribute to ancient ones that came with the property. Korab keeps recomposing his found-object "markers" until they finally disintegrate and return to the earth. He cut the procession of log slices from timber left by the roadside.

Korab found all kinds of possiblities in wooden cable spools abandoned by builders. He sometimes charred them for texture, often painted the interiors red, and rolled them into new configurations to enhance seasonal color changes in the garden.

bolism." The whole family participates in siting them and setting them up, "a kind of conceptual art in action." If these assemblies eventually self-destruct, and they do, he has a chance to try something new.

Long before I came to America I read in a collection of short stories by Henry Miller about an immigrant who managed to create his whole environment out of things discarded. It stuck so firmly in my sub-conscious that when I settled here and faced this country's throwaway economy, I started picking up things by the roadside. I passed over modern age rejects like tires and refrigerators, and went for wood and stone, worked by man, mementos of the countryside's farming past.

Large cable spools abandoned by builders were rolled home and ceremoniously charred for texture in a kind of fire dance. My son loved that. A barn was torn down nearby. When I learned that its beautiful hand-hewn beams were destined for the dump, I persuaded the trucker with a handsome tip to dump them at my place. Developers dug up stones rough cut by farmers or fancifully carved by retreating glaciers. They landed in my garden, perhaps until the next Ice Age.

Wooden beams and spools eventually collapsed, but man and nature have never failed to provide a new supply of materials. Logs left by the roadside, cut into rounds have a particular potential. Sometimes plain, sometimes painted, lined up, piled up, clustered, or spaced, each configuration of log slices seems made for its spot only to find, when reconfigured, an equally congenial setting somewhere else. The skeletons of dead lilacs evade the compost pile. Upside down trees have recently made appearances in the work of several well-known sculptors, but Korab resists claiming any deep significance for his lilacs. "I don't take myself so seriously as to call my markers ART. It's just *homo ludens* in action, playing with forms for my own joy. If others respond to them so much the better."

If there is a lesson to be learned from the very disparate collector's gardens we have looked at, it is that collection-building is a perfectly good motivation for making a garden just so long as the individual elements are fused into a whole.

Digression 6   Individualism, Community, Front Lawns

For a nation that claims to venerate rugged individualism we are curiously convention-bound in the way we usually organize the land around our houses. East to West, North to South, in cities and suburbs, on isolated farms and ranches we sash our houses with shrubs and lay down rugs of green grass before them. They may be incompatible with the soil and climate where we live; but we cling to front lawns and foundation plantings and struggle to maintain them. True, as already noted, we prize the openness of the layout. Even in the more paranoid new suburban enclaves, it is the whole development that is walled and gated, not the individual house. But an open space between house and street doesn't have to be given to mown grass, nor is a foliage miniskirt necessarily the best way to tie a house to the land. Where did these customary forms come from? Why this devotion to them? How much is individual preference? How much community pressure?

Affection for the lawn has the longer history. Some biologists even claim that it summons a genetic memory: the open savannas of Africa where humans first evolved. This seems a stretch. Researchers have found that people across many cultures prefer smooth ground and spaced trees in their everyday landscapes. Human beings find such a setting comfortable, investigators feel, because a smooth surface implies that the ground will be easy to walk on, while the trees add interest and focus, but the smooth surface doesn't have to be grass.[1] Mediterranean peoples by and large don't create their landscapes on a foundation of turf, or when they do, it is generally in imitation of northern European styles, such as the fashion for English landscapes in nineteenth century Italy. The case is much the same in China and Japan. You might expect the lawn to be part of the landscape vocabulary in the latter, since it has the kind of climate lawns like: damp. Yet, turf doesn't seem to have been used in Japanese gardens until after Japanese designers had seen the rolling lawns of England. They chose moss when they wanted a soothing sweep of green.

In his provocative examination of the front lawn, "Ghosts at the Door," J. B. Jackson proposes, to my mind more realistically, that in this country whatever our original ethnic origin, "We are all descendants, spiritually speaking, of the peoples of Great Britain and Ireland, of the Low Countries, and to a lesser extent of northern France and western Germany." And our lawns "are merely the civilized descendants of the Medieval pastures cleared among the trees."[2] Cleared land on which you could grow grass and feed cattle wasn't easy to come by in either northern Europe or much of North America. The forest ruled, and would quickly reclaim neglected land. Grassland demanded a considerable investment of time and hard work to create and to maintain. Small wonder that that grassland became over time a source of pride and pleasure. Studies have shown that lawns are cherished childhood memories for those who grew up playing on grass, and that such memories are powerful predictors of the surroundings they find attractive as adults.

Even in the Middle Ages the lawn was prized for more than just its utilitarian value, as Albertus Magnus makes clear in 1260. In discussing the planting of a pleasure garden he says that ". . . the sight is in no way so pleasantly refreshed as by fine and close grass kept short . . ."[3] Almost four hundred years later, Francis Bacon would repeat the sentiment in his essay "On Gardens" and his ideal garden, although more elaborate, shares many features with that of Albertus Magnus. The authors of American gardening books from McMahon to the present almost invariably begin any discussion of garden design with the lawn. Garden makers in the Northern Hemisphere seem always to have found it the ideal living ground plane on which to build either architectural or painterly volumes. That's not quite so true today: the books are as likely to tell you how to get rid of a lawn as how to create one. Before examining the reasons for its recent fall from environmntal grace we should see how it became such an American institution in the first place.

Pasturage indeed loomed large for the earliest English settlers, and they were quick to import the kinds of grass their cattle were accustomed to, not finding the native varieties optimally nutritious. On a less utilitarian level they carried in their minds the image of upper-class houses with simple ceremonial walled or fenced forecourts containing one or more panels of turf intersected by gravel walkways. From the beginning of the seventeenth century almost all the great English houses drawn by Smythson or Dankaerts or Swetzer or Kip and Knyff show just such an arrangement. Sometimes the panels were ornamented with trees or statues or, occasionally a pool; but most often the lawn was left unadorned. Just how soon the entrance court came to this country is hard to tell, but the Bodleian print of the late seventeenth-century Governor's Palace in Williamsburg shows one, laid out in what appear to be panels of lawn with topiary accents.

On March 16, 1721 William Byrd II notes in his diary that "This day we began to turf the bowling green," and later speaks of walking "about the garden to see my people lay the turf."[4] Just where the bowling green was at Westover can only be guessed; but it seems significant that the oval panel of turf at the entrance to Mount Vernon was often referred to as a bowling green in the eighteenth century. Most early mentions of turf or lawn refer to landscaping at country-estate scale so we can't be sure that ordinary homeowners made space for it on their grounds. But by the early nineteenth century and well before the invention of the lawnmower, travelers were reporting farm and village houses surrounded by neat lawns with a few trees or shrubs to ornament them in Western New York State.

> The houses are all delicately painted, their windows with green Venetian blinds, peeping gaily through fine young trees, or standing forward more exposed on their little lawns, green and fresh as those of England.[5]

and Foundation Planting

Similar descriptions would reappear as settlers, then travelers moved west to Ohio, Michigan, Illinois. Americans of modest means could own the land they lived on, and if they wanted to demonstrate ownership by imitating the great magnates of England there was no one to stop them. Many had clearly decided that a fenced grassground, how-ever severely miniaturized, provided a properly dignified approach to the front door. When Andrew Jackson Downing offered the following advice in his *Landscape Gardening* it seems that he was simply putting his imprimatur on an exist-ing custom and giving it a push:

> But there are many persons with small cottage places of little decided character, who have neither room, time, nor income, to attempt the improvement of their grounds fully. . . . How shall they render their places tasteful and agreeable, in the easiest manner? We answer, *by attempting only the simple and the natural*; and the unfailing way to secure this, is by employing as leading features only trees and grass.[6]

As the "modern" or "natural" style increased in popularity, acres of grass came to carpet the grounds of large country houses and middle-class villas. Still, the entrance lawn did not sweep all before it instantly in more modest establish-ments. What constituted the front yard was for quite a time a shifting mixture of individual taste and community custom and of equally shifting nomenclature. Some communities made a clear distinction between the dooryard garden—with its blend of fruit, flowers and vegetables—opposite the kitchen door, and the front yard of turf, trees, and perhaps a few shrubs between the parlor windows or the front door and the road. Others used the terms and types of planting inter-changeably. There were regional patterns: swept-earth yards in the rural South, hardpan or paved patios with plants in pots in California and the Southwest. Towns that took as models cities like Philadelphia with traditions of building houses right to the lot line didn't have front yards at all. In others, particularly in the "graceless villages" that marred the land for Downing and some of his correspondents they were unplanted dumping grounds or pig wallows.

In the minds of Downing and fellow critics it was up to individuals, "apostles of taste," to reform the customs and improve the looks of the graceless villages:

> . . . there are two great principles at the bottom of our national character, which the apostle of taste in the most benighted GRACELESS VILLAGE, may safely count upon. One of these is the *principle of imitation*, which will never allow a Yankee to be outdone by his neigh-bors; and the other, the *principle of progress*, which will not allow him to stand still when he discovers that his neighbor has really made an improvement.[7]

In some cases setting an example worked. Lyman Beecher told his children that when he and his wife arrived in Easthampton, Long Island in 1799

> . . . the town consisted of the plainest farm-houses, standing directly on on the street, with the wood-pile by the front door, and the barn close by. . . . Mine was the first orchard in East Hampton. People had had the impression that fruit would not do well so near the salt-water and laughed when they saw me setting out trees.
>
> It was not long, however, before others, seeing how well my orchard was thriving, began to set out trees. . . . In our front door-yard your mother had flowers and shrubs, and some of them are there yet. There is a snow-ball and a catalpa which she set out.
>
> Others saw this and did the same. The wood-piles were cleared away from the street in front of the houses, and door-yards made pretty, and shade-trees set out. And now you will not find many places prettier in sum-mer than East Hampton.[8]

Those shade trees set out along the streets may have encouraged the lawn's takeover of the front yard. Once big enough to truly provide shade they would seriously curtail the number and variety of flowers, fruits, and vegetables that could be grown in it. Or, could it have been that household-ers grew tired of having passersby reach over the fence and pick their fruit and flowers? The repetition of penalties pro-claimed by seventeenth-century New Amsterdam magis-trates indicates that the abuse was widespread, the penalties, ineffective. In 1850 Susan Fenimore Cooper was still com-plaining of the same casual garden thievery by adults and children alike. One solution: turf the front and move tempta-tions to the rear.

Probably much more influential was the idea that grass-grounds and street trees were the most significant ways in which a town or city could be made more orderly and attrac-tive. These civic amenities had appeared on the scene by the late seventeenth century and they were provided by a distinc-tively American mixture of individual enterprise, civic activism, and governmental legislation. Sometimes all three forces worked together, but usually one of the first two took the lead, with governmental endorsement after the program was under way. In 1695, Samuel Sewall records in his diary:

> I planted Two Locusts, two Elms at Wheelers pond, and one in Elm-Pasture near the Line over against the Middle-Elm. The middle Locust-Tree at Wheelers pond was set there the last year.

In his footnote to this passage, the editor, M. Halsey Thomas, notes that the town of Boston then ordered that since Sewall had planted the trees to shade the pond, he and his heirs had the exclusive right to cut them down and replant them.[9] In 1728, according to Rudy Favretti's research, it was the town that took on the planting of trees along one side of the Common.[10]

When street trees were first planted in New York seems undocumented, but since they were common in Holland they may well have predated English rule, even though they don't appear on the very detailed 1661 Castello plan. Perhaps with all the city's orchards, they weren't needed at that period. By 1730, Broadway, as depicted in the Lyne-Bradford map of the city, was still broad and lined with trees, and in 1750 Peter Kalm, the emissary of Linnaeus to North America, was so impressed by New York's street trees that he offered a detailed description:

> In the chief streets there are trees planted, which in summer give them a fine appearance, and during the excessive heat at that time afford a cooling shade. I found it extremely pleasant to walk in the town, for it seemed like a garden. The trees which are planted for this purpose are chiefly of two kinds: the water beech, or Linné's *Platanus occidentalis*, which is very plentiful and gives an agreeable shade in summer by its great and numerous leaves; and the locust tree, or Linné's *Robinia Pseud-Acacia*, which is also frequent . . . There are likewise lime trees and elms along these walks, but they are not by far so frequent as the others. One seldom met with trees of the same sort next to each other, they being in general planted alternately.[11]

In mixing their trees eighteenth-century tree-planters were wiser than their nineteenth-century followers as we learned in the 1940s when single-species plantings made it easy for Dutch elm disease to mow down countless avenues of centenarian elms. The pest that did in New York's eighteenth-century street trees and led to the mistaken impression that they only appeared in the city in the late nineteenth was human. The British force that occupied New York from 1776–1783 apparently cleared the entire island of Manhattan — and part of Long Island as well — of wood for fuel and fortifications. George Washington, reconnoitering on July 17, 1781, noted in his diary: "The Island is totally stripped of Trees, and wood of every kind; but low bushes (apparently as high as a Man's Waste) appear in places which were covered with wood in the year 1776." With the return of American control, came the return of shade trees to the streets. A 1793 print shows young trees, boxed for protection, lined up along the Battery, and an 1800 one, Lombardy poplars along Wall Street.[12]

In little more than a decade after the end of the revolution campaigns for civic improvement and beautification were launched in the towns and cities of the new republic, with New England in the lead, lawns and trees in the star parts. A major goal was the leveling, turfing, and fencing of the town commons. Far from being the tree-studded greenswards of present-day image, for most of the eighteenth century the commons of New England towns, originally intended as common pastures or paddocks for the town cows and drill grounds for the town militia, although sometimes

covered with scruffy grass, were often muddy, and usually rutted with the tracks of short-cutting carts. Boston had begun a gradual process of turning its Common into a public park by fencing it in 1739; but the town most often cited as a example was New Haven, and the man most held up as a model citizen was James Hillhouse. According to his biographer

> Since Theophilus Eaton and John Davenport . . . came to Quinnipiack in 1638, and laid out their beautiful town-plat around the open square which they reserved for their public buildings, their market-place and their graves, no man has ever done so much by personal influence and labor for the beauty of New Haven as was done by James Hillhouse.[13]

Hillhouse, who graduated from Yale in 1776, does seem to have been a remarkable man. A lawyer and real estate investor, he spent twenty years as congressman and senator, then the rest of his long life in a variety of responsible public positions in Connecticut. Some street trees had been planted in the early part of the century, and some improvements made to the New Haven common, but Hillhouse organized public subscriptions to level and grade the southern half and fence the whole. He also planted along the streets, often with his own hands, the elm trees from one of his farms that gave the town its epithet "Elm City" and encouraged other public-spirited citizens to do likewise. Hoping to close the nearly-full burial ground on the common — by then renamed the New Haven Green — he also organized a landscaped rural cemetery with lots sold by subscription, a new idea and one that took a while to catch on. Still, according to his older contemporary Timothy Dwight, president of Yale, foreign visitors found its grid of tree-bordered avenues impressive.

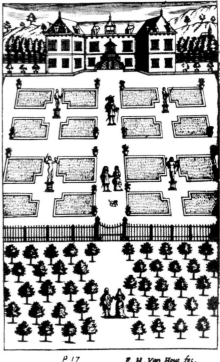

P 17   F. H. Van Hove fec.

Some current historians speculate that it might have been one influence on the design of Paris's Père Lachaise, which in turn influenced the creation of Mount Auburn, our first cemetery in the landscape style and one of the prime inspirations for the city park movement in the United States.

Some students at Yale in his day were certainly influenced by Hillhouse's activities and improvements. As fledgling lawyers and ministers like Oliver Wolcott, Jr. and Lyman Beecher moved into towns throughout the northeast they tried to persuade their fellow citizens to clean up their dooryards, turf the commons, and plant trees along the streets. Harvard, too, with the Boston Common as example, sent out its share of improvers and proselytizers for improvement. Success was spotty and uneven. Some towns like Hanover, New Hampshire resisted beautification until late in the nineteenth century despite efforts by Dartmouth College. Portsmouth, on the other hand, seems to have eagerly embraced the paving of sidewalks, and the planting of trees. In "The Glory of America: a century sermon" delivered at South Church in January 1801, the Reverend Timothy Alden boasts that one side of most streets have been "paved with very nice flat stones" and lists the streets planted with Lombardy poplars between 1792 and 1800:

> It ought to be added, that all these rows of trees have been set out, and neatly boxed, through the care and expense of a number of public spirited citizens. As trees are allowed by philosophers and physicians to render the air more salubrious and, as nothing can be more ornamental to a town, it is to be hoped that their laudable example will be followed until every street and vacant corner is replenished with the Lombardy poplar.

This passion for the Lombardy poplar was not just a New England phenomenon. We have already noted its presence in New York, and it is commonly said to have been introduced either by Michaux in 1787 or William Hamilton of Philadelphia in 1797. The latter date is clearly too late but the tree was indeed popular in Philadelphia, as numerous prints and engravings of the time demonstrate. Alas, Samuel Sewall doesn't say what kind of poplars he set out "in the Fore-yard to shade the windows from the Western sun in Summer." If they were Lombardy poplars this would date their introduction no later than 1705. Its elegant shape may have been the closest classically minded Americans could come to the cypress of the Mediterranean, but for them *Populus nigra's* real virtue was its speedy growth. "The planter is anxious for immediate effect—at least, planters in this country usually are." One could argue that Nathaniel Egleston's 1878 observation has yet to be proved wrong.[14] The Lombardy poplar continued to be planted long after it turned out to be brittle, short-lived, and often disruptive of drains and sewers. Andrew Jackson Downing tried valiantly to discourage its use and gradually the superior habits of elms, basswoods, and sugar maples claimed the streets for these natives.

Calls for village beautification and shade-tree planting recur in sermons, speeches, social improvement manuals, and horticultural books and magazines throughout the nine-

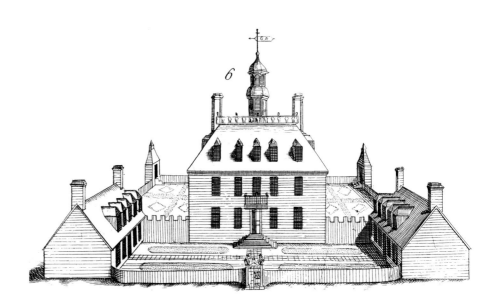

teenth century. Agricultural journals like *The New England Farmer*, 1823, *The Genesee Farmer*, 1831, and *The Yankee Farmer*, 1835 exhorted their readers to plant shade trees along village streets and in front of farmhouses, and there are paintings and prints of the period to testify that their words were heeded by many. Indeed, farmers had often been well ahead of townspeople in the tree-planting line, and by the middle of the nineteenth century many had also painted their houses "sleek" white and spruced up their front yards with lawns and flowers.[15] The drive for village improvement seems to have slackened during the Civil War, quite understandably, but it gained renewed vigor from the 1870s through the 1920s. Although it was often a component of the Colonial Revival gentrification that turned many pre-Revolutionary villages into summer resorts, the process could work in two directions.

Nathaniel Egleston uses the success of the Laurel Hill Association of Stockbridge as an example of the economic benefits to be derived from village improvement. The association was originally formed to preserve a wooded hill near the center of town. As it expanded its beautification activities throughout Stockbridge, property values went up and the town began to attract rich summer visitors, an unexpected boon to town merchants and local farmers. In York, Maine, on the other hand, it was summering Chicagoans who organized and raised the money for the Old York Historical and Improvement Society and hired the Chicago landscape architect O. C. Simonds, pillar of the Prairie School, to plan the York Village Green.[16]

Town greens often figured in the town plans of new settlements in the West if those towns were laid out by transplanted New Englanders; otherwise, courthouse squares or public squares served as central gathering spaces and settings for the principal public buildings. Some, where climate and soil were hospitable to grass, may have been turfed to start with; most boasted at least a few shade trees. Then, after the suc-

By the time the Governor's Place in Williamsburg, Virginia was recorded in what is called the Bodleian Plate (1737–1740) that fashion had crossed the Atlantic. A few scholars do label the oval panels in the forecourt flowerbeds, but it is far more likely that they were turfed like their English antecedents.

This engraving of the Boston Common drawn by Christian Remick, and dated by him to October 1, 1768 shows the tree-shaded promenade mentioned by visitors and street trees along Beacon Street, as well as John Hancock's house and garden and the beacon on Beacon Hill. It also shows the military drills for which the Common was used.

cess of New York's Central Park, no self-respecting city wanted to be without its own park landscaped on the lawn-and-tree model of the Northeast, whether or not that was a truly suitable way to go. Street trees moved west as well, but in more cases they were selected from varieties well adapted to local conditions, like the pepper trees, *Schinus molle*, that line Los Angeles boulevards in early photographs.

Perhaps what finally tipped the balance in favor of grass and trees as the proper setting for a house came from the design of the new planned suburbs like Riverside near Chicago, laid out in 1868 by Olmsted and Vaux who had created Central Park a decade earlier.

> We cannot judiciously attempt to control the form of the houses which men shall build, we can only, at most, take care that if they build very ugly and inappropriate houses, they shall not be allowed to force them disagreeably upon our attention. . . . We can require that no house shall be built within a certain number of feet of the highway, and we can insist that each house-holder shall maintain one or two living trees between his house and his highway-line.[17]

The setbacks that Olmsted and Vaux recommended were not a completely new idea. They had been reported more than a decade earlier as municipal requirements in Salt Lake City by a government surveyor,[18] and might well have existed elsewhere. But after 1868 curving tree-shaded streets lined with open lawns in front of houses would become a distin-

guishing mark of the well-to-do American suburb. Then, without the curves, of residential neighborhoods in towns, cities, and middle-class subdivisions. Unremarked, the responsibility for keeping the community green and shaded was shifting to the individual homeowner. True, associations of private citizens had initiated and financed village improvement societies: frugal town governments usually looked on beautification as frivolity. Increasingly such associations were replaced by development covenants that mandated lawns, trees, and a certain level of maintenance; or by informal but powerful neighborhood pressure on individuals. Although in some cases the town would plant and maintain street trees, in the more common twentieth-century scenario it would remove them to widen streets and accomodate an ever-growing army of automobiles.

The introduction of the lawn mower in the late 1850s, some twenty years after its invention in England, made these neighborhood lawns considerably easier to keep up. Advertisements of the period tout its ease of use by showing women and children as well as formally dressed men cheerfully pushing their mowers, or in some cases riding horse-drawn ones: riding mowers have been with us a long time. That men soon took over the care of the lawn is not too surprising. There was precedent: scything, the historic technique for cutting grass, was traditionally a masculine skill.

> He was as dignified with his coat off and with scythe in his hands, leading the mowers across the field, and cutting the widest swath of all, as when he stood conspicuous and honored in the Senate.[19]

There was propaganda: mowing was gentle exercise for the businessman, it promoted meditation and relaxing thoughts for the harried. And, added garden writers, who is not soothed by the smell of new-mown grass? Was hay fever less widespread in the nineteenth century one wonders. That lawn care also promoted competition as well as sociability among neighbors, was all to the good. The competitive spirit is far from being rare among gardeners. And lawns weren't thought to demand all the patience and nurturing—widely considered feminine attributes—that flowers and vegetables did. Smooth green turf signaled a man who took pride in himself and his surroundings, a good citizen. By the end of the nineteenth century the front lawn had become the nationally accepted visual expression of community spirit.

Those lawns didn't have to be bare. Judging from the strictures of the horticultural press they rarely were. To the tastemakers a few well-placed shrubs or a well-tended flower bed were acceptable; cast-iron deer and dogs, plaster Floras and Dianas were not. Nor were too many shrubs dotted about the property. Just when and why the shrubs migrated from the lawn and huddled up against the house to become that American innovation, foundation planting, is difficult to document. Certainly there is every evidence that houses up through the early years of the nineteenth century met the ground cleanly and directly, whether the foundations were exposed or buried. By mid-century Downing and others recommended the planting of a vine or two against the pillars of a piazza or the corners of a house to suggest *feeling* and a love of the beautiful. The illustrations in most pattern books showed vines and occasionally a few shrubs nestled up against houses, particularly the simplest ones. "A Cheap Cottage" in the February 1850 issue of *Godey's Magazine and Lady's Book* is tightly encircled by a strictly clipped hedge, but the accompanying text doesn't even mention the hedge or its location. Foundation planting seems to have crept into custom without much fanfare.

The first real discussion of the subject comes in Frank Scott's 1870 *Suburban Home Grounds*, and curiously he begins by saying that "It is becoming a fashion to decry the planting of shrubs in contact with dwelling houses." He attributes this attitude to health problems caused by packing yards with so many trees, shrubs, and vines that houses became dark and damp. He may have been aware of the conclusions drawn by a distinguished Boston physician, Henry Ingersoll Bowditch, from his pioneering statistical survey of the incidence of tuberculosis in Massachusetts. The bacterial cause of this scourge of New England—it killed Thoreau, most of Emerson's family, and eventually the philosopher himself—had not yet been discovered. Bowditch found that certain locations, and not just city slums, produced generations of victims even if successive owners came from different families.

> I know another homestead in which resides a family of wealth and refinement. It is a sweet rural cottage, overhung with clustering vines, delightfully situated among shade trees, thickly hemmed in by a shrubbery that Shenstone might have envied. . . . In the heats of our midsummer, every passerby would point out the spot as one to be selected for its perfect coolness of situation and quiet loveliness. But I fear it is most unhealthy . . .[20]

Four of the family's children had died of consumption, as did the previous owner of the house. Bowditch became convinced of the importance of sunlight and air circulation as preventive measures. "I have at times *thinned out* trees around a residence, where a family was growing up."

Scott was not about to let physicians' concerns impede the progress of foundation planting:

> . . . low-growing shrubs planted against the basement-walls of suburban houses, and rising only a few feet higher than the first floor, are not open to any such objections. A house that is *nested* in shrubs which seem to spring out of its nooks and corners with something of the freedom that characterizes similar vegetation springing naturally along stone walls and fences, seems to express the mutual recognition and dependence of nature and art . . .

Nathaniel Egleston, to the contrary, would banish shrubs and trees to the periphery of the lot:

> On all accounts, whether of health or aesthetic effect, there should be a clear space of some breadth around every house, where hardly so much as a shrub should break the smooth green of the turf or the clean sweep of gravel.[21]

It was aesthetic effect that concerned the young landscape architect, Charles Eliot, who was an even more emphatic proponent of foundation planting than Scott. Bewailing the dreariness of "The Suburbs in March" in the March 14, 1888 issue of *Garden and Forest*, he attributes it to the fact that "we have reduced our bits of ground to mere planes of shaven grass, from which the house walls rise stiff and unclothed." He names a dozen native shrubs and small trees, evergreen or boasting colorful berries or branches, which he says give the open country beauty even in the colorless half-way weeks between winter and spring when the snow is gone and the grass is dead. "Where are the houses which have bushes crowded around their bays and corners, as the wild bushes crowd the field walls, till they seem to be fairly grown to the ground?" Thick planting "to clothe the nakedness" of buildings is more than just an answer to the bleakness of March.

Eliot states his position forcefully in the opening sentence of a four-part series, "How to Mask the Foundations of a Country House" for the same magazine.[22] "Nothing is more essential to the beauty of a country-place than that the foundations of the house should be properly connected with the ground from which they spring." If the site is irregular and rocky and the architect designs the house to take advantage of it, he feels that a few strategically placed vines or ground-covers may be all that is needed. Sad to say, in his day as in ours, most often the site has been so leveled that "the house must stand like a box upon a floor." Flower beds won't do the

trick—they're bare in winter—and vines aren't sufficient. "Shrubs planted near the base of the house wall remove at once all appearance of isolation and nakedness, and nothing can help a building more than this." Planting should not be sparse but neither should the house "look as if it grew in a thicket." He advocated irregular groupings around the house, not continuous belts, and his advice on plants and placement is sound. Unfortunately as the idea took hold, its execution in the hands of the less talented bore little resemblance to the suggestions of a gifted designer. And take hold it did, as a drive through any residential district will demonstrate.

By the time Leonard Johnson's *Foundation Planting* came out in 1927—the only book I've been able to find devoted to the subject—many landscape architects had already had second thoughts about the notion. Among the more picturesque condemnations was Fletcher Steele's: "Little houses are belted with bulging shrubs as mud rolls out from under a footfall."[23] To today's eyes there's nothing very inspiring about Johnson's examples, and his criticisms and hints for improvement seem simply attempts to make the best of a bad job. But in fairness, the book was not intended for people who could afford a designer. Most of the houses shown are modest not high-style; and careful examination of the photographs reveals quite a few brick or concrete block foundations whose concealment is an act of mercy.

Exposed foundations offered an inducement to be sure, but photographs of houses from the mid-nineteenth century onward suggest additional unarticulated-but-felt reasons for

the stealthy, steady advance of foundation planting. The lines of eighteenth- and early nineteenth-century houses—Georgian, Federal, Greek Revival—tended to be horizontal, whereas those of later picturesque architectural styles tended to be vertical, and horizontal masses rest more comfortably on the land particularly where it is level. Furthermore, the American custom of building a house larger than would be in appropriate proportion to the size of its lot seems to call for some kind of planting to establish a connection and to mitigate the visual disproportion. Finally, more often than not developers tended to strip their property of trees and vegetation to make division and construction easier. Foundation planting was a quick fix for the barren landscapes around the houses they built. Once the idea took hold, and it certainly had by the 1930s, most Americans found a house without foundation planting unimaginable, whatever its architectural style, and however sharp the criticism directed at it by contemporary designers. Totally inappropriate foundation plantings even appeared around eighteenth-century houses in certain "historic" villages.

The popularity of lawn games that began in the mid-nineteenth century also had a role in clearing the lawn. Croquet, archery, lawn tennis, badminton, all needed a certain amount of shrub-free space. Then at the end of the century came golf, the biggest lawn-eater of them all. Golf demanded too much space for most private grounds, but golf clubs proliferated all across the country in the twenties and thirties. The kind of perfection golf-course grass was thought to

Opposite, top:
The lawn-and-tree front yard could be overdone, particularly if the trees were not thinned as they grew up and out. Their effectiveness in keeping any ray of the summer sun from reaching the house aroused concern on the part of nineteenth-century doctors.

Opposite, bottom:
A foundation planting of well-grouped youthful trees makes a graceful transition between a rather stolid Italianate mansion and its smoothly shorn lawn.

This page:
Trees grow. And homeowners won't discipline them. What was probably a neat foundation planting is well on its way to shrouding the entire façade of this house, having already covered the windows on the first floor. Both house and landscape suffer.

require had a profound and not particularly wholesome effect on the private lawn. Why can't my lawn be as smooth as a putting green? wondered the golfing homeowner. And set out to make it so.

The putting green's cossetted single-species carpet of shallow-rooted bentgrass was not really a good ideal for the home lawn's aspiration. True, the kind of grassground called a lawn has changed character repeatedly since the eighteenth century, which is probably why chroniclers of the lawn give so many different dates for its appearance in this country. The mown pasture grass of many early lawns was scarcely weed-free, and it generally turned brown in the hottest part of summer. It's not surprising that those who knew the perpetually verdant lawns of England denied that lawns existed in America, whatever Americans thought. By the mid-nineteenth century gardeners and nurserymen had given more study to the subject, and Downing, a great admirer of the British lawn, stated confidently that he had seen "admirable lawns wherever they have been properly treated. Fine lawns are therefore possible in the northern half of the Union." Proper treatment he said, consisted of "*deep soil, the proper kinds of grass, and frequent mowing.*" Deep soil—two feet was suggested—carefully prepared would insure deep roots, which could reach moisture even in dry periods. The soil should be good but not rich, and manure should be added only at the subsoil level and only if necessary. For seed he recommended

> a mixture of red-top (*Agrostis vulgaris*) and white clover (*Trifolium repens*), which are hardy short grasses and on the whole make the best and most enduring lawn for this climate. The proportion should be about three-fourths red-top to one fourth white clover.[24]

All the lawn needed once established, he said, was frequent mowing and rolling: no fertilization and no irrigation. Neither weeds nor insects were mentioned. Either they weren't much of a problem, or they were accepted as inevitable. Downing didn't attempt prescriptions for parts of the country he didn't know. But Northerners were already fanning out across the country in the 1840s, and they wanted lawns where the lawns of the Northeast would not grow. Seedsmen responded by importing, breeding, and testing grasses, hoping to find varieties suited to the varied soils and climates of the nation. This was a slow and not always successful process. Americans like quick results. And no one seemed willing to admit that lawns just don't belong in the desert. So began the processes of irrigation, fertilization, and pest control that would turn the late twentieth-century lawn into an ecological and public health menace.

The pressures and promises that garden writers and community groups, seedsmen, manufacturers of mowers, fertilizers, pesticides, and irrigation equipment, and lawn-care companies aimed at the suburban homeowner in search of a perfect lawn have been examined in exhaustive detail in several recent books. To cite just one example, clover continued to be a component of lawn mixes until after the Second

World War, and supplied enough nitrogen that lawns in areas where they belonged did not need fertilizing. Clover was transformed in the public mind from essential component of fine turf to weed in the fifties by a campaign from lawn-care providers and pesticide manufacturers. The newly developed pesticides that would kill dandelions and plantain also killed clover, so, to protect the pesticides, clover had to go. Enter chemical fertilizers!

By the 1980s studies began to document the role of runoff from these fertilizers in polluting lakes and streams, and of emissions from mowing equipment in polluting the air. The massive irrigation needed to grow grass in the arid West was seriously depleting the water supply. Lawns were found to be so saturated with pesticides that it was dangerous for children to play on them.

In the Middle West environmentalists have tried to replace front lawns with miniature restorations of the native prairie. Unfortunately neighbors often see these simply as neglected lawns where weeds ran wild, and invoke local weed laws to force their removal. Pioneering landscape architects like Darrel Morrison and Joan Nassauer have learned that making prairie "lawns" acceptable to the general public requires, along with education, designs demonstrating that the yard is being cared for. Borders of mown grass, clean white picket fences, even bird houses have proved successful in some places.[25]

Suggested environmentally friendly replacements for the chemical lawn are wide-ranging. Prairies would be as artificial as lawns in many parts of the country; so a search is on for attractive ground covers native to a locality or tolerant of local conditions even if not actually native. Some favor bringing back front-dooryard flower gardens. Since most front lawns are rarely used and play a purely visual role, giving front yards a variety of treatments might create some very interesting streetscapes. But such alternatives would probably demand more horticultural knowledge than lawns do, and would lack for many people the comfort of familiarity and easy community acceptance.

That lawns will vanish is highly unlikely. Their appeal to homeowners, designers, and the general public is too deep-rooted. And I can think of few surfaces more comfortable to play or just stretch out on. But even self-styled "defenders of the lawn" like Warren Schultz acknowledge that lawns will have to change and their care-givers give up their fervent perfectionism and the bad habits it has encouraged. In *A Man's Turf: The Perfect Lawn* Schultz offers a lightly ironic account of the many ways our love of the lawn led to its getting such a bad reputation, and concludes with suggestions for "proper treatment" that would have seemed quite familiar to Downing. And he has case histories from golf-course managers and turf farmers among others who have successfully applied them. With a combination of individual commitment, up-to-date ecological information, and a willingness to return to practices of the past, grassgrounds can be rehabilitated and given a positive place in the landscape. Rightly directed pressure from a well-informed community on both individual landowners and local governments can help.

The lawn represents the kind of orderly nature that studies have shown most people want around their dwellings.[26] And the conventional lawn-and-foundation front yard gives the individual the not-to-be-dismissed advantage of satisfying community ideals with his house's public face and of allowing him fairly free rein to express his own desires in its more private back yard.

Village improvement societies seem quaint today, out of scale with the giant metropolitan areas in which most Americans live, but how different really are they from privately funded associations like the Central Park Conservancy, which has assumed responsibilty for the maintenance of what is in fact public space? Larger in size and ambition but similar in motivation and structure, present-day descendants, associations like the land trusts and conservancies, seek to preserve private gardens, estates, farms, and ranches; save and expand city parks, gardens, and greenways on the premise that they contribute to livability, and livability promotes economic prosperity. Their adversaries, although similar, are larger and more powerful than those early civic improvers faced—giant corporations, sluggish bureaucracies, short-sighted politicians, aggressive developers—but such associations have already shown, as their predecessors did, that public opinion can be mobilized, votes and money gathered to direct development and preserve or create green spaces.

At the turn of the twentieth-century such McMansions as these lining a Milwaukee boulevard could have been found all across the country. Houses seem to overfill their lots whenever times are prosperous and they rarely advance the design of gardens.

Town and Suburban Gardens

Preceding page:
The wooden steps leading down to the pool have weathered right into harmony with the soft greens and grays of Thomas Church's plant palette for the Murray's garden. He chose plants that could withstand the strong winds of the hilltop and were, for the most part, deer-resistant.

Plan of E. N. Howell Garden:

1. Shrubbery border
2. Bank of roses
3. Vegetables, fruit, and cutting flowers
4. White pines and hemlocks
5. Cold frames and compost
6. Mixed dogwood
7. Hollyhocks
8. Lilacs
9. Sunken flower garden
10. Pool
11. Slope with native plantings
12. Boathouse

If you count the number of magazines in the United States that have the word country in their titles or measure the success of merchant designer Ralph Lauren you would think that this country was still the agrarian paradise that Thomas Jefferson hoped it would become. What you have witnessed in fact is the power of dream to disguise reality. The population of the United States, according to the census of 2000, was 248,709,873. Although the statistical breakdown is not available as of this writing, in 1990 more than three quarters of the population lived in metropolitan areas. Never mind the statistics, most Americans aspire to the country life even if they are apartment dwellers whose closest brush with the real thing is dressing up in country clothes on city weekends. A longing for the scents and sounds and sights of nature is certainly a component, but only one. Bound up in the mythic appeal of country living is belief in its healthfulness and in its freedom from urban dangers, real or imagined; nostalgia for a simpler, slower life; and an image of leisure and its pursuits, usually highly glamourized. Entwined with it and perhaps its underpinning is the almost overwhelming American desire to live in one's own house on one's own piece of land. (Prosperous apartment dwellers almost always have country houses.) The idea of country seems to be a code for the kind of independence we attach to home ownership, and have from the first northern European settlements. If it belongs to you, that piece of country doesn't have to be very big, and for most people it is not. But all those not-so-big houselots occupy a whole lot of land.

A closer look at the census figures suggests that we have really suburbanized rather than urbanized the United States. As a national average, three fifths of the population lives outside of the central city or central cities of its metropolitan area, that is, either in the suburbs, or in what the census calls rural areas within metropolitan areas and social commentators call exurbs or borderlands. Again, these figures don't tell the whole story. The residential districts around the densely constructed commercial core in most central cities are made up of single-family houses on lots big enough to have front and back yards just like those in small towns or suburban subdivisions. Sometimes such neighborhoods started as suburbs and were absorbed by the spreading city. Equally often, land outside of the commercial core was divided up initially, just as it had been in seventeenth-century Newbury,

Massachusetts, or the towns of Western New York State described by Frances Wright, to allow some open space on all sides of the house. Lot size almost always increases with the distance from downtown. The yards of residential neighborhoods swell into the gardens of the suburbs and gradually expand along a continuum that ends in the estates and farms of the exurbs.

For the most part the layout of town, city, and suburban residential property up until the end of World War II was the product of myriad decisions by individuals and small-scale developers and builders. Zoning laws were nonexistent, large scale financing rarely available. What is remarkable, as Sam Bass Warner, Jr., points out in his examination of Boston suburban growth from 1870 to 1900, is the consistency of the land planning under these circumstances.[1] Houselots were usually rectangular. Geometrically perfect, they usually were not. Some towns, particularly newer ones in the West and Midwest were laid out on a rigid grid, but more often surveys divided up the land in as rectilinear a manner as possible with allowances for rivers, existing roads, or other features of the terrain. Although other methods of land division exist in the United States, landscape historians like D. W. Meinig and John Reps consider this the most prevalent.

Except in the wealthiest suburbs, the lots were not large and differed little from those in cities and towns. The houses built on them were very large: McMansions are not a new phenomenon in this country, it's just that the lots are getting still smaller. When government policy and financing after World War II made possible the Levittowns and other gigantic housing tracts mass-produced for house-hungry veterans, almost nothing was done to change the pattern. Zoning laws might specify lot size, but the lots were still rectangular, and the houses often overlarge in proportion. Although the land had been bulldozed flat and featureless, curving streets and cul-de-sacs sometimes paid lip service to the topographically based streets of more sensitively laid out suburbs designed by landscape architects.

Privacy became a concern. Acreage provides insulation, but on a quarter-acre lot it takes planning to escape neighboring eyes. Many designers shared Fletcher Steele's objections to the open front lawn as an unusable reduction of private outdoor space, created "to make the place attractive to the neighborhood at the expense of personal comfort or convenience."[2] Providing such space was for him of fundamental importance in the design of a small lot:

> Indeed, the key to the real use of the garden area by the whole family will depend on easy accessibility from the house rooms and on finding a comfortable place to sit and live out of doors when they get out, well screened from neighbors.[3]

The house can be placed on its lot to maximize privacy in the garden, but if it is already on the site the garden-maker has no choice. There may be setback laws, or custom may rule. Sometimes neighborhood sentiment demands front lawns with foundation planting. Other cities and towns allow houses to open directly onto the street with garden space at the rear. Backyards are usually easier to make private but they are not always ideal in terms of sun and air circulation. Also, walls, fences, or hedges may be subject to height restrictions. Ideally the garden-maker would be allowed to site a house and shape its garden to make the most of the lot's orientation, the character of the terrain, and the views that can be seen from it, in addition to providing a comfortable level of screening. Unfortunately, this is more often the exception than the rule when it comes to a small yard or garden.

E. N. HOWELL GARDEN

Yet it does happen. One demonstration of the value of such an approach is E. N. Howell's garden in Dixon, Illinois. In 1909 he bought a long, narrow lot—100 feet by 300 feet, about two-thirds of an acre—running from the street to the Rock River. Although it was only five minutes from downtown by trolley, several friends considered it a strange purchase. But just the aspects of its topography that they found unpromising appealed to him: There was a ravine running across it and a steep bank down to the river. His first step was to consult a landscape architect and he made the fortunate choice of Ossian Cole Simonds. Howell told the author of a 1924 article about his garden in *The Garden Magazine* that:

> After going over the place we were so well agreed that practically no changes were made in the preliminary sketch. I then proceeded to carry out this plan to the letter with my own hands.[4]

They carefully located the house, built six years later, between the river and a large elm. By siting it at the top of the ridge overlooking the river, Simonds and Howell had about three-quarters of the lot left for the garden. The ravine area became a sunny sunken garden with a pool, flowerbeds, and places to sit sheltered on the north and west by banks of lilacs. It fulfilled Simonds's prescription for a front yard, which he defined as the space seen from the principal rooms of the house.

> From every viewpoint, it should appear beautiful enough to photograph or paint. A front yard should have open space to show sky, clouds and sunshine. The sky space is bounded preferably by the outlines of trees and bushes.[5]

In this case it was on the street side of the house, but in other designs Simonds located the "front yard" in what we would call the back of the house. On Howell's property there was still a lot of garden between the ravine and the city sidewalk. A grove of white pines provided a shady retreat on the inner edge of the entrance path along the western side of the lot. Beyond it a ten-foot-tall bank of prairie roses followed that path screening it from the vegetable garden. A loosely grouped thicket of prickly shrubs lined the sidewalk, in accord with Simonds's belief that

> …the public street should, in a large measure, be excluded from view, especially that part nearest the house. It has sometimes been said that a home owner should not be selfish, that he should allow the public to see his beautiful grounds. In answer to this, it may be

One of the determining factors in the placement of house and garden, the large elm tree already on the property marks the central axis in this view over beds of mingled flowers, fruit, and vegetables from just inside the street-screening shrubbery. The entrance drive is concealed behind the hedge of prairie roses and evergreens on the right.

Taking advantage of a ravine running across the lot, the owner, E. N. Howell, and the landscape architect, O. C. Simonds, created a sheltered sunken garden hedged with lilacs and furnished with benches on the opposite side from this view. Howell particularly enjoyed watching the wild birds that came to bathe in the pool.

A path winds down from porch to boathouse, in addition to a direct flight of steps. Paths, steps, and boathouse are completely hidden from both porch and river by the dense mixture of native shrubs, vines, and small trees planted on the cliffside. It is hard to imagine that this 1920s scene was five minutes from downtown Dixon, Illinois.

scape and as a healthy interesting occupation." By the time the house was started, Howell said, "the planting on the entire lot except where the house was to stand was in place and the plants which were to go near the house at its completion were growing in the vegetable garden ready for transplanting." E. N. Howell's garden was "a part of its owner," and that for O. C. Simonds "was the most perfect example of the landscape-gardener's art, but while the landscape-gardener may make the original design, in its most perfect form it must be developed, adopted and loved by its owner."[7]

ANNE SPENCER GARDEN

An equally imaginative fulfillment of Simons's ideal is the garden of the African-American poet Anne Spencer in Lynchburg, Virginia. Anne and her husband, Edward, met in college, married in 1901, the year after they graduated, and two years later moved to the house that Edward had built for them. The Spencers' lot was long and narrow like Howell's but it was smaller — 45 by 125 feet— and without much topographical variation. Spencer designed the garden herself, and did a brilliant job of giving an almost flat space movement, variety, surprise, and horticultural richness. Her garden and her physical involvement in it were as central to her daily life as the images and metaphors she drew from it were to her poetry. For seventy years, according to her biographer, J. Lee Greene, she spent almost all of her time working in it, when she wasn't writing or serving as the Dunbar High School librarian. But if she was the driving force, she could always count on the enthusiastic help of her husband, a very talented craftsman and builder, who also served as the city's first parcel postman. "Pop just let me do what I wanted," she told Greene. "If I liked it he did too."[8]

When they were caring for it the garden overflowed with flowers, a mix of old-fashioned favorites, new cultivars, and the occasional rarity packed into beds separated by grass paths. Its fame spread beyond Lynchburg and often the black intellectuals, writers, musicians, athletes, and politicians who had come to count on the Spencers' hospitality when they visited Virginia made special trips to see it at its peak of bloom.

Plants grew so tall and thick that privacy was not an issue, and in many of the period photographs it is hard to make out the garden's plan.

In Anne Spencer's last years illness limited her gardening time and after her death in 1975 the property was left to run wild. When Jane Baber White, a Lynchburg landscape designer, first saw the garden in 1983, it was so overgrown that it was difficult to see how imaginatively it had been laid out. After the Spencers' son, Chauncey, who lives across the street, walked through it with her and showed her photographs of what it had looked like in its prime, she could feel how deeply it had been loved. "I knew then that this little jewel of an abandoned garden deserved to be —indeed *had* to be —restored, and that I knew how to do it."[9] It was not to be an easy task, as White's account "The Restoration of a Poet's Garden" published in *The American Horticulturist*

The other side of the house overlooks a serene vista of the Rock River twenty feet below the cliff on which it is perched. Careful siting and planting conceal from a viewer on the porch the busy bridge downstream and present what seems untouched nature.

said that for the public a glimpse into such grounds, a glimpse leading to the exercise of one's imagination, is far more interesting than to have the property entirely exposed to view. Such glimpses can be provided without destroying privacy.[6]

The eastern side of the garden was home to fruit trees and berry bushes alongside the vegetable garden; then came coldframes and compost pile, and, nearest the house, a small lawn, which, according to the magazine writer, served as a child's playground.

On the river side of the house, the twenty-foot bank was thickly planted with native shrubs and vines, and the boathouse at the bottom so placed and planted out as to be invisible from both house and river. The plan exploits the topography of the lot so successfully that the working parts of the garden are screened from the pleasure-giving parts, yet all flow together seamlessly.

With plan in hand, Howell immediately began to propagate and raise the plants he would need from cuttings, nurseryman's plants, and material collected from the wild. "This has been of the very greatest benefit to me in acquiring knowledge of plants, their cultivation, their place in a land-

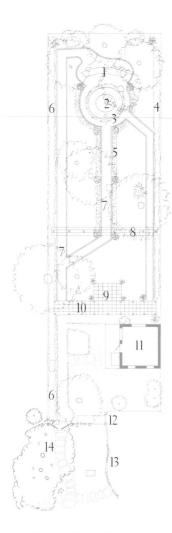

Anne Spencer Garden Restoration
Plan by Jane Baber White:

1. Bench
2. Pool
3. "Prince Ebo" fountain
4. Lilac hedge
5. English boxwood hedge
6. Herbaceous border
7. Gravel paths
8. Grape arbor
9. Minerva statue
10. Wisteria pergola
11. "Edankraal"
12. Blue lattice fence
13. Rose beds
14. Bulbs and groundcover

Above, right:
From earth covered with ivy
and violets, myriad little bulbs
thrust up blooms in early
spring to light the path that
leads from the back door of
the Spencer house through an
arch in the pale blue lattice
fence to the first "courtyard"
of the garden. Metal frames to
the left support the old-fashioned rose bushes that are just
beginning to leaf out.

makes very clear. Anne Spencer's house and garden had
been declared a Virginia Historic Landmark and placed on
the National Register in 1977, but restoring and maintaining
the house had already strained the financial resources of the
Friends of Anne Spencer Foundation. White realized that
restoration of the garden would have to be a separate operation and proceeded to organize it. Financial backing and
uncounted womanhours of volunteer labor were contributed
by her garden club, the Hillside Garden Club. Their efforts
were supplemented by skills, labor, and materials donated by
the city, the power company, boy scouts, college students,
and local businesses.

After considerable research the team decided to model
the restoration on the appearance of the garden in 1925, for
which they had considerable documentation. However, recognizing that money and hands for maintenance would
always be in short supply, White produced a simplified plan
that placed more emphasis on the bones of the garden than
on the flowers, and changed some materials to minimize
care. Grass paths were replaced by gravel, some flowerbeds
by patches of lawn, and privet hedges by easier-to-maintain
English boxwood without diminishing its appeal.

The garden is arranged as a rhythmic enfilade of spaces
more aptly described as courts rather than rooms, since they
are defined by lattice screens not walls. Steps lead down from
the back door of the house into what might be called the
antechamber. A paved parking space narrows it on the right
but this is well screened by a large bed of Spencer's own
selection of old-fashioned roses, rescued by the restorers. A
flagstone path swings to the left through groundcovers span-
gled with bulbs in the spring to a lattice arch in a lattice fence
painted a lovely soft blue. Typical of Edward Spencer's talent
for recycling, it was constructed from what had been the
original back porch of the house.

From the arch a path leads straight down the left side to
the bottom of the garden. The length of the path, between it
and the open wire boundary fence with its decorative iron
coping—a gift to Edward from Randolph Macon College—
lies a narrow flowerbed, a restrained remnant of Anne
Spencer's cottage-garden plantings. The different "courts"
open off it to the right. In the first one is the "cottage" called
Edankraal, a pun on the Spencers' first names added to the
African word for enclosure. According to Chauncey Spencer
his father built it so that his mother, who liked to sit in the
garden and write late into the night, would have a shelter.
Beyond Edankraal a wooden pergola supports "…wisteria
boughs / Dripping with the heavy honey of the Spring."[10]
This runs the width of the garden, extending over the path
and delineating the next court, within which a rectangular
latticework extension centered on the pergola encloses a statue of Minerva given to Spencer by friends. Now planted to
grass, this court is marked off by a grape arbor that hosts the
Concord and Niagara grapes celebrated in one of her poems.
From the arbor to the end of the garden the space is not
divided vertically but it has vertical accents—trees, shrubs,
and martin houses on tall poles—and the ground plane takes
on a lively pattern with additional paths balanced around a
central axis leading to a circular lily pool. Small as it is, there

is an amazing amount of variety to lure one through today's
serene and uncluttered garden, yet period photographs show
how effectively the design organizes the insatiable collecting
of a plant-loving gardener.

Successful suburban gardens don't have to be made by or
for gardeners. What is necessary is a real meeting of minds
between homeowner and designer, and that is founded on
honest communication. What does the owner like and like
to do in a garden? This is the essential question, but if the
designer is to give form to these wishes, he or she needs some
practical information as well. How much time and money is
the owner willing to spend on maintenance? What is the
budget, and if it is limited, can the project be done in stages?
On the other hand, the owner needs to be comfortable with
the way that the designer organizes outdoor space, and sure
that the latter is really listening to his needs.

ALLEN GARDEN

Good personal chemistry helps a lot. For Fletcher Steele,
the splendid small garden he designed for Charlotte and
Atkinson Allen was the beginning of a friendship that lasted
the rest of his life. Their lot, 90 by 200 feet, was similar in size
and shape to the gardens we have discussed, but the owners
were not interested in gardening. According to Robin Karson,
Steele's biographer, Charlotte Allen even claimed to hate
flowers and to consider green the only proper color for a garden.[11] This posed no problem for Steele, as his primary interest was in the shaping of space, and he felt that:

Beyond Edankraal, the garden house built for Anne Spencer by her husband, a T-shaped trellis roofed in wisteria shelters a statue of Minerva. A lilac hedge screens the right side of the garden from the neighbors. Along the other side (not shown) a narrow flowerbed backed by an open wire fence borders the path to the end of the garden.

The African head, called by the Spencers "Prince Ebo" was a gift from W .E. B. DuBois, and was made into a fountainhead for the pool. A thick wreath of liriope rings the pool, and boxwood hedges line the central path to the grape arbor. Dotted through the garden are martin houses, homes for the birds that kept it insect-free.

The green garden is particularly adapted to the needs of a small place. It can be designed so as to require a minimum of time and work to maintain. It needs little more than a restraining, guiding hand. Most of the real work can be done over a tea-cup in the shade. It is done in the mind.[12]

Eventually flowers would have a place, a limited one, in the Allen garden. What would really guide the design was a belief shared by the Allens and Steele that "beauty is found only in order and composition."[13]

The house, already under construction when Steele was hired, was L-shaped, with the principal rooms in a block parallel to the street, the kitchen and service rooms in a perpendicular wing extending back from the dining room along the driveway that hugged the north boundary of the property. Thus the backyard where the garden would be made was bounded by the house on two sides. The small setback-imposed front lawn he simply hedged. He immediately had a brick wall built the length of the south and east boundaries. Across the back of the garden area, he also built up a terrace, which extended between the garage and the back wall to the

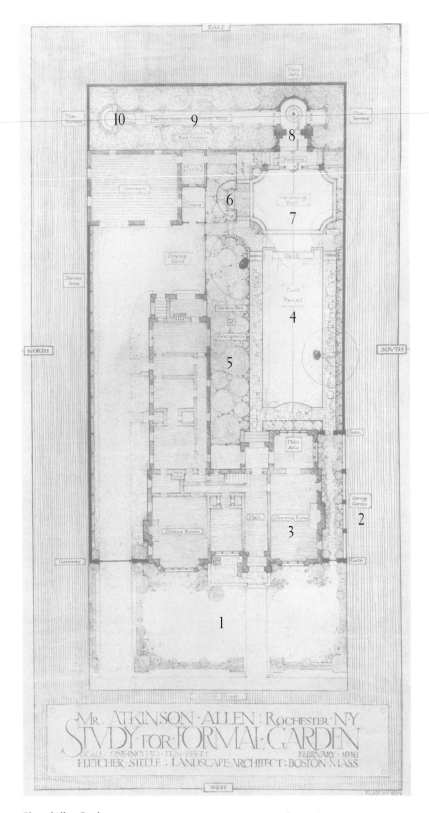

Plan of Allen Garden:

1. Front lawn
2. Spring Garden
3. Drawing room
4. Turf panel
5. Clipped evergreens
6. Saracen tent
7. Swimming pool
8. Arch framing Lachaise sculpture
9. Cedar Lined Terrace Walk
10. Tea House shown later replaced
    by a Calder mobile

north boundary, essentially turning house and garden into interlocking Ls. Raising the level of the ground at the back was a technique he often used in small gardens, not just to vary the terrain but also as an economical way to suggest a sunken garden. "A sunken garden," he wrote, "always seems to be particularly shut away from the world."

Despite its geometric precision, the garden is not bilaterally symmetrical: the main axis is centered on the drawing room, bisects a rectangular panel of grass, bordered by stone paved paths that extends from the paved covered terrace to the swimming pool, passes through the center of the pool to a seashell wall fountain and the terrace wall, terminating in an arch framing a monumental sculpture by Gaston Lachaise. A minor cross-axis runs across the pool to a teahouse in the shape of a Saracen tent. The major cross-axis is hidden: It runs on the raised terrace from the Lachaise along a gravel path flanked by marble urns set against a beech hedge to a Calder mobile at its northern end.

On the side bounded by the service wing of the house a wide bed of carefully clipped evergreens divided into bays displays a collection of specimen shrubs. The wall side has space only for a very narrow bed of ivy. On the swimming pool axis the Saracen Tent backed by a grove of mixed hawthorns is balanced by lilacs at the other end of the pool. A few larger trees, informally but carefully sited, provide rhythmic accents and shifting patterns of light and shade. "Definite geometrical areas," Steele felt, "require softening or they become stiff, dead things. The most welcome relief for lawns is found in deep irregular shadow, such as falls away from tall trees."[14]

Despite its swimming pool the Allen garden was not expected to host a great deal of active recreation. For Charlotte Allen, who kept the garden after her 1936 divorce, it was as much a visual refreshment as it was a comfortable setting for entertaining friends.

The idea of a garden to live in — not garden in — automatically suggests thinking of it as an outdoor room, as Steele considered the Allen garden. The idea was not new. Persian gardens, Indian gardens, Moorish gardens, Roman gardens, Spanish gardens, Italian Renaissance gardens all included spaces designed as open-air rooms. And all evolved in climates that permitted living out of doors for much of the year. For small houses in such climates, particularly in towns and cities, the patio, wholly or partly enclosed by roofed spaces, was the traditional, and common-sense, answer. The patio had a history in the southern United States from Florida to California or wherever the original settlers had come from Mediterranean Europe, but until the mid-twentieth century it had little influence on garden design in other parts of the country.

In his gridiron plan the military engineer who laid out New Orleans in 1722 for its founder, the Sieur de Bienville, followed a French tradition of dividing the blocks into long deep lots. Houses were built close to the street with enclosed

The crisp green architecture of Fletcher Steele's design is still meticulously maintained by the garden's current owner as this photograph taken a few years ago demonstrates. Uninhabited, the scene is restful; but it provided a perfect theater for the parties of the sociable woman for whom it was created.

gardens behind them in the original city, now the *Vieux Carré*, or French Quarter. Its early patios or courtyards, as residents prefer to call them, were not only arranged in a distinctive manner, but they are also the best documented in this country. The city's Notarial Archives contain beautifully drawn measured plans, elevations, and perspectives of houses and gardens dating from 1802 to 1903. Attention to detail was important because these were legal documents, so they usually depict planting beds, outbuildings, wells and cisterns, arbors, trellises, and paving. That the civil engineers who drew them up often had considerable artistic talent is a bonus.[15] Earlier documents like Gonichon's 1731 map of the city confirm that the lots had been arranged almost from the beginning as they were in the nineteenth century.[16]

HERMANN-GRIMA GARDEN

The courtyard of the Hermann-Grima House is an exactingly researched restoration that brings to life the documents in the Notarial Archives. Samuel Hermann, a wealthy merchant, built his house on St. Louis Street in the French Quarter in 1831. Hermann had emigrated to the city from Germany but his wife, Emerante, came from a Louisiana family, and their property was organized according to local tradition. It was an unusually large one, a T-shaped arrangement of long, narrow lots facing St. Louis, Dauphine, and Conti Streets. In 1844, after Hermann suffered financial reverses, it became the property of the Grima family who lived there until 1921. Three years later the house and the St. Louis Street courtyard lot attached to it were purchased by the Christian Woman's Exchange to provide inexpensive housing for working women. By 1963 there was less need for such housing and the board members of C. W. E. undertook the restoration of the house and the courtyard. Their research has been meticulous and ongoing. If new information indicates changes, they make them.

The Notarial Archives yielded building contracts and correspondence, but no plans. Fortunately the detached service wing remained intact, as did the 1831 flagstone paving and the outlines of the raised flowerbeds in the courtyard. Archaeological examination revealed a layer of brick paving and flowerbeds in the same long, narrow shape predating the Hermanns' ownership as well as a brick cooling pond and the foundation of the iron cistern. Excavation and analysis of the bricks indicated that the small building in the left rear corner of the courtyard had been built around 1790 as a stable. Researchers feel that it may have had a different use in later periods as the Hermanns had much larger stables in the Dauphine Street lot. Since it and the Conti Street lot are not owned by the C. W. E., archaeological examination has not been possible; but from her study of the Notarial Archives Suzanne Turner, the historian and landscape architect who designed the preservation plan for the courtyard, feels a good guess about their function can be made:

A feature that becomes obvious in the layout of larger lots comparable to the Hermann-Grima property is the careful way that the site was zoned according to use.

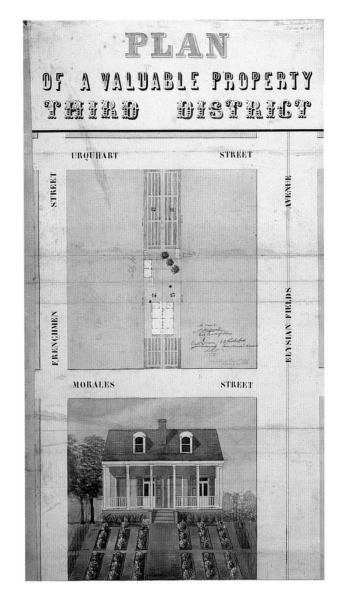

The less sightly household areas (privies, drying yards, woodpiles, etc.) were located at the farthest corners of the lot and walls and outbuildings were used to screen the more intensive work areas (stables, animal coops, vegetable gardens etc.) from the house and the main courtyard.[17]

The courtyard nearest the house may have contained the most ornamental plantings; but it also had to accommodate a great many practical activities. An examination of the structures in the Hermann-Grima Courtyard will give some idea of what these were. At the right rear corner is a giant cast-iron rainwater cistern, the source of household water for cooking, drinking, clothes- and dish-washing. Water from the well was usually too polluted—the city is almost at sea level so the water table is very high—to be used for anything except irrigating plants, cleaning flagstones, and putting out fires. The detached service wing is divided at ground level into an ironing room, a stair hall, a kitchen, a washroom for dishes, and a wine room with no interior openings from room to room. Obviously the courtyard was a much-used corridor, and a good bit of the cooking and washing likely spilled out into it.

Open wooden galleries connect the servants' (probably slaves') rooms on each of the top two floors of the service

Opposite, top:
When restoration of the Hermann-Grima House courtyard began, the detached service wing was intact and the outlines of the flowerbeds visible. Rooms for cooking, washing, ironing, and storage on the ground floor of the service building demanded a garden design that was both good to look at and efficiently organized for work.

Opposite, bottom:
Suzanne Turner, the landscape architect for the restoration, framed the raised brick-edged beds with clipped evergreen privet and, in the beginning, lined up kumquat trees down the center of each. Roses, which the Grima family is known to have grown, have replaced some kumquats since a large magnolia's demise let more sun into the garden.

This page:
In the absence of specific documents, watercolors like this image of an early nineteenth-century Creole front yard in the New Orleans Notarial Archives gave restorers information on how the long narrow beds, a distinctively local pattern also shown on courtyard layouts, might have been planted.

249

Los Angeles was still primarily a Hispanic city when this engraving was made in 1857, and it shows some of the varied ways in which patios were arranged, planted, and used. If they seem rather bare and mostly utilitarian, it is because water was in short supply: The massive irrigation projects of the Americans had not yet begun.

building. Originally both floors of the main house had open galleries across the back, but the arched openings of the loggia-like ground floor one were glassed in at some later time. These gave all the members of the household sitting spaces, sheltered from the hot sun and heavy rains, to enjoy the quiet and fresh air of the courtyard. That the courtyard or at least the large paved area adjacent to the house may also have been used for entertaining is suggested in an 1833 letter quoted by Shingo Dameron Manard in her account of the garden's restoration:

> By the by I must not forget to tell you of a most magnificent soiree M. Hermann gave last week, but was unfortunately much thwarted by the weather, which that day…proved must wretchedly bad, he was thus prevented of illuminating his court, and showing his Fireworks, which had already been prepared. But nevertheless out of three hundred and fifty persons invited, very few failed to come…[18]

No research was needed to establish the configuration of the raised beds: the outlines were right there, characteristically New Orleans in their long, narrow shapes and rhythmic, not quite symmetrical placement. What had been planted in them was another matter. Other than a reference to roses in a Grima family letter, there was no documentation. Still, travelers' accounts, letters, and nurserymen's newspaper advertisements provided the restorers with considerable information on what was grown in nineteenth-century New Orleans. That colorful shrubs and flowers were prized in a city where by all accounts horticultural interest ran high

might be expected. Less common in this country and noted by all visitors was the amount of fragrance, strong fragrance, in courtyard plantings. It really is not surprising that the inhabitants planted their gardens to counter the stench of the streets in a city with a semi-tropical climate and without a sanitation system.

If the illustrations in the archives didn't provide plant lists, they did offer ideas about the ways plants were arranged in the gardens. Neatness and order were the norm: low borders of precisely clipped evergreens, trees in rows, and, a distinctive habit, single lines of one kind of plant down the centers of the beds. It takes a vigilant and skillful gardener to achieve and sustain such tidiness in a city with a semitropical climate and abundant rainfall. As Suzanne Turner points out, "Because of the rapid rate of growth, the most formal of gardens will be transformed into a veritable jungle without constant maintenance." Understandably the very luxuriance of the city's natural surroundings would create a craving for neatness even if its original settlers had not come from that land of geometric order, France.

Houses in the parts of the Southwest first settled by immigrants of Hispanic origin characteristically formed hollow squares with each room opening into the central courtyard. In the California missions the patios were much larger and more often broadly rectangular in shape with masonry arcades or wooden ramadas around the perimeter. Such layouts, sensible responses to a hot and dry climate, were customary in the Spain and Mexico of the seventeenth and eighteenth centuries, which produced the immigrants and were equally traditional in the houses and temple compounds of preColumbian Mexico and in the pueblos of New Mexico and Arizona. In addition they were prescribed by the city planning ordinances of the Spanish Laws of the Indies. In the latter case, defense was the important motivation: Within his patio's four walls, the householder could protect his family, his livestock, and his tools. What the ordinances make very clear is that patios are open-air rooms for work. They stipulate that "each house in particular shall be so built that they may keep therein their horses and work animals," and that settlers should plant their seeds "in the farmlands that may be distributed."[19]

Visual or verbal records of the household patios of California, Arizona, and New Mexico and how they were used are scarce, but the Mexican one portrayed by Frederick Law Olmsted in 1853 probably gives an accurate picture of the activities they sheltered. When he and his brother made a brief excursion across the West Texas border, their horses and mule were led through one room of their host's house into "a house-court and garden, which was inclosed by high and strong palisades." As he describes the scene,

> A fanega of maize was then sent for to feed the horses, who, meantime, were rolling on the smooth ground of the court-yard, and drinking from the acequia which divided it from the garden. In this court-yard were several walnut and fig-trees, under which our horses were fastened. . . . Various vegetables were growing in the garden, but more maize than all else. [20]

Later on, the women of the household started to prepare "dinner in a corner of the yard, building a fire, chopping up meat and vegetables, and bringing out a metate to grind corn, which they then proceeded to slap into tortillas.

At the California missions, the patios and the gardens or *huertas* were distinct spaces. In 1829 when Alfred Robinson visited the patio at Santa Barbara, which would be later turned into a garden, it was still a workplace. After visiting the garden, he wrote, "we walked into the 'patio' or square, where carpenters, saddlers, and shoe-makers were at work, and young girls spinning and preparing wool for the loom." Early drawings of missions sometimes show a well or a cistern in the patio but no trees. Eugène Duflot de Mofras who visited California in the early 1840s did find a tree-filled interior courtyard at Mission San Luis Rey de Francia, and there may have been others where they could be irrigated.

What water was available was lavished on the *huertas* and they were what drew travelers' praises. They were planted in true vernacular garden fashion with a mixture of fruit trees and bushes, vegetables, herbs, and flowers, and defended by adobe walls or thick hedges of prickly-pear cactus. George Vancouver was enchanted with Mission San Buenaventura's *huerta* in 1793:

> . . . the garden of Buena Ventura far exceeded anything I had before met with in this region. . . not one species having yet been sown, or planted, that had not flourished, and yielded its fruit in abundance, and of excellent quality.[21]

Hugo Reid, who settled near Mission San Gabriel Arcangel in 1832 was equally enthusiastic about the improvements made to its *huertas* by Padre Jose Maria Zalvidea from 1805 to 1826:

> . . . it was to him that the after splendor of San Gabriel was due. He it was who planted the large Vineyards intersected with fine walks, shaded by fruit trees of every description, and rendered still more lovely by shrubs inspersed between—who laid out the orange garden, fruit and olive orchards—built the mill and dam—made fences of tunas (*cactus opuntia*) round the fields—made hedges of rose bushes—planted trees in the Mission square, with a flower garden and sun-dial in the centre. . .[22]

If Reid's description suggests a transformation of patio into pleasure garden it seems unusually early and may have been unique, but San Gabriel did have plenty of water. The garden did not last long. As Reid himself reports, little survived the secularization and sale of the missions by the Mexican government in 1834. In a few cases priests did build gardens within the patios, for example, the patio at Santa Barbara, transformed sometime after 1840 by Francisco Garcia Diego y Moreno, Bishop of the Two Californias.[23] But not immediately. Sir George Simpson of the Hudson's Bay Company visited a year or so later and reported that the monks were just beginning to weed and prune the neglected fruit trees in the walled five- or six- acre *huerta*, which was still producing a wide variety of vegetables and flowers.[24] Photographs of the Santa Barbara patio laid out as a garden, dating from the 1890s, were widely published and they did a lot to create the myth of the mission flower garden. Indeed flowers were grown at the missions. Some show up in analyses of adobe bricks. More important, if tantalizingly vague, is an entry that mentions flower seeds on a list of supplies sent to establish the first mission at San Diego in 1769.[25] But documents and common sense alike suggest that flowers were grown in the *huerta*. In the patio they would simply have been a snack for overnighting horses.

In ranch and town houses, the blending of the enclosed courtyard and the fruit-and-flower-filled *huerta* into the popular image of the romantic California patio celebrated by Helen Hunt Jackson in *Ramona* and in her 1883 articles for *The Century* magazine took form only after the Americans took over.

> In the western suburbs of Los Angeles is a low adobe house, built after the ancient style, on three sides of a square, surrounded by orchards, vineyards, and orange groves, and looking out on an old-fashioned garden, in which southernwood, rue, lavender, mint, marigolds, and gillyflowers hold their own bravely, growing in straight and angular beds among the newer splendors of verbenas, roses, carnations, and geraniums. On two sides of the house runs a broad porch, where stand rows of geraniums growing in odd-shaped earthen pots. . . . Whoever has the fortune to pass as a friend

In the space between the house and cottage (just beyond the right edge of the photograph) Church laid out planting beds around the existing gnarled native live oaks at Wild Horse Valley Ranch. Like his modernist peers, Church had no qualms about using ordinary materials in his designs, witness the asphalt that paves the open center of the courtyard.

across the threshold of this house finds himself transported, as by a miracle into the life of a half-century ago.[26]

Even twenty years ago may be stretching it, but it represents a more likely time span for such a patio than fifty. Yet, this is the image that guided most restorations of mission patios and private gardens in the late nineteenth and early twentieth centuries.

Like its East Coast counterpart, the Mission Revival style produced some very appealing gardens; but unfamiliar to many California immigrants, Mission Revival often lost out to the typical American open front lawn and backyard plan. The mid-twentieth century creators of the modern California garden—Church, Eckbo, Royston, Baylis, Halprin—had little use for either approach: One imitated the past, the other gave no privacy. But their gardens, which became the models for the post-World War II American backyard, descend from the Mission-Revival patio. Not in its details, but in its principles. It was the traditional expression of the idea that a garden should be enclosed, an extension of the house that served as both an open-air space for daily activities and an attractive setting for those activities. What the California landscape architects did was rethink the enclosed yard in terms of what twentieth-century families wanted to do in it. Some wanted sandboxes, swings, and bike paths for children that could be easily reworked when outgrown. Some wanted swimming pools, others were content with fountains or ornamental pools. Many wanted cooking areas, particularly places to grill meat and fish. And almost all wanted space and a good surface for tables and chairs. Given the amount of sunlight that made their year-round outdoor living possible, all wanted some degree of shade. They also wanted plants, but unless gardening was a hobby, they didn't want to spend much time on them. The titles of Church's and Eckbo's books, *Gardens Are For People* and *Landscape For Living* sum up the new approach.

In the hands of gifted designers who really knew their plants, even a seemingly self-contradictory wish list could be turned into a green and pleasant garden.

WILD HORSE VALLEY RANCH

A case in point is the garden created by Thomas Church for Mary Gary Harrison and her daughter and son-in-law, Edna and Don Murray, at Wild Horse Valley Ranch in the Napa Valley. In 1968, Church was at the height of his career and extremely busy. Persuasion was needed to convince him to take on the project, but it helped that the Murrays and Mrs Harrison had commissioned as architects for the house Wurster, Bernardi, and Emmons with whom Church had often collaborated.

The site was a hilltop commanding spectacular vistas to Mt. St. Helena at the far north, to Mt. Tamalpais and the tip of the Golden Gate Bridge to the south, then east to Mt. Diablo. The program was complicated. The house would have to serve at once as a country retreat for Mrs. Harrison, to be used from time to time, and a full-time residence for the Murrays, their three very active children, and a pack of

The splendid site chosen for the house and garden at Wild Horse Valley Ranch overlooks a landscape of hills, streams, woods, pastures, and distant ocean. The view from the rooftop also takes in such designed elements as the swimming pool and tennis courts, and the tangle of mostly native plants that cloaks the hillside.

Lower right:
Garrett Eckbo's redesign of his own property on commission from ALCOA in 1956 to test the potential of aluminum for garden structures became an instant icon of modern garden design. But it unintentionally reinforced the perception that constructed elements—hardscaping—were more important than plants.

Opposite:
Eckbo used standard, easily available aluminum fabrications—sheets, meshes, panels, rods, channels, and miscellaneous extrusions—to create complexly patterned screened pavilions.

pets, mostly dogs. The Murrays' twenty-six horses were stabled elsewhere on the property. What Willard Rand, the associate in charge—Wurster was in poor health—produced was two separate houses. For Mrs. Harrison he set a cottage on the western edge of the hilltop. For the Murrays he cantilevered a generous house over its southern brow, and then connected the two with a covered wooden walk on the north and east sides. This left an irregular court to be planted as a buffer between them, but it did not address all the challenges in the program. Church's landscaping would have to accommodate several different kinds of activities. If he placed a swimming pool on the hilltop there really wouldn't be room for anything else, so he set the pool into the hill a quarter mile below the house, where it had the same outlook but a different angle on the view. He laid out a separate area east of the big house so that dogs and children could spill out for strenuous play, leaving the courtyard to be shaped into a quiet garden with a generous central space in which tables and chairs could be set for adult luncheons or dinner parties. Here the view is withheld until you reach the steps that lead down to the pool or those up to the deck of the big house.

Church worked quickly and confidently. Mrs. Harrison told Phoebe Cutler that their three or four meetings at the ranch were "always and only at 6 AM. Tommy was a man of such great vision; he could look at a spot and see its potential. He never overwhelmed the natural beauty. He would enlarge it, center it and enhance it."[27] Working in the middle of construction debris from the almost-finished house he marked the seven gnarled oaks and the rock outcroppings to be saved as the bones of the design and laid out the planting beds with string and pieces of garden hose. He directed that the asphalt surface of the

parking area north of the compound be continued right through the courtyard, and it makes a handsome and restful background for the mix of textures and the harmonious blend of greens and grays and silvers that characterize the garden.

Plants had to be tough: the site was exposed to sun and wind, and they would not be pampered. Although the hill had been encircled with a deer-and-snake-resistant fence topped with fire-control sprinklers, there was still considerable potential for wildlife damage. Church knew his plants and knew the territory well. Both he and the local nurseryman and contractor, Leroy Lund, with whom he had worked previously and to whom he entrusted the planting, preferred to emphasize texture and leaf color.

Although the plants used were suited to Napa's Mediterranean climate—rainy winters, hot and dry summers—they did not include as many natives as Church would have liked, according to a post-planting inspection form consulted by Phoebe Cutler.[28] Taking into account the usual adjustments over time, they have held up well. When it came to the pool area Church's favorite native manzanita was combined with *Juniperus chinensis* 'Pfitzerana,' Australian grevillea, and Scotch broom to form a loose hedge. The hardscape materials are simple and typical of Church's work: a redwood deck and benches, and, surrounding the seventy-five-foot-long pool, exposed-aggregate concrete squares with redwood spacers.

ALCOA GARDEN

Church and his younger contemporaries like Eckbo, Halprin, and Royston were comfortable working with common materials, and really interested in new ones. A famous example is Garrett Eckbo's ALCOA Forecast Garden. In 1956 Aluminum Company of America's advertising agency asked Eckbo if he would consider exploring ways to use aluminum in the garden. He agreed to do so, using his own garden for his experiments. The metal, he found, had lots of advantages: It was easy to work, lightweight, didn't rust, and, if anodized, was highly resistant to corrosion. But it had one drawback for garden use: The heat conductivity that made it good for cookware eliminated its use for plant trellises. In his

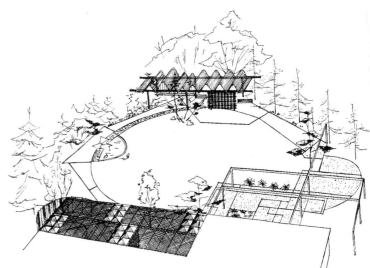

finished design, which was widely publicized in 1960, he created practical screening in complex patterns using standard aluminum fabrications.

To shade the sun-baked terrace between the living room and the studio, he built a roof of expanded aluminum mesh supported by a simple wood frame like that of the house. In four of the panels, triangular sheets of mesh were formed into rows of open pyramids, making the shifting patterns of light and shade still more intricate. A vertical expanded metal screen in the middle of the terrace veiled the view of the living room from the studio, and a curving fence of mixed mesh and solid panels closed off the studio end of the terrace. Anodized in shades of gold and bronze, the aluminum panels suited the house and made an attractive background for Eckbo's varied collection of plants.

Directly across the garden from the house, he built an open pavilion supported, again, with simple wooden framing. Waves of mesh in its natural aluminum color formed a ceiling of subtly varied silvery vaults. The fence along the back and a screen panel in front added two more patterns, anodized in gold. A concrete path, its exposed aggregate varying in color and texture, circled the lawn and linked house and pavilion. Midway between them on the eastern side it was interrupted by another Eckbo aluminum creation: a green-enameled fountain shaped like an origami flower, with waterspouts for stamens.

The ALCOA garden's extensive television and magazine exposure did not translate into aluminum latticework, however practical, dappling suburban backyards. Indeed the metal found its greatest acceptance cast or extruded into garden chairs, tables, and chaises, many quite traditional in style. The very complexity of Eckbo's constructions made them rather daunting models for most garden-makers, amateur or professional. What the garden's design really brought to the country's attention was the new aesthetic based on modern art and architecture. Given its sponsorship, hardscape—the current term for built forms—dominates the ALCOA garden. That was not always true of Eckbo's gardens and he wrote eloquently about plants and the way they shape space:

> Plant material, as an aggregation of units of unlimited variety in form, size, color and texture, has esthetic possibilites which have scarcely been scratched. The variety and richness of plants as a material for creative organization are limited only by questions of culture and maintenance, and by the scope and freedom of the plan conception.[29]

SHULMAN GARDEN

In his friend and neighbor, the distinguished architectural photographer Julius Shulman, Eckbo found just the kind of owner that O. C. Simonds had called for. Shulman not only loves plants but knows how to grow and place them.

In 1947, Shulman bought a two-acre hillside property, 1300 feet above sea level in a Los Angeles canyon. Free-way construction was accelerating in those years and the highway department wanted decomposed granite for substructure. As they excavated in the then uninhabited canyons they left behind flat pads, giving house builders a jump-start on grading. Shulman's was one hundred feet wide by forty feet deep, parallel to and backed on the north by a high hill. He commissioned Raphael Soriano to design a house for him and his wife and daughter and at the same time began consulting Eckbo on a landscape plan. The existing pad was not quite large enough for the house Soriano designed. To enlarge the pad and as a safety measure, Eckbo's site design called for the scrub-covered hill to be cut back forty-five degrees. Then began the construction of narrow terraces for planting, using broken concrete to form the undulating retaining walls. A neighbor's gardener had been building such walls; Shulman and Eckbo liked the way they looked. The terracing of the whole hillside took ten years to complete, but planting began as soon as there were terraces to plant.

The plan Shulman and Eckbo agreed on appears almost unstructured: some shaping of the land to make a slightly rolling lawn, a curving plant bed along the south edge, a low concrete retaining wall extending out from the house-long terrace, and a paved patio backed by a small pool between the house and Shulman's studio. Just the kind of simplicity that offers tremedous scope for development by a dedicated gardener.

That development has been continuous over the last fifty years and it has turned Soriano's rather austere modern house into a jungle pavilion. Shulman divides his jungle's progress into three stages. Early on he trained wisteria on the overhang to shade the living room and now it almost covers the south façade. By stage two the planting beds had matured and the lawn had become a pleasing flow of green between them. The effect, however attractive, became too difficult and time-consuming to maintain. Shulman turned the lawn into a brick terrace and path, the free-form planting areas into stepped rectangular brick-walled raised beds.

On the hillside, the grove of *Eucalyptus citriodora* planted by Eckbo seemed a bit lonely in the beginning as the slender trunks towered over seedling Monterey, Canary Island, and Aleppo pines, but the latter soon stretched up into a dark green backdrop for them. As the trees grew and plantings thickened Shulman threaded a series of trails, almost invisible from a distance, up and across the hill. On the open terraces and even under the trees he planted succulents as ground-covers: *Agaves americana* and *attenuata*, crassula, yuccas. If some of these seem large for that kind of use, the scale of the hill is such that the planting works visually as well as it does environmentally. The hillside has so far absorbed even the most torrential rains without run off, and it passes the yearly fire department landscape inspection with flying colors.

When Shulman proudly tells you that the redwoods he planted as twenty-eight-inch seedlings in 1959 are now eighty-five feet tall, with one five feet in diameter, you wonder what makes them thrive in a place with such hot, dry summers. The answer is that he discovered a small damp canyon about two hundred feet from the west end of the house where winter rains collected, and built a series of small pools that he can irrigate if the water supply gets too low. "The animals and birds love it. We've seen more than 75 dif-

In l947 Julius Shulman bought two acres in a canyon north of Los Angeles. His friend and landscape architect, Garrett Eckbo, came up with the simple plan shown when planting is beginning: concrete paths and low retaining wall to shape the lawn south of the house designed by Raphael Soriano, with a paved patio between the house and studio.

As the garden matured, ferns, flowers, and Shulman's favorite succulents filled expanding plant beds. Straight lines had swelled into curves, the lawn had lost ground, and even the house seemed camouflaged by shrubs and vines deployed for sun control. But at this stage the landscape was too hard to maintain even for its plant-loving owner.

Plants still rule in the garden's current stage; but they have been simplified and disciplined. A brick terrace and ramp and brick-edged raised beds replaced the lawn. Essentials planted early on remain: the wisteria over the screened area and the seventy-foot ficus tree in the nearest bed, both of which provide crucial shade to the house.

Opposite, top: Retaining walls of dry-laid broken concrete slabs anchor the contours of the hillside behind the house, creating flat spaces for planting beds and paths. In the first phase of development Eckbo chose the grove of graceful *Eucalyptus citriodora*, Shulman selected the conifers: Monterey pines in the foreground, baby Aleppo pines behind the eucalyptus.

Opposite, bottom: After years of growth, the eucalyptus trees are barely visible against the massive swell of Aleppo pines. Now the flower spikes of native yucca provide vertical accents in season, one of the several species of drought- and fire-resistant succulents that dominate the hillside plantings.

ferent species." It is not visible from the house and to reach it you have to follow a curving path designed to keep it concealed until you reach it.

Although Shulman found Eckbo "a very good advisor," they parted company over plant choices, particularly trees. Eckbo tended to prefer deciduous trees like sycamores and Brazilian pepper trees; Shulman evergreens, particularly pines. There were some practical reasons — evergreens provide shade and privacy all year — but emotional reasons seem stronger. "I spent my first ten years in a forest-surrounded farm in Connecticut, and after we moved to Los Angeles I was active in the Boy Scouts. I've always immersed myself in nature."[30] Now, having achieved optimum immersion, Shulman is engaged in removing selected branches to open up vistas through his jungle to the mountains and valley beyond.

As nineteenth-century writers like Downing had assured their readers, the small suburban garden can provide its owner with a large enough canvas for a lifetime of garden making. And since it began to engage their interest in the twentieth century, few landscape architects have been willing to give up commissions for private gardens, even small ones, no matter how many large public works they are called on to design. Many would echo Michael Van Valkenburgh's opinion that private gardens are smaller, and within limits always lies potential. "Even if they are not smaller, they nearly always happen faster. The work usually starts within a year. You can get your ideas out and get them built."

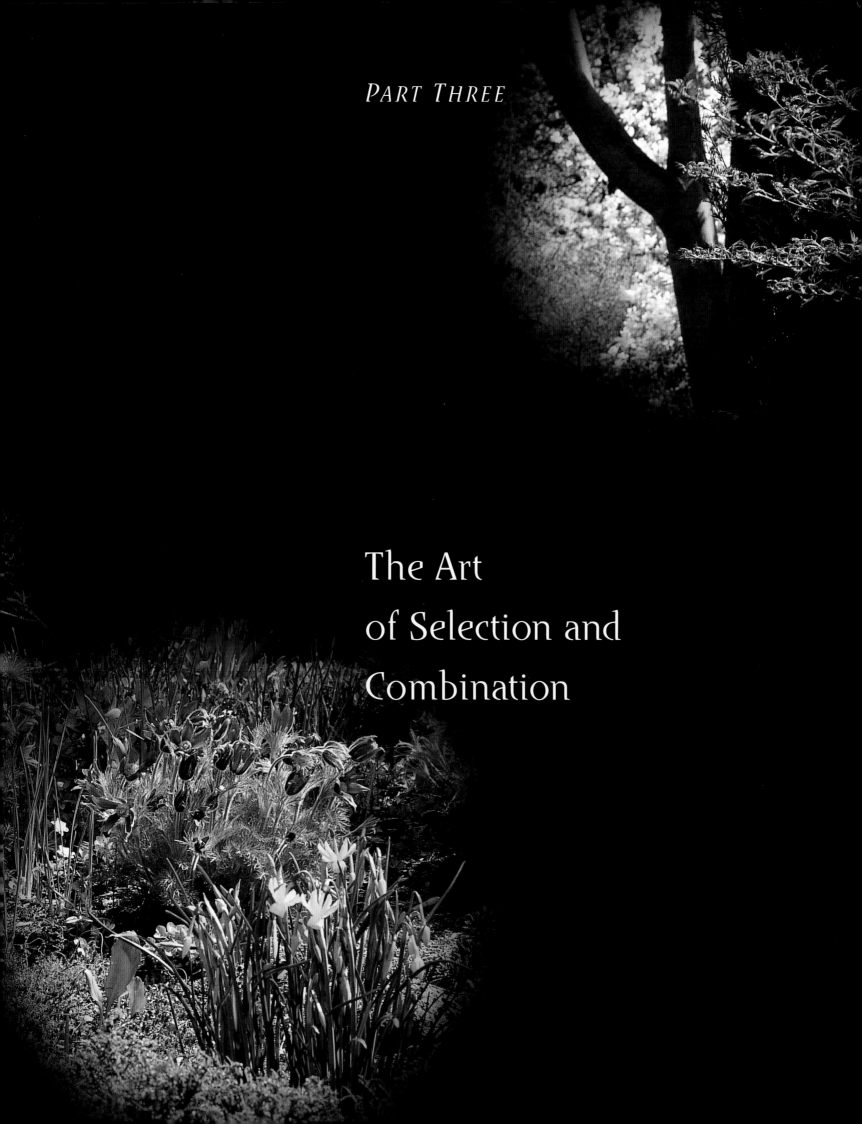

PART THREE

The Art
of Selection and
Combination

Four Portfolios of Twentieth-Century Gardens

A garden, or any designed landscape for that matter, cannot be a pure artistic expression for its creator in the way that a painting or a piece of sculpture can. It is subject to continual change by the forces of nature, and it is subject to the evolving needs of its owners, whether they make it or commission it. But because a very powerful one of those needs seems to be for order, and for the pleasure that comes from achieving order, looking at gardens in this country from the standpoint of artistry in design can be revealing even though artistry is not the whole story. If nothing else, it is fascinating to see how various are the ways in which individuals shape an order that pleases them. There are patterns that persist or recur after lapsing, a continuing tilt in the direction of usefulness, and above all, there is an American Attitude. You might call it "anything goes," but it is more discerning than that. American garden-makers never hesitate to borrow from other countries or cultures or eras, or to experiment with the newest idea they see in the media. But they are perfectly willing to break a composition up into its components, reorganize them, combine them with other design ideas, and adjust them to circumstances that seem polar opposites to their original employment. Both the natural world and created landscapes are simply considered resources to draw on.

Earlier chapters have analyzed the influences, precedents, strategies, concerns, and goals that American garden-makers have gathered into their design repertoire over the last four centuries. Let us now look at some of the ways in which some twentieth-century designers have drawn on that repertoire. Twentieth-century gardens did appear in those earlier chapters, but in those cases, the gardens, however distinctive in their final form, were developed primarily according to a single approach. Each of those that follow draws on several different elements to compose an original artistic expression. In all of these gardens, identifying sources of inspiration can add a fillip to appreciation, but it is the whole that is satisfying and memorable.

With black granite paths and glass boulders on a rectangular panel of blue glass gravel set in baby's tears, Topher Delaney's Garden of Historicism interprets Oriental ideas in a very modern way.

Recycling
The Past

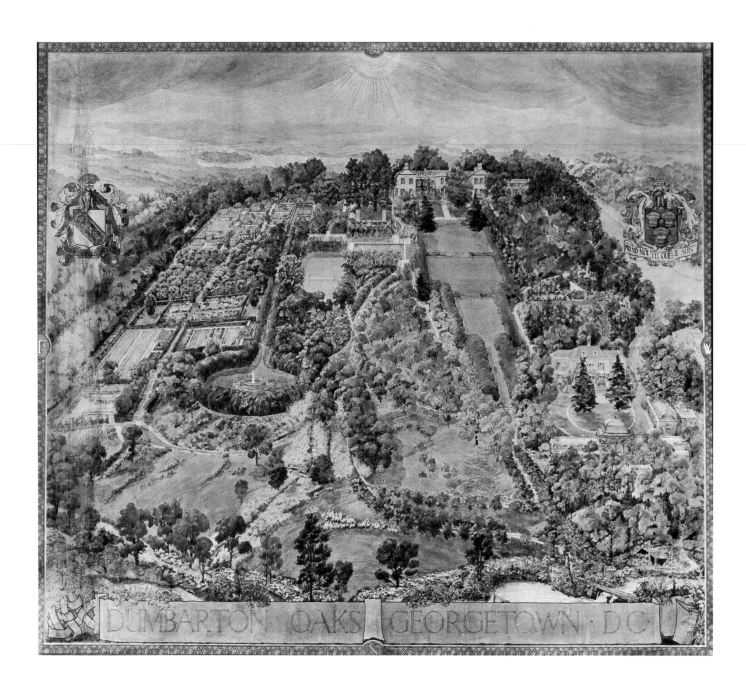

Preceding page:
"Nothing will ever be quite as beautiful as the rumpled masses of the Box as they follow the slope of the hill," Farrand wrote of the Box Walk. They have not needed replacement as has the boxwood that in her day walled the Ellipse at the hill's base, today delineated by an aerial hedge of pleached, precisely clipped hornbeam.

Above:
The garden as originally planned in a topographical view painted by Ernest Clegg in 1935 not long after Ambassador Bliss retired and he and his wife could live in and enjoy their new country estate in town. The structure remains nearly intact although many details have been changed: The Pebble Garden has replaced the tennis court, the naturalistic garden along the stream was given to the National Parks System.

DUMBARTON OAKS

According to its owner, next to her own garden in Maine, Dumbarton Oaks was Beatrix Farrand's favorite among all the gardens she made in her long career. When Ambassador and Mrs. Robert Woods Bliss bought the twenty-seven acre property in the Georgetown section of Washington, D. C. it had some fine trees as well as a much-added-to 1801 house on a high bluff from which the land sloped down in several directions. The gardens were created between 1922 and 1933, although the process of design refinement went on for thirty more years. In her last *Reef Point Gardens Bulletin* Farrand wrote, in the third person, that "as years passed she tried to heed Professor Sargent's advice to make the plan fit the ground and not twist the ground to fit a plan, and further-more to study the tastes of the owner."[1] At Dumbarton Oaks she did just that, although the ground was difficult, the own-ers had very definite preferences, and were absent on diplo-matic missions during many years of its creation. Fortunately

respect was mutual and mock-ups made and studied in place until agreement was reached. So close was the collaboration between Farrand and Mildred Bliss that the garden should be considered their joint handiwork. What these two perfectionists achieved was a seamless synthesis of European references and American appreciation of natural growth patterns in a series of outdoor rooms and terraces that turned a steep hillside and valley into a garden that simultaneously evokes serenity and invites exploration.

Separating their roles is not easy, but Mildred Bliss wanted a landscape that would have a sense of history behind it and remind her of gardens she had visited in Europe. She also had a real love of garden ornament. Beatrix Farrand gave the landscape its physical structure, and for her plants were fundamental to the design. Given her great horticultural knowledge, she was remarkably sparing in the number of different plants she used. It was her masterful ability to blend

and contrast shades and textures of green, and to weave them through and around the architectonic spaces that gives the landscape both unity and mystery. One is enticed to move through it to see just what surprise is around the corner. At times she shaped trees and shrubs, at others she let them grow free. Her compositions were varied but balanced, symmetrical at times, asymmetrical more often, and punctuated when needed with a single bold stroke like the monumental black oak that dominates the Green Garden.

The visions and the reasoning behind the decisions made by client and designer are explored in detail in *Beatrix Farrand's Plant Book for Dumbarton Oaks* which includes an appreciation by Mildred Bliss.[2] Beatrix Farrand wrote this remarkable book in 1941, the year after the Blisses gave the estate to Harvard University, as a guide to dealing with the changes that inevitably overtake a garden. If only all great gardens had such a guide!

On axis with the original 1801 block of the house, the North Vista reaches out to mixed evergreen and deciduous woods in three diminishing panels of lawn. The pruned magnolias and vines against the house show Farrand's skill in managing wall plantings.

Left:
The view west from a corner of the Green Garden across the Swimming Pool Terrace toward the wall embracing the North Vista gives a sense of the way that the walled gardens are stepped down the hill. In the foreground the limestone urn, imaginatively designed in the classical idiom, probably by Farrand's associate, Ruth Havey, epitomizes the quality of the stone and brickwork throughout the garden.

Overleaf:
Adapted from one in Rome, the secluded little outdoor theater with its beautiful brickwork and oval Lovers Lane Pool, is the most romantic of the individual gardens. At the far end, graceful silver maples arch over a path called Melisande's Allée that winds down toward the stream and what was once the naturalistic garden on the other side of it.

Above:
Forsythia Dell forms an early spring cascade of yellow between the rosy froths of Cherry Hill to the west and Crabapple Hill to the east. Farrand used such spectacular but short-lived swaths of color rarely and in the more informal parts of the garden at a distance from the house.

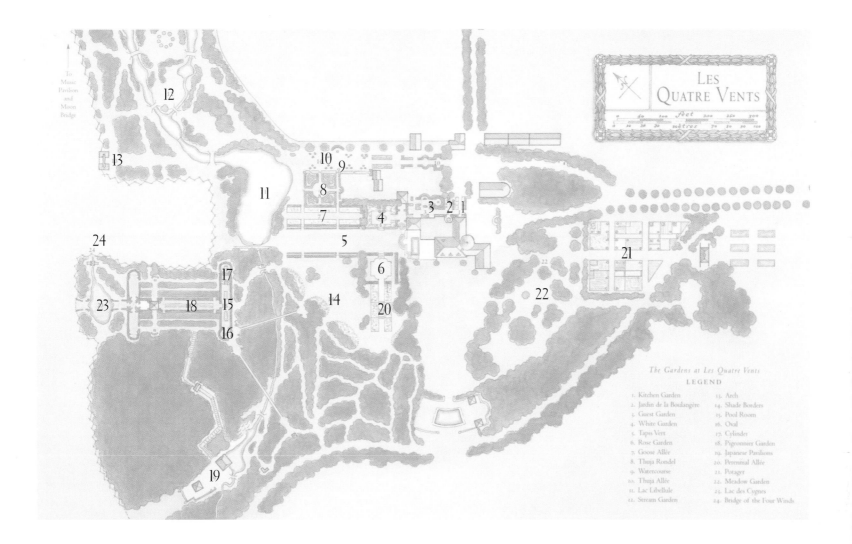

The Gardens at Les Quatre Vents
LEGEND

LES QUATRE VENTS

Not many private gardens on a truly grand scale were built in the last half of the twentieth century, but Francis H. Cabot's Les Quatre Vents is a notable exception, and given the energy and curiosity of its owner and creator it is probably not finished yet. He is, after all, the man who founded The Garden Conservancy, a break-through organization that helps the creators of outstanding American gardens find ways to preserve them. More than the actual acreage of his estate it is the diversity of its parts and the complexity of its organization that make it impossible to do more than sample its treasures. Much of its fascinating story must also be omitted in favor of a brief analysis of what makes it is so successful a garden of collections. Fortunately Cabot himself has written a charming, personal, and very illuminating history, *The Greater Perfection*, telling of his family's summer home in Quebec and of his struggles and triumphs in developing and expanding its gardens since he inherited it in 1965.

He could well be called "Capability" Cabot, since he seems to find any piece of land he looks at capable of being shaped into a delightful experience. He may simply open up a trail in the boreal forest, or satisfy the urge for a new and different garden by encroaching on the "unlimited encroachable space in the surrounding fields."[3] At the same time he has an omnivorous appetite for design ideas and garden structures wherever he finds them — Europe, the Orient, the United States. The follies at Les Quatre Vents bring into

modern times a long tradition that extends back at least as far as the Roman Empire. He'll tell you right away where an inspiration came from, but by the time it has passed through his imagination and been fitted to his land it has become truly his. Cabot considers himself primarily a horticulturist, and indeed he is a passionate and expert one. The growing season at Les Quatre Vents may be short but he takes full advantage of the deep-snowed winters and cool, misty summers of his Zone 4 climate. His perennials are spectacular. So are his collections of rarities, alpines, primulas, and prized Himalayan finds. Collections upon collections, but all orchestrated into a symphony.

Nearest to the house, Cabot has kept much of the landscape design made by his parents with the help of two of his uncles, an architect and an artist, but refined and embellished it. It is strongly axial and view-oriented as suits the French-style mansion, and composed for the most part of hedge-enclosed garden rooms. On the whole he has followed the same principles in creating his new gardens and garden-complexes even when they are at some distance and screened from the house. Hedges are formed mostly from the native thuja, which takes well to shearing; poplars serve as accents. These two species have a strong unifying presence in the garden, particularly thuja, both clipped and allowed to grow naturally, which also helps tie the designed landscape back to its forest and field surroundings.

Plan of Les Quatre Vents:

Opposite:
Francis Cabot inherited the sequence of gardens on the north-south cross axis just below the house. It runs from the Perennial Allée in the foreground to the hedge-enclosed Rose Garden, just visible at the top of the steps, picks up again across the *Tapis Vert*—the axial green carpet to the western view of the Laurentians—with the White Garden. Cabot has rebuilt the stonework, and greatly increased the variety and beauty of the plantings.

Left:
One isolated spot in the ravine reminded Cabot of Japanese landscapes, and he decided to build a Japanese pavilion as a quiet retreat. Patience was in order. The Japanese master carpenter who consented to build it required seven years, beginning with the choice of trees to cut for lumber. In fact, he built a platform with two pavilions of different dimensions. Cabot made paths, stepping stones, and a waterfall, but did not attempt a Japanese garden, which he feels does not translate well to this country.

This pigeonnier is for people, not pigeons, although its form was inspired by just such a traditional French farm structure. Rather, it serves as a view-shaper and as the linchpin for a complex of archchitectonic hedged garden rooms and water features. In its upper stories is an apartment with great charm and a glorious view.

The slope of the land dictated the shape and layout of the south-facing Potager's raised beds. Anne Cabot plants ornamental kales and cabbages to center the bed devoted to brassicas, and rings them with their edible cousins. She designs all the beds so that the harvest leaves them decorative, not desolate, but in a different pattern of flowers and vegetables each year.

Just as carefully designed and planted but informal in character are the spaces around a chain of lakes and brooks channeled from a stream that S-curves along the northwestern edge of the designed landscape, dropping into a ravine at one point. It took Cabot seven years to create a home for woodland perennials. He had to remove spruces killed by budworm, thin deciduous species, install barriers to separate prized specimens from aggressive natives, make trails, and devise irrigation methods. The result: a collection of meconopsis species to pale with envy most Americans who can't grow them, and primulas that bloom from May to October.

Anne Cabot, his wife, is the mistress of the Potager yet another garden type. It is she who designs its changing ornamental and productive patterns of fruit, vegetables, and flowers to cut. She also devised an evergreen knot garden outside the dining-room window, and a star mosaic in the patio of the Pigeonnier.

However tightly controlled at the core, the gardens at Les Quatre Vents are not really organized as a simple progression of spaces from strictly to loosely structured. The itinerary of a garden visit as designed by Cabot is very personal, but it effectively composes the garden as a series of contrasting experiences, with spots for rest and contemplation and lots of surprises, visual, aural, and kinetic along the way. And ideally a whole additional visit should be made just to appreciate the plantsmanship displayed.

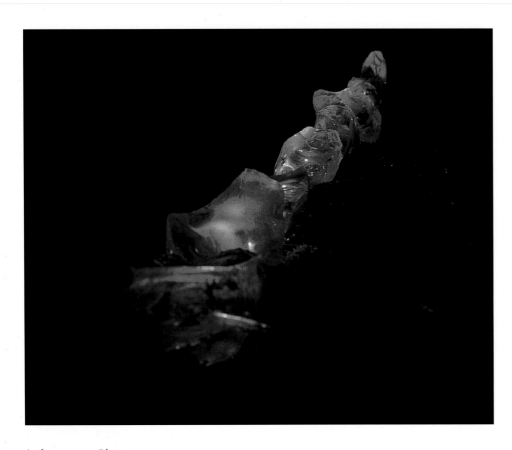

Art, architecture, and garden history form a reciprocally enriching triumvirate in a Palo Alto garden designed by Topher Delaney. The property is a bit less than an acre and it is packed with references, some straightforward, others ironic or punning. They don't strike you right away; it's the technology that dazzles first. Open the stainless steel and sandblasted glass front gate after dark and you are greeted by green glowing "boulders" of rough glass. The green is courtesy of fiberoptic lighting; seen in daylight the boulders are blue: the rocks of Ryoangi transmuted into glass for the entrance to a glass and steel house, or as she calls the space "Ryoangi à go-go."[4] But she has made no attempt to group these rocks in Japanese style, and you might well miss the allusion unless told.

The story is interesting. Eight years ago, Delaney created the back garden for a couple of dedicated gardeners. They loved the garden but eventually found the house inadequate. Instead of moving, they kept the garden and bulldozed the house, then hired Anne Fougeron, an architect recommended by Delaney, to make them a new one. To Delaney and to her clients the house Fougeron created suggested a contemporary interpretation of Paxton's Crystal Palace or a greenhouse, hence the lumps of cullet glass in the entry garden, the raw material from which the building's skin was fashioned. Design decisions were not always taken for aesthetic or symbolic reasons. The local government required that all water be drained on the site: no runoff allowed. The rectangular bed of glass gravel in the front garden helps solve that problem handsomely. A glittery base for glass boulders, it is also an eight-foot-deep French drain.

As if to announce "this is a green garden" the naturally blue boulders of rough glass glow green at nightfall, thanks to fiberoptics. The entry garden's narrow and subdued range of color, black and gray, green and blue hints at its Oriental inspiration.

Right:
From the entrance door, a polished slab of black granite runs through the courtyard and house to the back garden. In an allusion to the scholar's walk in a Chinese garden, a narrow serpentine path of the same black granite branches from the straight and wide, winding through a field of baby's tears to meet the crenellated wheelbarrow walk from the back garden.

On the other side of the house, the black granite slab forms a terrace flanked by billowing hedges of lavender, dappled with shade from a non-fruiting olive tree. Hidden paths in the lavender perpendicular to the terrace lead in one direction to an herb garden, in the opposite one to a fountain and a grid of calla lilies.

Vine-hung walls of metal mesh punctuated by cypresses mark the garden's boundaries. Another mesh wall hosts bougainvillea, trumpet vines, and climbing red roses, and delineates the trapezoidal garden room carpeted in lavender gravel from Barstow, California. The room expands in width from a foot at its northern end to twenty feet at the southern one, and the five openings in the wall range from one foot to five feet to give it the punning name of "gromen" in honor of its role as a sundial.

In the earlier garden at the rear, California's Mediterranean climate took a lead role in both space shaping and planting design. The site was flat, which made creating interesting outdoor spaces a challenge. Delaney placed low stucco walls to suggest terraces. Tall ochre and chartreuse panels call up Italian farmyards and the landscapes of the Mexican architect, Luis Barragán; lavender, olive trees, cypresses, and Seville orange trees in pots offer the scents and colors of Provence. A fence tapestried with bright blooming vines marks off a trapezoidal garden room, and there are rose and herb gardens.

The two gardens are a study in contrasts. The cool entry garden seems to call for slow and meditative motion. The warm and colorful courtyard invites all kinds of activities, from quiet contemplation to active sports.

At its southern end Delaney set a polished pink concrete pavement into the decomposed granite surface of the central court. Free-standing stucco walls set off one part for an orangerie. Across the court's northern end she built a raised bed for roses and in front of this "American Rose Garden" she lined up what appears to be a procession of wooden cubes. In fact, their square façades disguise their transformation by degrees from cubes to triangular polyhedrons.

Structuring The Small Garden

Preceding page:
Framing the view from the cottage toward the street—hidden by the overlapping yellow wall and the louvered fence—the arching fronds of *Dypsis cabadae*, an unusual small palm from Madagascar, contrast with the large yellow-splotched leaves of *Codiaeum variegatum* 'General Paget' to the right. Blocks of soft orange stone pave a serrated path through the black pebble mulch on the plant beds, a handsome water-conserving measure that Jungles employs throughout the grounds.

Plan: Overlapping walls and fences structure the enclosed gardens around the house but do not close in the space. Streetside plantings are just as colorful as interior ones.

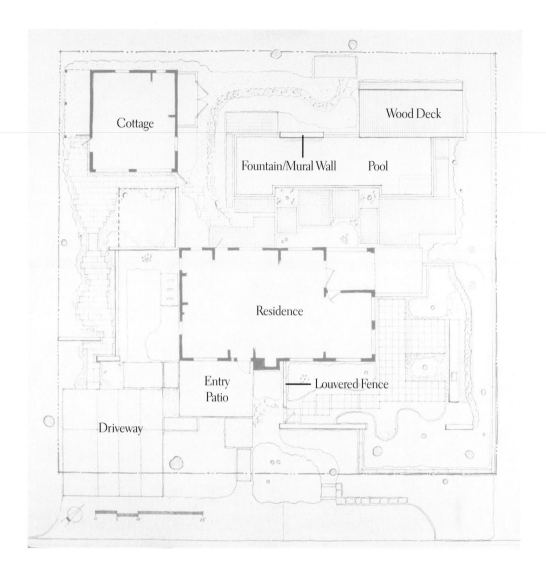

JUNGLES/YATES GARDEN

With his love of tropical and subtropical vegetation, and his home base in Florida, Raymond Jungles seems perfectly named for the landscape architecture profession, but jungle plants in the gardens he designs are held within a disciplined framework. He names Luis Barragán and the Brazilian painter and landscape architect Roberto Burle Marx as major influences on his approach to garden design. In fact both Jungles and his wife Debra Yates, an artist, revere Burle Marx as a mentor, and they traveled to Brazil to work and study with him almost every year. That Jungles uses some of their techniques—Barragán's colorful free-standing walls, Burle Marx's massed plantings—is apparent, but he configures and combines them in his own distinctive way.

The Key West garden created by Jungles for himself and Yates surrounds a house built by her father in the 1940s. The roughly half-acre fenced lot is divided into a series of separate but interconnected zones rotating around the house, the largest of which contains the swimming pool. Above the fountain, which faces the living-room windows is a tile mural by Burle Marx and his associate Haruyoshi Ono. This is the couple's tribute to friendship, since the fountain walls in most of Jungles' gardens are colored by Yates's bold and vibrant mosaic murals. A generous wooden deck, perfect for sunbathing, on one side of the pool balances a pattern of brick-paved squares, firm footing for tables and chairs, on the other side. Here and in the rest of the garden such hardscape elements provide a substantial counterpoint to the strong forms and patterns of its plants.

Jungles has had to meet several challenges in designing his home grounds. It holds his personal collection of tropical flora, many brought from Brazil, and it takes a good bit of self-restraint to keep a collection subordinate to design. In addition the garden serves as his laboratory for trying out new plants and ideas. His experiments would in themselves keep the garden changing without help from nature-the-bringer-of-hurricanes, which periodically decides to do some thinning. Tropical vegetation is generally large and his space is not, but the framework of walls and fences that seem to divide that space still further in fact creates multiple backgrounds to set off the sculptural forms of the plants. It is a tribute to his compositional skill that the garden, although containing more plants of more kinds than most of his commissioned projects, does not feel overcrowded.

In the foreground, pale tillandsia nestle at the foot of a palm from the Ryukyu islands, *Satakentia liukiuensis.* On the other side of the pool a vigorous allamanda vine reaches over the fountain wall to the tile mural by Roberto Burle Marx and Haruyoshi Ono. Color in this garden, as in most of Jungles' gardens, comes primarily from walls and paving. He does use some subtropical species like the *Vreisia versicolor* at the edge of the wooden deck that have brightly hued leaves, but for the most part plants are chosen for form, leaf shape, and texture. The yellow blossoms of the allamanda and the blue ones of a plumbago provide appealing accents but are not suited to playing the kind of major role that flower-color plays in an herbaceous border.

As we look across the entry patio, the open gate in the louvered fence gives a hint of the riches in the private garden beyond, among them a striking tropical black bamboo. In the street-side front garden, the vivid leaves of the shrub often called croton, *Codiaeum variegatum* 'Stoplight,' splash red against the fence. Beyond the pink wall another colorful croton cultivar joins the huge saucerlike fronds of *Licuala grandis,* the ruffled fan palm, and the swollen trunk of *Pseudophoenix vinifera,* the wine palm from Haiti.

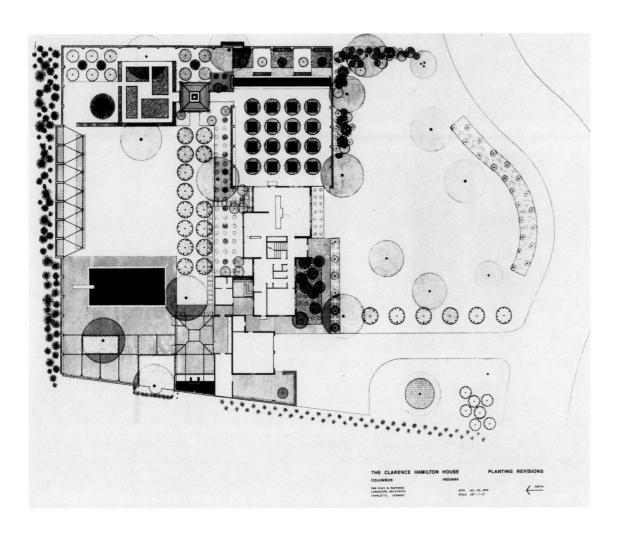

THE CLARENCE HAMILTON HOUSE   PLANTING REVISIONS

COLUMBUS   INDIANA

DAN KILEY & PARTNERS   DATE   DEC. 22, 1972
LANDSCAPE ARCHITECTS   SCALE   1/8" = 1'-0"
CHARLOTTE, VERMONT

NORTH ←

As the plan demonstrates, squares and rectangles play off each other to organize the walled garden, although the property is trapezoidal. The pergola along the western side of the swimming pool squares off the space by presenting a straight face to the garden. An allée of honey locusts parallel to the back of the house links dining and fountain pavilions. Across the opposite side of the lawn wisteria blankets the diagonal rafters of another pergola leading to an opening in the clipped hornbeam hedge that encloses the flowerbeds. On the east side of the house a grid of little-leaf lindens faces a line of jets in a shallow pool backed by ornamental cherries and ivy-covered walls.

Opposite, top:
A curving bed of *Vinca minor* accented by clipped cushions of yew defines the edge of the lawn without obscuring the view either to or from the house.

Opposite, bottom:
From the swimming pool terrace, the wisteria-heavy pergola offers deep shade to the left, the hornbeam hedge across the lawn hides secret spaces, and spurting jets beckon beyond the lattice-roof pavilion: This garden does not reveal all it has to offer at first view or from one vantage point. Individual areas may be symmetrical within, but their relationship is dynamic, and the visitor is continually enticed into exploration.

THE HAMILTON GARDEN

Were any proof needed that in the hands of a gifted and receptive designer the vocabulary of the architectural garden still has lots of lively possibilities, Dan Kiley's Hamilton Garden would supply it.[1] In 1965 Clarence and Muriel Hamilton asked Kiley to remake completely the landscaping of their small suburban house in Columbus, Indiana. Although he had only three-quarters of an acre to work with he created a garden that is strictly ordered but neither symmetrical nor static — criticisms often leveled at geometric layouts. In addition, his composition offers an imaginative solution to the challenge of providing privacy for the owners and still contributing to the attractiveness of the streetscape.

In front of the house Kiley set a fairly low-clipped hedge along the street side of the driveway and planted a row of sugar maples on the right-hand side. He kept some existing trees to accent the lawn, and defined its edge with a precise curved bed low enough not to seem a visual barrier. A seven-foot-high brick wall with several iron-fenced openings reminiscent of the *clairvoyées* in Baroque garden walls encloses the space beside and behind the house. On the other side of the back, or north, wall a mixed border of trees and shrubs fills out the property.

Within the walls Kiley created "a rich variety of spaces and experiences which are linked and united" geometrically.[2] The garden also provides for a variety of activities. It contains a swimming pool, a glassed-in pavilion for dining, a lattice-roofed fountain pavilion, and a hidden flower garden all seamlessly integrated into the design.

287

Low seating-walls corner the fountain pavilion. The allée of honey locusts aims straight for the dining pavilion at the other end of the garden, but lets the eye stray toward the double line of hedges in front of the house, or across the lawn to the swimming pool. Regularly spaced pilasters give depth to the extensive wall surfaces and Kiley carefully varied the plantings to make them interesting. Espaliered pyracanthas pattern the wall behind the diving board, and at night downlights turn the pilasters into glowing columns.

289

In the strict geometric grove of little-leaf lindens each tree is planted in a square bed of *Vinca minor* set into the gravel courtyard between the house and the shallow pool with its line of jets. Backing the fountain, a row of ornamental cherry trees contributes spring color. Red geraniums and, later in the year, white chrysanthemums tucked into the beds of *vinca* beneath the trees add seasonal accents.

The Arizona desert offers the landscape designer a truly bountiful palette of sculptural forms, delicate tracery, shades of green, and blossom colors. Martino knows these plants thoroughly and composes them expertly. In the patio outside the dining room, a striking cow's-tongue opuntia silhouetted against the wall balances a spiky ocotillo on the other side, both contrasting with the fine-spun foliage of a palo verde.

HAWKINSON GARDEN

The enclosed gardens created by Steve Martino for Jay Hawkinson in a suburb of Phoenix, Arizona take full advantage of the natural environment around them. A landscape architect famous for his pioneering plantings of desert flora in a city infamous for the amount of water it consumes trying to grow green grass lawns, Martino has demonstrated equal sensitivity to the region's architectural history in his imaginatively structured spaces. Hawkinson's lot had both constraints and advantages. Walling in the space for privacy was acceptable, which it might not have been in many communities; but the subdivision required that all walls visible from the street be painted bright white. As it was on a corner, views from two streets had to be taken into account. The area back of the house was not very deep but it opened on an open-space drainage wash, which meant that Martino could stretch its apparent extent by borrowing a vista of the natural landscape. In the first stage of the project, he developed this space as a patio off the dining room, building a wall just high

enough to screen the patio from a walkway built by the developer next to the drainage area. By placing the wall a few feet inside the boundary line he could control the planting on both sides, and the rich mixture of desert plants he used don't just frame the view, they flow right out into it. Also in stage one, Martino used a similar plant vocabulary to animate the white walls on the entrance side of the house. In fact, all the plants in the designed landscape are desert natives with low water requirements, and water is recaptured from the roof to augment the region's scanty rainfall, so that the need for additional water is minimized.

When the time came to proceed with landscaping the rather generous side yard, the second stage of the project, the client's needs were somewhat different. More houses had been built, there was more traffic on the streets, and more noise in the neighborhood. Hawkinson, a very busy corporate art director, needed quiet and privacy. Martino's design gave his client far more than a solution to the physical challenges

it addressed. Its sensuous and spatial pleasures combine to create a haven, a place apart, yet one completely connected to its desert surroundings. Just outside the kitchen door at street level is a dining terrace shaded by a yellow canvas sail swung from bright magenta poles. From this level, broad concrete steps set into the decomposed granite ground plane descend to a rounded sunken space that for Martino suggests a kiva, a circular below-ground ceremonial space found in Pueblo settlements since prehistoric times.

The two levels are smoothly linked by a raised plant bed that begins opposite the terrace and curves around the inside of the enclosing boundary wall. As it nears the corner, a second, higher wall behind it follows the same curve and creates in the corner a hidden triangular space with a narrow opening. On the other side of the opening, the higher wall continues until it meets the back boundary wall, the lower wall retaining the plant bed becomes lower. Visible through the opening is a circular fountain with a small jet, from which

water runs through a narrow channel to fall into a semi-circular pool. Invisible are the outdoor shower and storage room that flank the fountain behind the walls. The curving walls reflect the sound of water back into the space and increase its power to mask traffic noise.

Martino confirms that the warm tones of the walls in this part of the garden were inspired by the work of the Mexican architect, Luis Barragán, but the hues and harmony are Martino's, worked out on the spot with the owner by trial and error. If, as the designer says, the walls represent arms reaching out to the sun—the channel and jet are on axis with the summer-solstice sunrise—the simile is subtle, but perhaps a subliminal contribution to the garden's magnetism. Its essential quality, however, comes from a strong, clean, architectural structure that perfectly sets off the strong character of the native flora.

Two palo verde trees veil the entrance walk and front door of the house, their graceful forms courtesy of Martino's pruning.

The arcing walls of the sunken patio pivot around the water channel and pool with its eye-catcher concrete globe, which puts the lower wall levels in dynamic balance. Chosen to stand up to the desert sun, the wall colors are plant friendly, neither timid nor strident. In years where there has been enough rain, the desert becomes a brilliant mosaic of blossoms. From them Martino has selected red sage and penstemon, magenta-pink desert verbena, and yellow brittlebush, palo verde, and sweet acacia. But even after the flowering season, the agaves, ocotillos, and opuntias continue to animate the garden.

295

Opposite, top:
The divisions of the 70-foot-by-176-foot lot are geometric in spirit but flexible, not rigid. Contained spaces around the house relate to each other like those in an open-plan house. For the client the kitchen is truly the heart of the house and it looks out across the brick terrace to the long lawn. The small west-facing house at the far end is home to a daughter and her family. Both it and the main house have has been enlarged since the plan was drawn, but neither expansion really affects the landscape design. In the view from the house, a shadbush anchors the shrub border, primarily composed of native plants. Beyond the maple tree, already on the site, Child Associates planted a pair of Japanese Scholar trees, which seemed a suitable appropriation of a local planting tradition: There is a mature grove of these trees in the village.

Opposite, bottom:
Young rose bushes are just beginning their climb up the house to the trellises on the roof. Beyond the apple tree by the kitchen door, an herb bed runs along the house to the vine-covered pergola that shades the terrace. In the foreground, a newly planted Bradford pear.

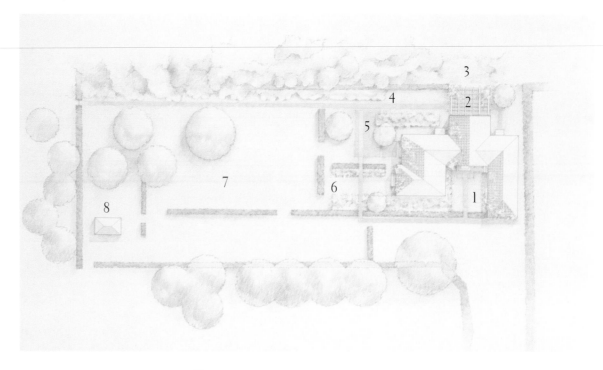

Plan:

1. Entry garden
2. Living room terrace
3. Native moorland
4. Hedgerow
5. Herb garden
6. Flowerbeds
7. Lawn
8. Daughter's house

A 'SCONSET GARDEN

Taking traditional elements from local gardens and reassembling them in a fresh way, the Boston landscape architect Susan Child and her team, Douglas Reed and Anita Berrisbeitia, created a diminutive modern landscape for the Nantucket summer residence of a Middle-Western couple. The hidden quarter-acre lot was once part of a large estate and the house started out as the estate's garage, which the architect, Edward O'Toole, enlarged and transformed into a shingled cottage that would not look out of place in the historic center of Siasconset (pronounced 'Sconset), and observes the time-honored island custom of covering the roof and walls with wooden lattices to encourage a blanket of summer roses. Child Associates, who participated in the project from the outset, found ideas for organizing the garden in the village, in its sea-captains' houses, streets, and parks but distributed them in a far from customary way.

Privet hedges do not tightly circumscribe the grounds as they do in the town's old-fashioned gardens. In some places

hedges define the boundaries; in others, sectioned, they mark spatial divisions, rooms within the garden, without really enclosing them. Susan Child calls them floating hedges. Inlaid in the grass ground, paths, and terraces of the same kind of old bricks that form the town pavements, direct movement, and suggest use. Planting beds, which repeat the long narrow footprint of the hedges, are big enough to satisfy the woman of the house, who is a dedicated cook and gardener, but not so big that their upkeep becomes a chore. This is a vacation house, after all.

On three sides other houses surround the property, but the fourth, the western side, adjoins protected native moorland. Almost the length of that edge of the garden, in contrast to the crisp-cut privet hedges, a tousled hedgerow combines mostly native shrubs with a few long-domiciled foreign-born ones like lilacs, rugosa roses, and peegee hydrandeas. Facing the moor, a pergola-covered terrace off the living room provides a perfect place to watch summer sunsets.

Opposite, top:
Concrete logs weave
through plantings of river
birch, iris, and Texas native
palmettos along the creek.
They offer a sturdy path
raised above soil that is frequently soggy — and an invi-
tation to run and jump for
the young and agile.

Opposite, bottoom:
From the kitchen terrace a
stainless-steel checker-plate
stairway floats down a hillside planted with redbuds,
Mexican elderberries, coral-
berries, and wax myrtles to
the fountain birdbath, which
interrupts the Mexican gravel path across the slope.
Black granite "logs" bridge
the water in what one might
consider a modern inter-
pretation of a traditional
Japanese bridge. The heap
of concrete logs shaping the
pool, however, is a very
twentieth-century caprice.

On the plan:

1. Path from street
2. Lawn
3. South stairs
4. Mexican gravel path
5. Stairs through bamboo grove
6. Stainless steel stairs
7. Fountain birdbath
8. North stairs
9. Concrete log path along creek

A GARDEN ON TURTLE CREEK

The house designed by Antoine Predock, an architect known
for his poetic concrete buildings, occupied most of the level
ground on the site overlooking Turtle Creek. The owners
then turned to Michael Van Valkenburgh, a landscape architect with an international practice who is the Charles Eliot
Professor of Landscape Architecture at the Harvard
Graduate School of Design. They commissioned him to
landscape the remaining acre, a steep hillside descending to
the creek bottom. They wanted a garden to walk in, and they
wanted it planted with vegetation native to Texas. The hillside was heavily wooded, so the first task was editing the
canopy to reduce the intense shade, a severe limitation on
plant choice, and to create views from the house. In order to
place trees just where wanted, the editing involved both
removal and replacement of native species like oaks, cotton-

woods, and pecans. The site had one other problem: Turtle
Creek periodically overflowed its banks, sometimes rising
halfway up the slope.

Van Valkenburgh cast a network of paths and stairs over
the hillside. He has always liked using industrial materials in
his landscape designs, and this one is no exception. A walkway of apparently random stainless steel checker-plate rectangles leads from the street around the south side of the
house to the south stairs, skirting the edge of the trapezoidal
lawn overlooking the garden. A concrete wall defines the
small lawn, and, making a mostly symbolic connection
between outdoors and indoors, carefully shorn turf covers
the treads of stairs to the library and the foyer. The risers are
concrete as are those of the south stairs, but on the latter the
treads are Mexican gravel. The stairs end at a clearly defined

Opposite page:
Unconventional "stepping
stones" of stainless-steel
checker-plate dance around
the house along the edge of
the lawn and out into the
hillside's ground ivy. The
lawn creeps up on the
house by taking over the
treads of the concrete stairs
to the library.

This page:
Spikes of equisetum punc-
tuate the ferns and ground
ivy that encroach on the
treads of the north stairs
with Van Valkenburgh's
encouragement. Just visible
at the bottom of the stairs is
Turtle Creek.

angled path of Mexican gravel that eventually terminates at the head of the north stairs, but a lot happens in between.

Following the path from south to north, the stroller comes first, on the right, to stairs down to the creek, this time of concrete hedged with black bamboo—not a native but carefully confined by a flush concrete wall. Farther on and to the left, a floating stair of checker-plate stainless steel rises to the kitchen door. Just beyond, the path suddenly turns into steeping stones—two black granite "logs"—across a shallow fountain birdbath backed by what seems a haphazard pile of concrete "logs" that suggest discarded building materials left in a construction-site puddle. Continuing along the path and descending the north stairs one comes upon more concrete logs tossed along the creek. They are there for a reason. They help solve a part of the flooding problem by providing a water-resistant raised walkway above the often sodden earth. Van Valkenburgh has given his clients a playful and unusual, but also beautiful and practical landscape.

Letting Plants Drive
The Design

Preceding page:
In autumn clumps of Japanese blood grass and a mop of pale yellow Hakone grass, *Hakonechloa macra albo-aurea*, contrast with textured greens of the conifers in the rock and alpine garden and echo the colorful foliage of shrubs in the border beyond. On the lawn between bed and border stands a rare weeping redwood, *Sequoia sempervirens pendulata* 'Pendula.'

This page:
Looking west over the terrace railings, beyond the luminous blossoms of the Chinese *Clematis lanuginosa* and the shade cast by an ancient apple tree, twin Alberta spruces mark the northern end of the apple-shaped rock and alpine garden. The western border holds a collection of conifers laced with shrubs and flowering trees.

Opposite:
A study in the art of composing foliage almost hides the front door of the house. Across the top the heavily veined leaves of the dogwood on the left balance the pink-splashed ones of *Actinidia kolmitka*, an ornamental cousin of the kiwi vine. Below them *Viburnum sieboldii* is backed by the fine dark foliage of *Viburnum davidii purpurea* 'Nana'. At the bottom the still finer texture of the bird's-nest spruce, *Picea abies* 'Nidiformis', which grows naturally into a cushion shape.

THE JANE KERR PLATT GARDEN

John and Jane Platt started with two and a half acres of neglected orchard on a high hill just west of Portland, Oregon, and by dint of long days and evenings dedicated to planting, pruning, weeding, and mowing—only in later years did they have help—created an extraordinary garden. John Platt wanted it named just for her, but in reality he was a true partner in its creation. It was he who found and bought the land with its eighteen-inch-deep fertile loam before they were married in 1939, and, among other feats of ingenious heavy lifting, he managed to haul the tons of dark, layered basalt from an abandoned quarry on Mount Hood that enabled the pair to build the rock garden areas. Jane Platt was the plantswoman, a role she came by naturally. Her father, Peter Kerr, was a highly regarded amateur horticulturist and his garden, Elk Rock, given by his daughters to the Episcopal Church, is now open to the public. She was also an artist. What the Platts accomplished was summed up in the cita-

tion when the Garden Club of America presented Jane Platt with its highest honor, the Mrs. Oakleigh Thorne Medal, in 1984: "For the establishment of an exquisite garden incorporating rare and difficult botanic material into a design of incredible harmony, beauty, and distinction."[1]

The highest part of the garden's rectangular site lies along the southern boundary, where a twenty-five-by-seventy-foot gravel terrace makes a softly enhancing background for flaming autumn foliage. From here the land slopes at first sharply, then gently down to the north and west. The house, designed by Pietro Belluschi, nestles into the slope on the eastern side. On the north, west, and south sides undulating planting beds ring the roughly acre-and-a-half central lawn, which plays host opposite the house to a large island bed. A particularly twentieth-century idea, island beds were popularized by the British nurseryman, Alan Bloom. The Platts' is apple-shaped in homage to the original orchard and its venerable remain-

ing trees, but it is planted as a rock-and-alpine garden and contains most of the garden's miniature conifer collection.

Jane Platt's tree collections — magnolias, stewartias, and conifers — include many of the garden's treasures, but what is even more inspiring is the way she has placed and combined so many very large trees without smothering what is a rather small space. With the exception of a large pin oak and a rare weeping redwood set as specimens in the lawn, most of the trees are planted in the perimeter beds and arranged so that they carry the eye into the forests and fields beyond the boundaries. The garden is, in fact, enclosed by hedges of Western red cedar or holly; but these are rarely visible. They are concealed by a rich understory of rhododendrons, witch hazels, winter hazels, and dogwoods, which also includes some less frequently seen small trees like *Davidia involucrata* and *Franklinia alatamaha*. At ground level, ferns and mosses in shady spots give way in sunny ones to bulbs and wildflowers, peonies, lilies, and roses to name only a few of the many different flowers that dapple the garden with color in spring and summer. John Platt estimated in 1987 that the garden contained more than 2,500 different species, yet it seems spacious and uncrowded. This is partly due to the large swaths of meticulously maintained lawn, and even more to the ruthless editing to which plantings are subjected. Jane Platt freely acknowledged that like all plant lovers she tended to overplant. Where she departed from the majority was in her ability to see that a cherished specimen had passed its prime or that two favorites were engaged in killing competition and to remove those that needed to go in order to preserve the health and beauty of the garden. Since her death in 1989, John Platt has kept up the garden in her spirit and to her standards, and recently their son David has taken up the responsibility for its continued health and development.

Spring flowers crowd stepping stone paths in the rock and alpine garden. In the foreground, miniature daffodils mingle with pasque flowers in shades of red and violet. The iris is a rare white form of *Iris magnifica*, the white magnolia is called Spring Snow.

Opposite:
Near the front of the house, a stone-paved path leads to an antic sculpture by Joel Shapiro. On one side of the path, butterburs, *Petasites japonicus*, hold up their saucer leaves. Tufts of autumn moor grass, *Sesleria autumnalis*, pattern the opposite side. Behind the statue the yellow blossoms of *Silphium perfoliatum* peek over a bank of grasses.

Left:
Drifts of miscanthis , pennisetum, and molinia, some of the designers' favorite grasses, billow down the hillside in back of the house. The ground-cover on the left side of the photograph is *Senecio aureus*, a native that in spring bursts into golden bloom.

THE DIAMOND GARDEN

The ridged and rocky thirty-five-acre property in Westchester County, New York, chosen by the Robert Diamonds for their country house was heavily wooded, but it offered both seclusion and a view. The bluff with the vista became the site for the house, a contemporary interpretation of the Shingle Style by the architectural firm of Shope, Reno, Wharton. To design the surrounding landscape, the Diamonds commissioned the Washington landscape architects Wolfgang Oehme and James Van Sweden, whose gardens are known for bold sweeping lines and contrasting plant masses. On the Diamond property Oehme and Van Sweden kept the native trees wherever they could, but cleared paths through them and created a new but natural-appearing understory. The entrance drive winds up the hill through the woods, passing around a meadow of shallow-rooted natives and grasses that handsomely cloaks the septic field, before arriving at the entrance courtyard. There are lots of grasses but no lawns in this garden. Massed plantings of ornamental grasses, an Oehme and Van Sweden trademark, layered with shrubs and perennials, flank the entrance. More grasses tumble down the steep bank between the terrace behind the house and a lower, sunny stone-paved terrace with three interconnected pools. Rustic stone paths lead into the woods from both ends of these terraces, as well as from the entrance courtyard. Set in a few selected spots pieces from the Diamonds' important collection of modern sculpture provide just the right punctuation for the soft textures and colors of the plants.

Because the site was so shaded, Oehme and Van Sweden had to eliminate many colorful plants from the plan. As a result the garden's coloring is subtle rather than bold, but it is planted in the sweeping masses of single species that typically structure their designs. They credit the gardens and ideas of Roberto Burle Marx for influencing their grand-scale painterly approach to animating the ground plane of a landscape. Both know their plants, and Oehme in particular is a consummate plantsman. This leads many observers to wonder why they plant so many of the same kinds repeatedly. They have well-thought-out reasons. Recognizing that the skilled maintenance required by intricate plant compositions is very hard to come by in this country, they plan their gardens for easy care. After thirty-some years of experience they have assembled a palette of reliable, hardy perennials and grasses from which they can select to suit the requirements of a specific site. They also plan their gardens for year round interest.[2] This explains at least part of their devotion to ornamental grasses. These grasses are as beautiful tawny and snow-covered in winter as they are green in summer or blooming in autumn. Both Oehme and Van Sweden studied in the Netherlands where ornamental grasses have long been widely used, and both were influenced by the gardens and writing of the German nurseryman Karl Foerster (1874–1970) and his many-layered plantings of grasses and perennials. American garden-makers really owe them a vote of gratitude for making his ideas better known on this side of the Atlantic.

Shallow cascades link the three lily pools set into a stone-paved terrace below the grass-covered slope, constructed with Oehme and Van Sweden's usual careful craftsmanship. They even consulted a Japanese expert on the placement of the large rocks in the pools. The yellow blossoms along the edge belong to *Ligularia dentata* 'Desdemona,' delicious to butterflies, distasteful to deer. To the left at the far end a sculpture by Barbara Hepworth marks the beginning of a path into the woods. To the right a birdhouse, one of many on the grounds, indicates the steps leading down to the swimming pool and pool pavilion.

Purple-tinged dwarf rhoeo edges a path through the rich vegetation. Warm accents: the orange flower-balls of the Brazilian *Stifftia crysantha* and the orange red leaves of *Cordyline fruticosa* 'Peter Buck.' The green tree behind the cordyline is *Clusia grandiflora*. Two members of the bromeliad family, *Neoregalia compacta* and *Aechmea smithiorum* showing a pink flower spike, cluster around the base of a foxtail palm.

THE LELAND MIYANO GARDEN

Another landscape designer whose point of view was strongly influenced by Roberto Burle Marx, is the Hawaiian Leland Miyano. Like his friend and mentor, whom he often visited in Brazil, Miyano started out as a sculptor and painter, endeavors that he still pursues in his spare time, but was seduced by his love of plants into his current career. And like Burle Marx he is a self-taught botanist and plant collector. His expert knowledge of cycads and palms is widely recognized.

Miyano's garden fills a one-acre corner lot about 500 feet above sea level at the foot of the Ko'olau mountains on the windward side of the island of Oahu. It was originally flat lawn with a gully on one edge, and a depression cut by a bulldozer to make a terrace. "I pushed and pulled that depression to give it a more organic shape, and piled up rocks and mounds of earth."[3] He has added hundreds of tons of basalt little by little without using heavy equipment. The soil was very good, a mixture of lava and humus washed down from the mountains. To make sure that Hawaii's torrential rains don't wash that soil from his garden he has constructed paths of split-face basalt and basalt cobbles arranging them in meanders to slow the water down so that it soaks into the ground.

The garden seems much bigger than it really is, partly because the house and the studio/garage are confined to one corner of the trapezoidal property, leaving the rest free for plants. In that corner stucco walls are arranged to give privacy from the street and yet allow air circulation. Chain-link fencing encloses the rest of the lot. Originally Miyano covered the fencing with vines, but in the garden's tropical climate they grew too fast and took too much work. Now he screens the boundaries with upright plants.

Planting has been a gradual process as he experiments with plants he has collected, not only in Brazil with Burle Marx, but also in Venezuela, the Philippines, and Australia. "The garden is very much a learning experience," he says, "since many plants are new to cultivation and I must find out

what conditions they need, how fast they will grow, and how large." Things do grow faster in the local environment, but as he points out "What many people don't realize is that there are seasons in the tropics: Plants go dormant and drop their leaves, which affects light levels. What you plant where is dependent on a set of interconnected conditions: wet and dry seasons, wind direction, and light levels, which are governed both by orientation and neighboring plantings. The side of a tree on which you place an epiphyte will determine how well it grows. It's as much a matter of air circulation as of light level." Miyano does not hesitate to remove plants if they do not do well or grow too big. His garden is designed to be low maintenance and contain only non-invasive vegetation, and he says he spends only a day a week working on it. He uses no pesticides or chemical fertilizers and relies on rainfall for watering.

Miyano's garden demonstrates that environmental sensitivity and a passion for plants need not preclude art. The net-

work of paths organizes the garden. Adapting a Burle Marx idea, he has bordered them with broad swaths of colorful groundcovers to give a strong sense of order to the garden's otherwise complex tapestry of tropical foliage arranged in a masterful orchestration of colors and textures. True to its experimental role, the garden is always changing, and one never knows just what will appear around a bend in a path. Miyano's latest project is trying to learn how to grow species endemic to Hawaii, many of which are now threatened. As anyone who has tried to domesticate wildlings knows, it is a real challenge to grow them successfully in a cultivated situation.

"We can't re-create a natural ecosystem; too much has changed in Hawaii. Too many species have been lost. Too many invasive species, animals and insects as well as plants, have come in. Instead, I am trying to create an ecosystem where compatible plants will grow as they would naturally, and at the same time can be composed in a work of art with harmonious relationships of color, form, and texture."

Trunks and branches of *Plumeria obtusa* 'Singapore Yellow' rise from a bed of scarlet pagoda flowers, *Clerodendrum Buchanani var. fallax*. Fronds of the dwarf date palm, *Phoenix Roebelenii*, finish off the right edge of the photograph.

This page:
From left to right at ground level artillery plant, or *Pilea serpillacea*, the South African succulent plectranthus, *Wikstroemia uva-ursi*, and more artillery plant make up a green polyphony. At the head of the zigzag path is a dwarf date palm and on the right side a *Cycas revoluta*, one of Miyano's large collection of these prehistoric plants.

Opposite:
Hidden in the garden's center a two-level pool fed by a recirculating pump fills the air with moisture to please the philodendrons, dieffenbachias, and crinums that fringe it.

Shaping and
Serving the Land

GAINESWAY FARM

In his introduction to *Abstracting the Landscape: The Artistry of A. E. Bye*, the catalog for a traveling exhibition, Neil Porterfield, the head of the landscape architecture department at Pennsylvania State University, states that "Arthur Edwin Bye is one of the most significant living landscape architects in the United States."[1] The profession agreed and in 1993 the American Society of Landscape Architects awarded him its top honor, the ASLA medal. In his fifty years of practice, A. E. Bye attracted a number of clients who were willing to give him great freedom to carry out his ideas. Among them were Mr. and Mrs. John Gaines, the owners of a large horse farm near Lexington, Kentucky, and his design for it is considered one of his masterpieces. Although he was commissioned to plan the entire property, on which he worked from 1974 to 1983, only the land related to their house and the views from it will be considered as a private designed landscape. Extensive as it looks, it is a small part of the whole.[2]

Bye worked in the tradition that shapes land for human use and enjoyment by abstracting forms found in nature. Keeping in mind the wishes of the owners, he looked for the essential natural character of a site, pared away everything extraneous to that essence, and built his composition to enhance it. He never hesitated to call in a bulldozer when it would serve his vision; but he was just as likely to build paths through a woodland or a bog and leave either almost untouched. He acknowledged that often his landscapes looked as if he had done nothing. They fit so seamlessly into the surrounding environment that the design seems inevitable.

Bye's intuitive grasp of the possibilities of a site was the product of a lifelong attentiveness to the natural world. At the suggestion of one of his students — he taught as long as he practiced — he took up photography to communicate what he saw in nature. "I became obsessed with the idea of mood in landscape. I felt it was a great necessity to return to my students each fall with photographs of serene landscapes or humorous landscapes or mysterious landscapes."[3] He admitted that this perception was "colored by our experiences and past associations" but found that it helped to isolate the characteristics that should inform a design.

In the case of Gainesway Farm, both the local geography and the intended use suggested an undulating pastoral landscape. Herds of bison had roamed the rolling Kentucky meadows before Americans settled there in the eighteenth century. The latter lost little time in importing what came to be called Kentucky bluegrass (*Poa pratensis*) to turn the lime rich soil into prime pasturage. And the Gaines house was a converted barn on a horse farm. Right around it, Bye and his associates, tapping into a local tradition of fine stonework, constructed retaining and screening walls to create terraces and planting beds. Existing trees stayed if they were in the right place; species native to the region were added where needed for shade or accent.

Bye's account of the inspiration for reshaping the vista from the terrace in his book, *Art into Landscape/Landscape into Art*[4] gives a vivid insight into his working methods:

> One spring evening in 1975 my client and I sat on his terrace and gazed northeast to his extensive meadow in the Kentucky Bluegrass country. It sloped downward several hundred feet to a fence in the apex of the valley and then gently upward a thousand feet or more to an open hilltop. As we watched his thoroughbred horses grazing, I asked if the fence was visually disturbing to him. To his affirmative reply, I said, "We can replace it with a Ha Ha fence. Surprisingly, he knew what a Ha Ha was and immediately directed me to build one . . .

With only a rough sketch on the back of an envelope to show his client what he had in mind, Bye proceeded to stake out the ha-ha on the ground. It took about three months to build the 450-foot fence of local stone, which echoes ones built long ago on the property. Then it took two more months of grading and sodding to make it disappear from the views where he wanted it to disappear. Unlike its eighteenth-century antecedents, which were designed to be completely invisible from the residence, this ha-ha in some places comes into view as a serpentine wall. The final step was rearranging the paddock fences on the distant hill to complement the line of the ha-ha. In contrast, the zigzag stone path from a gate in the ha-ha to the terrace, laid spontaneously without prior plan, took only a day to complete.

Bye solved the practical need — containing the horses but enhancing the vista — with a sculpturing of the land that provides ever-changing patterns of light and shade throughout the day and in every season.

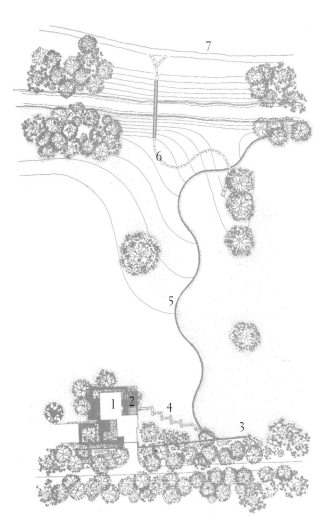

Plan:

1. House
2. Terrace
3. Existing wall
4. Zigzag path
5. Ha-ha
6. Stone path from lake
7. Lake

Top:
The vista across the stone ha-ha wall to the tracery of wooden paddock fences on the distant hillside is particularly dramatic in winter. Bye had the wall built of local stone in the style traditional in the area; but its curves represent a very modern distillation of the contours of the area's hills and valleys.

Below:
The zigzag walkway of rough limestone slabs, another example of Bye's preference for designing directly on the site without predetermined plans, took only a day to create.

MNEMONIC RIVER

When Janis Hall, a sculptor and an architect, decided to direct her talents to landscape design she joined A. E. Bye Associates. Three years later, in 1987, she became a partner and the firm name became A. E. Bye and Janis Hall. At times they worked together on a commission, but often they had separate projects. Mnemonic River, her treatment of a roughly two-acre section of a ten-acre property on the Massachusetts coast was her first independent undertaking. With it she demonstrated that even a quite small site is just as suited to sensitive, sculptural modeling as a large one. The owner's original impetus for requesting Hall's help was to find a solution to drainage problems in the area between the house and the shoreline. The owner was concerned that silt would build up in the tidal pool, damaging it and the carefully chosen native plantings around it, but she was receptive to Hall's desire to create a design that had aesthetic as well as practical value. Hall says that it was her first opportunity to take ideas she had explored in her small-scale sculptures to a full-scale landscape. "Instead of my hands shaping the clay, the bulldozer became my hands shaping the land."[5] She found working every day on the site with a very talented bulldozer operator exhilarating and enriching. "I hadn't thought about lights and shadows until I was standing there. Then I began to work with them and they became an integral part of the project." After her experience in architecture, where preestablished plans are a necessity, she has found very satisfying this freedom to improvise and incorporate unforeseen discoveries into a composition.

In retrospect she sees her design as inspired by the image of a river flowing down to the sea, hence its name. The serpentine line that separates it from the meadow, the woodland, and the pond represents for her the river's banks. The image didn't really come in to focus for her during the creating process. Like the drawn plan, it crystallized later.

The space was seeded with lawn grass for fire protection near the house, and reeds were replanted around the tidal pool. A. E. Bye had previously enriched the natural patterns in the adjacent meadow by adding more of what grew there naturally. Additional planting in the newly reshaped space was a joint operation carried out by Hall, Bye, and the owner, all of whom believe in using plants native to the site, which in this case include bayberries, inkberries, highbush blueberries, red cedars, downy shadblows, and endemic wildflowers.

The plan:

1. House
2. Meadow
3. Sculptured lawn
4. Tidal pool
5. Woodland
6. Projected library/garden folly

Top:
The site after the bulldozer had finished its work, but before topsoil was added, grass sown, and the pool shore replanted. Hall's photograph offers a rare chance to see the understructure of sculptured land.

Middle:
Throughout the seasons light and shade reshape the rolling contours of Mnemonic River. On a winter morning delicate shadows stripe the waves of earth revealed by a dusting of snow.

Bottom:
Spring sunlight gilds the mounds and picks up the dried grasses around the tidal pool.

321

Above:

The five-foot-wide entrance walk of crushed pink granite ends in a boulder-centered circle. From it a stepping-stone path curves through a "lawn" of velvety moss to the house. The casual-seeming groups of trees near the circle, placed to frame the view of the house, exemplify the garden's carefully composed naturalness.

SALT PONDS

The native landscape of Maine is a mosaic of rocks and water, evergreens and birches, mosses and ferns, so it is not surprising that when Patrick Chassé, who holds degrees in both botany and landscape architecture, designs gardens in his native state he often relies on these elements. Salt Ponds, on an island off the coast, is such a garden. In parts it appears that he has only cleaned up the woods and laid stepping-stone paths through them. In fact, the present landscape was created almost completely from the ground up, or, to be accurate, from the island's granite base up.

When the owners decided to build a Japanese-style house as a weekend retreat on the quite remote island, they called on Chassé, who has made many trips to China and Japan, and he worked with them and the fine craftsmen who built the house from the very beginning. He acknowledges that he has learned a great deal from Japanese gardens and he admires them, but he doesn't try to imitate them. The first step at Salt Ponds was examining and editing what was on the

site. Practically all of the spruce was senescent or dead, and the ground covers were not very healthy either. He stripped the roughly fifteen acres back to bedrock and brought in more rocks, gravel, topsoil, trees, and plants on the once-a-week ferry. One of the real challenges—the need for a septic field—he met by creating a sympathetic new landform with imported boulders to hide it.

Around the house and under the veranda that wraps all four sides, Chassé laid a rectangular frame of stone and gravel extending beyond the dripline of the roof with rock steps placed at strategic intervals, a very Japanese technique that, because of the veranda's shadow, makes the house seem to float on the land. The bridge over a gully between the house and the shore is the garden's other clearly Japanese-inspired element. He made a full-scale mock-up to ensure that the scale was right, and that the bridge, to be built with sturdy laminated carrying beams, looked as substantial as its construction.

Chassé prepared a well-edited palette of indigenous plants for the landscape: Spruces, birches, sheep laurel, lowbush blueberry, ferns, and mosses. His list was unexpectedly given a drastic reediting by voracious deer swimming ashore. A shipment of birches accidentally left lying on the dock was stripped overnight, and native plants they normally left alone in the wild, they ate to the ground if nursery-grown as those he brought in were. The principal survivors are spruces, birches — he bought large enough specimens so the crown was above the browse line — and mosses. The groundcover now consists mostly of mosses rather than the intricate tapestries of textures for which he is known, but he is an expert on mosses, and loves them. Except for the space right around the house, with its Oriental flavor, the garden seems uncontrived, a serene woodland opened up enough to invite easy exploration that offers a variety of sensory pleasures plus a few surprises.

Above:
Haircap moss, *Polytrichum commune,* upholsters much of the ground plane and Chassé enjoys pointing out that it is native both to Maine and Japan.

Left:
Rock-slabs piled to form steps provide access to the house from the broad panel of gravel and stone that frames the veranda. From the corner a stepping-stone path leads down through native grasses to a salt pond and beyond to the shore.

On a path between the
house and shore the
Japanese-inspired bridge
spans a gully that looks like
a natural streambed in dry
season but is actually a carefully constructed drainage
channel.

Right:
The owners have a collec-
tion of Korean tomb figures,
which Chassé has uncon-
ventionally but charmingly
tucked in among clusters of
boulders to surprise strollers
along paths in the wood.

THE VALENTINE GARDEN

The steep hillside provided splendid views of mountains and ocean. It also presented a substantial challenge to Isabelle C. Greene who was commissioned by Carol Valentine to landscape the site of her new house, a crisp, white, modern interpretation of Mediterranean village architecture designed by Paul Gray. It is always difficult to lay out a garden on land sloping down from a house, and this slope was exceptionally precipitous. To further complicate matters, the owner was granted only a very small water allowance. Greene, whose nation-wide landscape architecture practice is based in Santa Barbara, drew not just on her knowledge of the area but also on her training as a botanist and artist. Images from her extensive travels — rice paddies in Asia, terraced farms around the Mediterranean, and agricultural field patterns seen from the air in this country — also helped her arrive at a fascinating and very imaginative solution.

Boundary walls in the garden are stuccoed white like walls of the house. Three tiers filled with sun-loving plants hold the steep bank above the parking area, and a low wall with a Mexican vine called blood-trumpet, *Distictis buccinatoria,* trained against it defines the southern edge of the garden, separating it from the forest of live oaks below. Greene built up the south-facing hillside with layers of irregular terraces secured by walls of earth-toned textured concrete, their roughcast surface achieved by molding the concrete in forms lined with cedar shakes. Mass plantings of drought-tolerant succulents fill most of the terraces, minimizing the need for water, but since most beds are of moderate size a few can be more heavily irrigated allowing Mrs. Valentine to grow vegetables and flowers, particularly her favorite roses, in them. If she wishes to experiment with a plant or a pattern, she can change one section without having to redo the whole, and she does.

From the south terrace the modern marquetry spread out on the hillside comes into focus. Isabelle Greene likes to work with a palette of soft green, blue green, and silver foliage, colors characteristic of plants that grow in dry environments, an extremely useful preference for this thirsty site. These hues also harmonize perfectly with the dry stream of broken slates that cuts through the hillside beds, symbolically bringing water to them. Narrow beds of clipped santolina frame grapevines trained as standards on the broad stone paved landings between steps leading up to the house. Espaliered *Distictis buccinatoria* against the boundary wall is balanced by a fence of cordon-trained apple trees on the other side of the maintenance-cart path.

For the most part, the presence of water in this garden is both hidden — drip irrigation — and symbolic. A dry river of gray slate streams diagonally across it in a delta of rivulets and adds to the complexity of the colorful mosaic. Judiciously placed verticals — standard grapes, a pair of weeping mulberries with whitewashed trunks, a delicately framed pergola roofed with pleached crab apples — accent the mostly ground-hugging vegetation.

Not quite as colorful but no less complex is Greene's design for the small entry court, her response to the owner's wish for a Zen garden. On one side of the walkway a rock-centered pool of gray-blue granite chips with undulating edges of tan gravel patterns the ground, and irregular beds of shrubs and succulents line the walls. On the other side the gravel flows past a slate-edged pool of recirculating water fringed with the slender stems of cyperus and equisetum. As in the hillside garden there are endless details, contrasts of colors and textures to study and savor within the powerful and exciting overall compositions. The garden is a lesson that working with nature does not require giving up strong architectural form.

On one side of the entrance
court the only real water feature in the garden, a small
pool edged in roughly broken slate, hosts water-loving
papyrus and horsetail. The
dynamism of the design
springs from the tension
between the architectural
severity of the enclosing
walls and the informal,
almost casual-seeming
placement of plants and
rocks.

Timeline

A selected chronology of events in the history of American and World landscape and garden design prepared by the author in collaboration with Carly Hutchinson. Dates in the Ancient World are by nature approximate and many later ones represent the beginning of a process. Entries in capital letters refer to events in Central and South America.

THE AMERICAS		ASIA, AFRICA AND EUROPE
Earthen mounds and ridged fields at Watson Brake in Louisiana have been carbon-dated, but little is known about their use or their builders.	3200 BC	Sumerian people in Mesopotania build cities and invent writing (cuneiform)
	2800 BC	Step pyramid at Saqqara in Egypt is the first known building in stone.
	2600 BC	Oldest written account of an Egyptian garden: 2.5 acres with a "very large lake, fine trees," house, and pool. Nearly 600 years later, a doll-sized walled garden with pond and shade trees is buried in the tomb of Meketre, chancellor to Mentuhotep II.
At Poverty Point, near what is now Shreveport, Louisiana, the center of a culture that trades from Minnesota to the Caribbean, inhabitants build up over 400 years semi-circular terraces and mounds including a bird-shaped one: landscape design on a monumental scale. For the next 3000 years, a succession of mound- and pyramid-building cultures will arise and disappear in Middle and North America.	1730 BC	
THE OLMEC CULTURE, CHARACTERIZED BY MASSIVE STONE HEADS, FLOURISHES ON MEXICO'S EAST COAST.	1200 BC	
	1114 BC	Assyrian king Tiglath-Pileser I brings cedars and boxwood home from conquered lands. His gardens also contain wild and cultivated flowers, as well as oak and rare fruit trees.
	1000 BC	King Wen of the Zhou Dynasty builds a high earth terrace—Ling Tai—in Gaojing in Shanxi Province, digs a lake and fills the surrounding woods with tame animals. It is considered the first landscape created for entertainment.
	604 BC	Nebuchadnezzar II builds the Hanging Gardens of Babylon, terraces raised on stone vaults and watered from the Euphrates River.
During what is called the Woodland Period, extending to 1000 AD, ridged-field agriculture, including the decoratively laid out "garden beds" in Michigan, is practiced in and around the Mississippi Valley. A similar system has been found in the Andes.	500 BC	
	401 BC	Xenophon, a Greek historian, transliterates the Persian word for walled garden, *pairadaeza*, into the Greek, *paradeisos* from which comes the English word "paradise."
Hohokam people in Pueblo Grande, Arizona develop over the next 600 years an extensive irrigation system, farm plots, and communities with platform mounds and ball courts.	300 BC	
TEOTIHUACAN, NORTHEAST OF PRESENT-DAY MEXICO CITY, IS BY 500 AD ONE OF THE WORLD'S LARGEST CITIES, WITH CEREMONIAL PYRAMIDS, BROAD AVENUES, AND SUBURBAN DWELLINGS.	200 BC	
	54 BC	Cicero, famous as an orator, is also thought to have initiated decorative gardening in Rome. He builds a country garden for his brother, coins the epithet "topiarius" for an ornamental gardener.

THE AMERICAS   ASIA, AFRICA AND EUROPE

                                    55 AD   Pliny the Elder (23–79 AD) includes the art of gardening in his 37-volume
                                             Naturalis Historia. Between 97 and 107 AD, his nephew, Pliny the Younger, writes
                                             nine books describing his two villa gardens.

MAYAN CITY OF CARACOL IN WHAT IS NOW BELIZE DEVELOPS A NETWORK OF   560 AD
ROADS CONNECTING IT TO RINGS OF SUBURBS PREFIGURING TODAY'S URBAN
"SPRAWL."   699-
                                    761 AD   Poet and Painter Wang Wei paints a scroll of his garden, which is copied over and
                                             over in several media and becomes a major inspiration for Chinese garden-makers.

                                    840 AD   Walafrid Strabo writes *Hortulus* (The Little Garden) a poem on gardening.

Mounds and suburban villages also characterize Cahokia, a large city that   1050 AD
flourishes across the Mississippi from present-day St. Louis until 1150 AD.

                                    1238 AD Ibn Nasr begins construction of the Alhambra, a palace and garden complex
                                             overlooking Granada, Spain

                                    1250 AD The great civilizations of Ghana, Mali, and Zimbabwe grow up successively in
                                             subsaharan Africa over the 13th to 15th centuries.

                                    1260 AD Albertus Magnus writes *De Vegetabilis.*

                                    1289 AD *Sakuteiki,* the earliest horticultural treatise in Japan, is produced.

AZTECS CREATE TENOCHTITLAN IN A MEXICAN LAKE USING *CHINAMPAS,*   1325 AD
OFTEN CALLED FLOATING ISLANDS, EARTH-COVERED RAFTS ANCHORED TO
THE LAKE BOTTOM BY WILLOW-TREE ROOTS AS FOUNDATIONS. THE CITY'S
GARDENS AND FLOWERS WILL ASTONISH SPANISH INVADERS.

                                    1458 AD Michelozzi's Villa designed for Cosimo de Medici in Fiesole will be the proto-
                                             type for the Italian Renaissance garden.

Columbus lands in America for the first time.   1492 AD

                                    1499 AD The dry garden at Ryoangi Temple near Kyoto, thought to have been first laid out
                                             in 1430, is rebuilt after a 1488 fire.

THE EMPIRE OF THE INCAS BUILDS MACCHU PICHU IN THE ANDES.   1500 AD

                                    1504 AD Zahir-Ud-Din Muhammed also known as Babur builds his best-known garden,
                                             Bagh-I Wafa, in Kabul. In his autobiography, the *Babur-Nama,* he writes in detail
                                             about his gardens.

TENOCHTITLAN DESTROYED BY CORTES. SPANISH BUILD MEXICO CITY ON   1521 AD
ITS RUINS.

                                    1544 AD Botanical garden established in Pisa is followed by one in Padua (1545) and
                                             Florence (1550).

Spanish establish St. Augustine, Florida, the oldest permanent European city in   1565 AD
the United States.

                                    1573 AD Philip II of Spain promulgates planning rules for the Americas, The Laws for the
                                             Indies, which will shape settlements in the southern and western U.S.

                                    1601 AD Sir Francis Bacon's essay on Gardens

The first permanent English settlement, Jamestown, Virginia, is founded.   1607 AD

Santa Fe, New Mexico, is founded by the Spanish as a mission and exploration   1609 AD
center.

The Pilgrims land on Cape Cod, Massachusetts.

1620 AD — Mogul Emperor, Jahangir, creates the Shalimar-Bagh in Kashmir.

The Dutch West India Company founds the city of New Amsterdam on Manhattan Island. FIVE YEARS LATER IT CONQUERS PERNAMBUCO IN BRAZIL.

1625 AD

John Winthrop arrives in Boston. Sixteen years later he entertains French commissioners in his garden.

1630 AD — Shah Jahan builds the Taj Mahal and its garden in Agra as a tomb for his wife.

1634 AD — Ji Cheng publishes his landscape treatise, *Yüan Yeh*, *The Craft of Gardens*, in which he discusses the construction of the Chinese garden.

1661 AD — Louis XIV's finance minister, Nicolas Fouquet assembles a gifted team—André LeNôtre, garden designer; Louis LeVau, architect; Charles LeBrun, painter—to create Vaux-le-Vicomte. The king arrests him for looting the treasury and takes the team (and 1200 trees) from Vaux-le-Vicomte to make over a hunting lodge into the royal palace of Versailles.

Charleston, South Carolina is founded.

1670 AD

The earliest known formal garden in the U. S. is created on the Arthur Allen estate (now called Bacon's Castle) near Williamsburg, Virginia.

1680 AD

William Penn lays out Philadelphia, his " greene Country Towne." It becomes a hotbed of distinguished botanists, horticulturists, and scientists over the next 150 years.

1682 AD

1686 AD — William of Orange and his wife, Mary, who will become king and queen of England in 1688, begin building a palace and gardens at Het Loo in Holland.

1710-
1712 AD — Joseph Addison in *The Spectator* and Alexander Pope in *The Guardian* urge landscape designers to look to nature, not architecture, for guidance and inspiration.

New Orleans is founded by the Sieur de Bienville.

1718 AD

1731 AD — Philip Miller, curator of the Physic Garden in London, publishes his popular manual *The Gardener's Dictionary* following it with *The Gardeners Kalendar* a year later.

1738 AD — William Kent redesigns the garden at Rousham House in Oxfordshire and "calls in" the surrounding countryside.

The landscape at Middleton Place near Charleston, South Carolina, created over the next 10 years, adapts the architectural vista garden to American land forms.

1741 AD

1745 AD — Emperor Qian Long begins building the Summer Palace and its garden near Beijing.

1749 AD — Père Attiret writes the first complete description of a Chinese Garden by a European.

1751 AD — Lancelot "Capability" Brown, the most influential designer of the English landscape garden establishes his practice.

Martha Logan publishes *The Gardener's Kalendar,* based on her own experience, in the *South Carolina Gazette.*

1752 AD

1757 AD — Edmund Burke publishes *A Philosophical Enquiry into the Origin of Our Ideas of the Sublime and Beautiful*, which provides ideological underpinning for the English landscape garden.

George Washington inherits Mount Vernon and begins to design its landscape, a process to which he will be dedicated for the rest of his life.

1759 AD

1764 AD — Capability Brown is appointed Master Gardener at Hampton Court and lays out Blenheim Park. He will dominate English landscape design until his death in 1783.

Thomas Jefferson starts nearly sixty years of building and rebuilding his estate, Monticello, on a hill overlooking Charlottesville, Virginia, where, in 1817, he founds and designs the University of Virginia.

1768 AD

Franciscan Missionaries from Mexico found San Diego in Spanish California, the first of a chain of towns and missions extending up the coast to Santa Barbara (1823).

1769 AD

1788 AD Humphry Repton, a painter turned "improver" secures his first commission. Famous for his before-and-after Red Books, he is considered the principal successor to Brown.

1789 AD The Englisher Garten in Munich by Friedrich Ludvig von Sckell is the first public park designed as such.

A French engineer, Pierre L'Enfant, develops a complex plan for Washington, D. C. that adapts Baroque landscape design to the layout of a city.

1791 AD

1794 AD Uvedale Price publishes *Essays on the Picturesque* to promote a more romantic form of landscape garden.

The Louisiana Purchase. The territory that Jefferson buys from Napoleon more than doubles the size of the U. S.

1803 AD

An expedition headed by Meriwether Lewis and William Clark explores the Louisiana Territory, brings back a collection of hitherto unknown plants.

1804 AD The Royal Horticultural Society is formed in London.
Père Lachaise, the pioneer garden cemetery, is consecrated on a hill in Paris.

An Irish-born Philadelphia nurseryman, Bernard McMahon, writes *The American Gardener's Calendar*, a widely disseminated book adapting European horticultural practices to American conditions.

1806 AD

1816 AD After a trip to England Prince Hermann von Pückler-Muskau begins laying out his first picturesque landscape park on his estate near the then Polish border.

1817 AD Scottish author and designer John Claudius Loudon, invents a bendable wrought-iron glazing bar, permitting all glass conservatories. He goes on to publish *The Encyclopedia of Gardening* (1822) and *The Suburban Garden and Villa Companion* (1838) in addition to an influential periodical, *The Gardener's Magazine* (1826–38)

The first American horticultural society is formed in New York. It will close down in 15 years, re–form in 1900.

1818 AD

Pennsylvania Horticultural Society founded

1827 AD Leigh Hunt champions the planting innovation "bedding out" in *The Gardener's Magazine.*

Massachusetts Horticultural Society founded

1829 AD

1830 AD Edwin Budding invents the lawn mower.

Mt. Auburn Cemetery created as an innovative combination of arboretum and burying ground starts a trend to picturesque landscaped rural cemeteries.

1831 AD

1840 AD Kew Garden, formerly a royal preserve, opens to the public.

Andrew Jackson Downing publishes *A Treatise on the Theory and Practice of Landscape Gardening.*

1841 AD

1843 AD Birkenhead Park in Liverpool by Joseph Paxton impresses Downing and Olmsted on visits to England.

Salt Lake City, Utah is settled by Mormons under the leadership of Brigham Young.

1847 AD

Gold is discovered in California.
 Henry David Thoreau proclaims that "in Wildness is the preservation of the World"

1848 AD John Ruskin's *Seven Lamps of Architecture* kicks off the Arts and Crafts movement.

	1851 AD	Paxton is knighted for his creation of the Crystal Palace as the centerpiece of the Great Exhibition of the Works of Industry of all Nations in Hyde Park.
A. J. Davis lays out Llewellyn Park in West Orange, New Jersey, a picturesque suburb. 　Commodore Perry negotiates a treaty opening Japan to the West.	1853 AD	Baron Haussmann is appointed Prefect and begins remaking Paris into a city of broad tree-lined boulevards and creating, with the help of J.-C.-A. Alphand, new parks, revitalizing existing ones.
Henry Winthrop Sargent imports the lawnmower. By the 1870s Americans are manufacturing improved versions.	1855 AD	
	1857 AD	William Morris and his partners open a decorative arts company to promote the Arts-and-Crafts agenda.
With their Greensward Plan, Frederick Law Olmsted and Calvert Vaux win the commission to design Central Park in New York. 　After national money-raising campaign, Mount Vernon Ladies Association founded by Ann Pamela Cunningham buys Mount Vernon to preserve and restore it.	1858 AD	
President Lincoln signs a bill presenting Yosemite, and the Mariposa Big Tree Groves to California as a public park. 　George Perkins Marsh's *Man and Nature* examines the often disastrous consequences of human impact on the environment.	1864 AD	
	1870 AD	William Robinson publishes *The Wild Garden* initiating renewed interest in hardy herbaceous plants.
Congress designates more than two million acres in Wyoming to create Yellowstone, the first National Park.	1872 AD	
The Centennial Exposition in Philadelphia initiates the Colonial Revival movement.	1876 AD	
Charles Sprague Sargent, founder of the Arnold Arboretum, starts *Garden and Forest* magazine.	1888 AD	The first Arts-and-Crafts exhibition is held at the Regent's Street New Gallery in London.
Charles Eliot founds The Trustees of Reservations to preserve New England sites of historic or natural importance.	1891 AD	
	1892 AD	Sir Reginald Blomfield publishes *The Formal Garden in England.*
The World's Columbian Exposition in Chicago launches the "city beautiful" movement, popularizes Beaux-Arts eclecticism in architecture and landscape design.	1893 AD	
	1895 AD	The British National Trust is founded with a program similar to that of the Trustees of Reservations
Led by *House Beautiful*, a rush of illustrated magazines devoted to houses and gardens hits the newstands. In 1901 come *House & Garden, Country Life in America, The Garden,* and Gustav Stickley's *The Craftsman.*	1896 AD	
The American Society of Landscape Architects (ASLA) is founded by 10 distinguished practitioners.	1899 AD	With *Wood and Garden* Gertrude Jekyll begins a series of books and articles on design and color in the garden that are still highly influential.
Harvard University and MIT start Landscape Architecture degree programs.	1900 AD	
Juliette Low founds the Lowthorpe School of Landscape Architecture for Women since Harvard will not admit them	1901 AD	
	1909 AD	Georges Braque and Pablo Picasso invent Cubism.
The Garden Club of America, a consortium of state garden clubs, forms in Philadelphia.	1913 AD	Edwin Lutyens begins work on the Viceroy's (now the Prime Minister's) Palace in New Delhi and its modern version of the moghul garden.

The National Park Service is formally established.

1916 AD

1919 AD — The Bauhaus school, dedicated to integrating art and industrial production, is founded by Walter Gropius in Weimar, moves to Dessau six years later.

1925 AD — Under the supervision of J. C. N. Forestier, the gardens at the Exposition Internationale des Arts Décoratifs et Industriels Modernes in Paris demonstrate a wide variety of innovative designs that will later be characterized as Art Deco and Art Moderne.

John D. Rockefeller, Jr., begins restoring Colonial Williamsburg (Virginia's capital 1699 to 1781) with Arthur Shurcliff as planner and landscape architect.

1926 AD

Brookgreen Gardens, the first U.S. garden designed as an outdoor sculpture gallery, is created in South Carolina.

1931 AD

1933 AD — Nazi Germany shuts down the Bauhaus. Its teachers, including Herbert Bayer, Mies van der Rohe, Walter Gropius, and Marcel Breuer, flee to England and the United States.

1935 AD — English landscape architects Geoffrey Jellicoe and Russell Page form a partnership, begin designing Ditchley Park for Ronald and Nancy Tree.

Walter Gropius becomes dean of Harvard's Graduate School of Design, inspires three landscape architecture students—Garrett Eckbo, James Rose and Dan Kiley—to challenge the relevance of Beaux-Arts instruction.

1937 AD

ROBERTO BURLE MARX, INSPIRED BY MODERN ART, DESIGNS A FREE-FORM TROPICAL GARDEN FOR A ROOF OF THE MINISTRY OF EDUCATION AND HEALTH IN RIO DE JANEIRO, BRAZIL. HE WILL CONTINUE TO CREATE DISTINCTIVE AND HIGHLY INFLUENTIAL GARDENS UNTIL HIS DEATH IN 1991.

1938 AD

1939 AD — World War II begins

Post-World-War-II government subsidies for suburban housing promote proliferation of developments like Levittown on Long Island.

1946 AD

President Truman signs legislation creating the National Trust for Historic Preservation.
  Aldo Leopold's *Sand County Almanac*, published
  MEXICAN ARCHITECT, ENGINEER AND LANDSCAPE ARCHITECT LUIS BARRAGÁN DESIGNS MEXICO CITY SUBDIVISION, EL PEDREGAL, AND ITS GARDENS.

1949 AD — Jellicoe and Page begin successful independent practices.

Rachel Carson's *Silent Spring* urges Americans to consider the impact of chemical pesticides.

1962 AD

In *Design with Nature* Ian McHarg sets out a blueprint for landscape and urban design that is environmentally responsible.

1969 AD

1977 AD — Gilles Clément, one of an innovative group of young landscape designers in France, begins work in an abandoned pasture on what he calls *Le Jardin en Mouvement*. With a few shrubs clipped into hedge fragments or balls for contrast and stability, plants are left to follow natural growth cycles and move about as they wish with minimum editing.

The Garden Conservancy is founded to help owners find ways to preserve outstanding private gardens.

1989 AD

1992 AD — The first Festival des Jardins de Chaumont-sur-Loire. Each year French and foreign designers are given a theme and invited to come up with exciting ideas for small gardens.

Notes

INTRODUCTION

1. Alexis de Tocqueville, *Democracy in America*, Vol. I, 326.
2. Alexis de Tocqueville, *Democracy in America*. Vol. II, 3.
3. John Winthrop, *Winthrop's Journal 1630–1649*, 286.
4. Dr. Alexander Hamilton, *Gentleman's Progress* (The Itinerarium of Dr. Alexander Hamilton 1744), edited by Carl Bridenbaugh, 103.

PART 1 CHAPTER 1

1. Gilbert L. Wilson, *Buffalo Bird Woman's Garden*. Originally published in 1917 as *Agriculture of the Hidatsa Indians: An Indian Interpretation*, 16.
2. Bartram, William, *Travels and Other Writings*, including *Travels through North & South Carolina, Georgia, East & West Florida*, Part II, Chapter 4, 100–01.
3. Schoolcraft, Henry Rowe, *Information Respecting the History, Condition and Prospects of the Indian Tribes of the United States*, 16.
4. Cronon, William, *Changes in the Land: Indians, Colonists, and the Ecology of New England*, 42–81.
5. U. P. Hedrick, *A History of Horticulture in America*, 57.
6. Donck, Adriaen Van Der, *A Description of the New Netherlands*, (1656), 27.
7. Danckaerts, Jasper, *The Journal of Jasper Danckaerts 1679–1680*, in *Original Narratives of Early American History*, 44.
8. Thomas, Gabriel, *An Historical and Geographical Account of Pensilvania and of West New-Jersey*, 1698, 332.
9. Jackson, John Brinckerhoff, "Nearer Than Eden," *The Necessity for Ruins and Other Topics*, 32.
10. Lawson, William, *A New Orchard and Garden* with *The Country Housewifes Garden for Herbs of Common Use*, 57.
11. *Winthrop Papers*. Vol. III, Boston, The Massachusetts Historical Society, 1947, 48.
12. William Bradford, *Descriptive and Historical Account of New England in Verse* quoted in Ann Leighton, *Early American Gardens "For Meate or Medicine,"* 31.
13. *Plants and People*. Dublin Seminars for New England Folklife, Annual Proceedings 1995, 70.
14. John Parkinson, *A Garden of Pleasant Flowers*, 5.

PART 1 CHAPTER 2

1. Humphry Repton, *The Art of Landscape Gardening* including *Sketches and Hints on Landscape Gardening* (1795), and *Theory and Practice of Landscape Gardening* (1803), 140.
2. Walter Kendall Watkins, "The Hancock House and its Builders" John Hancock to James Glin, December 20, 1736. *Old Time New England* (LXVII: July 1926) 2–19.
3. Rev. Peter Whitney, *History of Worcester County*, 1793. quoted in *Gardens of Colony and State*, Vol. I, 107.
4. Joseph Addison, *The Spectator*, No. 414, 25 June 1712, in *The Genius of the Place*, 143.
5. Alexander Pope, essay from *The Guardian*, 1713, in *The Genius of the Place*, 207.

6. Joseph Addison, *The Spectator*, No. 414, 25 June, 1712, in *The Genius of the Place*, 142.
7. William Byrd, *History of the Dividing Line Run in the Year 1728. The Writings of "Colonel William Byrd of Westover in Virginia, Esquire,"* 296.
8. Daniel J. Boorstin, *The Americans: The Colonial Experience*, 319–20.
9. Harriott Horry Ravenel, *Eliza Pinckney*, in the series *Women of Colonial and Revolutionary Times*, 53.
10. Barbara Paca-Steele (with St.Clair Wright), "The Mathematics of an Eighteenth Century Wilderness Garden," *Journal of Garden History* Vol. 6, No. 4, 299.
11. François-Jean, Marquis de Chastellux, *Travels in North America in the Years 1780, 1781, and 1782*, 1963, 118, 380.
12. Francois Alexandre Frédéric, duc de La Rochefoucauld-Liancourt, *Voyage dans les Etats-Unis d'Amerique fait en 1795, 1796 et 1797*, (Author's translation) 86–87.
13. John Brinckerhoff Jackson, "Nearer than Eden," *The Necessity for Ruins and Other Topics*, 32.
14. D. W. Meinig, *The Shaping of America*, Vol. I: *Atlantic America 1492–1800*, 248.
15. Thomas Jefferson, letter to William Hamilton from Washington, July 1806, in *Thomas Jefferson's Garden Book*, 323–24.

PART 1 CHAPTER 3

1. Fredrika Bremer, *The Homes of the New World; Impressions of America*, 47.
2. John Claudius Loudon, *The Suburban Gardener and Villa Companion*, 108.
3. D. W. Meinig, *The Shaping of America*, Vol. II: *Continental America 1800–1867*, 222.
4. Norman B. Wilkinson, *E. I. du Pont, Botaniste: The Beginning of a Tradition*, 52.
5. Kathleen McClelland, "Pioneer Gardeners in Utah," *The Historical Gardener: Plants and Garden Practices of the Past*, Summer, 1994, 2–3, 12.
6. Frederick Law Olmsted, *A Journey Through Texas* (1853–54), 1860, reprint 1969, 129–30.
7. Kenneth T. Jackson, *Crabgrass Frontier*, 12.
8. Frederick Law Olmsted, and Calvert Vaux, *Preliminary Report upon the proposed Suburban Village at Riverside near Chicago*. 1868.
9. Frederick Law Olmsted, "Plan for a Small Homestead," *Garden & Forest*, May 2, 1888, 111.
10. Frederick Law Olmsted, *To the Board of Commissioners of the Central Park*, May 20, 1858 in *Creating Central Park, 1957–1861. The Papers of Frederick Law Olmsted*, Vol. III, 133.

PART 1 CHAPTER 4

1. Charles Adams Platt, *Italian Gardens*, (reprint 1993), 16.
2. Guy Lowell, ed., *American Gardens*, introduction.
3. Mrs. Schuyler Van Rensselaer, *Art Out-of-Doors*, 160, 167.
4. Henry Winthrop Sargent, Supplement to the Sixth Edition of Andrew Jackson Downing's *A Treatise on the Theory and Practice of Landscape Gardening* (1859), 432.
5. Henry James, *The American Scene* (1907) with three essays from "Portraits of Places" edited by W. H. Auden, 322.
6. Gustav Stickley, "Craftsman Gardens for Craftsman Homes," *More Craftsman Homes* (reprint 1982), 168.
7. Barbara Wells Sarudy, *Gardens and Gardening in the Chesapeake 1700–1805*, 7.

8. Victoria Padilla, *Southern California Gardens: An Illustrated History*. (1961), 166.
9. David C. Streatfield, *California Gardens: Creating a New Eden*, 175.
10. Wilhelm Miller, *The Prairie Spirit in Landscape Gardening*, Bulletin 184, Illinois Agricultural Experiment Station, 1915, 5.

PART 1 CHAPTER 5

1. Phoebe Cutler, *The Public Landscape of the New Deal*, 85.
2. Thomas D. Church, "The Small California Garden: Chapter I: A New Deal for the Small Lot." *California Arts & Architecture*, May 1933, 16.
3. Thomas Church, "Designing the Small Lot Garden," *California Arts & Architecture*, July 1933, 16.
4. Garrett Eckbo, "Small Gardens in the City: A Study of Their Design Possibilities." *Pencil Points*, September 1937. Reprinted in *Garrett Eckbo: Philosophy of Landscape. Process Architecture 90*, August 1990, 116–120.
5. James Rose, "Freedom in the Garden" *Pencil Points*, October 1938. Reprinted in Treib, Marc, Editor. *Modern Landscape Architecture: A Critical Review*, 68–70.
6. Garrett Eckbo, *An Interview with Garrett Eckbo*, 10
7. Dorothée Imbert, "A Model for Modernism: The Work of Pierre-Émile Legrain," *Modern Architecture: A Critical Review*, 92–107.

PART 2 CHAPTER 1

1. Didymus Mountain (Thomas Hill), *The Gardeners Labyrinth* (1594), 1982 ed., 26.
2. John Parkinson, *A Garden of Pleasant Flowers: Paradisi in Sole Paradisus Terrestris* (1629) reprint 1976, 7.
3. Francis Bacon, Lord Verulam, *The Essays, No. 46: Gardens* (1625), 1852, 162.
4. Paula Deitz, "Formal Garden, Oldest in the U.S., Grows Again," *The New York Times*, Thursday, May 11, 1989, Section C, 112.
5. Philip Vickers Fithian, *Journal and Letters 1767–1774*, John Rogers Williams, ed. 1900, 105.
6. Thomas D. Church, *Gardens Are For People*, 15.
7. Thomas D. Church, ibid., 209.
8. Celia Thaxter, *An Island Garden* (1894), reprint 1985, 26–27.
9. Beatrice Simpson, All quotations come from conversations with the author.

DIGRESSION 1

1. Joan Parry Dutton, *Enjoying America's Gardens*, New York, 1958, 301.
2. Christopher Tunnard, *The City of Man*, New York, Scribner, 1953, 110.
3. Samuel Maverick, "A Briefe discription of New England" c. 1660. *Massachusetts Historical Society Proceedings* 2nd Series I (1884–85, 235.
4. Peter Kalm, *Travels in North America*. The English Version of 1770 revised from the original Swedish by Adolph B. Benson, ed., 1987, 117.
5. Fredrika Bremer, *The Homes of the New World: Impressions of America*. Mary Howitt, trans., Vol. 2, 182.
6. *Winthrop Papers*, "Essay on the ordering of towns." Vol. III, 184.
7. Ivor Noel Hume, *Digging for Carter's Grove* 1974, 36–38.
8. *Thomas Jefferson's Garden Book 1766–1824*, 377.
9. J. B. Jackson, "A New Kind of Space." *Landscape* 18, no. 1, 1969, 34.
10. Lewis Allen, *Rural Architecture* (1852), 129.

11. Andrew Jackson Downing, *The Theory and Practice of Landscape Gardening* (1841; New York, 1967), 295.

12. Fred E. H. Schroeder, *Front Yard America* (Bowling Green, Ohio, 1993), 80–81.

13. Frank J. Scott, *The Art of Beautifying Suburban Home Grounds* 1870, Vol. I, 61.

14. Nathaniel Egleston, *Villages and Village Life with hints for their improvement* (New York, 1878), 139.

15. Sylvester Baxter, *Garden and Forest* (1890), 594.

16. Madame de La Tour du Pin (1770–1853), *Memoirs*. Felice Harcourt, trans. and ed., 1971, 235.

17. Peter Kalm, op. cit., 121.

18. Mrs. Ann MacVicar Grant, *Memoirs of an American Lady*, reprint, 1903, 76.

19. John Michael Vlach, "Afro-Americans," *America's Architectural Roots: Ethnic Groups that Built America*. Dell Upton, ed., 45.

20. George Kubler and Martin Soria, *Art and Architecture in Spain and Portugal and Their American Dominions* 1500 to 1800, 62–63.

21. Samuel Gaillard Stoney, *Plantations of the Carolina Low Country*, 48.

22. Hugh Morrison, *Early American Architecture*, 120.

23. Erik Larsen, *Frans Post, interprète du Brésil*, 73; and Clarival do Prado Valladares and Luiz E. de Mello Filho. *Albert Eckhout: A Presença da Holanda no Brasil Século XVII*, 37.

24. *Letters & Papers of John Singleton Copley and Henry Pelham* 1739–1776, 136–37.

25. Andrew Jackson Downing, op.cit., 326.

26. Donald G. Mitchell, *Rural Studies with Hints for Country Places*, 325.

27. Charles Henderson, *Henderson's Picturesque Gardens*, 54.

28. Mrs. Francis King, *The Beginner's Garden*, 11.

29. Christopher Grampp, "Gardens for California Living." *Landscape*, Vol. 28, No. 3, 1985, 42.

PART 2 CHAPTER 2

1. John and Ray Oldham, *Gardens in Time*, 150.

2. Franklin Hamilton Haslehurst, *Gardens of Illusion: The Genius of André Le Nostre*, 3.

3. Humphry Repton, *The Art of Landscape Gardening*, 61.

4. John Hancock to James Glin, December 20, 1736; William Grigg, October 4, 1736. in Walter Kendall Watkins "The Hancock House and its Builders." *Old Time New England* (XVII:July 1926) 2–19.

5. Robert Beverley, *The History and Present State of Virginia* (1705), 128.

6. Henry A. M. Smith, "The Ashley River: its Seats and Settlements." *The South Carolina Historical and Genealogical Magazine*, Vol. XV (January 1919), 118.

7. Alexander Pope, *An Epistle to Lord Burlington*, 1731.

8. John James, *The Theory and Practice of Gardening*, 20.

9. Rundlet-May Family Manuscript Collection. Society for the Preservation of New England Antiquities Library and Archives.

10. George Washington, *Diary*. March 11, 1747.

11. George Washington, *Diary*. April 5, 1760.

12. *A Catalogue of the Washington Collection in the Boston Athenaeum.*, 189–221.

13. Andrew Burnaby, *Travels Through the Middle Settlements in North America in the Years 1759 and 1760*, 67.

14. George Washington to Samuel Vaughan, November 12, 1787.

15. George Washington to Lund Washington, New York, August 19, 1776.

16. George Washington. *Diary*. October 10, 1789.

17. Jacquetta M. Haley, *Pleasure Grounds: Andrew Jackson Downing and Montgomery Place with Illustrations by Alexander Jackson Davis*, 12.

18. Andrew Jackson Downing, All quotations from "A Visit to Montgomery Place" *The Horticulturist*. Volume 2, No. 4, 153–160.

19. Charles Eliot, "Old Montgomery Place" *Garden and Forest*. Vol. III, no. 108 March 19, 1890, 139.

20. John Brinckerhoff Jackson, "The Almost Perfect Town" *Landscapes*, 120.

21. E. J. Hooper, *The Western Farmer and Gardener*. 197–198.

22. Frederick Law Olmsted to Frederick J. Kingsbury, 20 January, 1891. In Laura Wood Roper, *FLO: A Biography of Frederick Law Olmsted*, 416.

23. Frederick Law Olmsted to George W. Vanderbilt. 12 July 1889. Olmsted Papers. in Charles E. Beveridge and Susan L. Klaus *The Olmsteds at Biltmore*, 3.

24. Frederick Law Olmsted, *Report Upon a Projected Improvement of the Estate of the College of California at Berkeley, near Oakland* in Sutton. Civilizing American Cities, 270.

25. Telephone conversation with William E. Alexander, Landscape and Forest Historian, Biltmore Estate.

DIGRESSION 2

1. John Muir, Wilderness Essays, 253–4.

2. Captain Arthur Barlowe, *The First Voyage Made to the Coasts of America*, 1584 in *Early English and French Voyages, chiefly from Hakluyt, 1534–1608*, 1952 ed., 228.

3. William Bradford, *Of Plymouth Plantation 1620–1647*, 70.

4. Master Ralph Lane, *Account of the Particularities of the Imployments of the Englishmen left in Virginia*, 1586 in *Early English and French Voyages*, 257.

5. Bernard McMahon, *The American Gardener's Calendar*, 72.

6. The Rev. John Frederick Schroeder, *Tenth Anniversary Address to The Horticultural Society of New York*, 22.

7. U. P. Hedrick, *The Land of the Crooked Tree*, 130–32.

8. Sarah Bayliss Royce, *A Frontier Lady: Recollections of the Gold Rush and Early California*, 123.

9. Fredrika Bremer, *The Homes of the New World; Impressions of America*, 209.

10. Mrs. Ann MacVicar Grant, *Memoirs of an American Lady*, 72.

11. Liberty Hyde Bailey, *Garden-Making*, 138.

12. *The Garden Magazine*. April 1917, page 198.

13. François Auguste René Chateaubriand, *Travels in America*. Richard Switzer, trans., 44.

14. Thomas Ashe, *Travels in America, performed in the year 1806*, 7.

15. Ralph Waldo Emerson, "Nature" in *Essays: First and Second Series*, 382.

16. Henry David Thoreau, "A Week on the Concord and Merrimack Rivers." from *The Works of Thoreau* (1937), 85.

17. Henry David Thoreau, "Autumnal Tints." *The Works of Thoreau*, 174.

18. Henry David Thoreau, ibid., 170.

19. Charles William Eliot, Charles Eliot, *Landscape Architect*, reprint 1971, 4.

20. Charles William Eliot, ibid., 215–16.

21. Frank A. Waugh, *The Landscape Beautiful*, 128–29.

22. Alexis de Tocqueville, "A Fortnight in the Wilds" in *Journey to America*. J. P. Mayer, ed., 372.

PART 2 CHAPTER 3

1. Sir Uvedale Price, *An Essay on the Picturesque*. (1794) in The Genius of the Place, 356.

2. René Louis, marquis de Girardin, *An Essay on Landscape* (1783), 50.

3. Margaret Law Callcott, ed. *Mistress of Riversdale: The Plantation Letters of Rosalie Stier Calvert 1795–1821*, 84.

4. René Louis, marquis de Girardin, ibid., 24.

5. Andrew Jackson Downing, *A Treatise on the Theory and Practice of Landscape Gardening*. 6th ed. (1859) facsimile ed. 1967. 25.

6. Melanie Louise Simo, *Loudon and the Landscape*, 80.

7. Benson J Lossing, *Vassar College and its Founder*, 60.

8. Robert M. Toole, "Springside: A. J. Downing's only extant garden," *Journal of Garden History* 1989, Vol. 9, No. 1, 20–39.

9. Benson J. Lossing, op. cit., 63.

10. Andrew Jackson Downing, "A Few Hints on Landscape Gardening" *The Horticulturist*. November 1851, 122.

11. Andrew Jackson Downing, *Landscape Gardening*, 60 note.

12. Andrew Jackson Downing, ibid., 312.

13. John Drayton Hastie, *The Story of Magnolia Plantation and its Gardens . . . Their First 300 Years*, 3.

14. Jens Jensen, as told to Ragna B. Eskil, "Natural Parks and Gardens" in *The Saturday Evening Post*. March 8, 1930, 169.

15. Robert Grese, "Abstractions of Nature." *Garden Design*, Autumn, 1988, 75.

16. Jens Jensen. *Siftings*, reprint 1990, 35.

17. Ted Nierenberg, *The Beckoning Path: Lessons of a Lifelong Garden*. Text by Mark Kane, 11.

DIGRESSION 3

1. Timothy Dwight, *Travels in New England and New York*, Vol. I, 7.

2. Donald G. Mitchell, *Rural Studies with Hints for Country Places*, 184.

3. Andrew Jackson Downing, *A Treatise on the Theory and Practice of Landscape Gardening*, 6th ed. 1859, 101.

4. George Washington Cable, *The Amateur Garden*, 75.

5. Timothy Dwight, op. cit., Vol. II, 324.

6. Bronson Alcott, *The Journals of Bronson Alcott*. Odell Shepard, ed., 117.

7. Thomas G. Fessenden, *The New American Gardener*, 15th ed., 109.

8. Andrew Jackson Downing, "On the Improvement of Country Villages" in *Rural Essays*, 230.

9. Timothy Dwight, op. cit., Vol. II, 347.

10. Andrew Jackson Downing, "The New York Park" in *Rural Essays*, 152.

11. George Washington Cable, op. cit., 43.

12. Andrew Jackson Downing, "On the Improvement of Country Villages" in *Rural Essays*, 234.

13. Catherine E Beecher and Harriet Beecher Stowe, *The American Woman's Home*, 295.

14. Henry Ward Beecher, *Plain and Pleasant Talk about Fruits, Flowers and Farming*, 1874 edition, 50.

15. The Rev. John Frederick Schroeder, "Tenth Anniversary Address to the Horticultural Society of New York," 8.

16. Andrew Jackson Downing, "A Talk about Public Parks and Gardens" in *Rural Essays*, 146.

PART 2 CHAPTER 4

1. Mark Laird, *The Flowering of the Landscape Garden: English Pleasure Grounds 1720–1800*, 142–44.
2. Andrew Jackson Downing, "Hints on Flower-Gardens" *The Horticulturist.* April, 1847, 9.
3. John Claudius Loudon, *The Suburban Gardener and Villa Companion*, 216.
4. Humphry Repton, *The Art of Landscape Gardening, including his Sketches and Hints on Landscape Gardening and Theory and Practice of Landscape Gardening*, 144.
5. Frank J. Scott, *The Art of Beautifying Suburban Home Grounds*, 103.
6. Caroline Kirkland, *A New Home . . . Who'll Follow*, 1839.
7. Frank J. Scott, op. cit., 105.
8. Anna B. Warner, *Gardening by Myself*, reprint 1924, 60.
9. Mrs. Schuyler Van Rensselaer, *Art Out-of-Doors*, 147.
10. Elias A. Long, *Ornamental Gardening for Americans*, 208.
11. Liberty Hyde Bailey, *Garden Making*, 2.
12. Bonnie Blodgett, Unpublished research.
13. Elaine Greene, "Of Time and the Garden" *House & Garden*, May 1986, 166–171.
14. Susan Fenimore Cooper, *Rural Hours*, 127–128.
15. Charles Fletcher Lummis, "The Carpet of God's Country" *Land of Sunshine/Out West.* May, 1905, 307.
16. Arthur A. Shurcliff, *Autobiography of Arthur A Shurcliff*. Privately printed. Society for the Preservation of New England Antiquities Library and Archives.
17. Arthur A. Shurcliff, "Some Old New England Flower Gardens" *New England Magazine.* December, 1899, 422–26.
18. Elizabeth Hope Cushing, "The Work of 'Our Own Hands': The Evolution of the Arthur A. Shurcliffs' Summer Residence at Ipswich." *Old Time New England*, Vol. 78, No. 268 (Fall/Winter 2000), 42–66.

DIGRESSION 4

1. J. E. Spingarn, "Henry Winthrop Sargent and The Landscape Tradition at Wodenethe" reprinted in *Landscape Architecture*, October 1938, 24.
2. Anne Peterson, "Women Take the Lead in Landscape Art." *New York Times.* March 13, 1938, D5.
3. Gilbert Imlay, *A Topographical Description of the Western Territory of North America*, 169.
4. Thomas G. Fessenden, *The New American Gardener*, 110.
5. Andrew Jackson Downing, " On Feminine Taste in Rural Affairs" in *Rural Essays*, 45–47.
6. Henry Ward Beecher, *Plain and Pleasant Talk about Fruits, Flowers and Farming* (1859) 117.
7. Beth Mattocks, "Gardening Pioneers of Colorado" *Pioneer American Gardening*, 237.
8. Margaret H. Davidson, "Agriculture of the Dakotas" *Pioneer American Gardening*, 252.
9. Lucile Winifred Reynolds, *Leisure-time Activities of a Selected Group of Farm Women*, 4, 7, 13.
10. Jane Colden, *Botanic Manuscript of Jane Colden*, Introduction, 23.
11. John H. Plumb, "Britain & America: The Cultural Heritage," *The English Heritage*, 8.
12. Elise Pinckney, *Thomas and Elizabeth Lamboll: Early Charleston Gardeners*, 11.
13. Harriott Horry Ravenel, *Eliza Pinckney*, 224.
14. Laura Viancour, "Lady Jean Skipwith of Prestwould." in *The Influence of Women on the Southern Landscape*, 55.

15. Elizabeth K. Langhorne, Edward Lay, William D. Riely, *A Virginia Family and Its Plantation Houses*, 97.
16. Mrs. Ann MacVicar Grant, *Memoirs of an American Lady*, 71.
17. Catharine E. Beecher and Harriet Beecher Stowe, *The American Woman's Home*, 311.
18. Mariana Griswold Van Rensselaer, *Accents as Well as Broad Effects.* David Gebhard, ed., 8.
19. Mrs. Schuyler Van Rensselaer, *Art Out-of-Doors.* 185.
20. Rebecca Warren Davidson, "Introduction to the Reprint Edition." *The Spirit of the Garden.* xii.
21. Judith Tankard, *The Gardens of Ellen Biddle Shipman*, 29.
22. James Yoch, *Landscaping the American Dream*, 10–20.
23. Guy Lowell quoted in Mary Bronson Hartt, "Women and the Art of Landscape Gardening." *The Outlook.* March 28, 1908, 699.
24. Diana Balmori, "Campus Work and Public Landscapes" in Balmori, McGuire, and McPeck. *Beatrix Farrand's American Landscapes.* 137–39.
25. Susan Davis Price, *Minnesota Gardens: An Illustrated History*, 29.
26. Marjorie Gibbon Battles and Catherine Colt Dickey, *Fifty Blooming Years*, 18.
27. Virginia Lopez Begg, "Frances Duncan: The 'New Woman' in The Garden." *Journal of the New England Garden History Society*, Vol. 2 (Fall 1992), 33.

PART 2 CHAPTER 5

1. Fredrika Bremer, *The Homes of the New World: Impressions of America*, 370.
2. Catharine Maria Sedgwick, *Letters from Abroad to Kindred at Home*, 206.
3. Alan Emmet, *So Fine a Prospect*, 87.
4. Keith N. Morgan, *Charles A. Platt: The Artist as Architect*, 18.
5. Edith Wharton, *Italian Villas and Their Gardens*, 5.
6. Claudia Lazzaro, *The Italian Renaissance Garden*, 11, 26.
7. Edith Wharton, op. cit., 7.
8. Phoebe Cutler, "The Villas of Rome and Gardens at Home." *Journal of the New England Garden History Society*, Vol. 8, 7.
9. Phoebe Cutler, ibid., 10.
10. Edward S. Prior, M. A., "American Garden-Craft from an English Point of View," *House & Garden*, November 1903, 207–08.
11. Reginald Blomfield, *The Formal Garden in England*, 10.
12. Patricia Nelson O'Brien, *Filoli*. (Master of Landscape Architecture thesis, University of California, Berkeley, 1975), 7–8.
13. Christopher McMahon and Timmy Gallagher, *The Gardens at Filoli*, 16.
14. Bruce Porter, "Art & Architecture in California," in Zoeth Skinner Eldredge, *History of California*. Vol. 5, 463.
15. Bruce Porter, Introduction to Porter Garnett. *Stately Homes of California.* (Boston, 1915)
16. McMahon and Gallagher, op. cit., 21.
17. Mariana Griswold Van Rensselaer, "Japanese Gardening" *Garden and Forest.* January 30, 1889, 52.
18. Clay Lancaster, *The Japanese Influence in America*, 197–98.
19. Gustav Stickley, *Craftsman Homes*, 119.
20. T. Kaori Kitao, "Rocks, Islands, Mountains and the Japanese Garden." *Japanese Gardens*, Brooklyn Botanic Garden Record (1990), 6.
21. Dean Cardasis, Telephone interview, July 2000.
22. James C. Rose, "The Sensible Landscape" in *Landscape.* Vol. 10, 227–30.

23. James C. Rose, *Creative Gardens*, 22.
24. Auguste Bernard Duhaut-Cilly, *A voyage to California, the Sandwich Islands & around the world in the years 1826–29*, 234, note 4.
25. Edward S Morse, *Glimpses of China and Chinese Homes.* 58, 206–07.
26. Ji Cheng, *The Craft of Gardens*.
27. Osvald Siren, *Gardens of China*, 5.
28. *The New York Chinese Scholar's Garden Interpretive Guide*, 1.
29. Herbert Croly, *Willard Straight*, and Louis Graves. *Willard Straight in the Orient; with illustrations from his sketch-books.*
30. Osvald Siren, *Gardens of China*, 5
31. Lester Collins, *Innisfree: An American Garden*, 39.

DIGRESSION 5

1. U.S. Census Bureau, *Geographical Mobility: March 1998– March 1999* (updates), 20–531.
2. Albert C. Manucy, *The Houses of St. Augustine: notes on the architecture from 1565 to 1821*, 55.
3. Richard Westmacott, *African-American Gardens and Yards in the Rural South*, 79.
4. Catherine M. Howett, "A Southern Lady's Legacy: the Italian 'Terraces' of La Grange, Georgia" in *The Journal of Garden History*, Vol. 2, No. 4, Oct–Dec 1982, 347.
5. Suzanne Turner, "Roots of a Regional Garden Tradition: The Drawings of the New Orleans Notarial Archives." In *Regional Garden Design in the United States*, 187.
6. Mark Laird, *The Flowering of the English Landscape Garden*, 70.
7. *Vick's Monthly Magazine.* Vol. I, May 1878, 139.
8. Henry Winthrop Sargent, Supplement to Andrew Jackson Downing. A *Treatise on the Theory and Practice of Landscape Gardening*, facsimile 1967, 538.
9. Andrew Jackson Downing, "A Few Hints on Landscape Gardening" in *Rural Essays*, 120.
10. Wilhelm Miller, *The Prairie Spirit in Landscape Gardening*, 5.
11. Charles Keeler, *The Simple Home*, 15.
12. Jens Jensen, as told to Ragna B. Eskil, "Natural Parks and Gardens" *The Saturday Evening Post*, March 8, 1930, 170.
13. Paul R. Baker, *The Fortunate Pilgrims: Americans in Italy 1800–1860*, 20.
14. Mabel Osgood Wright, *The Garden of a Commuter's Wife*, 86, 250.

PART 2 CHAPTER 6

1. Elisabeth B. MacDougall, Introduction. *Music in Stone: Great Sculpture Gardens of the World*, 14–16.
2. Kenneth L. Ames, "Contextualizing the Morris Arboretum." In *Victorian Landscape in America: The Garden as Artifact*, 5–15.
3. Tom Krenitsky, Unpublished article.
4. Tom Krenitsky, Telephone interview.
5. Tom Krenitsky, Telephone interview.
6. William Hertrich, *The Huntington Botanical Gardens*, 1905–1949, 27.
7. Joe Clements, Telephone interview.
8. Warren Manning to Frank A. Seiberling, June 23, 1911.
9. Susan Child, "Warren Manning 1860–1938: The Forgotten Genius of the American Landscape." *Journal of the New England Garden History Society*, Vol. 1, Fall, 1991, 32.
10. Jennifer Yoos, "Conversation with Vincent James, George Hargreaves and James Carpenter" *a+u* 98: II 18–26.

11. Paula Deitz, "In the Line of Beauty" *Gardens Illustrated*. June 2000, 46.

12. Balthazar and Monica Korab. All quotes are from telephone interviews with the Korabs or notes supplied by them.

DIGRESSION 6

1. Rachel Kaplan, Stephen Kaplan and Robert L. Ryan, *With People in Mind: Design and Management of Everyday Nature*, 12.

2. John Brinckerhoff Jackson, *Landscape*. Autumn, 1951, 8.

3. Albertus Magnus, *On Vegetables and Plants*. in John Harvey, *Mediaeval Gardens*, 6.

4. William Byrd of Virginia, *The London Diary (1717–1721) and Other Writings*. Louis B. Wright and Marion Tinling, eds., 507, 510.

5. Frances Wright D'Arusmont, *Views of Society and Manners in America*. (September 3, 1818 to mid May 1820) Paul R. Baker, ed., 95.

6. Andrew Jackson Downing, *A Treatise on the Theory and Practice of Landscape Gardening*, 6th ed., 63.

7. Andrew Jackson Downing, "On the Improvement of Country Villages" *Rural Essays*, 230.

8. Barbara M. Cross, ed., *The Autobiography of Lyman Beecher*, 66.

9. Samuel Sewall, *The Diary of Samuel Sewall 1674–1729*. M. Halsey Thomas, ed., 329.

10. Rudy J. Favretti, "The Ornamentation of New England Towns: 1750–1850" *Journal of Garden History*. Vol. 2 No. 4 (Oct–Dec 1982). 329–30.

11. Peter Kalm, *Travels in North America* 1987 ed., 131.

12. I. N. Phelps Stokes, *The Iconography of Manhattan Island, 1498–1909*. reprint 1967, 59, 72.

13. Leonard Bacon, *Sketch of the life and public services of Hon. James Hillhouse of New Haven: With a Notice of his Son, August Lucas Hillhouse*, 51.

14. Nathaniel Hillyer Egleston, *Villages and Village Life with Hints for Their Improvemen*,. 83.

15. *The Farm*. from the Dublin Seminars for New England Folklife, Annual Proceedings 1986, 43.

16. Lucinda A, Brockway, "The Colonial Revival Landscape 'Tempus Fugit': Capturing the Past in the Landscape of the Piscataqua". "A *Noble and Dignified Stream*" *The Piscataqua Region in the Colonial Revival, 1860–1930*. Bibliography no. 18.

17. Frederick Law Olmsted and Calvert Vaux, *Preliminary Report upon the Proposed Suburban Village at Riverside, Near Chicago*, 24.

18. John W. Reps, *The Making of Urban America: A History of City Planning in the United States*, 472.

19. Leonard Bacon, op. cit., 45.

20. Henry Ingersoll Bowditch, *Topographical Distribution and Local Origin of Consumption in Massachusetts*, 94.

21. Nathaniel Hillyer Egleston, op. cit., 85.

22. Charles Eliot, "How to Mask the Foundations of a Country House" I-IV; "Design in the Surroundings of Houses". *Garden and Forest*. July 14, 31, August 14, 28, 21, 1889.

23. Fletcher Steele, *Design in the Little Garden*, 33.

24. Andrew Jackson Downing, "A Chapter on Lawns." Rural Essays, 185.

25. Joan Iverson Nassauer, "Messy Ecosystems, Orderly Frames." *Landscape Journal*. November 1995, 168–69.

26. Rachel Kaplan and Stephen Kaplan, *The Experience of Nature: A Psychological Perspective* 101.

PART 2 CHAPTER 7

1. Sam Bass Warner, Jr., *Streetcar Suburbs: The Process of Growth in Boston (1870–1900)* 67–116.

2. Fletcher Steele, *Design in the Little Garden*. 10.

3. Fletcher Steele, ibid., 24.

4. Arthur C. Eldredge, "Making a Small Garden Look Large" *The Garden Magazine*. Vol. 38, No. 6 (February 1924) 332–35.

5. O. C. Simonds, *Landscape-Gardening*. 141.

6. O. C. Simonds, ibid., 152.

7. O. C. Simonds, ibid., 150.

8. J. Lee Greene, *Time's Unfading Garden: Anne Spencer's Life and Poetry*, 160.

9. Jane Baber White, "Restoration of a Poet's Garden." *American Horticulturist*, October 1987, 27.

10. Anne Spencer, [Thou are come to us, O God, this year] in J. Lee Greene, *Time's Unfading Garden*, 182.

11. Robin Karson, *Fletcher Steele, Landscape Architect: An Account of the Gardenmaker's Life, 1885–1971*. 33.

12. Fletcher Steele, *Design in the Little Garden* 30.

13. Fletcher Steele, ibid., 17.

14. Fletcher Steele, ibid., 30.

15. Suzanne Turner, "Roots of a Regional Garden Tradition: The Drawings of the New Orleans Notarial Archives" *Regional Garden Design in the United States*, 165.

16. Samuel Wilson, Jr., Introduction. *A New Orleans Courtyard 1830-1860: The Hermann-Grima House*, 2.

17. Suzanne Turner, "A Preservation Plan for the Hermann-Grima House," *A New Orleans Courtyard 1830–1860*, 26.

18. Shingo Dameron Manard. "Recreating a Period Garden" *A New Orleans Courtyard 1830–1860*, 5.

19. Dora P. Crouch, Daniel J. Garr, and Axel L. Mundigo, *Spanish City Planning in North America*. 16, 17

20. Frederick Law Olmsted, *A Journey Through Texas*, 348–49.

21. George Vancouver, *Vancouver in California 1792–1794: The Original Account of George Vancouver*, 229.

22. Hugo Reid, *The Indians of Los Angeles County: Hugo Reid's letters of 1852*, 82.

23. Thomas Brown, *Landscapes and Gardens of the Mission Era*. Unpublished talk delivered September 1980, 16.

24. Sir George Simpson, *Narrative of a Journey Round the World, during the Years 1841 and 1842*, 216.

25. Thomas Brown, "Gardens of the California Missions" *Pacific Horticulture*. Spring 1988, 7.

26. Helen Hunt Jackson, *Glimpses of California and the Missions*. (Articles first published in The Century, 1883), 192.

27. Phoebe Cutler, "Thomas Church's Wild Horse Valley Ranch." Unpublished research.

28. Phoebe Cutler, ibid.

29. Garrett Eckbo, *Landscape for Living*, 95.

30. Julius Shulman, Telephone conversations, June 2001.

PART 3 PORTFOLIO 1

1. Beatrix Farrand, *The Bulletins of Reef Point Gardens*, 112.

2. Diane Kostial McGuire, ed., *Beatrix Farrand's Plant Book for Dumbarton Oaks*, xxi.

3. Francis H. Cabot, *The Greater Perfection*, 60.

4. Topher Delaney, Conversations with the author.

PART 3 PORTFOLIO 2

1. Although Clarence and Muriel Hamilton have died and the garden is now owned and cared for by Enkei America Inc., it is always referred to by the name of the original owners.

2. Dan Kiley, "The Hamilton Garden," *Process Architecture: Landscape Design: Works of Dan Kiley*, No. 33, 28.

PART 3 PORTFOLIO 3

1. John W. S. Platt, "Oregon Eden," *House & Garden*, February 1987, 144.

2. James Van Sweden, *Gardening with Nature*, 19–20, 38–41.

3. All Leland Miyano quotations are from telephone conversations with the author.

PART 3 PORTFOLIO 4

1. Catherine Howett, ed., *Abstracting the Landscape: The Artistry of Landscape Architect A. E. Bye*, 13.

2. Gainesway Farms, originally 500 acres, has grown to 1500 acres since it was sold to Mr. and Mrs. Graham J. Beck, the present owners, in 1989.

3. A. E. Bye, *Art into Landscape, Landscape into Art*. 2nd ed., 168.

4. Ibid., 101.

5. Author's interview with Janis Hall.

Bibliography

A Catalogue of the Washington Collection in the Boston Athenaeum. Compiled by Appleton P. C. Griffin; appendix by William Coolidge Lane [Cambridge, University Press: J. Wilson and Son] The Boston Athenaeum, 1897.

Abstracting the Landscape: The Artistry of Landscape Architect A. E. Bye. Catherine Howett, ed., State College: Pennsylvania State University Press, 1990.

Alcott, Bronson. *The Journals of Bronson Alcott.* Selected and edited by Odell Shepard. Boston: Little Brown, 1938.

Alden, Rev. Timothy. *The Glory of America: A Century Sermon.* delivered at South Church, Portsmouth, New Hampshire, January 4, 1801.

Allen, Lewis F. *Rural Architecture.* New York: C. M. Saxton, 1852.

Anderson, Edgar. *Plants, Man and Life.* Boston: Little, Brown and Company, 1952.

Appelbaum, Stanley. *The Chicago World's Fair of 1893.* New York: Dover Press, 1980.

Architectural Record: The restoration of Colonial Williamsburg in Virginia. Reprinted from December 1935 issue. New York: F. W. Dodge, c. 1935.

Ashe, Thomas. *Travels in America, Performed in the Year 1806.* London, 1809.

Bacon, Francis, Lord Verulam. *The Essays, No. 46, Gardens* (1625). London: William Pickering, 1852.

Bacon, Leonard. *Sketch of the Life and Public Services of Hon. James Hillhouse of New Haven: With a Notice of His Son, August Lucas Hillhouse.* New Haven, 1860.

Bailey, Liberty Hyde. *Garden-Making.* Chicago: The Garden-Craft Series, 1902.

Bailyn, Bernard. *The Peopling of British North America: An Introduction.* New York: Vintage, 1988.

Baker, Paul R. *The Fortunate Pilgrims: Americans in Italy, 1800-1860.* Cambridge: Harvard University Press, 1964.

Balmori, Diana, Diane Kostial McGuire, Eleanor M. McPeck. *Beatrix Farrand's American Landscapes.* Sagaponack N. Y.: Sagapress, 1985.

Barlow, Elizabeth, and William Alex. *Frederick Law Olmsted's New York.* New York: Praeger, 1972.

Bartram, John. *The Correspondence of John Bartram 1734–1777.* Edmund Berkeley and Dorothy Smith Berkeley, eds. Gainesville: University Press of Florida, 1992.

Bartram, John and William. *John and William Bartram's America: Selections from the Writings of the Philadelphia Naturalists.* Helen Gere Cruickshank, ed. New York: Devin-Adair, 1957.

Bartram, William. *Travels and Other Writings,* including *Travels through North & South Carolina, Georgia, East & West Florida.* Philadelphia, 1791. New York: The Library of America, 1996.

Battles, Marjorie Gibbon and Catherine Colt Dickey. *Fifty Blooming Years 1913–1963.* The Garden Club of America, 1963.

Byrd, William. *The London Diary (1717–1721) and Other Writings.* Louis B. Wright, and Marion Tinling, eds. New York: Oxford University Press, 1958.

——*The Secret Diary of William Byrd of Westover 1709–1712.* Louis B. Wright, and Marion Tinling, eds. Richmond, Va.: Dietz Press, 1941.

Betts, Edwin M., and Hazlehurst Bolton Perkins. *Thomas Jefferson's Flower Garden at Monticello.* Revised and enlarged by Peter J. Hatch. Charlottesville: University Press of Virginia, 1986.

Beveridge, Charles E. and Klaus, Susan L. *The Olmsteds at Biltmore,* NAOP Workbook Vol. 5, Bethesda, Md., National Association for Olmsted Parks, 1995.

Beverley, Robert. *The History and Present State of Virginia* (1705). Louis B. Wright, ed. Chapel Hill: University of North Carolina Press, 1947.

Beecher, Catherine E. and Harriet Beecher Stowe. *The American Woman's Home.* New York: J. B. Ford, 1870.

Beecher, Henry Ward. *Plain and Pleasant Talk about Fruits, Flowers and Farming.* New York: Derby & Jackson, 1859.

——*Plain and Pleasant Talk about Fruits, Flowers and Farming.* New edition with additional matter from recent writings published and unpublished. (First 86 pages new material) New York: J. B. Ford, 1874.

Benes, Peter, ed. *The Farm. Annual Proceedings of the Dublin Seminars for New England Folklife.* Boston: Boston University, 1988.

——*New England Prospect: A Loan Exhibition of Maps at the Currier Gallery of Art.* Boston: Boston University, 1981.

——*Plants and People. Annual Proceedings of The Dublin Seminar for New England Folklife.* Boston: Boston University, 1996.

Birch, William. *The Country Seats of the United States of North America: With Some Scenes Connected with Them.* Springland, near Bristol, Pennsylvania, 1808–1809.

Birnbaum, Charles and Robin Karson, eds. *Pioneers of American Landscape Design.* New York: McGraw-Hill, 2000.

Blomfield, Reginald. *The Formal Garden in England* (1892). London: Waterstone, 1985.

Bolton, Herbert Eugene, ed. *Fray Juan Crespi: Missionary Explorer on the Pacific Coast 1769–1744.* Berkeley: University of California Press, 1927.

Boorstin, Daniel J. *The Americans: The Colonial Experience.* New York: Vintage Books, 1958.

Bowditch, Henry Ingersoll. *Topographical Distribution and Local Origin of Consumption in Massachusetts.* Boston: Massachusetts Medical Society, 1862.

Boyd, William K.., ed. *William Byrd's Histories of the Dividing Line Betwixt Virginia and North Carolina.* Raleigh: North Carolina Historical Commission, 1929.

Bradford, William. *Of Plymouth Plantation 1620–1647.* New York: Modern Library, 1981.

Bremer, Fredrika. *The Homes of the New World; Impressions of America.* (Trip Sept 1849 to Sept 1851) Translated by Mary Howitt. London: Arthur Hall, Virtue & Co., 1853.

Bridenbaugh, Carl. *Cities in the Wilderness.* New York: Ronald Press, 1938.

Brissot de Warville, J. P. *Nouveau voyage dans les Etats Unis de l'Amerique Septentrionale fait en 1788.* Paris, chez Buisson, avril 1791.

Brooks, Van Wyck. *The Flowering of New England 1815–1865.* New York: E. P. Dutton, Modern Library Edition, 1936.

Brown, Jane. *Beatrix: The Gardening Life of Beatrix Jones Farrand, 1872–1959.* New York: Viking, 1995

Bryant, William Cullen, ed. *Picturesque America.* London: Cassell and Co., Ltd., 1894–1897.

Buckingham, James Silk. *The Slave States of America.* London, 1842. Excerpted in *The Rambler in Georgia: Travellers' Accounts of Frontier Georgia.* Mills Lane, ed. Savannah: The Beehive Foundation, 1990.

Burnaby, Andrew. *Travels through the Middle Settlements in North America in the Years 1759 and 1760.* Reprinted from the third edition of 1798. New York, 1904.

Bushman, Richard L. *The Refinement of America: Persons, Houses, Cities.* New York: Knopf, 1992.

Bye, A. E. *Art into Landscape, Landscape into Art.* Second ed. Mesa, Arizona: PDA Publishers, 1988.

Byne, Mildred Stapely, and Arthur Byne. *Spanish Gardens and Patios.* Philadelphia: J. B. Lippincott, 1928.

Cable, George Washington. *The Amateur Garden.* New York: Charles Scribner's Sons, 1914.

Cabot, Francis H. *The Greater Perfection.* A Hortus Press Book. New York: W. W. Norton, 2001.

Callcott, Margaret Law, ed. *Mistress of Riversdale: The Plantation Letters of Rosalie Stier Calvert 1795–1821.* Baltimore: Johns Hopkins University Press, 1991.

Carter, George; Patrick Goode, and Laurie Kedrum. *Humphry Repton Landscape Gardener 1752–1818.* Norwich: Sainsbury Centre for Visual Arts, 1982.

Chaco and Hohokam: Prehistoric Regional Systems in the American Southwest. Patricia L. Crown and W. James Judge, eds. Santa Fe: School of American Research Press, 1991.

Chastellux, François-Jean, marquis de. *Travels in North America in the Years 1780, 1781, and 1782.* Revised translation by Howard G. Rice, Jr. Chapel Hill: North Carolina University Press, 1963.

Chateaubriand, François-Auguste René de. *Travels in America* (from a visit in 1791). Richard Switzer, trans. Lexington: University of Kentucky Press, 1969.

Church, Thomas D. *Gardens Are for People.* New York: Reinhold, 1955.

——*Your Private World.* San Francisco: Chronicle Books, 1969.

Church, Thomas D. with Grace Hall and Michael Laurie. *Gardens Are For People.* Second ed. New York: McGraw-Hill, 1983.

Cleveland, H.W.S. *Landscape Architecture as Applied to the Wants of the West.* Originally published 1873. Pittsburgh: University of Pittsburgh Press, 1965.

Cohen, Paul E. and Robert T. Augustyn. *Manhattan in Maps: 1527-1995.* New York: Rizzoli, 1997.

Colden, Jane. *Botanic Manuscript of Jane Colden.* Edited by H. W. Rickett and Elizabeth C. Hall: Chantecleer Press, 1963.

Collins, Lester. *Innisfree: An American Garden.* Sagaponack, N. Y.: Sagapress/Harry N. Abrams, 1994.

Common Places. Readings in American Vernacular Architecture. Dell Upton and John Michael Vlach, eds. Athens: The University of Georgia Press, 1986.

Conder, Josiah. *Landscape Gardening in Japan, with the Supplement of 40 Plates.* Reprint of 1912 ed., originally published in 1893. New York: Dover, 1964.

Cook, Clarence. *The House Beautiful.* (1877) Unabridged reprint of 1881 ed. New York: Dover, 1995.

Cooper, Susan Fenimore. *Rural Hours.* New York: George P. Putnam, 1850.

Copley, John Singleton. *Letters & Papers of John Singleton Copley and Henry Pelham 1739–1776.* Massachusetts Historical Society Collections, Vol. 71. The Massachusetts Historical Society, 1914.

Croly, Herbert. *Willard Straight.* New York: MacMillan, 1924.

Cronon, William. *Changes in the Land: Indians, Colonists, and the Ecology of New England.* New York: Hill and Wang, 1983.

——*Nature's Metropolis: Chicago and the Great West.* New York: W. W. Norton, 1991.

Cross, Barbara M., ed. *The Autobiography of Lyman Beecher.* Cambridge: Belknap Press/Harvard, 1961.

Cutler, Phoebe. *The Public Landscape of the New Deal.* New Haven: Yale University Press, 1985.

Cutler, William Parker, and Julia Perkins Cutler, *Life, Journals and Correspondence of Rev. Manasseh Cutler, LL.D.* (1888) Athens: Ohio University Press, 1987.

Danckaerts, Jasper. *The Journal of Jasper Danckaerts 1679-1680.* Reprint in *Original Narratives of Early*

American History. New York: Barnes and Noble, 1969.

Davis, John. *Travels of Four Years and a Half in the United States of America during 1798, 1799, 1800, 1801, and 1802*. New York: Henry Holt, 1909.

D'Arusmont, Frances Wright. *Views of Society and Manners in America (1818–1820)*. Paul R. Baker, ed. Cambridge: Belknap Press/Harvard, 1963.

de Forest, Elizabeth Kellam. *The Gardens & Grounds at Mount Vernon: How George Washington Planned and Planted Them*. Mount Vernon, Virginia: The Mount Vernon Ladies Association of the Union, 1982.

Doell, M. Christine Klim. *Gardens of the Gilded Age*. Syracuse, N. Y.: Syracuse University Press, 1986.

Dezailler d'Argenville, Antoine-Joseph. *The Theory and Practice of Gardening* (Paris, 1709). John James, trans., London, 1712. Gregg International Publishers, Ltd., 1969.

Donck, Adriaen Van der. *A Description of the New Netherlands*. (1656) Thomas F. O'Donnell, ed. Syracuse, N.Y.: Syracuse University Press, 1968.

Downing, Andrew Jackson. *A Treatise on the Theory and Practice of Landscape Gardening*. Sixth ed. (1859), with a supplement by Henry Winthrop Sargent. Facsimile, New York: Funk & Wagnalls, 1967.

——*Cottage Residences* (1873). Published as *Victorian Cottage Residences* with a new preface by Adolf K. Placzek. New York: Dover, 1981.

——*Rural Essays*. George William Curtis, ed. New York: George P. Putnam and Company, 1893. Reprint. New York: Da Capo Press, 1974.

——*The Architecture of Country Houses* (1850). Reprint, New York: Dover, 1969.

Drury, John. *Historic Midwest Houses*. Minneapolis: The University of Minnesota Press, 1947.

Duflot de Mofras, Eugene. *Travels on the Pacific Coast* (1840, 1841,1842). 2 vols. Annotated by Marguerite Eyer Wilbur, ed. and trans. Santa Ana: Fine Arts Press, 1937.

Duhaut-Cilly, Auguste-Bernard. *A voyage to California, the Sandwich Islands & Around the World in the Years 1826–1829*. Translated by August Fruge and Neal Harlow, eds. Berkeley: University of California Press, c. 1999.

Dumbarton Oaks Colloquia on the History of Landscape Architecture: II (1972) *The Picturesque Garden and Its Influence Outside the British Isles*; VI (1978) *John Claudius Loudon and the Early Nineteenth Century in Great Britain*; VIII (1982) *Beatrix Jones Farrand (1872–1959): Fifty Years of American Landscape Architecture*; XI (1987) *Prophet with Honor: The Career of Andrew Jackson Downing (1815–1852)*; XII (1988) *The Dutch Garden in the Seventeenth Century*; XIII (1989) *Garden History: Issues, Approaches, Methods*; XIV (1990) *The Vernacular Garden*; XV (1991) *Regional Garden Design in the United States*. Washington, D.C., Dumbarton Oaks Trustees for Harvard University, 1974–95.

Dutton, Joan Parry. *Enjoying America's Gardens*. New York: Reynal Company, 1958.

Dwight, Timothy. *Travels in New England and New York*. Barbara Miller Solomon, ed., with Patricia M. King. Cambridge: Belknap Press/ Harvard, 1969.

Earle, Alice Morse. *Old-Time Gardens*. New York: Macmillan, 1901.

Early English and French Voyages, Chiefly from Hakluyt, 1534–1608: From Original Narratives of Early American History. New York: Barnes & Noble, 1952.

Eaton, Leonard. *Landscape Artist in America: The Life and Work of Jens Jensen*. Chicago: The University of Chicago Press, 1964.

Eckbo, Garrett. *An Interview with Garrett Eckbo*. Michael Laurie, interviewer. Watertown, Mass.: The Hubbard Educational Trust, 1990.

——*Landscape for Living*. New York: An Architectural Record Book with Duell, Sloan & Pearce, F. W. Dodge Corp., 1950.

Egleston, Nathaniel Hillyer. *Villages and Village Life with Hints for Their Improvement*. New York, 1878.

Eighteenth Century Life: "British and American Gardens." Robert P. Maccubbin and Peter Martin, eds. Williamsburg: College of William and Mary and The Colonial Williamsburg Foundation, 1984.

Eliot, Charles William. *Charles Eliot, Landscape Architect*. (1902) Reprint, Freeport, N. Y.: Books for Libraries Press, 1971.

Eliot, Jerad. *Essays upon Field Husbandry in New England and Other Papers 1748–1762*. New York: AMS Press, 1967.

Emerson, Ralph Waldo. *Essays & Lectures*. New York: The Library of America, c.1983.

——*Essays: First and Second Series*. New York: Harper & Row. Originally published by T.Y. Crowell, 1926.

——*Selected Essays*. New York: Viking Penguin, 1982.

Emmet, Alan. *So Fine a Prospect*. Hanover and London: University Press of New England, 1996.

Farrand, Beatrix. *The Bulletins of Reef Point Gardens*. Reprinted with an introduction by Paula Deitz. Bar Harbor, Maine: The Island Foundation, 1997.

Fein, Albert. *Frederick Law Olmsted and the American Environmental Tradition*. New York: George Braziller, 1972.

Ferri-Pisani, Lieutenant-Colonel Camille. *Prince Napoleon in America, 1861*. Translated by Georges J. Joyaux. Bloomington: Indiana University Press, 1959.

Fessenden, Thomas G. *The New American Gardener*. 1828. Boston: Otis, Broaders, & Company, 1842.

Fithian, Philip Vickers. *Journal and Letters 1767–1774*. John Rogers Williams, ed., for The Princeton Historical Association. Princeton, N. J.: The University Library, 1900.

Fleming, Nancy. *Money, Manure & Maintenance: Ingredients for the Successful Gardens of Marian Coffin*. Weston, Mass.: Country Place Books, 1995.

Fleming, Ronald Lee and Lauri A. Halderman, *On Common Ground: Caring for Shared Land from Town Common to Urban Park*. Harvard, Mass.: Harvard Common Press, c.1981

French, Jere Stuart. *The California Garden*. Washington, D.C., Landscape Architecture Foundation, 1993.

Gardens of Colony and State. Alice G. B. Lockwood, ed. and compiler, for The Garden Club of America. Vols. I and II. New York: Charles Scribner's Sons, 1931, 1934.

Gardiner, John and David Hepburn. *The American Gardener, Including A Treatise on Gardening by a Citizen of Virginia* (by John Randolph, first published 1804). Washington City, 1826.

Garnett, Porter. *Stately Homes of California*. Introduction by Bruce Porter. Boston: Little Brown, 1915.

Gilbert, Alma M. and Judith Tankard. *A Place of Beauty: The Artists and Gardens of the Cornish Colony*. Berkeley, CA, Ten Speed Press, 2000.

Girardin, R. L. marquis de. *An Essay on Landscape*. Translated by Daniel Malthus. 1783. Reprinted with *A Tour to Ermenonville*. 1785. New York: Garland Publishing, 1982.

Gothein, Marie Luise. *A History of Garden Art*. 2 vols., London: J. M. Dent & Sons, 1928.

Grant, Mrs. Ann MacVicar. *Memoirs of an American Lady*. First ed., London 1808, based on stay from 1758–68. New York, 1903.

Graves, Louis. *Willard Straight in the Orient; With Illustrations from his Sketch-books*. New York: Asia Publishing Company, 1922.

Greene, J. Lee. *Time's Unfading Garden: Anne Spencer's Life and Poetry*. Baton Rouge: Louisiana State University Press, 1977.

Greenough, Horatio. *Form and Function: Remarks on Art*. Harold A. Small, ed., Berkeley: University of California Press, 1947.

Grese, Robert E. *Jens Jensen: Maker of Natural Parts and Gardens*. Baltimore: Johns Hopkins University Press, 1992.

Griffen, Sarah L. and Kevin D. Murphy, eds. *"A Noble and Dignified Stream" The Piscataqua Region in the Colonial Revival, 1860-1930*. York, Maine: Old York Historical Society, 1992.

Griswold, Mac, and Eleanor Weller. *The Golden Age of American Gardens*. New York: Harry N. Abrams, 1991.

Gutowski, Robert R., ed. *Victorian Landscape in America: The Garden as Artifact*. Proceedings from the Centennial Symposium, June 16, 1988. Philadelphia: Morris Arboretum of the University of Pennsylvania, 1989.

Haley, Jacquetta M., ed. *Pleasure Grounds: Andrew Jackson Downing and Montgomery Place with Illustrations by Alexander Jackson Davis*. Tarrytown: Sleepy Hollow Press, 1988.

Hamilton, Dr. Alexander. *Gentleman's Progress. The Itinerarium of Dr. Alexander Hamilton 1744*. Carl Bridenbaugh, ed. Chapel Hill, 1948.

Handlin, David P. *The American Home*. Boston: Little, Brown & Company, 1979.

Hansen, Marcus Lee. *The Atlantic Migration 1604–1860*. Cambridge: Harvard University Press, 1940.

Harvey, John. *Mediaeval Gardens*. London: B. T. Batsford, Ltd., 1981.

Hastie, John Drayton. *The Story of Magnolia Plantation and its Gardens . . . Their First 300 Years*. Charleston, S.C.: Magnolia Plantation, 1984.

Hastie, Marie Clinton. *Magnolia-on-the-Ashley*. Charleston, c. 1931.

Hazlehurst, Franklin Hamilton. *Gardens of Illusion: The Genius of André Le Nostre*. Nashville: University of Tennessee Press, 1980.

Hedrick, U. P. *A History of Horticulture in America to 1860*. (1950) With an addendum of books published from 1861–1920 by Elizabeth Woodburn. Portland, Oregon: Timber Press, 1988.

Hedrick, U. P. *The Land of the Crooked Tree*. New York, Oxford University Press, 1948. Reprint, Detroit: Wayne State University Press, 1986.

Henderson, Charles. *Henderson's Picturesque Gardens and Ornamental Gardening Illustrated*. New York: Peter Henderson & Co., 1908.

Henderson, Peter. *Gardening for Pleasure*. New York: Orange Judd, 1886.

Hertrich, William. *The Huntington Botanical Gardens, 1905–1949*. Personal Recollections. San Marino, Calif.: The Huntington Library, 1949.

Hill, Anna Gilman. *Forty Years of Gardening*. New York: Frederick A. Stokes Company, 1938.

Hollingsworth, Buckner. *Her Garden Was Her Delight*. New York: Macmillan, 1962.

Hooper, E. J. *The Western Farmer and Gardener*. Cincinnati: J. A. and U. P. James, 1850.

Hunt, John Dixon and Peter Willis. *The Genius of the Place: The English Landscape Garden 1620–1820*. New York: Harper & Row, 1975.

Hutcheson, Martha Brookes Brown. *The Spirit of the Garden*. Boston: The Atlantic Monthy Press, c. 1923. Reprint ed. Introduction by Rebecca Warren Davidson. Amherst: University of Massachusetts Press in association with the Library of Landscape History, 2001.

Imlay, Gilbert. *A Topographical Description of the Western Territory of North America*. Third ed. (London, 1797). Reprint, New York: Augustus M. Kelley, 1969.

The Influence of Women on the Southern Landscape. Proceedings of the Tenth Conference on Restoring Southern Gardens and Landscapes. October 5–7, 1995. Winston Salem, N. C.: Old Salem, 1997.

Jackson, Faith Reyher. *Pioneer of Tropical Landscape*

Architecture: William Lyman Phillips in Florida. Gainesville: The University Press of Florida, 1997.

Jackson, Helen Hunt. *Glimpses of California and the Missions.* (Articles first published in *The Century* in 1883) Boston: Little, Brown & Company, 1911.

Jackson, John Brinckerhoff. *A Sense of Place, a Sense of Time.* New Haven: Yale University Press, 1994.

——*American Space: The Centennial Years 1865–1876.* New York: W.W. Norton, 1972.

——*Landscape in Sight.* Helen Lefkowitz Horowitz, ed. New Haven: Yale University Press, 1997.

——*Landscapes.* Ervin H. Zube, ed. Amherst: The University of Massachusetts Press, 1970.

——*The Necessity for Ruins and Other Topics.* Amherst: The University of Massachusetts Press, 1980.

——*The Southern Landscape Tradition in Texas.* Number 1 in The Anne Burnett Tandy Lectures in American Civilization. Fort Worth: Amon Carter Museum, 1980.

Jackson, Kenneth. *Crabgrass Frontier. The Suburbanization of the United States.* New York, Oxford, 1985.

James, Henry. *The American Scene* (1907), with three essays from "Portraits of Places." W. H. Auden, ed. New York: Scribner's, 1946.

Jellicoe, Geoffrey and Susan. *The Landscape of Man: Shaping the Environment from Prehistory to the Present Day.* Van Nostrand Reinhold (paperback) 1982.

Jenkins, Virginia Scott. *The Lawn: A History of an American Obsession.* Washington: Smithsonian Institution Press, 1994.

Jensen, Jens. *Siftings.* Originally published 1939. Reprint, Baltimore: Johns Hopkins University Press, 1990.

——*The Clearing.* Chicago: Ralph Fletcher Seymour, 1949.

Ji Cheng. *The Craft of Gardens.* Translated by Alison Hardie. New Haven: Yale University Press, 1988.

Johnson, Gerald W. and Charles Cecil Wall. *Mount Vernon: The Story of a Shrine.* New York: Random House, 1953.

Johnson, Edward. *Wonder-working Providence of Sions Saviour in New England.* London, 1654. Reprint in *Original Narratives of Early American History.* J. Franklin Jameson, ed. New York: Barnes and Noble, 1967.

Johnson, Jory, and Frankel, Felice, photographer. *Modern Landscape Architecture: Redefining the Garden.* New York: Abbeville Press, 1991.

Johnson, Leonard H. *Foundation Planting.* New York: A. T. De La Mare, 1927.

Jonas, Patricia. *Japanese-Inspired Gardens: Adapting Japan's Design Traditions for Your Garden.* Brooklyn, N. Y.: Brooklyn Botanic Garden, 2001.

Josselyn, John. *New-England's Rarities Discovered.* 1672. Reprint, Boston: Massachusetts Historical Society, 1972.

Kalm, Peter. *Travels in North America.* The English Version of 1770 revised from the original Swedish by Adolph B. Benson, ed. New York: Dover, 1987.

Kaplan, Rachel and Stephen Kaplan. *The Experience of Nature: A Psychological Perspective.* Cambridge: Cambridge University Press, 1989.

Kaplan, Rachel, Stephen Kaplan, and Robert L. Ryan. *With People in Mind: Design and Management of Everyday Nature.* Washington, D.C.: Island Press, 1998.

Karson, Robin. *Fletcher Steele, Landscape Architect: An Account of the Gardenmaker's Life, 1885–1971.* New York: Harry N. Abrams/Sagapress, 1989.

Kassler, Elizabeth B. *Modern Gardens and the Landscape.* New York: The Museum of Modern Art, 1964.

Keeler, Charles. *The Simple Home.* (1904) Santa Barbara: Peregrine Smith, Inc., 1979.

Kemble, Frances Anne. *Journal of a Residence on a Georgian Plantation in 1838–39, 1863.* Savannah: Beehive Press, 1992.

Keswick, Maggie. *The Chinese Garden.* U.S. ed., New York: Rizzoli, 1978.

Kiley, Dan and Jane Amidon. *The Complete Works of America's Master Landscape Architect.* Boston: Bulfinch Press/Little, Brown & Company, 1999.

King, Mrs. Francis. *The Beginner's Garden.* New York: Charles Scribner's Sons, 1927.

——*The Well-Considered Garden.* New York: Charles Scribner's Sons, 1922.

Kirkland, Caroline. *A New Home—Who'll Follow.* By Mrs. Mary Clavers (pseud.) Boston: C. S. Francis, 1839.

Kolodny, Annette. *The Land before Her: Fantasy and Experience of the American Frontiers, 1630–1860.* Chapel Hill: University of North Carolina Press, 1984.

Kubler, George, and Martin Soria. *Art and Architecture in Spain and Portugal and Their American Dominions 1500 to 1800.* Baltimore: Penguin Books, 1959.

Laird, Mark. *The Flowering of the Landscape Garden: English Pleasure Grounds 1720–1800.* Philadelphia: University of Pennsylvania Press, 1999.

Lancaster, Clay. *The Japanese Influence in America.* New York: Walton H. Rawls, 1963.

Langhorne, Elizabeth, K. Edward Lay, William D. Riely. *A Virginia Family and Its Plantation Houses.* Charlottesville: The University Press of Virginia, 1987.

Langley, Batty. *New Principles of Gardening.* 1727. John Dixon Hunt, ed. New York: Garland Publishing, 1982.

La Rochefoucauld-Liancourt, François-Alexandre Frédéric, duc de. *Voyage dans les Etats-Unis d'Amerique fait en 1795, 1796 et 1797.* Paris, 1799.

La Tour du Pin, Madame de. (1770–1853) *Memoirs.* Felice Harcourt, ed. and trans. New York: The McCall Publishing Company, 1971.

Larsen, Erik. *Frans Post, interprète du Brésil.* Amsterdam: Colibris, 1962.

Lawson, William. *A New Orchard and Garden.* (1618) bound with John Marriot, *Knots for Gardens* (1623) and Ralph Austen, *A Treatise of Fruit Trees together with The Spirituall Use of an Orchard.* (1653). John Dixon Hunt, ed. New York: Garland Publishing Company, 1982.

Lazzaro, Claudia. *The Italian Renaissance Garden.* New Haven: Yale University Press, 1990.

Leigh, Frances Butler. *Ten Years on a Georgia Plantation since the War.* (1866–1877) 1883. Savannah: Beehive Press, 1992.

Leighton, Ann. *American Gardens of the Nineteenth Century "For Comfort and Affluence."* Amherst: The University of Massachusetts Press, 1987.

——*American Gardens in the Eighteenth Century "For Use or For Delight."* Boston: Houghton Mifflin, 1976.

——*Early American Gardens "For Meate or Medicine."* Boston: Houghton Mifflin, 1970.

Lewis, Oscar. *Here Lived the Californians.* New York: Rinehart, 1957.

Long, Elias A. *Ornamental Gardening for Americans.* New York: Orange Judd Company, 1907.

Lossing, Benson J. *Vassar College and its Founder.* New York: C. A. Alvord, 1867.

Loudon, John Claudius. *An Encyclopedia of Gardening.* Reprint of 1835 ed. New York: Garland Publishing, 1982.

——*The Suburban Gardener and Villa Companion.* Reprint of 1838 ed., New York: Garland Publishing, 1982.

Lowell, Guy, ed. *American Gardens.* Boston: Bates and Guild, 1902.

Magnani, Denise. *The Winterthur Garden.* New York: The Henry Francis du Pont Winterthur Museum and Harry N. Abrams, 1995.

Major, Judith K. *To Live in the New World: A. J. Downing and American Landscape Gardening.* Cambridge, Mass.: MIT Press, 1997.

Manard, Shingo Damaron, ed. *A New Orleans Courtyard 1830–1860: The Hermann-Grima House.* New Orleans: Christian Woman's Exchange, 1996.

Manucy, Albert C. *The Houses of St. Augustine: Notes on the Architecture from 1565 to 1821.* St. Augustine: St. Augustine Historical Society, 1962.

Marsh, George Perkins. *Man and Nature.* Originally published 1864. Cambridge: Harvard University Press, 1965.

Martin, Peter. *The Pleasure Gardens of Virginia.* Princeton: Princeton University Press, 1991.

Marx, Leo. *The Machine in the Garden.* New York: Oxford University Press, 1964.

Maverick, Samuel. "A Briefe discription of New England" c. 1660. *Massachusetts Historical Society Proceedings*, 2nd series I (1884–85).

McAndrew, John. *The Open-Air Churches of Sixteenth-Century Mexico.* Cambridge: Harvard University Press, 1965.

McGuire, Diane Kostial, ed. *Beatrix Farrand's Plant Book for Dumbarton Oaks.* Washington, D. C., Dumbarton Oaks, 1980.

——*Gardens of America: Three Centuries of Design.* Charlottesville, Va; Thomasson-Grant, 1989.

McHarg, Ian L. *Design with Nature.* Paperback ed. Garden City, N. Y.: Doubleday/Natural History Press, 1971.

McMahon, Bernard. *The American Gardener's Calendar.* Philadelphia: B. Graves, 1806.

McMahon, Christopher and Timmy Gallagher. *The Gardens at Filoli.* San Francisco: Pomegranate Artbooks, 1994.

Meanings of the Garden. Proceedings of A Working Conference to Explore the Social, Psychological and Cultural Dimensions of Gardens. Mark Francis and Randolph T. Hester, eds. Jr. Davis: University of California, 1987.

Meek, A.. and Turner, Suzanne. *The Gardens of Louisiana: Places of Work and Wonder.* Baton Rouge: Louisiana State University Press, 1997.

Mendieta, Fray Geronimo (1525–1604) *Historia Eclesiastica Indiana.* Madrid: Edition Atlas, 1973.

Meinig, D. W. *The Shaping of America* Vol. 1: *Atlantic America 1492–1800.* New Haven: Yale University Press, 1986. Vol. 2: *Continental America 1800–1867.* New Haven: Yale University Press, 1993. Vol. 3: *Transcontinental America, 1850–1915.* New Haven: Yale University Press, 1998.

Meinig, D. W., ed. *The Interpretation of Ordinary Landscapes.* New York: Oxford University Press, 1979.

Menzies, Archibald. *Journal of Vancouver's Voyage.* April to October 1792. C. F. Newcombe, M. D., ed. Archives of British Columbia, Memoir No. V., Victoria, B.C., 1923.

Miller, Philip. *The Gardeners Kalendar.* London, 1748. (eighth ed).

Miller, Wilhelm. *The Prairie Spirit in Landscape Gardening.* Bulletin 184, Illinois Agricultural Experiment Station. Urbana: University of Illinois, 1915.

Mitchell, Donald G. *Rural Studies with Hints for Country Places.* New York: Charles Scribner & Co., 1867.

Mitchill, Samuel Latham. *Address Delivered to The Horticultural Society of New-York.* August 29, 1826.

Moore, Charles W., William J. Mitchell, and William Turnbull, Jr. *The Poetics of Gardens.* Cambridge: MIT Press, 1988.

Morgan, Keith N. *Charles A. Platt: The Artist as Architect.* Cambridge, Mass.: The Architectural History Foundation and MIT Press, 1985.

Morrison, Hugh. *Early American Architecture.* New York: Dover Publications, 1987.

Morse, Edward S. *Glimpses of China and Chinese homes.* Boston: Little, Brown & Company, 1902.

Morse, Edward S. *Japanese Homes and Their Surroundings*. Published 1886. New York: Dover Publications, 1961.

Morton, George. *Mourt's Relation or Journal of the Plantation of Plymouth* (London: John Bellamie, 1622). Reprint, George B. Cheever, ed., New York: John Wiley, 1848.

Mountain, Dydymus (Thomas Hill). *The Gardeners Labyrinth* (1594). John Dixon Hunt, ed. New York: Garland Publishing, 1982.

Muir, John. *The Story of My Boyhood and Youth*. San Francisco: Sierra Club Books, 1988.

——*Wilderness Essays*. Salt Lake City: Gibbs Smith, 1980.

Murray, The Hon. Charles Augustus. *Travels in North America during the Years 1834, 1835 & 1836*. New York: Harper & Brothers, 1839.

Music in Stone: Great Sculpture Gardens of the World. Text by Sidney Lawrence and George Foy; Introduction by Elisabeth MacDougall; Foreword by John Train; Photographs by Nicolas Sapieha. New York: Scala Books, 1984.

Myers, Albert Cook, ed. *Narratives of Early Pennsylvania, West New Jersey and Delaware 1630–1707*. Reprint in *Original Narratives of Early American History*. New York: Barnes and Noble, 1946.

Narratives of Early Virginia 1606–1625: Reprint in *Original Narratives of Early American History*. New York: Barnes and Noble, 1952.

Nash, Roderick. *Wilderness and The American Mind*. Third ed., New Haven: Yale University Press, 1982.

The New York Chinese Scholar's Garden Interpretive Guide. New York: The Staten Island Botanical Garden, 1999.

Nichols, Frederick Doveton and Ralph E. Griswold. *Thomas Jefferson Landscape Architect*. Charlottesville: University Press of Virginia, 1978.

Niemcewicz, Julian Ursyn. *Under Their Vine and Fig Tree*. Metchie J. E. Budka, ed. and trans. Vol. XIV in the *Collections of The New Jersey Historical Society at Newark*. Elizabeth, N. J.: Grassman, 1965.

Nierenberg, Ted. *The Beckoning Path: Lessons of a Lifelong Garden*. New York: Aperture Foundation, Inc., 1993.

Noel Hume, Audrey. *Archaeology and the Colonial Gardener*. Williamsburg: The Colonial Williamsburg Foundation, 1974.

Noel Hume, Ivor. *Digging for Carter's Grove*. Williamsburg: The Colonial Williamsburg Foundation, 1974.

O'Brien, Patricia Nelson. *Filoli*. Master of Landscape Architecture thesis, University of California, Berkeley, 1975.

Olmsted, Fredrick Law. *A Journey in the Back Country*. Originally published 1860. New York: Burt Franklin, 1970.

——*A Journey Through Texas*. (1853–54) Originally published 1860. New York: Burt Franklin, 1969.

——*Civilizing American Cities. A Selection of Frederick Law Olmsted's Writings on City Landscape*. S. B. Sutton, ed. Cambridge: MIT Press, 1979.

——*The Papers of Frederick Law Olmsted*. Charles Capen McLaughlin, editor-in-chief. Vol. I: *The Formative Years: 1822–1852*. Vol. II: *Slavery and the South*. Vol. III: *Creating Central Park*. Volume IV: *Defending the Union, The Civil War and the U. S. Sanitary Commission*. Vol. V: *California Frontier*. Vol. VI: *The Years of Olmsted, Vaux & Company*. Baltimore, Johns Hopkins University Press, 1977–1992.

Olmsted, F. L., and Calvert Vaux. *Prelimary Report upon the proposed Suburban Village at Riverside, near Chicago*. New York: Sutton, Bowne & Co., 1868.

Olmsted, Frederick Law, Jr., and Theodora Kimball, eds. *Frederick Law Olmsted, Forty Years of Landscape Architecture, 1822–1903*. New York, 1928.

Osgood, Frances S. *The Poetry of Flowers and Flowers of Poetry to Which are Added A Simple Treatise on Botany with Familiar Examples, and A Copious Floral Dictionary*. New York: J. C. Riker, 1853.

Padilla, Victoria. *Southern California Gardens: An Illustrated History*. Published by arrangement with the University of California Press. Santa Barbara: Allen A. Knoll, 1994.

Parkinson, John. *A Garden of Pleasant Flowers*. Originally published as *Paradisi in Sole: Paradisus Terrestris*. London 1629. New York: Dover, 1976.

Pinckney, Elise. *Thomas and Elizabeth Lamboll: Early Charleston Gardeners*. Charleston, S. C.: The Charleston Museum, 1969.

Platt, Charles Adams. *Italian Gardens*. (1894) with an overview by Keith N. Morgan and additional plates by Charles A. Platt. Portland Ore.: Sagapress/Timber Press, 1993.

Plumb, John H. "Britain & America: The Cultural Heritage," *The English Heritage*. Frederic Youngs, Jr., et al., eds. St. Louis: Forum Press, 1978.

Porter, Bruce. "Art and Architecture in California," in Eldredge, Zoeth Skinner, *History of California*. New York: Century History Co., c. 1915.

Portillo y Diez de Sollano, Alvaro del. *Descubrimientos y Exploraciones en las Costas de California*. Madrid, 1947.

Price, Susan Davis. *Minnesota Gardens: An Illustrated History*. Afton, Minn.: Afton Historical Society Press, 1995.

Ramsey, Leonidas W., and Charles H. Lawrence. *The Outdoor Living Room*. New York: Macmillan, 1932.

Ravenel, Harriott Horry. *Eliza Pinckney*. Reprint in *Women of Colonial and Revolutionary Times*. New York: Charles Scribner's Sons, 1896.

Reid, Hugo. *The Indians of Los Angeles County: Hugo Reid's Letters of 1852*. Annotated by Robert F. Heizer, ed. Los Angeles: Southwest Museum, 1968.

Relf, Diane, ed. *The Role of Horticulture in Human Well-Being and Development*. Portland, Ore.: Timber Press, 1992.

Reps, John W. *The Making of Urban America: A History of City Planning in the United States*. Princeton: Princeton University Press, 1965.

Repton, Humphry. *The Art of Landscape Gardening, including Sketches and Hints on Landscape Gardening, 1795, and Theory and Practice of Landscape Gardening, 1803*. John Nolen, ed. Boston: Houghton, Mifflin and Company, 1907.

Reynolds, Lucile Winifred. *Leisure-time Activities of a Selected Group of Farm Women*. A Part of a Dissertation submitted to the faculty of the Division of the Biolocgical Sciences in candidacy for the degree of Doctor of Philosophy. 1935. Private ed., University of Chicago Libraries, 1939.

Richardson, Robert D., Jr. *Emerson: The Mind on Fire*. Berkeley: University of California Press, 1995.

Roper, Laura Wood. *FLO: A Biography of Frederick Law Olmsted*. Baltimore: Johns Hopkins University Press, 1973.

Rose, James C. *Creative Gardens*. New York: Reinhold, 1958.

——*Gardens Make Me Laugh*. 1965. New ed. Baltimore: Johns Hopkins University Press, 1990.

——*The Heavenly Environment*. Hong Kong: New City Cultural Service Ltd.,1987.

——*Modern American Gardens—Designed by James Rose*. Text by Marc Snow (pseud.) New York: Reinhold, 1967.

Royce, Sarah Bayliss. *A Frontier Lady: Recollections of the Gold Rush and Early California*. New Haven: Yale University Press, 1932.

Russell, Howard S. *Indian New England before the Mayflower*. Hanover, N. H.: University Press of New England, 1980.

Sarudy, Barbara Wells. *Gardens and Gardening in the Chesapeake 1700–1805*. Baltimore: Johns Hopkins University Press, 1998.

Saunders, William S., ed. *Daniel Urban Kiley: The Early Gardens*. New York: Princeton Architectural Press, 1999.

Schaw, Janet. *Journal of a Lady of Quality*. New Haven: Yale University Press, 1922.

Schoolcraft, Henry Rowe. *Information Respecting the History, Condition and Prospects of the Indian Tribes of the United States: Collected and Prepared under the Direction of the Bureau of Indian Affairs per Act of Congress of March 3, 1847*. Philadelphia: Lippincott, Grambo & Co., 1853.

Schroeder, Fred E. H. *Front Yard America: The Evolution and Meanings of A Vernacular Domestic Landscape*. Bowling Green, Oh.: Bowling Green State University Popular Press, c. 1993.

Schroeder, the Rev. John Frederick. *The Intellectual and Moral Resources of Horticulture: An Anniversary Discourse, Pronounced before the New-York Horticultural Society at the Annual Celebration, August 26, 1828*. New York, Published at the request of the society, 1828.

Schultz, Warren. *A Man's Turf: The Perfect Lawn*. New York: Clarkson Potter, 1999.

Schuyler, David. *The New Urban Landscape*. Baltimore: Johns Hopkins University Press, 1988.

Scott, Frank J. *The Art of Beautifying Suburban Home Grounds*. New York: D. Appleton & Co., 1870.

Scully, Vincent J., Jr. *The Shingle Style*. New Haven: Yale University Press, 1995.

Sedgwick, Catharine Maria. *Letters from Abroad to Kindred at Home, by the Author of 'Hope Leslie,' 'Poor Rich Man and the Rich Poor Man,' 'Live and Let Live,' &c., &c*. New York: Harper, 1841.

Sewall, Samuel. *The Diary of Samuel Sewall 1674–1729*. M. Halsey Thomas, ed. New York: Farrar, Straus and Giroux, 1973.

Silver, Timothy. *A New Face on the Countryside: Indians, Colonists, and Slaves in South Atlantic Forests, 1500–1800*. Cambridge: Cambridge University Press, 1990.

Simo, Melanie Louise. *Loudon and the Landscape*. New Haven: Yale University Press, 1988.

Simonds, Ossian Cole. *Landscape-Gardening*. Reprint of 1920 ed. with new introduction by Robert Grese. Amherst: University of Massachusetts Press, 2000.

Simpson, Sir George. *An Overland Journey around the World during the Years 1841 and 1842*. Philadelphia: Lea and Blanchard, 1847.

Siren, Osvald. *China and Gardens of Europe of the Eighteenth Century* (originally published 1950). Washington, D. C.: Dumbarton Oaks Research Library and Collection, 1990.

——*Gardens of China*. New York: Ronald Press, 1949.

Slosson, Elvinia, compiler. *Pioneer American Gardening*. New York: Coward-McCann, 1951.

Soloman, Barbara Stauffacher. *Green Architecture and the Agrarian Garden*. New York: Rizzoli, 1988.

Sousa-Leão, Joaquim de. *Frans Post 1612–1680*. Amsterdam: L. Van Gendt & Co., 1973.

Spencer, Darrell. *The Gardens of Salem: The Landscape History of a Moravian Town in North Carolina*. Winston Salem, N.C.: Old Salem, Inc., 1997.

Spirn, Anne Whiston. *The Granite Garden*. New York: Basic Books, 1984.

Spongberg, Stephen A. *A Reunion of Trees*. Cambridge: Harvard University Press, 1990.

Starr, Kevin. *Americans and the California Dream 1850–1915*. New York: Oxford University Press, 1973.

Steele, Fletcher. *Design in the Little Garden*. Boston:

The Atlantic Monthly Press, 1924.

——*Gardens and People*. Boston: Houghton Mifflin, 1964.

Stickley, Gustav. *Craftsman Homes*. Republication of second New York ed. (1909). New York: Dover, 1979.

——*More Craftsman Homes*. Republication of 1912 ed. New York: Dover, 1982.

Stilgoe, John R. *Borderland: Origins of the American Suburb, 1820–1939*. New Haven: Yale University Press, 1988.

——*Common Landscape of America, 1580 to 1845*. New Haven: Yale University Press,1982.

Stokes, I. N. Phelps. *The Iconography of Manhattan Island, 1498–1909*. (Originally New York, Robert H. Dodd, 1915) New York, Arno Press, 1967.

Stoney, Samuel Gaillard. *Plantations of the Carolina Low Country*. Charleston, S. C.: Dover Publications and The Carolina Art Association, 1989.

Streatfield, David. *California Gardens: Creating a New Eden*. New York: Abbeville Press, 1994.

The Archaeology of Garden and Field. Naomi F. Miller and Kathryn L. Gleason, eds. Philadelphia: University of Pennsylvania Press, 1994.

The Colonial Revival in America. Alan Axelrod, ed. Published for The Henry Francis du Pont Winterthur Museum. New York: W. W. Norton, 1985.

Tankard, Judith. *The Gardens of Ellen Biddle Shipman*. Sagaponack, N. Y.: Sagapress, 1996.

Thaxter, Celia. *An Island Garden*. With a new introduction by John M. Kingsbury. Ithaca, New York: Bullbrier Press, 1985.

The House and Garden. Essays by Pauline C. Metcalf and Valencia Libby. Roslyn, N. Y.: Nassau County Museum of Art, 1986.

Thomas Church, Landscape Architect. Regional Oral History Office, The Bancroft Library. 2 vols. Interviews conducted by Suzanne B. Riess. Berkeley: University of California, 1978.

Thomas Jefferson's Garden Book 1766–1824 with relevant extracts from his other writings. Annotated by Edwin Morris Betts. Philadelphia: The American Philosophical Society, 1985.

Thoreau, Henry David. *The Maine Woods*. New York: Harper & Row, 1987.

——*The Natural History Essays*. Salt Lake City: Gibbs Smith Publisher, Peregrine Smith Books, 1980.

——*The Works of Thoreau*. Selected by Henry Seidel Canby, ed. Boston: Houghton Mifflin, 1937.

Thouin, Gabriel. *Plans Raisonnés de Toutes les Espèces de Jardins*. Originally published 1820. Paris, Inter-Livres, n.d.

Tice, Patricia M. *Gardening in America, 1830–1910*. Rochester, N. Y.: The Strong Museum, 1984.

Tichi, Cecelia. *New World, New Earth: Environmental Reform in American Literature from the Puritans through Whitman*. New Haven: Yale University Press, 1979.

Tocqueville, Alexis de. *Democracy in America*. Vols. I and II. New York: Vintage, 1945.

——*Journey to America*. J. P. Mayer, ed. New Haven: Yale University Press, 1960.

Torquemada, Fray Juan de. *Monarquia Indiana*. Facsimile of 1723 ed. 3 vols. Mexico: Editorial Porrua, 1969.

Treib, Marc, ed. *Modern Landscape Architecture: A Critical Review*. Cambridge: MIT Press, 1993.

Treib, Marc and Dorothée Imbert. *Garrett Eckbo: Modern Landscapes for Living*. Berkeley: University of California Press, 1997.

Trollope, Frances. *Domestic Manners of the Americans*. (First ed., 1832, reprinted from fifth ed., 1839) London: George Routledge and Sons, Ltd., 1927.

Tunnard, Christopher. *The City of Man*. New York: Scribner, 1953.

——*Gardens in the Modern Landscape*. Second (revised) ed. New York: Charles Scribner's Sons, 1948.

Upton, Dell, ed. *America's Architectural Roots: Ethnic Groups that Built American*. Washington, D.C., 1986.

Valladares, Clarival do Prado, and Mello Filho, Luiz Emydigio de. *Albert Eckhout: A Presença da Holanda no Brasil Século XVII*. Rio de Janeiro, Ediçoes Alumbramento, 1989.

Vancouver, George. *Vancouver in California 1792–1794: The Original Account of George Vancouver*. Annotated by Marguerite Eyer Wilbur, ed. Los Angeles: Glen Dawson, 1953.

Van Rensselaer, Mariana Griswold. *Accents as Well as Broad Effects*. David Gebhard, ed. Berkeley: University of California Press, 1996.

Van Rensselaer, Mrs. Schuyler. *Art Out-of-Doors*. London: T. Fisher Unwin, 1893.

——*Art Out-of-Doors*. Second ed., 1925.

Van Sweden, James. *Gardening with Nature*. New York: Random House, 1997.

Van Valkenburgh, Michael. *Transforming the American Garden: 12 New Landscape Designs*. Cambridge: Harvard University Graduate School of Design, 1986.

Van Valkenburgh, Michael, curator. *Built Landscapes: Gardens in the Northeast*. Brattleboro, Vt.: Brattleboro Museum & Art Center, 1984.

Vaux, Calvert. *Villas & Cottages*. (1864) Reprint: New York: Dover, 1970.

Walker, Peter, and Melanie Simo. *Invisible Gardens: The Search for Modernism in the American Landscape*. Cambridge, Mass.: MIT Press, 1994.

Warner, Anna B. *Gardening by Myself*. 1871. Reprint: The Constitution Island Association, 1924.

Warner, Sam Bass, Jr. *Streetcar Suburbs*. Cambridge: Harvard University Press, 1978.

Washington, George. *Diaries*. Vols. I–IV. John C. Fitzpatrick, A.M, ed. New York: Houghton Mifflin Company, 1925.

Waterman, Thomas Tileston. *The Mansions of Virginia 1706–1776*. Chapel Hill: University of North Carolina Press, 1946.

Watts, May Theilgaard. *Reading the Landscape*. New York: Macmillan, 1957.

Watts, William. *The Seats of the Nobility and Gentry in a Collection of the most interesting and Picturesque Views*. 1779. John Dixon Hunt, ed. New York: Garland Publishing, 1982.

Waugh, Frank A. *The Landscape Beautiful*. New York: Orange Judd Company, 1910.

Westmacott, Richard. *African-American Gardens and Yards in the Rural South*. Knoxville: The University of Tennessee Press, 1992.

Wharton, Edith. *Italian Villas and Their Gardens*. New York: The Century Company, 1904.

Whitehill, Walter Muir. *Dumbarton Oaks: The History of a Georgetown House and Garden, 1800–1966*. Cambridge: Belknap Press Harvard, 1967.

Williamson, Tom. *Polite Landscapes: Gardens and Society in Eighteenth-Century England*. Stroud, Gloucestershire: Alan Sutton, 1995.

Wilson, Gilbert L. *Buffalo Bird Woman's Garden*. Originally published in 1917 as *Agriculture of the Hidatsa Indians: An Indian Interpretation*. St. Paul: Minnesota Historical Society Press, 1987.

Winthrop Papers. Vols. I–V. The Massachusetts Historical Society, 1947.

Winthrop, John. *Winthrop's Journal 1630–1649*. In series, *Original Narratives of Early American History*. New York: Charles Scribner's Sons, 1908.

Wood, William. *New England's Prospect* (1635). Reprint, Alden T. Vaughan, ed., Amherst: University of Massachusetts Press, 1977.

Woodward, Evan Morrison. *Bonaparte's Park and the Murats*. Trenton: MacCrellish & Quigley, 1879.

Woodward, Evan Morrison. *History of Burlington and Mercer counties, N. J.; with bigraphical sketches of many of their pioneers and Prominent Men*. Philadelphia: Everts & Peck, 1883.

Wright, Mabel Osgood. *The Garden of a Commuter's Wife, recorded by the gardener*. New York: Macmillan, 1902.

Wright, Mary and Russell. *Guide to Easier Living*. New York: Simon and Schuster, 1950.

Yoch, James. *Designing the American Dream: The California Gardens of Florence Yoch*. New York: Abrams/Sagapress, 1989.

Zaitzevsky, Cynthia. *Frederick Law Olmsted and the Boston Park System*. Cambridge: Belknap Press/Harvard, 1982.

ARTICLES AND PERIODICALS

Antiques. August 1986. Streatfield, David C. "The Garden at Casa del Herrero."

California Arts & Architecture. May 1933. Church, Thomas D. "The Small California Garden: Chapter I: A New Deal for the Small Lot"; July, 1933. "Designing the Small Lot Garden"; April, 1934. "Planting the Small Garden."

Century: May 1906; March 1907; August 1907; September 1910; October 1910.

Country Life in America. Entire run, especially Vol. 1 no.1–Vol. 31 no. 3 (1901–17).

Garden & Forest. Vol.1–10 (1888–97).

Garden Design. 1982–2001.

The Garden Magazine. 1905–24.

Godey's Magazine and Lady's Book. Philadelphia, 1850–68.

The Horticulturist. 1846–60.

House & Garden. 1901–93.

House Beautiful. 1944–65.

Journal of Garden History: Vol. 2, No. 4 (Oct–Dec 1982); Vol. 6, No. 4 (Oct–Dec 1986); Vol. 9, No.1. (1989); Vol. 9, No. 3 (June–Sept, 1989); Vol. 16, No. 1 (Jan–Mar 1996); Vol. 16, No. 2 (Apr–Jun 1996); Vol. 17, No. 1 (Jan–Mar 1997).

Journal of the New England Garden History Society. Vols. 1–8.

Landscape: Autumn, 1951; Vol 18, No.1 (1969); Vol. 28, No. 3 (1985).

Landscape Journal. November, 1995. Nassauer, Joan Iverson. "Messy Ecosystems, Orderly Frames."

Landscape Architecture. 1982–2001. Also: Spingarn, J. E. "Henry Winthrop Sargent and the Landscape Tradition at Wodenethe," October 1938, 28-39; McGuire, Diane Kostial. "Early Site Planning on the West Coast."

New England Magazine. Shurcliff, Arthur A. "Some Old New England Flower Gardens," December 1899.

Nineteenth Century. Beveridge, Charles E. "Frederick Law Olmsted's Theory on Landscape Design," Summer, 1977.

Old Time New England. Vol. 17 (July 1926); Vol. 78, No. 268 (Fall/Winter 2000). Boston: The Society for the Preservation of New England Antiquities.

Out West Magazine. Lummis, Charles. "The Carpet of God's Country." Los Angeles: F. A.Pattee & Co., 1905.

The Outlook. March 28, 1908. Lowell, Guy quoted in Hartt, Mary Bronson. "Women and the Art of Landscape Gardening."

Pacific Horticulture. 1985–2001.

Process: Architecture. No. 4. *Lawrence Halprin*; No. 33. *Landscape Design: Works of Dan Kiley*; No. 90. *Garrett Eckbo: Philosophy of Landscape*.

Sunset 1928–2001.

Vick's Monthly Magazine. Vol. I (1878); Vol. II (1879). Rochester, New York.

Index

Illustration Credits

Acknowledgments

When I started my research for this book I was an editor at Condé Nast Publications and my colleagues rather doubted that I would ever manage to finish the project, in spite of the company's support at the time. Still, some cheered me on, and fifteen years later I have indeed finished, thanks to the many, many people who have helped and encouraged me.

I WISH TO EXPRESS MY DEEPEST GRATITUDE TO:

The librarians, archivists, and curators whose assistance was crucial: Catha Grace Rambusch at The Catalog of Landscape Records in the United States; Cynthia Cathcart at Condé Nast; Linda Lott at Dumbarton Oaks; Flora Nyland at The F. Franklin Moon Library, SUNY ESF; Mary Daniels, Ann Whiteside, and Alix Reiskind at the Frances Loeb Library, Graduate School of Design, Harvard University; Sally Spier Stassi at Historic New Orleans; Alissa Rosenberg at the Minnesota Historical Society; Renée Nisivoccia at the Morris County Parks Commission; Mildred Deriggi at the Long Island Studies Institute, Nassau County Museum; Marie Long at The LuEsther T. Mertz Library, New York Botanical Garden; Paula Healy at the Archives of American Gardens, Smithsonian Institution; Lorna Condon and Rebecca Aaronsen at the Society for the Preservation of New England Antiquities; Joel Smith at the Frances Lehman Loeb Art Center, Vassar College; and most especially Katherine Powis at the Library of the Horticultural Society of New York.

The garden and landscape historians who have generously shared information and leads, beginning with the late Isidore Smith and including William Howard Adams, Virginia Lopez Begg, Bonnie Blodgett, Abbott Lowell Cummings, Phoebe Cutler, Paula Dietz, Alan Emmet, John Dixon Hunt, Elizabeth Igleheart, Valencia Libby, William Bryant Logan, Timothy Steinhoff, David Streatfield, Judith Tankard, Suzanne Turner, Nancy Wetzel, and James Yoch.

The landscape architects and professional garden designers, many of whom also wear historian hats, for the information and insights they have given me. Charles Birnbaum, the late A. E. Bye, Dean Cardasis, Patrick Chassé, Susan Child, Topher Delany, Isabelle Greene, Robert Grese, Janis Hall, Raymond Jungles, Dan Kiley, Leland Miyano, Patricia O'Donnell, Dean Sheaffer, James Van Sweden, Michael Van Valkenburgh, Jane Baber White.

The garden owners, many of them also the creators of those gardens and three of them the photographers as well, who have shared their knowledge and enthusiasm: Francis Cabot, J. Drayton Hastie, Balthazar and Monica Korab, Tom Krenitsky, Edna Murray, Ted Nierenberg, Julius Shulman, Babs Simpson, Carol Valentine.

The directors, horticulturists, curators, and press officers at historic gardens who have found plans and photographs, provided information and historic documentation, and shown endless patience in answering my questions: William Alexander at Biltmore Estate; Elisabeth Baldwin at the William Paca Garden; Jana Christian and Mark Heppner at Stan Hywet; Carol City, Michele Pecoraro, and Kathy Roncarati at Plimoth Plantation; Joe Clements at the Huntington Gardens; Shelley Drulard at Middleton Place; Diane Galt at Casa del Herrero; Catherine Grosfils at Colonial Williamsburg; Stephen Moses at the Hermann-Grima House; Pamela Pollack at Sonnenberg; Michael Short at the Ohme Gardens; Lucy Tolmach at Filoli; Gary Wetzel at the Society for the Preservation of New England Antiquities.

The artists — Harry Bates, Michael Maskarinec, Kenneth and Teresa Pascual, Richard Tobias — and the photographers who contributed: Jacques Dirand, Felice Frankel, Mick Hales, Darrel Holler, Sean Kernan, Bruce Krobusek, Robert Lorenzson, Russell MacMasters, Peter Margonelli, Richard Nicol, Marina Schinz, Curtice Taylor, the late John Vaughan, Alan Ward, Donald Wong, Doug Young. And also John Crowley, consultant, and Diana Gongora, picture researcher, who were of great help in gathering images from museums and libraries.

The friends who offered suggestions and shared special knowledge — Douglas Brenner, Christin Gangi, Elaine Greene, Robert Levering, Ronaldo Maia, Senga Mortimer, and James O'Brien — and most especially those who gave me help way beyond the call of friendship — Fleur Champin, Carly Hutchinson, Roberta Knapp, Ngaere Macray and David Seeler, and Marilyn Schafer.

The people at Abrams who pulled the book into its final shape, first and foremost Margaret L. Kaplan, who over the last few years alternately encouraged my progress and gently prodded me to stop researching and finish writing, providing invaluable advice along the way. My editor, Elaine Stainton, a joy to work with, as was the book's designer, Robert McKee. And Holly Jennings, who helped with the endless-seeming details of organizing the visual material.

My family, whose support was important in so many ways that I can't begin to count them all. From my parents' example came the life-long fascination with the world of nature, with growing plants and making gardens that eventually inspired this book. The encouragement and help — whenever and whatever needed — provided by my brother, Lauren F. Otis, my sister-in-law, Helen, and their children — Climena, Lauren H., and Nathaniel — have continually recharged my energy and lifted my spirits, not to speak of the tangible contributions made by the photographic skills of the two Laurens, father and son.

Endsheets: Path along the Ashley River in the gardens at Magnolia Plantation, near Charleston, S.C. Photograph © Mick Hales

Project Director: Margaret L. Kaplan
Editor: Elaine M. Stainton
Photo Consultant: John Crowley
Designer: Robert McKee
Production Director: Hope Koturo

Library of Congress Cataloging-in-Publication Data

Otis, Denise.
  Grounds for pleasure : four centuries of the American garden / Denise Otis.
     p. cm.
  Includes bibliographical references (p.   ) and index.
  ISBN 0-8109-3273-3
  1. Gardens — United States — Design — History.
  2. Landscape design — United States — History.
  3. Gardening — United States — History.
  I. Title.
  SB466.U6 O84 2002
  712'.0973 — dc21

                          2002002196

Printed and bound in Hong Kong
10 9 8 7 6 5 4 3 2 1

Harry N. Abrams, Inc.
100 Fifth Avenue
New York, N.Y. 10011
www.abramsbooks.com

Abrams is a subsidiary of

LA MARTINIÈRE
G R O U P E